When should I travel to get the best airfare?
Where do I go for answers to my travel questions?
What's the best and easiest way to plan and book my trip?

frommers.travelocity.com

Frommer's, the travel guide leader, has teamed up with **Travelocity.com**, the leader in online travel, to bring you an in-depth, easy-to-use resource designed to help you plan and book your trip online.

At **frommers.travelocity.com**, you'll find free online updates about your destination from the experts at Frommer's plus the outstanding travel planning and purchasing features of Travelocity.com. Travelocity.com provides reservations capabilities for 95 percent of all airline seats sold, more than 47,000 hotels, and over 50 car rental companies. In addition, Travelocity.com offers more than 2,000 exciting vacation and cruise packages. Travelocity.com puts you in complete control of your travel planning with these and other great features:

> **Expert travel guidance from Frommer's** - over 150 writers reporting from around the world!
>
> **Best Fare Finder** - an interactive calendar tells you when to travel to get the best airfare
>
> **Fare Watcher** - we'll track airfare changes to your favorite destinations
>
> **Dream Maps** - a mapping feature that suggests travel opportunities based on your budget
>
> **Shop Safe Guarantee** - 24 hours a day / 7 days a week live customer service, and more!

Whether traveling on a tight budget, looking for a quick weekend getaway, or planning the trip of a lifetime, Frommer's guides and Travelocity.com will make your travel dreams a reality. You've bought the book, now book the trip!

Travelocity.com
A Sabre Company

Frommer's®

A New Star-Rating System & Other Exciting News from Frommer's!

In our continuing effort to publish the savviest, most up-to-date, and most appealing travel guides available, we've added some great new features.

Frommer's guides now include a new **star-rating system.** Every hotel, restaurant, and attraction is rated from 0 to 3 stars to help you set priorities and organize your time.

We've also added **seven brand-new features** that point you to the great deals, in-the-know advice, and unique experiences that separate travelers from tourists. Throughout the guide look for:

Finds	Special finds—those places only insiders know about
Fun Fact	Fun facts—details that make travelers more informed and their trips more fun
Kids	Best bets for kids—advice for the whole family
Moments	Special moments—those experiences that memories are made of
Overrated	Places or experiences not worth your time or money
Tips	Insider tips—some great ways to save time and money
Value	Great values—where to get the best deals

We've also added a **"What's New"** section in every guide—a timely crash course in what's hot and what's not in every destination we cover.

Other Great Guides for Your Trip:

Frommer's Europe

Frommer's Vienna & the Danube Valley

Frommer's Prague & the Best of the Czech Republic

Frommer's Europe from $70 a Day

Frommer's Road Atlas Europe

Hanging Out in Europe

Frommer's®

Budapest & the Best of Hungary

4th Edition

by Joseph S. Lieber & Christina Shea

with Erzsébet Barát

Here's what the critics say about Frommer's:

"Amazingly easy to use. Very portable, very complete."

—*Booklist*

"The only mainstream guide to list specific prices. The Walter Cronkite of guidebooks—with all that implies."

—*Travel & Leisure*

"Complete, concise, and filled with useful information."

—*New York Daily News*

"Detailed, accurate, and easy-to-read information for all price ranges."

—*Glamour Magazine*

WILEY

Wiley Publishing, Inc.

About the Authors

All four of **Joseph S. Lieber**'s grandparents emigrated from Eastern Europe at the turn of the last century, settling in New York City, where he was born and raised. Mr. Lieber lived in Hungary in the early 1990s, teaching English and researching the first edition of this book. He is presently practicing law in Boston.

Christina Shea served as a Peace Corps volunteer in Hungary. Subsequently, she directed Peace Corps language-training programs in Lithuania and Kyrghyzstan. She is the author of the novel *Moira's Crossing* (St. Martin's Press 2000).

Erzsébet Barát was born in Kunhegyes, a small town in the Great Hungarian Plain. She currently lives in Szeged, where she is an associate professor of English at Attila József University. She earned her Ph.D. in Linguistics from Lancaster University, in England. Her dissertation concerns the oral histories of Hungarian women.

Published by:

Wiley Publishing, Inc.

909 Third Ave.
New York, NY 10022

ISBN 0-7645-6581-8
ISSN 1086-2188

Editor: Naomi P. Kraus
Production Editor: M. Faunette Johnston
Cartographer: John Decamillis
Photo Editor: Richard Fox
Production by Wiley Indianapolis Composition Services

For information on our other products and services or to obtain technical support, please contact our Customer Care Department within the U.S. at 800-762-2974, outside the U.S. at 317-572-3993 or fax 317-572-4002.

Wiley also publishes its books in a variety of electronic formats. Some content that appears in print may not be available in electronic formats.

Manufactured in the United States of America

5   4   3   2

Contents

List of Maps

This book is dedicated to the brave and wonderful people of New York City and to the glorious city itself, which stands taller than ever in the aftermath of September 11.

Acknowledgments

The authors wish to thank their many friends and helpers in Hungary, including Tamás Tóth, Réka Fekete, Andrea Varállyay, and the Bereczki family. And finally, we thank Aryeh T. Lieber and Marcel M. Lieber for being such curious and bright-eyed boys.

An Invitation to the Reader

In researching this book, we discovered many wonderful places—hotels, restaurants, shops, and more. We're sure you'll find others. Please tell us about them, so we can share the information with your fellow travelers in upcoming editions. If you were disappointed with a recommendation, we'd love to know that, too. Please write to:

Frommer's Budapest & the Best of Hungary, 4th Edition
Wiley Publishing, Inc. • 909 Third Avenue • New York, NY 10022

An Additional Note

Please be advised that travel information is subject to change at any time—and this is especially true of prices. We therefore suggest that you write or call ahead for confirmation when making your travel plans. The authors, editors, and publisher cannot be held responsible for the experiences of readers while traveling. Your safety is important to us, however, so we encourage you to stay alert and be aware of your surroundings. Keep a close eye on cameras, purses, and wallets, all favorite targets of thieves and pickpockets.

New! Frommer's Star Ratings & Icons

Every hotel, restaurant, and attraction listing in this guide has been ranked for quality, value, service, amenities, and special features using a star-rating scale. In country, state, and regional guides, we also rate towns and regions to help you narrow down your choices and budget your time accordingly. Hotels and restaurants in the Very Expensive and Expensive categories are rated on a scale of one (highly recommended) to three stars (exceptional). Those in the Moderate and Inexpensive categories rate from zero (recommended) to two stars (very highly recommended). Attractions, towns, and regions are rated according to the following scale: zero stars (recommended), one star (highly recommended), two stars (very highly recommended), and three stars (must-see).

(Finds   (Fun Fact   (Kids   (Moments   (Overrated   (Tips   (Value

The following abbreviations are used for credit cards:

AE	American Express	DISC	Discover	V	Visa
DC	Diners Club	MC	MasterCard		

FROMMERS.COM

Now that you have the guidebook to a great trip, visit our website at **www.frommers.com** for travel information on nearly 2,000 destinations. With features updated regularly, we give you instant access to the most current trip-planning information available. At Frommers.com, you'll also find the best prices on airfares, accommodations, and car rentals—and you can even book travel online through our travel booking partners. At Frommers.com, you'll also find the following:

- Daily Newsletter highlighting the best travel deals
- Hot Spot of the Month/Vacation Sweepstakes & Travel Photo Contest
- More than 200 Travel Message Boards
- Outspoken Newsletters and Feature Articles on travel bargains, vacation ideas, tips & resources, and more!

What's New in Budapest & Hungary

The best news for visitors to Hungary this year is the lack of bite it will have on their wallets. Inflation in Hungary continues to run at a 10 to 15% annual rate, but the strong US dollar combined with the ever-declining Hungarian forint means that the prices of many goods and services have remained fairly constant from year to year for dollar-wielding visitors. Indeed, many of the prices in this book are actually lower in terms of dollars than they were two years ago! That said, the current global economic uncertainty, along with the unforeseeable impact of the introduction of the euro, makes one wonder if this trend will continue.

And though we list a host of new things to see and do in Hungary below, the preeminent experience here is still an old favorite. If you ask us, the status of **Pécs** as the best kept secret in Hungary can't last for much longer. Each time we visit, the town is more beautiful than ever. Do yourself a favor and go now before the tourist crowds eventually discover it.

PLANNING YOUR TRIP Because the Hungarian forint is now fully convertible, there are no longer any restrictions regarding re-exchange of unused forints back into foreign currency. Consequently, unlike in the past, visitors need not retain their currency exchange receipts as proof of lawful exchange, nor need they any longer exercise caution in not buying more forints than are likely to be used while in Hungary. For more on currency matters, see "Money," in chapter 2, "Planning Your Trip to Budapest."

GETTING TO KNOW BUDAPEST A long-planned new metro line—the green line—remains the subject of bitter political wrangling between Budapest Mayor Gábor Demszky and the central-right national government. Though the city won a drawn-out legal battle over subsidization of the project, the government is refusing to comply with the court's order to fund it. If and when it is ever completed, the green line will run from Keleti Station in Pest across the river to Southern Buda, a part of the city that is not presently served by the metro. This will go a long way towards opening up that seldom-visited part of town to foreign tourists. For more on public transportation in Budapest, see "Getting Around," in chapter 3, "Getting to Know Budapest."

A new free English-language weekly publication called *Look* contains extensive listings of films, concerts, and other cultural events. Other useful Hungarian publications are listed under "Fast Facts," in chapter 3, "Getting to Know Budapest."

WHERE TO STAY A Swiss investor group recently won a tender offer to purchase the historic but crumbling **New York Coffeehouse** and plans to renovate and re-open it as a five-star hotel. This decision came at the end of a long public debate over the future of the historic building, during which various other ideas—including using the building as the home of the controversial new National Theater (the old theater was destroyed in a fire)—were considered and ultimately rejected.

Speaking of renovations and new hotel construction, a group of Cypriot and Canadian investors are rescuing the **Gresham Palace,** the once-grand Art Nouveau structure at the head of the Chain Bridge in Pest, from its long-time state of woeful disrepair. They're converting it into yet another luxury hotel (of the Four Seasons variety). The *Budapest Sun* forecasts that it will be "one of the most expensive hotels in Europe" when work is completed in late 2002. Thanks to the efforts of local green activists, who achieved their first notable success in Budapest, the center of the stately and historic Roosevelt Square will not be converted into a parking lot for the hotel. The original plan was to raze the small park in the middle of the square, home to trees more than a hundred years old. The lot will now be built underground.

The former Hotel Centrál, one of our favorite off-the-beaten-track hotels, reopened in 2001 as the **Hotel Andrássy** after an ambitious renovation. Located in an exclusive embassy neighborhood just off Pest's Andrássy út, a minute's walk from Heroes' Square and the City Park, this fine hotel is just a 25-minute walk to the center of Pest.

Check out chapter 4, "Where to Stay in Budapest," for more on Budapest's accommodation options.

WHERE TO DINE   Although a new law requires all restaurants to offer a nonsmoking section, the fact is that most barely comply. You should expect restaurants, *especially cafes,* to be as smoky as they've ever been.

Several new restaurants have recently opened in Budapest. For instance, **Antique Restaurant,** recently opened by an ambitious female member of the famous Légrádi restaurant family, is a combination antique shop/stylish restaurant that offers live Hungarian music every evening. The kitchen proudly offers to cook up any exquisite meal on the premises to satisfy any palate.

Articsóka is another welcome addition to the Budapest dining scene. A complex consisting of a restaurant, cafe, roof terrace, art gallery and theater, this establishment features a carefully designed Moorish interior along with excellent fare. It is already a favorite dining place of Hungarian show biz and media celebrities, and on Friday evenings there is a free theater performance of excellent quality.

A number of new and exciting cafes and bistros have recently opened up along **Andrássy ut** between Oktogon and Deák tér, turning this historic street into a concentrated hub of nightlife. With tables on the street, and a stylish young clientele, these places are bringing a bit of Paris to the Budapest landscape. For cafe recommendations, see "Traditional Coffeehouses," in chapter 5, "Where to Dine in Budapest."

EXPLORING BUDAPEST   The famed **crown jewels of St. Stephen** were ceremoniously moved from the National Museum to their current home in the Parliament as part of Hungary's second millenium celebration in 2000.

The **Zsigmond Kun Folk Art Museum,** housed in a small apartment, is one of our favorite little museums in all of Hungary. Sadly, founder Mr. Zsigmond Kun died in 2001 at the ripe old age of 100. For almost a century, Uncle Zsigmond, as he is fondly called by all who knew him, traveled around Hungary collecting and documenting the country's folk art. Following his death, the museum closed for renovation, but is expected to re-open by Christmas 2002.

Budapest's wonderful 100-year-old **merry-go-round,** in the city amusement park, was recently restored to its original, delightful grandeur. The riders still must actively pump to keep the horses rocking, while authentic Wurlitzer music plays. No visit to Budapest is complete without a ride on this merry-go-round and on the lovely Ferris wheel.

For other cool things to see and do in Budapest, see chapter 6, "Exploring Budapest."

BUDAPEST SHOPPING   The city of Budapest is now awash in huge new Western-style malls. As a general matter, we tend to avoid such malls in favor of smaller local shops, but you might want to check out the amazing **"Tropicarium"** at a mall in southern Buda called Campona. The Tropicarium features both an aquarium—the largest in Central Europe—and a miniature rain forest, with snakes, alligators and the like (there's even rain!). There's also a bowling alley and an 11-screen multiplex cinema at the mall.

The very newest shopping mall in town is the **West End Center,** right behind Nyugati railway station. This is the first mall to be built right in central Pest.

Expensive new boutiques dot the landscape in central Pest. One of particular note is run by the controversial designer **Tamás Náray,** and bears his name. The shop has no telephone, although given the prices here, it is safe to assume the business could afford a phone line.

For more on Budapest's best shopping, see chapter 8, "Budapest Shopping."

BUDAPEST AFTER DARK   Prices for concerts, opera and theater have risen more steeply than any other prices since the last edition of this book. Still, there are few if any events in Budapest beyond the means of the average Western budget traveler.

Jazz clubs are taking hold in Budapest. Several new spots have opened to go along with the more established ones from the 1990s. We recommend several hot places, including **Fat Mo's Music Club** (great food, too), **Old Man's** (catch the Hungarian blues legend Hobo) and **TRAFO** (located in a funky old converted electric power station). Cover charges are minimal or non-existent.

A complete rundown of Budapest's nightlife can be found in chapter 9, "Budapest After Dark."

THE DANUBE BEND   The annual **Visegrád International Palace Tournament** has grown in scale in recent years and is now a must-see for medieval enthusiasts—it is an authentic medieval festival replete with dueling knights on horseback, early music, and dance.

In Esztergom you will find a new sign of better days ahead for peaceful co-existence in Central Europe. Notwithstanding deeply rooted tensions between the Hungarians and Slovaks, Esztergom is once again connected by **bridge** across the Danube to the Slovak town of Sturovo. The Germans blew up the previous bridge connecting these towns in World War II. Until 2001, all that remained was a curious stump on the river's edge, along with four unconnected pylons in the river, stark monuments to the German rampage in Europe as well as to the continuing regional hostilities.

For more suggestions on what to do in the Danube region, see chapter 10, "The Danube Bend."

SOUTHERN HUNGARY: THE GREAT PLAIN & THE MECSEK HILLS   The heart of **Szeged,** the proud capital of the Hungarian Great

Plain (and the paprika capital of the world), is the main pedestrian-only "walking street," Karász utca. This street has just undergone a thorough and loving reconstruction, and is filled with a host of interesting little shops. There is no finer place to stroll in all of Hungary than down the Karász utca on a lovely summer evening, winding your way from one pastry shop to the next.

For other great things to do in the South of Hungary, see chapter 13, "Southern Hungary: The Great Plain & the Mecsek Hills."

1

The Best of Budapest

Budapest's extraordinary ambience can be felt everywhere. From the old women selling boxes of raspberries in the heart of downtown Pest, cars careening by on all sides, to the young boys playing soccer in the green foothills of Buda, where the air is fresh and clean, this city and its people take you in and hold you tight. Budapest is a remarkable and yet wholly unpretentious place. Explore it fully. Turn off any of the main boulevards and you'll quickly find yourself in a quiet residential neighborhood. The rich scent of a hearty *gulyás* (stew) wafts from a kitchen window. A woman with a brightly colored kerchief tied about her head sweeps the sidewalk with a homemade broom. Cigarette smoke fogs the cavelike entryway of the corner pub, and the sign on the door states that beer is served as early as 7am. Rows of salamis hang in the window of the grocery store next door. In the park across the way, men play chess in the shade of chestnut trees, young lovers kiss on a bench, and the famed Hungarian pedigree dog, the *vizsla,* can be glimpsed darting through the trees. Below, you'll find our personal take on the best experiences the city has to offer.

1 Favorite Little Adventures

The many grand attractions of the city are all described in this book, and are certainly worth a visit. For us, however, exceptional beauty and fascination are to be found in the city's day-to-day self. Consider, for instance, the following small adventures off the beaten track.

- **Discovering the Courtyards of Budapest:** Budapest's residential streets are truly enchanting, but it is inside the courtyards of the buildings that the city's greatest secret is held: Budapesters are villagers at heart. Fruit trees and flower gardens flourish, cats lounge in the sun, and jars of pickled vegetables line the window ledges. Nearly every apartment building in this city has an open-air courtyard in its center, where pensioners sit on the common balconies smoking cigarettes,

gossiping, and watching the children race around the yard, dodging flower pots and laundry racks. The main entrance doors to many apartment buildings are left unlocked during the daytime hours. See chapter 7, "Strolling Around Budapest," for further wanderings.

- **Exploring the Neighborhood Markets:** There is scarcely a neighborhood in Budapest without its own outdoor produce market. Professional vendors mix with elderly peasants who are in for the day with a wagon of fresh-picked fruits and veggies. Everything is fresh and inexpensive. Shop for a picnic lunch or simply wander around soaking up the vibrant workaday atmosphere. See "Shopping A to Z," in chapter 8, "Budapest Shopping," for more on market shopping.

- **Riding the Trams:** Armed with your daily transit pass, get the lay of the land and more from the windows of the city's many trams. Board a tram and ride it to the terminus and back, or disembark along the way fo a closer look around—a great and economical way to spend a rainy day. See "Getting Around," in chapter 3, "Getting to Know Budapest," for details on public transportation.

- **Packing a Picnic for the City Park:** On a nice summer day, it seems that all of Budapest has come to City Park to enjoy the weather and each other's company. Children of all ages fill the playgrounds and linger by the entrances of the amusement park, the zoo, and the circus. Bathers flock to the historic Széchenyi Baths. Mostly, though, people come just to stroll, a time-honored pastime in Central Europe. See "Parks, Gardens & Playgrounds," in chapter 6, "Exploring Budapest."

- **Taking a Walk in the Buda Hills:** It's hard to believe that such an expanse of hilly forest is right here within the capital city. There are hiking trails aplenty; every Budapest native has a favorite. Ask around. See chapter 6, "Exploring Budapest," for more of the Buda Hills.

- **Strolling Through the Jewish District:** Budapest has the largest Jewish population of any city on the European continent (outside Russia). Pest's historic Jewish neighborhood, run-down but relatively unchanged, resonates with the magic and tragedy of the past. See "Walking Tour 4: The Jewish District," in chapter 7, "Strolling Around Budapest."

2 The Best Places to Enjoy a Sunset

- **From the Riverside:** Locals and visitors alike stroll along the Danube bank (Pest side) in the early evening, taking in the changing light over the shimmering water. Find a free bench, or venture out onto one of the bridges that span the Danube to enjoy a different view of the glorious river that snakes its way through the very soul of Central Europe.

- **From the Ferris Wheel:** The beautiful old yellow Ferris wheel in Budapest's amusement park will lift you gently up into the evening air. At the apex of the long, slow ride you will have an astonishing view of the entire city and the falling sun. See p. 120.

- **From the Tower of Saint Stephen's Church:** This is the highest point in Pest; from here, the only barrier to the horizon is smog or haze (on a bad day). For those who can handle it, the long, arduous ascent makes the vista all the more pleasurable. Others can ride the newly installed lift to the top. See p. 107.

3 Favorite Off-the-Beaten-Track Museums

- **Zsigmond Kun Folk Art Museum:** For almost the entirety of the 20th century a fellow named Zsigmond Kun traveled the back roads of Hungary, collecting and cataloging all manner of folk art. On display here in his former apartment are ceramics and brandy flasks, tapestries and chairs, sheep bells, shepherds' hats, and hundreds of other examples of Hungarian folk art. See p. 115.

Hungary

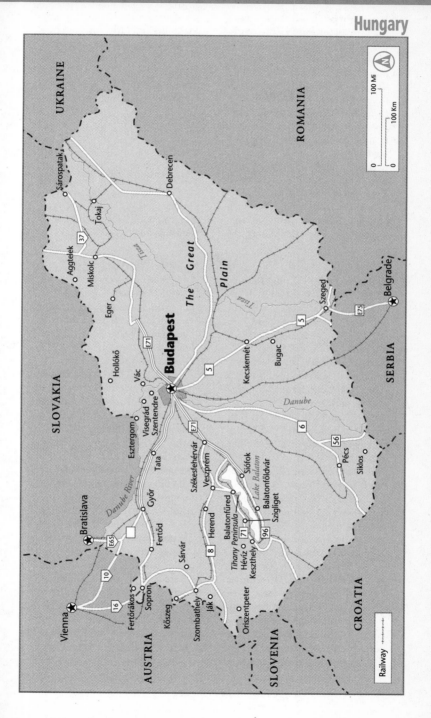

UKRAINE

ROMANIA

100 Mi

100 Km

Sárospatak

Debrecen

Tokaj

37

Aggtelek

Miskolc

Eger

The Great

Plain

Tisza

Tisza L.

Belgrade

Szeged

E75

E71

Budapest

Hollókő

Vác

SLOVAKIA

5

Kecskemét

Bugac

SERBIA

5

Visegrád
Szentendre

Esztergom

Tata

Danube

6

E71

Székesfehérvár

56

Pécs

Siklós

Győr

Veszprém

Siófok

Lake Balaton

Balatonföldvár

Szigliget

Danube River

Fertőd

Herend

Balatonfüred

71

96

Bratislava

E65

Sárvár

8

Tihany Peninsula

Hévíz

Keszthely

10

CROATIA

16

Fertőrákos

Sopron

Kőszeg

Szombathely

Ják

Őriszentpeter

Vienna

AUSTRIA

SLOVENIA

Railway

- **Imre Varga Collection:** This small museum features the sensitive, piercing work of Imre Varga, Hungary's best-known contemporary sculptor. Of particular note is the shaded garden where Varga's forlorn, broken figures stand and sit on benches resting. See p. 115.
- **Postal Stamp Museum:** Generations of philatelists the world over have admired the artistic creations of Magyar Posta. Here you'll find rack after rack of the country's finest stamps. See p. 111.
- **Transport Museum:** This vast and wonderful museum features large-scale models of all sorts of vintage vehicles—trains, motorcycles, bikes, early model cars, antique horse buggies, and more. Kids adore this fabulous trip through history. See p. 120.
- **Statue Park:** This desolate and wind swept outdoor museum displays a number of fine examples of statues that once dominated the landscape—both urban and rural—of Central and Eastern Europe and the Soviet Union. The place is a bit like an elephant dying ground, covered with the Socialist realist detritus of modern history, oddly compelling in its vanished power. See p. 112.

4 Favorite Places to Kill an Hour

- **A Bench on the Danube Promenade:** Find an empty bench on this heavily trafficked pedestrian walkway on the bank of the Danube. Sit back and drink in Budapest.
- **Margaret Island:** This lovely park in the middle of the river between Buda and Pest is beautifully maintained, with fountains, floral gardens, green fields, and the like. Find yourself a piece of green and settle down for a while. See p. 116.
- **The Baths:** There is no place quite like the baths to unwind. The city's fabled thermal waters invite you to loosen up, slow down, and relax. See "Spa Bathing & Swimming: Budapest's Most Popular Thermal Baths," in chapter 6, "Exploring Budapest."
- **A Traditional Coffeehouse:** Imperial Budapest is long, long gone, but a few of the trappings still remain. None is quite so pleasant as the traditional, ornate coffeehouse, symbol of turn-of-the-20th-century–Budapest. Coffee and sweets are still very inexpensive, and customers may linger for hours without drawing any unkind looks from the waiters. See "Traditional Coffeehouses," in chapter 5, "Where to Dine in Budapest."
- **A Bench on Tóth Árpád sétány:** This is the perfect alternative to the Danube Promenade, for those who prefer a quiet urban bench to one on a main thoroughfare. Tóth Árpád sétany is a surprisingly untraveled street, with great benches but few pedestrians, that runs the entire length of the Castle District, on the Buda side (that is, the non-Danube side). See "Walking Tour 2: The Castle District," in chapter 7, "Strolling Around Budapest."
- **A Borozó:** Wine cellars are everywhere in Budapest, capital city of a wine-loving land. Each cellar has its own house wine, its own local clientele, and a chair with your name on it. See "The Bar Scene," chapter 9, "Budapest After Dark."

5 Favorite Experiences Outside of Budapest

- **Cruising the Danube:** There is nothing like a boat ride on a fine sunny day. From Budapest, head up the river to the charming towns of Szentendre and Visegrád along the Danube Bend. See "Exploring the Danube Bend," chapter 10, "The Danube Bend."
- **Visiting the Margit Kovács Museum (Szentendre):** The highly original works of Hungary's best-known ceramic artist are displayed in this expansive museum in a lovely village on the Danube Bend. Kovács's unique sculptures of elderly women and her folk-art-influenced friezes of village life are especially moving. See p. 178.
- **Hiking in the Hills Outside Szigliget:** You can hike up to the fantastic ruins of a 13th-century castle above this scenic little village in the Lake Balaton region, or go a few miles farther north and hike up into hills covered with vineyards. See "Szigliget," chapter 11, "The Lake Balaton Region."
- **Swimming in the Thermal Lake at Hévíz:** Even in the bitterest spell of winter, the temperature in Europe's largest thermal lake seldom dips below 85° to 90°F. Hungarians swim here year-round, and you can, too! If

you're here in winter, it'll be a particularly memorable experience. See p. 194.
- **Climbing the Eger Minaret:** This beautiful, small city in northern Hungary is home to one of the country's most impressive Turkish ruins: a 14-sided, 110-foot-tall minaret. Those who succeed in climbing the steep, cramped, spiral staircase are justly rewarded with a spectacular view. See p. 198.
- **Exploring Pécs:** When you wander around this delightful city in southern Hungary, you'll discover why it's known as the 2,000-year-old city. Pécs is home to one of Hungary's most pleasing central squares and some great examples of Turkish architecture. See "The 2,000-Year-Old City of Pécs," chapter 13, "Southern Hungary: The Great Plain & the Mecsek Hills."
- **Sampling Szeged's Fruit and Vegetable Market:** At the main open-air market behind the bus station, in this town near the Serbian and Romanian borders, local farmers sell their bounty of peaches, apricots, cherries, and pears, as well as fresh flowers, and of course, dried paprika wreaths. See p. 215.

6 Best Hotel Bets

- **Best Historic Hotel:** The splendid, sprawling **Hotel Gellért**, XI. Gellért tér 1 (© **1/385-2200**), first opened in 1918, is still one of the city's most elegant and charming hotels. The Art Nouveau Gellért Baths are the most popular in Budapest. See p. 63.
- **Best for Business Travelers:** The **Kempinski Hotel Corvinus**, V. Erzsébet tér (© **800/426-3135** in North America, or 1/429-3777),

is the hotel of choice for corporate visitors, with conference facilities, a state-of-the-art business center, and an efficient staff. See p. 60.
- **Best for a Romantic Getaway:** Any of the pensions in the Buda Hills would be suitable, but the **Vadvirág Panzió**, II. Nagybányai út 18 (© **1/275-0200**), is particularly fetching, surrounded as it is by sloping gardens and terraces. See p. 73.

- **Best for Families:** Parents will appreciate the location of the **Hotel Liget,** VI. Dózsa György út 106 (© 1/269-5300), across the street from City Park's zoo, amusement park, and circus. See p. 68.
- **Best Moderately Priced Hotel: Hotel Astra Vendégház,** I. Vám u. 6 (© 1/214-1906), opened in 1997, is perfectly situated in Buda's quaint Watertown neighborhood, just a 10-minute walk from the Castle District, and minutes from the Danube embankment. See p. 64.
- **Best Budget Hotel:** The accommodations at **Charles Apartment House,** I. Hegyalja út 23 (© 1/201-1796), are comfortable and clean flats—with bathrooms and fully equipped kitchens—in Buda apartment buildings. See p. 66.
- **Best Pension:** The charming **Gizella Panzió,** XII. Arató u. 42/b (© 1/249-2281), built into the side of a hill, has a lovely view of the valley in a quiet neighborhood that's relatively easy to reach by bus. The rooms are quaint and sunny. See p. 71.

- **Best Location:** This one is a tie between the only two hotels in Buda's elegant and timeless Castle District: The **Hilton Budapest,** I. Hess András tér 1–3 (© 1/488-6600), is a luxurious place right next door to the Matthias Church and the Fisherman's Bastion, while **Hotel Kulturinnov,** I. Szentháromság tér 6 (© 1/355-0122), is a modest guest house just across the square. See p. 67.
- **Best Service:** At the **San Marco Guest House,** III. San Marco u. 6 (© 1/388-9997), the charming proprietors, who speak fluent English, are happy to go out of their way to provide guests with whatever they need: restaurant reservations, theater tickets, train schedules, and more. See p. 70.
- **Best View:** You'll either see the full Pest skyline or overlook the delightful streets of the Castle District at the **Hilton Budapest,** I. Hess András tér 1–3 (© 1/488-6600), widely considered the city's classiest hotel. See p. 67.

7 Best Dining Bets

- **Best for a Romantic Dinner:** At **Náncsi Néni Véndéglője,** II. Órdögárok út 80 (© 1/397-2742), high up in the Buda Hills, you can dine in the casual elegance of an outdoor garden in summer, with live music at night. See p. 95.
- **Best Decor:** The huge branches of a wonderful old tree create a canopy under which guests dine by candlelight in the interior courtyard at **Kis Buda Gyöngye,** III. Kenyeres u. 34 (© 1/368-6402). See p. 96.
- **Best View:** You won't be able to pronounce the restaurant's name, but the view from a terrace table at

lovely **Udvarház a Hármashatárhegyen,** I. Hármashatár-hegyi út 2 (© 1/388-8780), is beyond words. High in the Buda Hills, you'll enjoy a great panoramic view. See p. 95.
- **Best Wine List: Gundel,** XIV. Állatkerti út 2 (© 1/322-1002), the city's fanciest and most famous restaurant, complements its traditional dishes prepared in innovative ways with a fabulous and extensive wine list. See p. 90.
- **Best Gulyás:** While fine gulyás abound in this town, you surely won't be disappointed with the offering at **Malomtó Étterem,** II.

Frankel Leó u. 48 (© **1/326-2847**). See p. 96.

- **Best Wild Game:** At **Aranyszarvas,** I. Szarvas tér 1 (© **1/375-6451**)—the restaurant's name means the Golden Stag—enjoy savory venison stew, pheasant, and wild boar. See p. 91.
- **Best Vegetarian:** At **Marquis de Salade,** VI. Hajós u. 43 (© **1/302-4086**), the cooks from around the world prepare an amazing assortment of delicious vegetarian dishes. **Govinda,** V. Belgrád rakpart 18 (© **1/318-1144**), the riverside Indian

restaurant run by the Hare Krishnas, comes in a close second here. See p. 87.

- **Best Coffeehouse: Művész Kávéház,** VI. Andrássy út 29 (© **1/352-1337**), just across from the Opera House, is a certifiable classic and is open late—the perfect location for a coffeehouse. See p. 98.
- **Best Pastries:** Our favorite pastry shop is the century-old, utterly charming little **Ruszwurm Cukrászda,** I. Szentháromság u. 7 (© **1/375-5284**), located in the heart of the Castle District. See p. 98.

2

Planning Your Trip to Budapest

Now that you've decided to travel to Budapest, you must have dozens of questions. Do I need a visa? What currency is used in Hungary, and can I get my hands on some at home? Will any festivals take place during my trip? What's the best route to get there? This chapter is devoted to providing answers to these and other questions.

1 Visitor Information & Entry Requirements

VISITOR INFORMATION

For general country information and a variety of pamphlets and maps before you leave, contact the government-sponsored **Hungarian National Tourist Office,** 150 E. 58th St., New York, NY 10155 (© **212/355-0240;** fax 212/207-4103; htnewyork@ hungarytourism.hu). In London, the **Hungarian National Tourist Office** is at 46 Eaton Place, London SW1X 8AL (© **823-1032;** fax 823-1459; htlondon @hungarytourism.hu). The Hungarian National Tourist Office's main website, a great source of information, is **www. hungarytourism.com.**

A website with dozens of links to a large variety of Budapest-related sites is **www.fsz.bme.hu/hungary/budapest/ bplinks;** also check out **www.fsz.bme. hu/hungary/qgeneral.html** while you are there. Another site with lots of helpful information for visitors is **www.vista.hu,** the website of the **Vista Visitor Center** (see "Visitor Information," in chapter 3, "Getting to Know Budapest"). The Budapest city government also has a decent site; visit it at **www.fph.hu.** Find general city information at **www.budapest.com.** To get news about Hungary, check out the Hungarian News Agency at **www.mti. hu/news/default.htm.** It's updated daily.

ENTRY REQUIREMENTS

DOCUMENTS Citizens of the United States, Canada, the Republic of Ireland, and the United Kingdom need only a valid passport to enter Hungary. Citizens of Australia and New Zealand need a visa as well as a passport; contact the nearest Hungarian embassy for details and requirements concerning visas.

CUSTOMS You're allowed to bring duty-free into Hungary 250 cigarettes, 2 liters of wine, and 1 liter of spirits. There is no limit to the amount of money you may bring into the country. However, you may not bring into the country or take out of the country more than 1,000,000 forints in Hungarian currency.

Returning **U.S. citizens** who have been away for at least 48 hours are allowed to bring back, once every 30 days, $400 worth of merchandise duty-free. You'll be charged a flat rate of 4% duty on the next $1,000 worth of purchases. Be sure to have your receipts handy. On mailed gifts, the duty-free limit is $100. You cannot bring fresh foodstuffs into the United States; tinned foods, however, are allowed. For more information, contact the **U.S. Customs Service,** 1300 Pennsylvania Ave., NW, Washington, DC 20229 (© **800/973-2867;**

202/354-1000) and request the free pamphlet *Know Before You Go.* It's also available on the web at www.customs. gov. (Click on "Traveler Information" then "Know Before You Go".)

For a clear summary of **Canadian** rules, write for the booklet *I Declare,* issued by **Revenue Canada, 2265** St. Laurent Blvd., Ottawa K1G 4KE (© **506/636-5064**). Canada allows its citizens a Can$750 exemption, and you're allowed to bring back, duty-free, one carton of cigarettes, 1 can of tobacco, 40 imperial ounces of liquor, and 50 cigars. In addition, you're allowed to mail gifts to Canada valued at less than Can$60 a day, provided they're unsolicited and don't contain alcohol or tobacco (write on the package "Unsolicited gift, under $60 value"). All valuables should be declared on the Y-38 form before departure from Canada, including serial numbers of valuables you already own, such as expensive foreign cameras. *Note:* The $750 exemption can only be used once a year and only after an absence of 7 days.

U.K. citizens returning from a non-EC country have a customs allowance of 200 cigarettes; 50 cigars; 250g of smoking tobacco; 2 liters of still table wine; 1 liter of spirits or strong liqueurs (over 22% volume); 2 liters of fortified wine, sparkling wine or other liqueurs; 60cc (ml) perfume; 250cc (ml) of toilet water; and £145 worth of all other goods, including gifts and souvenirs. People under 17 cannot have the tobacco or alcohol allowance. For more information, contact **HM Customs & Excise,** Passenger Enquiry Point, 2nd Floor

Wayfarer House, Great South West Road, Feltham, Middlesex, TW14 8NP (© **0181/910-3744;** from outside the U.K. 44/181-910-3744), or consult their website at **www.open. gov.uk**.

The duty-free allowance in **Australia** is A$400 or, for those under 18, A$200. Upon returning to Australia, citizens can bring in 250 cigarettes or 250 grams of loose tobacco and 1.125 liters of alcohol. If you're returning with valuable goods you already own, such as foreign-made cameras, you should file form B263. A helpful brochure, available from Australian consulates or Customs offices, is *Know Before You Go.* For more information, contact **Australian Customs Services,** GPO Box 8, Sydney NSW 2001 (© **02/6275-6666** in Australia; 202/797-3189 in the U.S.), or go to **www.customs.gov.au**.

The duty-free allowance for **New Zealand** is NZ$700. Citizens over 17 can bring in 200 cigarettes, or 50 cigars, or 250 grams of tobacco (or a mixture of all three if their combined weight doesn't exceed 250 g); plus 4.5 liters of wine and beer, or 1.125 liters of liquor. New Zealand currency does not carry import or export restrictions. Fill out a certificate of export, listing the valuables you are taking out of the country; that way, you can bring them back without paying duty. Most questions are answered in a free pamphlet available at New Zealand consulates and Customs offices: *New Zealand Customs Guide for Travellers, Notice no. 4.* For more information, contact **New Zealand Customs,** 50 Anzac Ave., P.O. Box 29, Auckland (© **09/359-6655**).

2 Money

CURRENCY

The basic unit of currency in Hungary is the **forint (Ft)**. Coins come in denominations of 1, 2, 5, 10, 20, 50, and 100 Ft. Banknotes come in denominations of 200, 500, 1,000, 5,000, 10,000 and 20,000 Ft

Over the past several years, the U.S. dollar has gained against the Hungarian forint at roughly the same or even a greater rate than inflation in Hungary. The result, each year, has been a U.S. dollar that, in general, goes as far or farther in Hungary than it did the previous year. Of course, we cannot predict whether this trend will continue. At any rate, Hungary continues to be considerably less expensive for travelers than most Western countries. Labor-intensive services, such as picture framing, tailoring, shoe and watch repair, and the like, are particularly inexpensive.

As of this writing, the rate of exchange is $1 = 280 Ft (or 100 Ft = 36¢), and this is the rate used to calculate all the U.S. dollar prices in this book. Of course, exchange rates will fluctuate over time.

Note: Several hotels and pensions in Budapest list their prices in U.S. dollars, and many list them in euros, the new currency of the European Union. This is done solely as a hedge against forint inflation, as Hungary is not actually a member of the European Union. All hotels in Budapest accept payment in Hungarian forints as well as foreign currencies. We have converted prices given in euros in this book into dollars based on an exchange rate of 1.1€ = $1, the rate at press time. This rate is, of course, subject to fluctuations.

CHANGING MONEY

The best official rates for both cash and traveler's checks are obtained at banks. Exchange booths are also located throughout the city center, in train stations, and in most luxury hotels, but exchange booths almost uniformly offer lower rates than banks. This is particularly true of one Inter Change chain, which offers a rate up to 20% lower than the going bank rate, depending on the amount you exchange. ATMs are found in front of banks throughout the city. You may withdraw forints at the daily exchange rate from your home

account through the Cirrus and PLUS networks (see "ATMs," below).

Since June 2001, with the full convertibility of the Hungarian forint, there are no longer any restrictions regarding re-exchange of forints back into your currency. Consequently, unlike in the past, you need not retain your currency exchange receipts as proof of exchange.

BLACK MARKET The black market no longer serves a particularly useful purpose for tourists, as it once did. The bands of Middle Eastern money changers that were once a permanent fixture of Keleti Station (in front of official exchange booths at the side of track 6 by the entrance of the international ticket office) can still be found in reduced numbers, offering an exchange rate just 2% to 3% higher than the official rate. You are highly unlikely to be cheated by them, though you have only a small margin to gain by trading with them. However, you should regard with extreme suspicion anyone who accosts you on the street wanting to change money, especially someone offering you a rate more than 2% to 3% better than the official one. Such a person is certainly out to cheat you.

HARD CURRENCY

It makes sense to have some cash on hand. At some banks and at all exchange booths you will get a better rate when exchanging cash. Dollars might also come in handy at flea markets.

TRAVELER'S CHECKS

Traveler's checks are accepted for exchange at most banks and exchange offices, including the **American Express** office between Vörösmarty tér and Deák tér in central Pest, at V. Deák Ferenc u. 10, 1052 Budapest (© **1/235-4330** or 1/235-4300; fax 1/267-2028). Many hotels (but not stores) also accept them as payment.

The Hungarian Forint

For American Readers   At this writing $1 = approximately 280 Ft (or 100 Ft = 36¢), and this was the rate of exchange used to calculate the dollar values given in this chapter.

For British Readers   At this writing £1 = approximately 400 Ft (or 100 Ft = 25p), and this was the rate of exchange used to calculate the pound values in the table below.

Note: The rates given here fluctuate and may not be the same when you travel to Hungary. Therefore, this table should be used only as a guide:

Ft	U.S.$	U.K.£	Ft	U.S.$	U.K.£
5	.02	.01	3,000	10.80	7.50
10	.04	.03	4,000	14.40	10.00
25	.09	.06	5,000	18.00	12.50
50	.18	.13	6,000	21.60	15.00
75	.27	.19	7,000	25.20	17.50
100	.36	.25	8,000	28.80	20.00
200	.72	.50	9,000	32.40	22.50
300	1.08	.75	10,000	36.00	25.00
400	1.44	1.00	15,000	54.00	37.50
500	1.80	1.25	20,000	72.00	50.00
750	2.70	1.87	25,000	90.00	62.50
1,000	3.60	2.50	30,000	108.00	75.00
1,500	5.40	3.75	40,000	144.00	100.00
2,000	7.20	5.00	50,000	180.00	125.00

You are likely to get a slightly lower exchange rate with traveler's checks than with cash, especially at exchange booths. Be aware that if you should wish to cash in your traveler's checks for dollars at the American Express office, you will end up losing 7% since they first exchange the checks for forints and then buy the forints back for dollars.

ATMS

There are numerous ATMs throughout Budapest that are connected to the **Cirrus** (© 800/424-7787; www. mastercard.com) and **Plus** (© 800/ 843-7587; www.visa.com) networks, as well as credit card accounts. Look for them at the airport or on the street in front of banks. You may withdraw money from your account in Hungarian forints only, at the official daily exchange rate. In our experience, the ATMs of "OTP" banks are the most convenient when it comes to walking around in town and those of "MKB" are most convenient in shopping centers, while the ATMs of "K&H" banks are totally unreliable.

If you plan to use an ATM, be sure you know your four-digit PIN access number before you leave home and be sure to find out your daily withdrawal limit before you depart.

CREDIT & CHARGE CARDS

Credit and charge cards are widely accepted throughout Budapest. All first- and second-class hotels, many pensions, and all of the more expensive

What Things Cost in Budapest	U.S.$	£
Taxi from Ferihegy II airport to the city center (depending on which fleet)	11.00–22.00	7.79–15.59
Metro from Nyugati Station to Deák tér	36¢	.26
Local telephone call	78¢	.55
Double room at the Hilton (Very Expensive)	193–281	136.75–201.20
Double room at the Hotel Victoria (Expensive)	91.00	64.47
Double room at Hotel Kulturrinov (Moderate)	64.00	45.35
Double room at Hotel MEDOSZ (Inexpensive)	44.00	31.17
Dinner for one, without wine, at Kis Buda Gyöngye (Expensive)	8–12	5.67–8.50
Dinner for one, without wine, at Malomtó Étterem (Moderate)	4–8	2.83–5.67
Dinner for one, without wine, at Makkhetes Vendéglő (Inexpensive)	3–6	2.13–4.25
Half liter of beer	1–1.50	.71–1.06
Coca-Cola	80¢–1.50	.57–1.06
Cup of coffee	1–2	.71–1.42
Roll of ASA 100 Kodacolor film, 36 exposures	4.50	3.19
Admission to the Hungarian National Museum	1.70	1.20
Movie ticket	2.50	1.77
Opera ticket	13–35	9.21–24.80

restaurants in Budapest accept at least one major card. Many—but not all—boutiques, art galleries, antiques stores, crystal and china stores, and trendy shops in the city center also accept credit and charge cards. Inexpensive restaurants and shops that cater more to locals than tourists generally do not. Look for the applicable stickers in the window. Some shops require you to produce some additional form of ID, such as your passport or driver's license.

WHAT TO DO IF YOUR WALLET GETS STOLEN
Be sure to block charges against your account the minute you discover a card has been lost or stolen. Then be sure to file a police report.

Almost every credit card company has an emergency 800-number to call if your card is stolen. They may be able to wire you a cash advance off your credit card immediately, and in many places, they can deliver an emergency credit card in a day or two. The issuing bank's 800-number is usually on the back of your credit card—though of course, if your card has been stolen, that won't help you unless you record the number elsewhere.

Citicorp Visa's U.S. emergency number is ☎ **800/336-8472.** American Express cardholders and traveler's check holders should call ☎ **800/221-7282.** MasterCard holders should call ☎ **800/307-7309.** Otherwise, call the toll-free number directory at ☎ 800/555-1212.

Odds are that if your wallet is gone, the police won't be able to recover it for you. However, it's still worth informing the authorities. Your credit card company or insurer may require a police report number or record of the theft.

If you choose to carry traveler's checks, be sure to keep a record of their serial numbers separate from your checks. You'll get a refund faster if you know the numbers.

If you need emergency cash over the weekend when all banks and American Express offices are closed, you can have money wired to you from **Western Union** (© **800/ 325-6000;** www.westernunion.com/). You must present valid ID to pick up the cash at the Western Union office. However, in most countries, you can pick up a money transfer even if you don't have valid identification, as long as you can answer a test question provided by the sender. Be sure to let the sender know in advance that you don't have ID. If you need to use a test question instead of ID, the sender must take cash to his or her local Western Union office, rather than transferring the money over the phone or online.

3 When to Go

THE CLIMATE
Budapest has a relatively mild climate—the annual mean temperature in Hungary is 50°F. Nevertheless, summer temperatures often exceed 80° to 85°F, and sweltering hot, humid days are typical in July. January is the coldest month, averaging 30°F, though temperatures can dip well below that on any given day. Be prepared for damp and chilly weather in winter. Spring is usually mild and, especially in May and June, wet. Autumn is usually quite pleasant, with mild, cooler weather through October.

Budapest's Average Daily Temperatures

	Jan	Feb	Mar	Apr	May	June	July	Aug	Sept	Oct	Nov	Dec
Temp. (°F)	30	34	38	53	62	68	72	71	63	52	42	35
Temp. (°C)	−1	1	3	12	17	20	22	22	17	11	6	2

HUNGARY CALENDAR OF EVENTS
With a little luck, your trip to Budapest will coincide with one or more of the city's cultural events. Keep in mind, though, that during some of them, particularly the Spring Festival and the Formula One Grand Prix in mid-August, hotel rooms are particularly hard to come by. All inquiries about ticket availability and location of events should be directed to Budapest's main tourist information office, **Tourinform,** with a main office at Sütő u. 2, 1052 Budapest (© **1/317-9800;** fax 1/317-9656; www.tourinform.hu). It's open daily from 8am to 8pm, and to 3pm on weekends in winter. There's also a branch office at Liszt Ferenc tér 11. (© **1/322-4098;** fax 1/342-2541) that's open daily from 10am to 10pm, and to 6pm in winter.

HOLIDAYS
January 1 (New Year's Day), March 15 (National Holiday), Easter Sunday and Easter Monday, May 1 (May Day), Whit Monday, August 20 (St. Stephen's Day), October 23 (Republic Day), November 1 (All Saints' Day), and December 25–26 (Christmas). Shops, museums, and banks are closed on all holidays.

March
Budapest Spring Festival. For 2 weeks, performances of everything from opera to ballet, from classical music to drama, are held at all the major halls and theaters of Budapest. Simultaneously, temporary exhibitions open in many of

Budapest's museums. Tickets are available at the **Festival Ticket Service,** V. 1081 Rákóczi út 65 (© **1/333-2337**), and at the individual venues. Mid- to late March.

Hollókő's Easter Festival. During Easter in this charming small town in northeastern Hungary, villagers wear national costumes and participate in a folk festival. Traditional song, dance, and foods are featured. For information, contact the Hungarian Arts Festivals Federation (© **36/1-318-8165;** www.arts festivals.hu). Easter.

May–June

Book Fair. Publishers set up kiosks throughout central Pest to display the year's newly released titles. The main attractions, such as authors' dedication sessions, are located in Vörösmarty tér. Most books are in Hungarian, of course, but there are always beautiful books on art, architecture, and other subjects. Last week of May or first week of June.

June–August

Open-Air Theater Programs. A rich variety of open-air performances are given throughout Budapest. Highlights include opera and ballet at the Margaret Island Open-Air Theater, folklore and dance at the Buda Park Theater, musicals in Városmajor Theater, and classical music recitals in the Dominican Courtyard at the Hilton Hotel. For information, contact the Hungarian Arts Festivals Federation (© **36/1-318-8165;** www.artsfestivals.hu). June through August.

Organ Concerts. Concerts are given in the Matthias Church, in the lovely Castle District of Buda. See p. 109 for details. June through August.

Organ Concerts. Budapest's largest church, St. Stephen's Basilica, hosts organ concerts. See p.107. July through August.

Summer Opera and Ballet Festival. This 10-day festival is the only time to see a summer performance at the wonderful Hungarian State Opera House in Budapest. Tickets are available at the **Opera House** box office at VI. Andrássy út 22 (© **1/332-7914**) or at the **National Philharmonic Ticket Office,** V. Vörösmarty tér 1 (© **1/318-0281**). July or August.

International Palace Tournament, Visegrád. Each summer, this ancient town on the Danube hosts an authentic medieval festival replete with dueling knights on horseback, early music, and dance. Second weekend in July.

International Guitar Festival. Esztergom. This stately little town on the Danube hosts the guitar festival, which features performers from around the world. Classical concerts are performed in the Basilica. For information, contact Gran Tours, Esztergom at Széchenyi tér 25, (© **33/413-756**). First week of August every other year; the next festival is scheduled for 2003.

Formula One Grand Prix. One of the European racing circuit's most important annual events is held at Budapest's HungaroRing. Call © **36/2-844-4444** or check out **www.hungaroring.hu**. Second weekend in August.

Pepsi Island (Pepsi-sziget). Óbuda Island in the Danube. Established in 1994 as Hungary's very own "Woodstock," Pepsi-sziget is a weeklong music festival that draws young people from all over Europe. The event features foreign and local rock, folk, and jazz groups on dozens of stages playing each day from early afternoon to the wee hours of the morning. Camping is available. Pick up a program schedule at **Tourinform** or check out their website. Usually begins in the second week of August.

Traditional Handicraft Fair. The Castle District is the site of a 3-day annual handicraft fair, which draws vendors from across Hungary and from Hungarian enclaves in neighboring countries, especially Romania. The wares are generally handmade and of high quality. This is a part of the St. Stephen's Day (August 20) celebrations.

St. Stephen's Day. This is Hungary's national day. The country's patron saint is celebrated with cultural events and a dramatic display of fireworks over the Danube at 9pm. Hungarians also celebrate their Constitution on this day, as well as ceremoniously welcome the first new bread from the recent crop of July wheat. August 20.

National Jewish Festival. In 1999, this new annual festival arrived on the Hungarian cultural scene. The festival features a variety of Jewish-related events—from klezmer music to a book fair, from ballet to cabaret—held in various locations in Budapest. For information, contact the **Tourism and Cultural Center of the Budapest Jewish Community,** 1075 Budapest, Síp u. 12. (✆ **36/1-343-0420;** www.interdnet. hu/Zsido/zsikk/festival_en.html).

Szeged Summer Festival. Szeged, the proud capital of the Great Plain, is home to a summer-long series of cultural events (ballet, opera, rock opera, open-air theater). If you find that many of the concert halls and

theaters in Budapest are closed (as is often the case in the summer months), board a southbound train. For information, call ✆ **62/471-411.** June through August.

September

Budapest International Wine Festival. This festival, in Budapest's Castle District, features wine tastings, displays, and auctions, as well as folk and classical music performances. All 22 wine regions of Hungary are represented. The sponsor is the **Hungarian Viniculture Foundation,** XII. Hertelendy u. 1/b (✆ **1/355-1847;** fax 1/202-2390; www. bacchus.hu/english/eng_index.htm). Long weekend in early September.

Budapest International Fair. For 10 days, Budapest's HungExpo grounds are filled with displays of Europe's latest consumer goods. Contact ✆ **36-1/263-6000;** www. hungexpo.hu. Mid-September.

Budapest Art Weeks. In celebration of the opening of the fall season, special classical music and dance performances are held for 3 weeks in all the city's major halls. For information, contact the Hungarian Arts Festivals Federation (✆ **36/1-318-8165;** www.artsfestivals.hu). The festival's traditional start is September 25, the day of Béla Bartók's death.

Contemporary Music Weeks. Held in conjunction with the Budapest Art Weeks, this 3-week festival also features performances in all the capital's major halls. For information, contact the Hungarian Arts Festivals Federation (✆ **36/1-318-8165;** www.artsfestivals.hu).

STAYING HEALTHY

No shots or inoculations are required for entry to Hungary. To be on the safe side, bring enough of any pre-

scription or other medication you may need. Even if you do, it is good practice to take along a copy of all prescriptions—in their generic forms—in case you run out of any meds. Sunscreen and other toiletries are readily available.

If you worry about getting sick away from home, consider purchasing **medical travel insurance** and carry your ID card in your purse or wallet. In most cases, your existing health plan will provide the coverage you need. See the section on insurance below for more information.

If you suffer from a chronic illness, consult your doctor before your departure. For conditions like epilepsy, diabetes, or heart problems, wear a **Medic Alert Identification Tag** (© 800/ 825-3785;   www.medicalert.org), which will immediately alert doctors to your condition and give them access to your records through Medic Alert's 24-hour hotline.

And don't forget sunglasses and an extra pair of contact lenses or prescription glasses.

Contact the **International Association for Medical Assistance to Travelers (IAMAT)** (© 716/754-4883 or 416/652-0137;   www.sentex.net/ ~iamat) for tips on travel and health concerns in the countries you're visiting and lists of local, English-speaking doctors. Any foreign consulate can provide a list of area doctors who speak English. If you get sick, consider asking your hotel concierge to recommend a local doctor—even his or her own. You can also try the emergency room at a local hospital; many have walk-in clinics for emergency cases that are not life-threatening. You may not get immediate attention, but you won't pay the high price of an emergency room visit (usually a minimum of $300 just for signing your name).

INSURANCE
TRAVEL INSURANCE AT A GLANCE

Check your existing insurance policies before you buy travel insurance of any kind. You're likely to have partial or complete coverage. But if you need

some, ask your travel agent about a comprehensive package. The cost of travel insurance varies widely, depending on the cost and length of your trip, your age and overall health, and the type of trip you're taking.

For information, contact one of the following popular insurers:

- **Access America** (© 800/284-8300; www.accessamerica.com/)
- **Travel Guard International** (© 800/826-1300; www.travel guard.com)
- **Travel Insured International** (© 800/243-3174; www.travel insured.com)
- **Travelex Insurance Services** (© 800/228-9792; www.travelex-insurance.com)

MEDICAL INSURANCE

Emergency medical treatment is provided free of charge in Hungary, but you'll have to pay for prescription medications and for non-emergency care.

Most health insurance policies cover you if you get sick away from home—but check, particularly if you're insured by an HMO. With the exception of certain HMOs and Medicare/Medicaid, your medical insurance should cover medical treatment—even hospital care—overseas. However, most out-of-country hospitals make you pay your bills up front, and send you a refund after you've returned home and filed the necessary paperwork. Members of **Blue Cross/ Blue Shield** can now use their cards at select hospitals in most major cities worldwide. Call © **800/810-BLUE** (www.bluecares.com/blue/bluecard/ wwn) for a list of participating hospitals.

If you require additional insurance, try one of the following companies:

- **MEDEX International,** 9515 Deereco Rd., Timonium, MD 21093-5375 (© **888/MEDEX-00** or 410/453-6300; fax 410/453-6301; www.medexassist.com).

- **Travel Assistance International,** 9200 Keystone Crossing, Suite 300, Indianapolis, IN 46240 (© **800/821-2828;** www.travel assistance.com), For general information on services, call Worldwide Assistance Services, Inc., at © **800777-8710.**

The cost of travel medical insurance varies widely. Check your existing policies before you buy additional coverage. Also, check to see if your medical insurance covers you for emergency medical evacuation: If you have to buy a one-way, same-day ticket home and forfeit your nonrefundable roundtrip ticket, you may be out big bucks.

LOST-LUGGAGE INSURANCE

On international flights (including US portions of international trips), baggage is limited to approximately $9.07 per pound, up to approximately $635 per checked bag. If you plan to check items more valuable than the standard liability, you may purchase "excess valuation" coverage from the airline, up to $5,000. Be sure to take any valuables or irreplaceable items with you in your carry-on luggage. If you file a lost luggage claim, be prepared to answer detailed questions about the contents of your baggage, and be sure to file a claim immediately, as most airlines enforce a 21-day deadline.

CAR RENTAL INSURANCE (LOSS/DAMAGE WAIVER OR COLLISION DAMAGE WAIVER)

If you hold a private auto insurance policy, you probably are covered in the U.S., but not abroad, for loss or damage to the car, and liability in case a passenger is injured. The credit card you used to rent the car may provide some coverage for you abroad.

Car rental insurance probably does not cover liability if you caused the accident. Check your own auto insurance policy, the rental company policy, and your credit card coverage for the extent of coverage: Is your destination covered? Are other drivers covered? How much liability is covered if a passenger is injured? (If you rely on your credit card for coverage, you may want to bring a second credit card with you, as damages may be charged to your card and you may find yourself stranded with no money.)

Car rental insurance costs about $20 a day.

5 Tips for Travelers with Special Needs

FOR TRAVELERS WITH DISABILITIES

Buses and metros in Budapest are not equipped for people with disabilities, and many hotels, restaurants, and museums are generally not accessible to wheelchairs. However, Hungarians are accustomed to helping people with disabilities get on and off buses, up and down stairs, etc. You will find people to be very helpful and generous in this respect.

Most disabilities shouldn't stop anyone from traveling. There are more options and resources out there than ever before.

AGENCIES/OPERATORS

- **Flying Wheels Travel** (© **800/ 535-6790;** www.flyingwheels travel.com) offers escorted tours and cruises that emphasize sports and private tours in minivans with lifts.

- **Access Adventures** (© **716/889-9096**), offers customized itineraries for a variety of travelers with disabilities.

- **Accessible Journeys** (© **800/ TINGLES** or 610/521-0339; www.disabilitytravel.com) caters specifically to slow walkers and wheelchair travelers and their families and friends.

ORGANIZATIONS

- **The Moss Rehab Hospital** (© **800/397-2681;** www.above beyondtours.com) offers gay and lesbian tours worldwide and is the exclusive gay and lesbian tour operator for United Airlines. **Now, Voyager** (© **800/255-6951;** www.nowvoyager.com) is a San Francisco–based, gay-owned and operated travel service.

PUBLICATIONS

- *Out and About* (© **800/929-2268** or 415-644-8044; www.out andabout.com) offers guidebooks and a newsletter 10 times a year packed with solid information on the global gay and lesbian scene.
- *Spartacus International Gay Guide* and *Odysseus* are good, annual English-language guidebooks focused on gay men, with some information for lesbians. You can get them from most gay and lesbian bookstores, or order them from **Giovanni's Room** bookstore, 1145 Pine St., Philadelphia, PA 19107 (© **215/923-2960;** www.giovannisroom.com).
- *Gay Travel A to Z: The World of Gay & Lesbian Travel Options at Your Fingertips,* by Marianne Ferrari (Ferrari Publications; www.ferrariguides.com), is a very good gay and lesbian guidebook series.

FOR SENIORS

Don't be shy about asking for discounts, but always carry some kind of identification, such as a driver's license, that shows your date of birth. Also, mention the fact that you're a senior citizen when you first make your travel reservations. For example, many hotels offer seniors discounts. In most cities, people over the age of 60 qualify for reduced admission to theaters, museums, and other attractions, and discounted fares on public transportation.

Members of **AARP,** formerly the American Association of Retired Persons, 601 E St. NW, Washington, DC 20049 (© **800/424-3410** or 202/434-2277; www.aarp.org), get discounts on hotels, airfares, and car rentals. AARP offers members a wide range of benefits, including *Modern Maturity* magazine and a monthly newsletter. Anyone over 50 can join.

The Alliance for Retired Americans, 8403 Colesville Rd., Suite 1200, Silver Spring, MD 20910 (© **301/578-8422;** www.retiredamericans.org), offers a newsletter six times a year and discounts on hotel and auto rentals; annual dues are $13 per person or couple. *Note:* Members of the former National Council of Senior Citizens receive automatic membership in the Alliance.

AGENCIES/OPERATORS

- **Grand Circle Travel** (© **800/221-2610** or 617/350-7500; www.gct.com) offers package deals for the 50-plus market, mostly of the tour-bus variety, with free trips thrown in for those who organize groups of 10 or more.
- **Elderhostel** (© **877/426-8056;** www.elderhostel.org) arranges study programs for those age 55 and over (and a spouse or companion of any age) in the U.S. and in more than 80 countries around the world. Most courses last five to seven days in the U.S. (2 to 4 weeks abroad), and many include airfare, accommodations in university dormitories or modest inns, meals, and tuition.

FAMILY TRAVEL

Children are treated like royalty in Hungarian culture, pampered not just by parents and extended family members, but also by shopkeepers, train conductors and all sorts of other people whose paths they cross in everyday life. Budapest has numerous attractions geared to children, from the zoo, circus, and amusement park in Pest's City Park to a range of museums, including ones dedicated to science, natural history, and transportation. There is even a miniature children's railway running through the hills of Buda, with children in official Hungarian railway dress serving as conductors. And in this land of sweet teeth, there are fresh pastries and ice cream cones sold everywhere, seemingly from every open window along the commercial thoroughfares. We have been traveling here with young children for the past six years and have no regrets—neither will you.

PUBLICATIONS

- *Family Travel Times* is published 6 times a year by **Travel with Your Children** (© **888/822-4388** or 212/477-5524; www.travelwith yourkids.com). Subscriptions are $39 a year for quarterly editions and include a weekly call-in service for subscribers. A free publication list and a sample issue are available online.

WEBSITES

- **Family Travel Network** (www. familytravelnetwork.com) offers travel tips and reviews of family-friendly destinations, vacation deals, and thoughtful features such as "What to Do When Your Kids Are Afraid to Travel" and "Kid-Style Camping."
- **Travel with Your Children** (www.travelwithyourkids.com) is a comprehensive site offering sound advice for traveling with children.

FOR STUDENTS & OTHERS UNDER 26 YEARS

If you're planning to travel outside the U.S., you'd be wise to arm yourself with a **international student ID card,** which offers substantial savings on rail passes, plane tickets, and entrance fees. It also provides you with basic health and life insurance and a 24-hour help line. The card is available for $22 from the **Council on International Educational Exchange,** or CIEE (www.ciee. org). The CIEE's travel branch, **Council Travel Service** (© **800/226-8624;** www.counciltravel.com), is the biggest student travel agency in the world. **STA Travel** (© **800/781-4040;** www. statravel.com) is another travel agency catering especially to young travelers, although their bargain-basement prices are available to people of all ages.

In Canada, **Travel CUTS** (© **800/ 667-2887** or 416/614-2887; www. travelcuts.com), offers similar services. In London, **Campus Travel** (© **0171/ 730-3402;** www.campustravel.co.uk), opposite Victoria Station, is Britain's leading specialist in student and youth travel.

Express, the former state-run student travel agency, remains a valuable resource for students. Among other things, Express sells the **International Student Identity Card** (ISIC) and **International Youth Hostel Federation** card (IYHF) (for the ISIC card, you need to bring a photo; the nearest photo booths are at V. Október 6 u. 22 and at Nyugati railway station). The main office of Express is located at V. Szabadság tér 16 (© **1/331-6393**); it's open Monday through Thursday from 8:30am to 4:30pm, and Friday from 8:30am to 2:30pm.

The **Hungarian Youth Hostel Federation,** on the fourth floor of VII. Almássy tér 6, near Blaha Lujza tér, Red line, (© **1/352-1572,** ext. 203), is another good source of information and discounts for young travelers. Pick up an IYHF card (no photo required) for 1,500 Ft ($5.50). The office is open Monday through Friday from 8am to 4pm. There is also a useful youth travel agency called

Mellow Mood Ltd., located at VII. Baross tér 15 (© **1/331-6393**) (Baross utca on tram 4, 6). It's open Monday through Friday from 8am to 4pm.

FOR WOMEN

NANE, an organization to help women in the case of rape and/or domestic abuse, operates a hot line in Hungarian and English; call © **1/ 267-4900.** Leave a message if necessary. The **International Women's Club Foundation** (© **1/225-3078;** the line is active only from 10am to noon daily) meets regularly and welcomes new members.

6 Getting There

BY PLANE

The flying time to Budapest from New York is just over 9 hours; from London, it is approximately 2½ hours.

You may want to consider flying to Vienna to keep down your travel costs. You can easily get a train from Vienna to Budapest, so you won't have to spend a night in the wallet-busting Austrian capital if you don't want to.

NEW AIR TRAVEL SECURITY MEASURES

In the wake of the terrorist attacks of September 11, 2001, the airline industry began implementing sweeping security measures in airports. Expect a lengthy check-in process and extensive delays. Although regulations vary from airline to airline, you can expedite the process by taking the following steps:

- **Arrive early.** Arrive at the airport at least 2 hours before your scheduled flight.
- **Try not to drive your car to the airport.** Parking and curbside access to the terminal may be limited. Call ahead and check.
- **Don't count on curbside check-in.** Some airlines and airports have stopped curbside check-in altogether, whereas others offer it on a limited basis. For up-to-date information on specific regulations and implementations, check with the individual airline.
- **Be armed with plenty of documentation.** A government-issued photo ID (federal, state, or local) is now required. You may need to show this at various checkpoints. With an e-ticket, you may be required to have with you printed confirmation of purchase and perhaps even the credit card with which you bought your ticket. This varies from airline to airline, so call ahead to make sure you have the proper documentation. And **be sure that your ID is up-to-date:** an expired driver's license, for example, may keep you from boarding the plane altogether.
- **Know what you can carry on— and what you can't.** Travelers in the United States are now limited to one carry-on bag, plus one personal bag (such as a purse or a briefcase). The FAA has also issued a list of newly restricted carry-on items; see the box "What You Can Carry On—and What You Can't."
- **Prepare to be searched.** Expect spot-checks. Electronic items, such as a laptop or cellphone, should be readied for additional screening. Limit the metal items you wear on your person.
- **It's no joke.** When a check-in agent asks if someone other than you packed your bag, don't decide that this is the time to be funny. The agents will not hesitate to call an alarm.
- **No ticket, no gate access.** Only ticketed passengers will be allowed beyond the screener checkpoints, except for those people with specific medical or parental needs.

> ### ⌐Tips What You Can Carry On—And What You Can't
>
> The Federal Aviation Administration (FAA) has devised new restrictions on carry-on baggage, not only to expedite the screening process, but to prevent potential weapons from passing through airport security. Passengers are now limited to bringing just one carry-on bag and one personal item onto the aircraft (previous regulations allowed two carry-on bags and one personal item, like a briefcase or a purse). For more information, go to the FAA's website www.faa.gov.apa/pr/index.cfm. The agency has released a new list of items passengers are not allowed to carry onto an aircraft:
>
> **Not permitted:** knives and box cutters, corkscrews, straight razors, metal scissors, metal nail files, golf clubs, baseball bats, pool cues, hockey sticks, ski poles, ice picks.
>
> **Permitted:** nail clippers, tweezers, eyelash curlers, safety razors (including disposable razors), syringes (with documented proof of medical need), walking canes and umbrellas (must be inspected first)
>
> The airline you fly may have **additional restrictions** on items you can and cannot carry on board. Call ahead to avoid problems.

THE MAJOR AIRLINES

Delta Airlines (✆ 800/241-4141, 800/361-9783 from eastern Canada, 0800/414-767 in London) and **Malév** (✆ 800/877-5429, 800/262-5380, or 800/223-6884), the former Hungarian state airline, offer nonstop service between North America and Budapest. (Most Delta-issued tickets are actually for Malév planes.) Other leading carriers include **Lufthansa** (✆ 800/645-3880), **British Airways** (✆ 800/247-9297), and **Austrian Air** (✆ 800/843-0002).

BUDAPEST'S AIRPORTS

Until quite recently, Budapest was served by two adjacent airports, **Ferihegy I and Ferihegy II,** located in the XVIII district in southeastern Pest. However, Ferihegy I has now been turned over to NATO for military use, so Ferihegy II (which has a **Terminal A** and a **Terminal B**) is the place for all civilian flights. There are several main information numbers: For arrivals, try ✆ 1/296-5052; for departures, call ✆ 1/296-5883; and for general information, call ✆ 1/296-7155. Make sure you pick up a copy of the free **LRI Airport Budapest Magazine** while at the airport, as it contains a wealth of valuable phone numbers and transportation-related information, as well as articles on Hungary.

All arriving flights are international since there is no domestic air service in Hungary. All arriving passengers pass through the same Customs gate and emerge into the bustling arrival hall of the airport.

Though extended and modernized over the past few years, the airport remains quite small. In each terminal, you will find several accommodation offices, rental-car agencies, shops, and exchange booths. Note that exchange rates are generally less favorable here than in the city, so you may not want to change very much money at the airport.

Twenty-four-hour **left-luggage service** is available at Terminal B (✆ 1/296-8802). Finally, since Hungary is still a non-EU country, its airport has one of Europe's rapidly dwindling number of genuine duty-free shops.

BY TRAIN

Countless trains arrive in Budapest from most corners of Europe. Many connect through Vienna, where 11 daily trains depart for Budapest from either the Westbahnhof or Sudbahnhof station. Six daily trains connect Prague and Budapest, while one connects Berlin with Budapest and two connect Warsaw with Budapest.

The train trip between Vienna and Budapest takes about 3½ hours and costs approximately $50 one-way in first class, $33 one-way in second class. Hungarian railway offers a great deal for short-term visitors coming from Vienna: a round-trip second class ticket for $50, valid up to four days that includes a free pass for all public transport in Budapest. For more information on Vienna trains, contact the **Austrian National Tourist Board,** 500 Fifth Ave., Suite 800, New York, NY 10110 (© **212/944-6885**); 11601 Wilshire Blvd., Suite 2480, Los Angeles, CA 90025 (© **310/477-3332**); 30 St. George St., London W1R 0AL (© **020/7629-0461**); 2 Bloor St. E., Suite 3330, Toronto, ON M4W 1A8 (© **416/967-3381**); or 1010 Sherbrooke St. W., Suite 1410, Montréal, PQ H3A 2R7 (© **514/849-3708**).

GETTING AROUND HUNGARY BY TRAIN

Train travel within Hungary is generally very efficient; trains almost always depart right on time and usually arrive on time. In the train stations, departures (*érkező vonatok*) are listed on the yellow poster, while arrivals (*induló vonatok*) are listed on the white poster. You can access a full, user-friendly timetable on the Web, at **elvira.mav informatika.hu.** As you must conduct your search in Hungarian, it is helpful to know that *honnan* means "from where," *hova* means "to where,"

ma means "today," *holnap* means "tomorrow" and *keres* means "ask" or, in this context, "search."

A train posted as *személy* is an interminable local train, which stops at every single village and town on its route. A *sebes* (speedy) train makes more selective stops, but is, essentially, another type of local train. Always opt for a *gyors* (fast) or Intercity train to get to your destination in a timely manner. All Intercity trains (but no other domestic trains) require a seat reservation (*helyjegy*), costing 340 Ft ($1.25); ask for the reservation when purchasing your ticket. On Intercity trains, you must sit in your assigned seat. All intercity trains now comply strictly with a new law imposing constraints on smoking in public spaces; they have a single car designated for smokers, while the rest of the train is non-smoking. If you want a seat in the smoking car, you need to ask for *dohányzó* when buying your ticket. The gyors train is typically an old, gritty, rumbling train with the classic eight-seat compartments. The Intercity, a state-of-the-art, clean, modern train without compartments, is said to travel faster, but our experience has shown us that there's seldom more than 15 to 30 minutes difference between the two in terms of speed.

During the day, obtain **domestic train information** over the phone by dialing © **1/461-5400** and **international train information** at © **1/461-5500**. Purchase tickets at train station ticket windows or from the MÁV Service Office, VI. Andrássy út 35 (© **1/322-80482**), open 9am to 6pm Monday through Friday.

TRAIN PASSES

MÁV now offers 7-day and 10-day tourist passes, good for rail travel throughout Hungary. A 7-day pass costs 10,100 Ft ($36), while a 10-day pass goes for 14,540 Ft ($52). In Hungary, all passes are validated at a station ticket window or at the **MÁV**

Service Office (☎ 1/322-8082) when purchased.

Besides the 7- and 10-day tourist passes, regional passes, such as **European East Pass** (for Austria, Hungary, the Czech Republic, and Poland), are also available. The European East Pass is good for first-class unlimited rail access in Austria, the Czech Republic, Hungary, Poland, and Slovakia. You must purchase the pass from a travel agent or Rail Europe (see contact information below) before you leave for Europe. A pass for any 5 days of unlimited train travel in a month-long period costs $210 for adults, $105 for children ages 4 to 11. A pass for any 10 days of unlimited train travel in a 1-month period costs $330 for adults, $165 for children ages 4 to 11. If you plan to visit only one European country or region, bear in mind that a country or regional pass will cost less than a Eurailpass.

EURAILPASS   The **Eurailpass** entitles travelers to unlimited first-class travel over the 100,000-mile (160,900km) national railroad network in all western European countries, except Britain, and including Hungary in eastern Europe. It's also valid on some lake steamers and private railroads. A Eurailpass may be purchased for as short a period as 15 days or as long as 3 months. The passes are not available to residents of the countries where the pass is valid or to residents of the United Kingdom.

The Eurailpass, which is ideal for extensive trips, eliminates the hassles of buying tickets—just show your pass to the ticket collector. You should note, however, that some trains require seat reservations. Also, many of the trains have couchettes, or sleeping cars, for which an additional fee is charged.

The pass cannot be purchased in Europe, so you must secure one before leaving on your trip. It costs $572 for 15 days, $740 for 21 days, $918 for 1 month, $1,298 for 2 months, and $1,606 for 3 months. Children under 4 travel free if they don't occupy a seat (otherwise they are charged half fare); children under 12 are charged half fare.

If you're under 26, you can obtain unlimited second-class travel, wherever Eurailpass is honored, on a **Eurail Youthpass,** which costs $644 for 1 month, $910 for 2 months.

Groups of two or more people can purchase a **Eurail Saverpass** for 15 days of discounted travel in first class for $486, or get a month of travel for $780. To be entitled to the discount, the members of the group must travel together.

The **Eurail Flexipass** allows passengers to visit Europe with more flexibility. It's valid in first class and offers the same privileges as the Eurailpass. However, it provides a number of individual travel days, which can be used over a much longer period of consecutive days. That makes it possible to stay in one city and yet not lose a single day of discounted travel. There are two passes: $674 for 10 days of travel within 2 months and $888 for 15 days of travel within 2 months. Children 4 to 11 are charged 50% of the adult fares.

In addition, a **Eurail Youth Flexipass** is good for travelers under 26. Two passes are available: $473 for 10 days of travel within 2 months and $622 for 15 days of travel within 2 months.

These passes are available from travel agents in North America, or you can contact **Rail Europe** by calling ☎ 800/848-7245 or surfing over to **www.raileurope.com.**

For British travelers, many different rail passes are available in the U.K. for travel in Europe. Stop in at the **International Rail Centre,** Victoria Station, London SW1V 1JY (☎ 0171/834-2345); or Wasteels, 121 Wilton

Rd., London SW1V 1JZ (© **0171/ 834-7066**).

BY BUS

Inland and international buses will eventually arrive at and depart from two terminals (see below) after the Erzsébet tér station (formerly the main station) finally shuts its doors; indeed, by the time this book hits the shelves, it may be closed. Until then, buses to and from Western Europe and points in Hungary west of the Danube call at the **Erzsébet tér bus station** (© **1/ 485-2100** domestic information; 1/485-2162 international information), just off Deák tér in central Pest. All three metro lines converge on Deák tér. Buses to and from Eastern and Central Europe, as well as points in Hungary east of the Danube, call at the **Népstadion bus station** (© **1/ 252-2995** domestic information; 1/252-1896 international information). Take the Red line metro to Népstadion. Buses to and from the Danube Bend and other points north of Budapest call at the **Árpád híd bus station** (© **1/320-9229** or 1/317-9886). Take the Blue line metro to Árpád híd. (It can be difficult to get through to the bus stations over the telephone and to reach an English speaker. Your best bet is to gather your information in person or try the Tourinform office.)

BY CAR

Several major highways link Hungary to nearby European capitals. The **E60** (or M1) connects Budapest with Vienna and points west; this highway was recently expanded into a multi-lane motorway and is now a toll road from the Austrian border to the city of Györ. The **E65** connects Budapest with Prague and points north.

The **border crossings** from Austria and Slovakia (from which countries most Westerners enter Hungary) are hassle-free. In addition to your passport, you may be requested to present your driver's license, vehicle registration, and proof of insurance (the number plate and symbol indicating country of origin are acceptable proof). A green card is required of vehicles arriving from Bulgaria, France, the former USSR, Greece, Poland, Italy, Romania, and Israel. Hungary no longer requires the International Driver's License. Cars entering Hungary are required to have a decal indicating country of registration, a first-aid kit, and an emergency triangle. For traffic regulations, see "Getting Around," in chapter 3.

Driving distances are: from Vienna, 154 miles (248 km); from Prague, 347 miles (560 km); from Frankfurt, 590 miles (952 km); and from Rome, 802 miles (1,294 km).

BY HYDROFOIL

The Hungarian state shipping company **MAHART** operates hydrofoils on the Danube between Vienna and Budapest in the spring and summer months. It's an extremely popular route, so you should book your tickets well in advance. In North America or Britain, contact the Austrian National Tourist Board (see "By Train" above). In Vienna, contact MAHART, Handelskai 265 (© **43/729-2161;** fax 43/ 729-2163).

From April 3 through July 2 the MAHART hydrofoil departs Vienna at 9am daily, arriving in Budapest at 2:30pm, with a stop in Bratislava when necessary (passengers getting on or off). From July 3 to August 29 two hydrofoils make the daily passage, departing Vienna at 8am and 1pm, arriving in Budapest at 1:30 and 6:30pm, respectively. From August 30 to November 1, the schedule returns to one hydrofoil daily, departing Vienna at 9am and arriving in Budapest at 2:30pm. Customs and passport control begin 1 hour prior to departure. The one-way fare is 830 AS ($55) and round-trip fare is 1,150 AS ($77) (We use the exchange rate of $1 to AS 15 for these purposes.) Children 5 years and under not requiring seats ride free; children between the ages of 6 and 15 are half price. Eurailpass holders also receive a discount, as long as they buy the ticket before boarding. ISIC holders also receive a discount. The Budapest office of **MAHART** is

at V. Belgrád rakpart (© **1/318-1704** or 1/318-1880). Boats and hydrofoils from Vienna arrive at the international boat station next door to the MAHART office on the **Belgrád rakpart,** which is on the Pest side of the Danube, between the Szabadság and Erzsébet bridges.

7 Planning Your Trip Online

Researching and booking your trip online can save time and money. Then again, it may not. It is simply not true that you always get the best deal online. Most booking engines do not include schedules and prices for budget airlines, and from time to time you'll get a better last-minute price by calling the airline directly, so it's best to call the airline to see if you can do better before booking online.

On the plus side, Internet users today can tap into the same travel-planning databases that were once accessible only to travel agents—and do it at the same speed. Sites such as **Frommers.com**, **Travelocity.com**, **Expedia.com**, and **Orbitz.com** allow consumers to comparison shop for airfares, access special bargains, book flights, and reserve hotel rooms and rental cars.

But don't fire your travel agent just yet. Although online booking sites offer tips and hard data to help you bargain shop, they cannot endow you with the hard-earned experience that makes a seasoned, reliable travel agent an invaluable resource, even in the Internet age. And for consumers with a complex itinerary, a trusty travel agent is still the best way to arrange the most direct flights to and from the best airports.

Still, there's no denying the Internet's emergence as a powerful tool in researching and plotting travel time. The benefits of researching your trip online can be well worth the effort.

Last-minute specials, such as weekend deals or Internet-only fares, are offered by airlines to fill empty seats. Most of these are announced on Tuesday or Wednesday and must be purchased online. They are only valid for travel that weekend, but some can be booked weeks or months in advance. Sign up for weekly e-mail alerts at airline websites or check mega-sites that compile comprehensive lists of last-minute specials, such as **Smarter Living** (smarterliving.com) or **WebFlyer** (www.webflyer.com).

Some sites, such as Expedia.com, will send you **e-mail notification** when a cheap fare becomes available to your favorite destination. Some will also tell you when fares to a particular destination are lowest.

TRAVEL PLANNING & BOOKING SITES

Keep in mind that because several airlines are no longer willing to pay commissions on tickets sold by online travel agencies, these agencies may either add a $10 surcharge to your bill if you book on that carrier—or neglect to offer those carriers' schedules.

The list of sites below is selective, not comprehensive. Some sites will have evolved or disappeared by the time you read this.

- **Travelocity** (www.travelocity.com or www.frommers.travelocity. com) and **Expedia** (www.expedia. com) are among the most popular sites, each offering an excellent range of options. Travelers search by destination, dates, and cost.
- **Orbitz** (www.orbitz.com) is a popular site launched by United,

Frommers.com: The Complete Travel Resource

For an excellent travel-planning resource, we highly recommend **Frommers.com** (www.frommers.com). We're a little biased, of course, but we guarantee that you'll find the travel tips, reviews, monthly vacation giveaways, and online-booking capabilities thoroughly indispensable. Among the special features are our popular **Message Boards,** where Frommer's readers post queries and share advice (sometimes even our authors show up to answer questions); **Frommers.com Newsletter,** for the latest travel bargains and inside travel secrets; and Frommer's **Destinations Section,** where you'll get expert travel tips, hotel and dining recommendations, and advice on the sights to see for more than 2,500 destinations around the globe. When your research is done, the **Online Reservation System** (www.frommers.com/booktravelnow) takes you to Frommer's favorite sites for booking your vacation at affordable prices.

Delta, Northwest, American, and Continental airlines. (Stay tuned: At press time, travel-agency associations were waging an antitrust battle against this site.)

- **Qixo** (www.qixo.com) is another powerful search engine that allows you to search for flights and accommodations from some 20 airline and travel-planning sites (such as Travelocity) at once. Qixo sorts results by price.
- **Priceline** (www.priceline.com) lets you "name your price" for airline tickets, hotel rooms, and rental cars. For airline tickets, you can't say what time you want to fly—you have to accept any flight between 6am and 10pm on the dates you've selected, and you may have to make one or more stopovers. Tickets are nonrefundable, and no frequent-flyer miles are awarded.

SMART E-SHOPPING

The savvy traveler is armed with insider information. Here are a few tips to help you navigate the Internet successfully and safely.

- **Know when sales start.** Last-minute deals may vanish in minutes. If you have a favorite booking site or airline, find out when last-minute deals are

released to the public. (For example, Southwest's specials are posted every Tuesday at 12:01 am central time.)

- **Shop around.** If you're looking for bargains, compare prices on different sites and airlines—and against a travel agent's best fare. Try a range of times and alternative airports before you make a purchase.
- **Stay secure.** Book only through secure sites (some airline sites are not secure). Look for a key icon (Netscape) or a padlock (Internet Explorer) at the bottom of your web browser before you enter credit card information or other personal data.
- **Avoid online auctions.** Sites that auction airline tickets and frequent-flier miles are the number-one perpetrators of Internet fraud, according to the National Consumers League.
- **Maintain a paper trail.** If you book an e-ticket, print out a confirmation, or write down your confirmation number, and keep it safe and accessible—or your trip could be a virtual one!

ONLINE TRAVELER'S TOOLBOX

Veteran travelers usually carry some essential items to make their trips easier. Following is a selection of online tools to bookmark and use.

- **Visa ATM Locator** (www.visa.com), for locations of Plus ATMs worldwide, or **MasterCard ATM Locator** (www.mastercard.com), for locations of Cirrus ATMs worldwide.
- **Foreign Languages for Travelers** (www.travlang.com). Learn basic terms in more than 70 languages and click on any underlined phrase to hear what it sounds like. *Note:* Free audio software and speakers are required.
- **Intellicast** (www.intellicast.com) and **Weather.com** (www.weather.com). Gives weather forecasts for all 50 states and for cities around the world.
- **Cybercafes.com** (www.cybercafes.com) or **Net Café Guide** (www.netcafeguide.com/mapindex.htm). Locate Internet cafes at hundreds of locations around the globe. Catch up on your e-mail and log onto the web for a few dollars per hour.
- **Universal Currency Converter** (www.xe.net/currency). See what your dollar or pound is worth in more than 100 other countries.
- **U.S. State Department Travel Warnings** (www.travel.state.gov/travel_warnings.html). Reports on places where health concerns or unrest might threaten U.S. travelers. It also lists the locations of U.S. embassies around the world.

8 Recommended Reading

BOOKS

A good number of the best books on Hungary are now out of print. If you can't find a given book in a bookstore or on the Internet, your best bet is to check in a university library. Many books published by Corvina, a Budapest-based English-language press, are recommended below. They can be purchased at English-language bookstores in Budapest, or you can write for a free catalog: **Corvina kiadó,** P.O. Box 108, Budapest H-1364, Hungary.

HISTORY & POLITICS For a general history of Hungary, there's still nothing better than C. A. McCartney's *Hungary: A Short History* (Aldine, 1962), which is unfortunately out of print and difficult to find. *A History of Hungary* (Indiana University Press, 1990), edited by Peter Sugar, is an anthology with a number of good essays. *The Habsburg Monarchy,* 1809–1918 (London: Hamish Hamilton, 1948), by A. J. P. Taylor, is a readable analysis of the final century of the Austro-Hungarian empire.

The Holocaust in Hungary: An Anthology of Jewish Response (University of Alabama Press, 1982), edited and translated by Andrew Handler, is notable for the editor's excellent introduction. Elenore Lister's *Wallenberg: The Man in the Iron Web* (Prentice Hall, 1982) recounts the heroic life of Raoul Wallenberg, written against the chilling backdrop of Nazi-occupied Budapest.

Joseph Rothschild has written two excellent surveys of 20th-century Eastern European history, both with large sections on Hungary. They are *East Central Europe Between the Two World Wars* (University of Washington Press, 1974) and *Return to Diversity: A Political History of East Central Europe Since World War II* (Oxford University Press, 1989).

MEMOIRS Two memoirs of early-20th-century Budapest deserve mention: *Apprentice in Budapest: Memories of a World That Is No More* (University of Utah Press, 1988) by the anthropologist Raphael Patai; and *Budapest 1900* (Weidenfeld & Nicolson, 1989), by John Lukacs, which captures the feeling of a lively but doomed imperial city at the turn of the century. Post-communist Budapest is described in Marion Merrick's *Now You See It, Now You Don't; Seven Years in Hungary 1982–89* (Mágus 1998). Another book of note is *In Search of the Mother Book*, a memoir by the American feminist literary figure Susan Rubin Suleiman, who fled Hungary after World War II and returned to the land of her birth in the late 1980s.

CULTURE   *The Cuisine of Hungary* (Bonanza Books, 1971), by the famous Hungarian-born restaurateur George Lang, contains all you need to know about the subject. Tekla Domotor's *Hungarian Folk Beliefs* (Corvina and Indiana University Press, 1981) covers witches, werewolves, giants, and gnomes. Zsuzsanna Ardó's *How to Be a European: Go Hungarian* (Biográf, 1994) is a witty little guidebook to Hungarian culture, etiquette, and social life.

Julia Szabó's *Painting in Nineteenth Century Hungary* (Corvina, 1985) contains a fine introductory essay and over 300 plates. In our opinion, the best tourist-oriented coffee-table book available in Budapest is *Budapest Art and History* (Flow East, 1992), by Delia Meth-Cohn.

FICTION   Not all the best examples of Hungarian literature are available in translation, but look for the following: *Gyula Illyés's The People of the Puszta* (Corvina, 1979), an unabashedly honest look at peasant life in the early 20th century; György Konrád's *The Case Worker* (Penguin, 1987), a portrayal of a political system in disrepair; Péter Esterházy's *Helping Verbs of the Heart* (Weidenfeld & Nicolson, 1991), a gripping story of grief following a parent's death; István Örkény's *The Toth Family* and *The Flower Show* (New Directions, 1966), the first an allegorical story about fear and authority, the second a fable about different types of reality in modern life; Zsolt Csalog's *Lajos M., Aged 45* (Budapest: Maecenas, 1989), an extraordinary memoir of life in a Soviet labor camp; Kálmán Mikszáth's *St. Peter's Umbrella* (Corvina, 1962); and Zsigmond Móricz's *Seven Pennies* (Corvina, 1988), a collection of short stories by one of Hungary's most celebrated authors.

3

Getting to Know Budapest

In this chapter, you'll find a host of practical information you will need during your stay in Budapest—from neighborhood orientation to listings of the cheapest rental-car agencies, from how to use a pay phone to how to avoid taxi hustlers. Glance through this chapter before your arrival, and consult it during your stay.

1 Orientation

ARRIVING

BY PLANE   The easiest way into the city is probably the **Airport Minibus** (☎ 1/296-8555; fax 1/296-8993), a public service of the LRI (Budapest Airport Authority). The minibus, which leaves every 10 or 15 minutes throughout the day, takes you directly to any address in the city. From either terminal, it costs 1,800 Ft ($6.50); the price includes luggage transport. The trip takes from 30 minutes to an hour, depending on how many stops are made. The Airport Minibus desk is easily found in the main hall. Minibuses also provide the same efficient service returning to the airport; arrange for your pickup *one full day in advance*. The minibus will pick up passengers virtually anywhere in the Budapest area.

LRI also runs an **Airport-Centrum** shuttle bus, which leaves every half hour (5am to 9pm) from the airport. Passengers are dropped off at Erzsébet tér, across from the Kempinski Hotel and just off Deák tér, where all three metro lines converge. The price is 800 Ft ($2.90). You can also take the LRI Airport-Centrum bus to return to the airport. Tickets are sold aboard the bus. The trip takes between 30 and 40 minutes.

We strongly discourage the use of cabs from the **Airport Taxi** fleet (☎ 1/296-6534), which is notoriously overpriced. A ride downtown from one of these cabs might cost as much as twice the fare of a recommended fleet (see "Getting Around" below). Unfortunately, for reasons no one has been able to explain to us with a straight face, cabs from the Airport Taxi fleet are the only cabs permitted to wait for fares on the airport grounds. However, dozens of cabs from the cheaper fleets we recommend are at all times stationed at roadside pull-outs just off the airport property, a stone's throw from the terminal, waiting for radio calls from their dispatchers. All it takes is a phone call from the terminal and a cab will be there for you in a matter of minutes. For three or more people traveling together (and maybe even two people), a taxi from a recommended fleet to the city will be cheaper than the combined minibus fares, at approximately 3,000 Ft ($10.80). A taxi from the airport to downtown takes about 20 to 30 minutes.

It's also possible to get to the city by public transportation; the trip takes about 1 hour total. Take the red-lettered **bus no. 93** to the last stop, Kőbánya-Kispest. From there, the Blue metro line runs to the Inner City of Pest. The cost is two transit tickets, which is 200 Ft (75¢); tickets can be bought from the automated vending machine at the bus stop (coins only) or from any newsstand in the airport.

BY TRAIN   Budapest has three major train stations: Keleti pályaudvar (Eastern Station), Nyugati pályaudvar (Western Station), and Déli pályaudvar (Southern Station). The stations' names, curiously, correspond neither to their geographical location in the city nor to the origins or destinations of trains serving them. Each has a metro station beneath it and an array of accommodation offices, currency-exchange booths, and other services.

Most international trains pull into bustling **Keleti Station** (© 1/314-5010), a classic steel-girdered European train station located in Pest's seedy Baross tér, beyond the Outer Ring on the border of the VII and VIII districts. Tourists are met here by various hustlers offering rooms and taxis. The Red line of the metro is below the station; numerous bus, tram, and trolleybus lines serve Baross tér as well.

Some international trains arrive at **Nyugati Station** (© 1/349-0115), another classic designed by the Eiffel company and built in the 1870s. It's located on the Outer Ring, at the border of the V, VI, and XIII districts. A station for the Blue line of the metro is beneath Nyugati, and numerous tram and bus lines serve busy Nyugati tér (formerly Marx tér).

Few international trains arrive at **Déli Station** (© 1/375-6293), an ugly modern building in central Buda; the terminus of the Red metro line is beneath the train station.

MÁV operates a minibus that will take you from any of the three stations to any point in the city for 1,100 Ft ($4) per person, or between stations for 700 Ft ($2.50) per person. To order the minibus, call © **1/353-2722.** Often, however, a taxi fare will be cheaper, especially for groups of two or more travelers (see "Getting Around," later in this chapter).

BY BUS   The **Erzsébet tér bus station** is just off Deák tér in central Pest, where all three metro lines converge. The Red metro line stops at the **Népstadion bus station,** and the Blue line goes to the **Árpád híd bus station.**

VISITOR INFORMATION

Since Budapest is undergoing rapid change, published tourist information is often out of date. The best information source in the city is **Tourinform** (© **1/317-9800** or 1/317-8992; www.hungarytourism.hu), the office of the Hungarian Tourist Board. Centrally located at V. Sütő u. 2, just off Deák tér (reached by all three metro lines) in Pest, the office is open daily from 8am to 8pm. There is now a second branch of Tourinform as well, in the bustling entertainment district of Liszt Ferenc tér, open daily from 10am to 10pm (Liszt Ferenc tér is just down the street from Oktogon, reached by yellow line of the metro or tram No. 4 or 6). The staff in both offices speaks English and dispenses advice on all tourist-related subjects, from concert tickets to pension rooms, from train schedules to horseback riding.

Another very useful information source is **Vista Visitor Center** at V. Paulay Ede u. 7 (© **1/267-8603;** www.vista.hu), a 5-minute walk from Deák tér (reached by all three metro lines) in Pest. This travel agency/cafe is open Monday through Friday from 8am to 10pm, and Saturday and Sunday from 10am to 10pm. Best used as an in-country travel resource (as well as a meeting point for foreigners), Vista also has a great deal of information on Budapest (as well as Internet access; see "Fast Facts: Budapest," later in this chapter).

You can also access city information through the **"Touch Info"** user-friendly computer terminals located at the airport, at Déli Railway Station, at several of the larger metro stations, and in the market hall at Fővám tér.

Of the various free information pamphlets you will find at tourist offices, pubs and elsewhere in the city, the most useful is probably *Look,* a free English-language weekly publication with extensive film and concert listings that was first published in 2001. The listings in *Pesti Est,* a free mainly Hungarian-language weekly that is widely available at clubs, bookstores, and other such places, are more extensive but harder, obviously, for the nonnative to understand. Two other useful free monthly publications are *Programme in Hungary* and *Budapest Panorama,* both available at tourist offices and hotels. These contain information on scheduled cultural events.

The *Budapest Sun,* an English-language weekly newspaper, also has listings for concerts, theater, dance, movies, and other events, along with restaurant reviews and the occasional interesting article; it's available at most hotels and many newsstands. It is also available online at www.budapestsun.com; you can search back issues as well at this website. A similar resource, now available only online, is the former print publication *Budapest Week,* found at www.budapestweek.com.

CITY LAYOUT

You'll follow this section much better with a map in hand. The city of Budapest came into being in 1873, the result of a union of three separate cities: **Buda, Pest,** and **Óbuda.** Budapest, like Hungary itself, is defined by the **River Danube** (Duna). The stretch of the Danube flowing through the capital is fairly wide (the average width is 400m/1,325 ft.), and most of the city's historic sites are on or near the river. Eight bridges connect the two banks, including five in the city center. The Széchenyi Chain Bridge (Lánchíd), built in 1849, was the first permanent bridge across the Danube. Although blown up by the Nazis, it was rebuilt after the war.

MAIN STREETS & SQUARES

PEST   On the right bank of the Danube lies Pest, flat as a *palacsinta* (pancake), spreading far into the distance. Pest is the commercial and administrative center not just of the capital, but of all Hungary. Central Pest, the term used in this guide, is that part of the city between the Danube and the semicircular **Outer Ring** boulevard (Nagykörút), stretches of which are named after former Austro-Hungarian monarchs: Ferenc körút, József körút, Erzsébet körút, Teréz körút, and Szent István körút. The Outer Ring begins at the Pest side of the Petőfi Bridge in the south and wraps itself around the center, ending at the Margit Bridge in the north. Several of Pest's busiest squares are found along the Outer Ring, and Pest's major east-west avenues bisect it at these squares.

Central Pest is further defined by the **Inner Ring** (Kiskörút), which lies within the Outer Ring. It starts at Szabadság híd (Freedom Bridge) in the south and is alternately named Vámház körút, Múzeum körút, Károly körút, Bajcsy-Zsilinszky út, and József Attila utca before ending at the Chain Bridge. Inside this ring is the **Belváros,** the historic Inner City of Pest.

Váci utca (distinct from Váci út) is a popular pedestrian shopping street between the Inner Ring and the Danube. It spills into **Vörösmarty tér,** one of the area's best-known squares. The **Dunakorzó** (Danube Promenade), a popular evening strolling place, runs along the river in Pest, between the Chain

> ### ℭ Hungarian Address Terms
>
> Navigating in Budapest will be easier if you are familiar with the following words (none of which are capitalized in Hungarian):
>
> | | |
> |---|---|
> | utca (abbreviated as u.) | street |
> | út | road |
> | útja | road of |
> | körút (abbreviated as krt.) | boulevard |
> | tér | square |
> | tere | square of |
> | köz | alley or lane |
> | liget | park |
> | sziget | island |
> | híd | bridge |
> | sor | row |
> | part | riverbank |
> | pályaudvar (abbreviated as pu.) | railway station |
> | állomás | station |

Bridge and the Erzsébet Bridge. The historic Jewish district of Pest is in the **Erzsébetváros** (Elizabeth Town), between the two ring boulevards.

Margaret Island (Margit-sziget) is in the middle of the Danube. Accessible via the Margaret Bridge or Árpád Bridge, it's an enormously popular park with restricted vehicular traffic.

BUDA & ÓBUDA   On the left bank of the Danube is Buda; to its north, beyond the city center, lies Óbuda. Buda is as hilly as Pest is flat. Streets in Buda, particularly in the hills, are not as logically arranged as those in Pest.

The two most dramatic points in central Buda are Castle Hill and Gellért Hill. **Castle Hill** is widely considered the most beautiful part of Budapest. A number of steep paths, staircases, and small streets go up to Castle Hill, although no major roads do. The easiest access is from Clark Ádám tér (at the head of the Chain Bridge) by funicular or from Várfok utca (near Moszkva tér) by foot or bus. Castle Hill consists of the royal palace itself, home to numerous museums, and the so-called **Castle District,** a lovely medieval neighborhood of small, winding streets, centered around Holy Trinity Square (Szentháromság tér), site of the Gothic Matthias Church. There's little traffic on Castle Hill, and the only industry is tourism.

Gellért Hill, to the south of Castle Hill, is named after the martyred Italian bishop who aided King István I (Stephen I) in his conversion of the Hungarian nation to Christianity in the 10th and 11th centuries. A giant statue of Gellért sits on the side of the hill, and on top is the Citadella, a fortress built by the Austrians.

An area of parks lies between Castle Hill and Gellért Hill, in the historic **Tabán** neighborhood, an impoverished quarter razed for hygienic reasons in the early 20th century. A few Tabán buildings still stand, on the eastern edge of the quarter.

Below Castle Hill, along the Danube, is a long, narrow neighborhood known as the **Watertown** (Víziváros). The main street of Watertown is Fő utca (Main Street).

Central Buda, the term used in this guide, is a collection of mostly low-lying neighborhoods below Castle Hill. The main square of central Buda is **Moszkva tér,** just north of Castle Hill. Beyond Central Buda, mainly to the east, are the Buda Hills.

Óbuda is on the left bank of the Danube, north of Buda. Although the greater part of Óbuda is modern and drab, it boasts both a beautiful old city center and the impressive Roman ruins of **Aquincum.** Unfortunately, the road coming off the Árpád Bridge slices the old city center in half, destroying its integrity. The historic center of the old city is **Fő tér** (Main Square), a square as lovely as any in Hungary. **Óbuda Island** (Óbudai-sziget) is home to a huge and underused park and is the site each August of Hungary's own annual "Woodstock" music festival, called "Pepsi sziget" (Pepsi Island). For more on this event, see the "Hungary Calendar of Events," in chapter 2, "Planning Your Trip to Budapest."

FINDING AN ADDRESS   Locating addresses in Budapest can be daunting at first, largely because of the strangeness of the Hungarian language. However, with a little practice and a good map, you should meet with success.

Budapest is divided into 22 districts, called *kerülets* (abbreviated as *ker.*). A Roman numeral followed by a period should precede every written address in Budapest, signifying the kerület; for example, XII. Csörsz utca 9 is in the 12th kerület. Because many street names are repeated in different parts of the city it's very important to know which kerület a certain address is in. If the address you seek doesn't have a Roman numeral preceding it, you can also tell the kerület from the four-digit postal code. The middle two digits represent the kerület; thus, Csörsz utca 9, 1123 Budapest will be in district XII. The most popular neighborhoods for tourists are the V. kerület (the Inner City of Pest) and the I. Kerület (Buda's Castle District).

A common mistake made by visitors is to confuse **Váci út,** the heavily trafficked main road that goes from Nyugati Station toward the city of Vác, with **Váci utca,** the pedestrian-only street in the Inner City. Similarly, visitors sometimes mistake Vörösmarty utca, a station on the Yellow metro line, with Vörösmarty tér, the terminus of the same Yellow metro line. Read signs carefully—Hungarian is a language with a fine sense of detail. Refer to the "Hungarian Address Terms" box above.

Street signs are posted on buildings and give the name of the street or square, the kerület, and the building numbers found on that block. Even- and odd-numbered buildings are on opposite sides of the street. Numbers are seldom skipped; often you'll end up walking longer than you expected to reach a given number.

Many street names have been changed since 1990, reverting for the most part back to their pre–World War II names, though on a handful of central streets with politically evocative former names, like Lenin körút (now Teréz körút) and Nép-köztársaság út ("People's Republic Road," now Andrássy út), the old signs, for symbolic reasons, have been left up alongside the new, with red slashes through them. But the great majority of streets offer no such hint to the uninitiated.

Floors in buildings are numbered European style, meaning that the first floor is one flight up from the ground floor (*földszint*), and so on. Addresses are usually written with the floor number in Roman numerals and the apartment number in Arabic numerals. For example, XII. Csörsz utca 9, IV/3 is on the fourth floor, Apartment 3.

STREET MAPS   A good map can save you much frustration in Budapest. Western-made maps are sold throughout Budapest, but Cartografia, a Hungarian company, makes two maps that are substantially cheaper and cover Budapest in great detail. The Cartografia foldout map is fine, but if you find its size awkward you should pick up Cartografia's *Budapest Atlas*. Both maps are available throughout central Pest at kiosks and bookstores. Public transportation lines are shown on the maps, but, in places, the map is too crowded to make the lines out clearly. The BKV térkép (Budapest Transportation Authority map), available from metro ticket windows, is therefore recommended as a complement (see "Getting Around," below). If you plan on any hiking excursions in the Buda Hills, you should pick up the *A Budai Hegység map, no. 6* of the *Cartografia Turistatérképe* (Touring Map) series.

Our favorite **map stores** in Pest, where you can also pick up maps of other cities in Hungary, the Budapest-by-Bike map, and international maps are **Globe Map Shop,** at VI. Bajcsy-Zsilinszky út 37 (© **1/312-6001**), open Monday through Friday from 9am to 5pm (metro: Arany János utca on the Blue line); and **Térképkirály** (Map King), at V. Sas u. 1 (© **1/266-0561**), open Monday through Friday from 9am to 7pm (metro: Deák tér). You can also find maps in most of the bookstores recommended in chapter 8, "Budapest Shopping."

And, for the wired folks among you, there is an excellent (and free) Budapest map with great search capabilities online at **www.fsz.bme.hu/hungary/budapest/cgi-bin/search**.

NEIGHBORHOODS IN BRIEF

Pest

Inner City (Belváros) The historic center of Pest, the Belváros is the area inside the Inner Ring, bound by the Danube to the west. Many of Pest's historic buildings are found in the Belváros, as well as the city's showcase luxury hotels and most of its best-known shopping streets.

Leopold Town (Lipótváros) Just to the north of the Belváros, Lipótváros is considered a part of central Pest. Development began here at the end of the 18th century; it soon emerged as a center of Pest business and government. Parliament, plus a number of government ministries, courthouses, banks, and the former stock exchange, are all found here. Before the war, it was considered a neighborhood of the "high bourgeoisie."

Theresa Town (Terézváros) The character of Terézváros is defined by Andrássy út, the great boulevard running the length of it from Hero's Square through Oktogon and down into the Inner City. This grand street has been regaining its reputation of elegance: Andrássy út is once again the "best address" in town. The Teréz körút section of the Outer Ring cuts through Terézváros; Oktogon is its major square. The area around Nagymező utca is the city's theater district.

Elizabeth Town (Erzsébetváros) Directly to the southeast of Terézváros, Erzsébetváros is the historic Jewish neighborhood of Pest. During the German occupation of 1944–45, a ghetto was constructed here. This district is still the center of Budapest Jewish life, though it is exceedingly run-down and is by no means as vibrant a place as it once was.

Joseph Town (Józsefváros) One of the largest central Pest neighborhoods, József-város is to the southeast of Erzsébetváros. It has long had a reputation of being the seediest part of Pest, and for all appearances this reputation is a deserved one. József körút, the neighborhood's segment of the

Outer Ring, is a center of prostitution and pornography.

Buda

Castle District (Várnegyed) The city's most beautiful and historic district dates to the 13th century. On a plateau above the surrounding neighborhoods and the Danube beyond, the Castle District is defined by its medieval walls. The immense Buda Palace and its grounds fill the district's southern end. The northern end is home to small winding streets, Matthias Church, the Fisherman's Bastion, and the Hilton Hotel.

Watertown (Víziváros) The long, narrow neighborhood wedged between the Castle District and the Danube, the Víziváros is historically a quarter where fishermen and small artisans reside. Built on the steep slope of Castle Hill, it has narrow alleys and stairs instead of roads in many places. Its main street, Fő utca, runs the north-south

length of the Víziváros, parallel to and a block away from the river.

Buda Hills The Buda Hills are numerous remote neighborhoods that feel as if they're nowhere near, let alone within, a capital city. By and large, the hills are considered a classy place to live. Neighborhoods are generally known by the name of the hill on which they stand.

Rose Hill (Rózsadomb) This is the part of the Buda Hills closest to the city center and one of the city's most fashionable and luxurious residential neighborhoods.

Óbuda

Óbuda is a mostly residential area now, its long Danube coastline once a favorite spot for workers' resorts under the old regime. Most facilities have been privatized, so a large number of hotels are found here. The extensive Roman ruins of **Aquincum** and the beautifully preserved old-town main square are Óbuda's chief claims to fame.

2 Getting Around

BY PUBLIC TRANSPORTATION

Budapest has an extensive, efficient, and inexpensive public transportation system. If you have some patience and enjoy reading maps, you can easily learn the system well enough to use it wisely. The system, however, is not without its drawbacks. The biggest disadvantage is that except for 17 well-traveled bus and tram routes, all forms of transport shut down for the night at around 11:30pm (see "Night Service," below). Certain areas of the city, most notably the Buda Hills, are beyond the reach of this night service, and taxis are thus required for late-night journeys. Another problem with the system is that travel can be quite slow, especially during rush hour. A third disadvantage, pertinent mostly to tourists, is that Castle Hill can be reached in only three ways by public transportation, all of which are quite crowded in busy tourist seasons. Finally, and perhaps most important, crowded public transport is the place where you are most likely to be targeted by Budapest's professional pickpockets (see "Safety," in "Fast Facts: Budapest," later in this chapter).

FARES All forms of public transportation in Budapest require the self-validation of pre-purchased tickets (*vonaljegy*), which cost 100 Ft (36¢) apiece (children under 6 travel free); single tickets can be bought at metro ticket windows, newspaper kiosks, and the occasional tobacco shop. There are also automated machines in most metro stations and at major transportation hubs, but the older ones are not too reliable. On weekends and at night it can be rather difficult to find an open ticket window, so buy enough to avoid the trouble of constantly having to

Budapest at a Glance

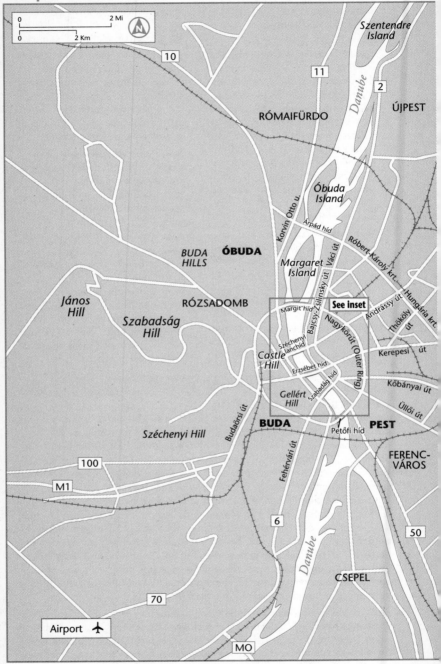

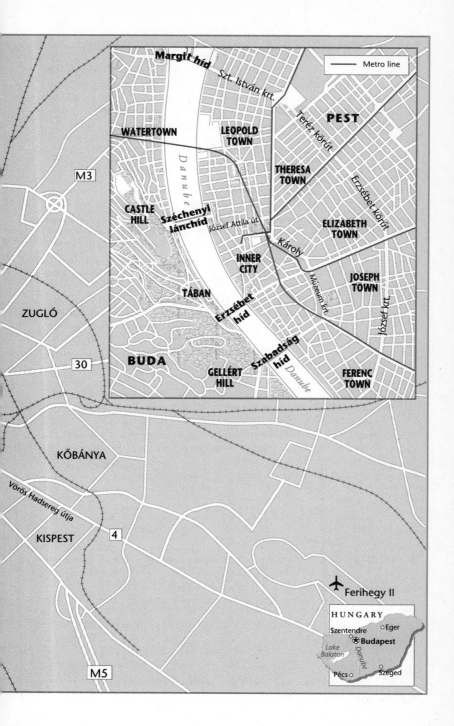

replenish your stock. For 950 Ft ($3.40) you can get a 10-pack (*tizes csomag*), and for 1,850 Ft ($6.65), you can get a 20-pack (*huszas csomag*).

While this standard ticket is valid on the metro, three new types of optional metro tickets were introduced several years ago, making ticket buying a bit more complicated. A "metro section ticket" (*metrószakaszjegy*), at 70 Ft (25¢), is valid for a single metro trip of three stations or less. A "metro transfer ticket" (*metróátszállójegy*), at 160 Ft (60¢), allows you to transfer from one metro line to another on the same ticket, without any limit to the number of stations you may travel. And a "metro section transfer ticket" (*metró-szakaszátszállójegy*), at 110 Ft (40¢), allows you to transfer from one metro line to another, but only for a trip totaling five or fewer stops.

For convenience, we recommend that you purchase a day pass or multiday pass while in Budapest. Passes are inexpensive and need only be validated once, saving you the hassle of having to validate a ticket every time you board. A pass will probably save you some money, too, as you are likely to be getting on and off public transportation all day long. Day passes (*napijegy*) cost 800 Ft ($2.90) and are valid until midnight of the day of purchase. Buy them from metro ticket windows; the clerk validates the pass at the time of purchase. A 3-day pass (*turistajegy*) costs 1,600 Ft ($5.75) and a 7-day pass (*hetijegy*) costs 1,950 Ft ($7); these have the same validation procedure as the day pass.

For longer stays in Budapest, consider a 2-week pass (*kéthétibérlet*) at 2,500 Ft ($9), or a monthly pass (*havibérlet*) or 30-day pass (*30 napos bérlet*), both at 3,820 Ft ($13.75). Such passes are available only at major metro stations, and you need to bring a regulation passport photo.

Dark-blue uniformed inspectors (who even now flip out a hidden red armband when approaching you—a remnant of the not-too-distant past when they traveled the metro in plain clothes) frequently come around checking for valid tickets, particularly at the top or bottom of the escalators to metro platforms. On-the-spot fines of 1,500 Ft ($5.40) are assessed to fare dodgers; pleading ignorance generally doesn't work. Given how inexpensive public transport is, risking a time-consuming altercation with metro inspectors is probably not worth it. Metro tickets are good for 1 hour for any distance along the line you're riding, except for metro section tickets (*metrószakaszjegy*), which are valid only for 30 minutes. You may get off and reboard with the same ticket within the valid time period.

The **Budapest Card,** a tourist card that we do not particularly recommend (it does not pack any value), combines a 3-day *turistajegy* (transportation pass) with free entry to certain museums and other discounts.

SCHEDULES & MAPS   All public transport operates on rough schedules, posted at bus and tram shelters and in metro stations. The schedules are a little confusing at first, but you'll get used to them. The most important thing to note, perhaps, is when the last ride of the night departs: Many a luckless foreigner has waited late at night for a bus that won't be coming until 6am!

The transportation map produced by the Budapest Transport Authority (*BKV térkép*) is available at most metro ticket windows for 250 Ft (90¢). Since transportation routes are extremely difficult to read on most city maps, we suggest that you buy one of these handy maps. In addition, on the map's reverse side is a full listing of routes, including the all-important night-bus routes.

NIGHT SERVICE   Most of the Budapest transportation system closes down between 11:30pm or midnight and 5am. There are, however, 17 night routes

(13 bus and four tram), and they're generally quite safe. A map of night routes is posted at many central tram and bus stops, and a full listing appears on the BKV transportation map. The number 78 night bus follows the route of the Red metro line, while the number 182 night bus follows the route of the Blue metro line. Though night buses often share the same numbers as daytime routes (with an É suffix, meaning *éjszaka,* or night), they may actually run different routes. Night buses require the standard, self-validated ticket. Skipping stops is prevalent on night buses, so pay attention.

UNDERPASSES   Underpasses are found beneath most major boulevards in Budapest. Underpasses are often crowded with vendors, shops, and the like, and many of them have as many as five or six different exits, each letting you out onto a different part of the square or street. Signs direct you to bus, tram, trolleybus, and metro stops, often using the word *fele,* meaning "toward." (Note that although Budapest is a very safe city, especially when compared to American cities of comparable size, underpasses tend to be among the more menacing places late at night, as various lowlifes enjoy hanging out in these subterranean confines.)

Directions given throughout this book use a metro station as a starting point whenever possible. In cases where that's simply impossible, other major transportation hubs, such as Móricz Zsigmond körtér in southern Buda, are used as starting points.

BY METRO

You'll no doubt spend a lot of time in the Budapest metro. The system is clean and efficient, with trains running every 3 to 5 minutes from about 4:30am until about 11:30pm. The main shortcoming is that there are just three lines, only one of which crosses under the Danube to Buda. (A fourth line is planned, but it will be several years at least before ground is broken.) The three lines are universally known by color—Yellow, Red, and Blue. Officially, they have numbers as well (1, 2, and 3 respectively), but all Hungarians refer to them by color and all signs are color coded. All three lines converge at **Deák tér,** the only point where any meet.

The **Yellow (1) line** is the oldest metro on the European continent. Built in 1894 as part of the Hungarian millennial celebration, it has been refurbished and restored to its original splendor. Signs for the Yellow line, lacking the distinctive colored M, are harder to spot than signs for the Blue and Red lines. Look for signs saying *földalatti* (underground). Each station has two separate entrances, one for each direction. The Yellow line runs from Vörösmarty tér, site of Gerbeaud's Cukrászda in the heart of central Pest, out the length of Andrássy út, past the Városliget (City Park), ending at Mexikói út, in a trendy residential part of Pest known as Zugló. So, depending on the direction you're heading, enter either the side marked IRÁNY MEXIKÓI ÚT or IRÁNY VÖRÖSMARTY TÉR. Incidentally, somewhere in the middle of the line is a stop called Vörösmarty utca; this is a small street running off Andrássy út and should not be confused with the terminus, Vörösmarty tér. (However, at each of these stops you will find a splendid traditional coffee house, Gerbaud and Lukács, respectively.) It's worth taking a ride on this line, with its distinct 19th-century atmosphere.

The **Red (2)** and **Blue (3) lines** are modern metros and to reach them you descend long, steep escalators. The Red line runs from Örs vezér tere in eastern Pest, through the center, and across the Danube to Batthyány tér, Moszkva tér, and finally Déli Station. Keleti Station is also along the Red line. The Blue line runs from Kőbánya-Kispest, in southeastern Pest, through the center, and out to Újpest-Központ in northern Pest. Nyugati Station is along the Blue line.

On the street above stations of both the Red and Blue lines are distinctive colored M signs. Tickets should be validated at automated boxes before you descend the escalator. When changing lines at Deák tér, you're required to validate another ticket (unless you have a special "metro transfer ticket"). The orange validating machines are in the hallways between lines but are easy to miss, particularly if there are big crowds.

BY BUS

There are about 200 different bus (*busz*) lines in greater Budapest. Many parts of the city, most notably the Buda Hills, are best accessed by bus. Although buses are the most difficult to use of Budapest's transportation choices, with patience, (and a BKV map) you'll be able to get around in no time. With the exception of night buses, most lines are in service from about 4:30am to about 11:30pm. Some bus lines run far less frequently (or not at all) on weekends, while others run far more frequently (or only) on weekends. This information is both on the reverse of the BKV transportation map and on the schedules posted at every bus stop.

Black-numbered local buses constitute the majority of the city's lines. Red-numbered buses are express; generally, but not always, the express buses follow the same routes as local buses with the same number, simply skipping certain stops along the way. If the red number on the bus is followed by an *E* the bus runs nonstop between terminals (whereas an *É*—with an accent mark—signifies *éjszaka*, meaning night). Depending on your destination, an express bus may be a much faster way of traveling. A few buses are labeled by something other than a number; one you'll probably use is the *Várbusz* (Palace Bus), a minibus that runs between Várfok utca, up the steep staircase from Buda's Moszkva tér, and the Castle District. The buses themselves have always been blue, though now some express buses are beginning to appear in red.

Tickets are self-validated on board the bus by the mechanical red box found by each door. You can board the bus by any door. Unlike metro tickets, bus tickets are valid not for the line, but for the individual bus; you're not allowed to get off and reboard another bus going in the same direction without a new ticket. Tickets cannot be purchased from the driver.

The biggest problem for bus-riding tourists is the drivers' practice of skipping stops when no one is waiting to get on and no one has signaled to get off. To signal your intention to get off at the next stop, press the button above the door (beware—some drivers open only the doors that have been signaled). Most stops don't have their names posted; a list of stops is posted inside all buses, but if stops are skipped you may lose track. Chances are, though, that the Hungarians riding a given bus will know exactly where your stop is, and people are generally enthusiastic about helping foreigners on buses. You can also ask the driver to let you know when he has reached your stop.

Avoid buses in central areas during rush hours, since traffic tends to be quite bad. It pays to go a bit out of your way to use a metro or tram at these times instead, or simply to walk.

BY TRAM

You'll find Budapest's 34 bright-yellow trams (known as *villamos* in Hungarian) very useful, particularly the nos. 4 and 6, which travel along the Outer Ring (*Nagykörút*), and the nos. 47 and 49, which run the Inner Ring.

Tickets are self-validated on board. As with buses, tickets are valid for one ride, not for the line itself. Trams stop at every station, and all doors open, regardless of whether anyone is waiting to get on. The buttons near the tram doors are for emergency stops, not stop requests.

When a tram line is closed for maintenance (a not infrequent occurrence), replacement buses ply the tram route. They go by the same number as the tram, with a *V* (for *villamos*) preceding the number.

BY TROLLEYBUS

Red trolleybuses are electric buses that receive power from a cable above the street. There are only 14 trolleybus lines in Budapest, all in Pest. Of particular interest to train travelers is no. 73, the fastest route between Keleti Station and Nyugati Station. All the information in the "By Bus" section above regarding boarding, ticket validation, and stop-skipping applies to trolleybuses as well.

BY HÉV

The **HÉV** is a suburban railway network that connects Budapest to various points along the city's outskirts. There are four HÉV lines; only one, the Szentendre line, is of serious interest to tourists (see chapter 10, "The Danube Bend").

The terminus for the Szentendre HÉV line is Buda's Batthyány tér, also a station of the Red metro line. The train makes 10 stops in northern Buda and Óbuda en route to Szentendre. Most hotels, restaurants, and sights in those areas are best reached by the HÉV (so indicated in the directions given throughout this book). To reach Óbuda's Fő tér (Main Square), get off at the Árpád híd (Árpád Bridge) stop.

The HÉV runs regularly between 4am and 11:30pm. For trips within the city limits, the cost is one transit ticket, self-validated as on a bus or tram. Tickets to Szentendre cost 250 Ft (90¢) (minus 100 Ft/36¢) for the portion of the trip within city limits if you have a valid day pass). HÉV tickets to destinations beyond the city limits are available at HÉV ticket windows at the Batthyány tér station, at the Margit híd station, or from the conductor on board (no penalty assessed for such purchase).

BY COGWHEEL RAILWAY & FUNICULAR

Budapest's **cogwheel railway** (*fogaskerekű*) runs from Városmajor, across the street from the Hotel Budapest on Szilágyi Erzsébet fasor in Buda, to Széchenyi-hegy, one terminus of the Children's Railway (Gyermek Vasút) and site of Hotel Panoráma. The cogwheel railway runs from 4:30am to 11pm, and normal transportation tickets (self-validated on board) are used. The pleasant route twists high into the Buda Hills; at 100 Ft (36¢), it is well worth taking just for the ride.

The **funicular** (*sikló*) connects Buda's Clark Ádám tér, at the head of the Széchenyi Chain Bridge, with Dísz tér, just outside the Buda Castle. The funicular is one of only two forms of public transportation serving the Castle District (the Várbusz and bus no. 16 are the other possibilities; see "By Bus," above). An extremely steep and short ride (and greenhouse-hot on sunny days), the funicular runs at frequent intervals from 7:30am to 10pm (closed on alternate Mondays). Tickets cost 400 Ft ($1.40) for adults and 300 Ft ($1.15) for children going up; 300 Ft ($1.15) and 200 Ft (75¢) coming down.

BY TAXI

We divide Budapest taxis into two general categories: organized fleets and private taxis. If you only follow one piece of advice in this book, it's this: Do business with the former and avoid the latter. Because taxi regulations permit fleets (or private drivers) to establish their own rates (within certain parameters), fares vary greatly between the different fleets and among the private unaffiliated drivers.

The best rates are invariably those of the larger fleet companies. We particularly recommended Fő Taxi (© 1/222-2222). Other reliable fleets include Volántaxi (© 1/466-6666), City Taxi (© 1/211-1111), Tele5 (© 1/355-5555), and 6×6 (© 1/266-6666). Call one of these companies from your hotel—or ask the clerk to call for you—even if there are other private taxis waiting around outside. The same applies to restaurants. You will seldom, if ever, wait more than 5 minutes for a fleet taxi in any but the most remote of neighborhoods. Following our advice, Frommer's reader M.M.L. took a Fő Taxi from the train station to his hotel for 550 Ft ($2). When he left for the station a few days later he asked the clerk to call him a Fő Taxi, but the clerk responded "No need. We have Hotel Taxi." That "hotel taxi" ended up costing M.M.L. 1,200 Ft ($4.35) for the same trip.

Finally, you are most likely dealing with a dishonest driver if he asks you to pay for his return trip, asks to be paid in anything but forints, or quotes you a "flat rate" in lieu of running the meter. One exception to these rules of thumb is the fixed rate of 2,800 Ft ($10.10) offered by Tele5 from the city center to the airport; this is a tad less than two Airport Minibus fares (though with tip it would be more).

If you desire a station wagon, ask for a *"kombi"* when calling for your taxi.

Tipping is usually not more than 10%. Hungarians usually round the bill up. If you think you have been cheated by the driver, then you certainly should not tip.

Though most people call for a taxi or pick one up at a taxi stand (a stand is basically any piece of sidewalk or street where one or more drivers congregate), it is possible to hail one on the street, though the base rate will be slightly higher. At taxi stands in Budapest, the customer chooses with whom to do business; go with a cab from one of the recommended fleets, even if it's not the first in line.

Additional pointers are found in the brochure *Taking a Taxi in Budapest,* available at Tourinform and elsewhere.

BY CAR

There's no reason to use a car for sightseeing in Budapest. You may, however, wish to rent a car for trips out of the city (see chapters 10–13). Although Hertz, Avis, National, and Budget offices can be found in town and at the airport, marginally better deals can be had from some of the smaller companies. You are urged to reserve a rental car as early as possible. If you reserve from abroad, ask for written confirmation by fax or e-mail. If you don't receive confirmation, it's wise to assume that the reservation has not been properly made.

We have quoted rates for the least expensive car currently listed by each of these recommended agencies.

Denzel Europcar InterRent, VIII. üllői út 60–62, 1082 Budapest (© 1/477-1080; fax 1/477-1099), offers the Suzuki Swift for 4,500 Ft ($16.20) per day (insurance included), plus 45 Ft (16¢) per kilometer. They also have a rental counter at the airport (© 1/296-6610), but here you pay an additional 11% airport tax.

LRI Airport Rent-A-Car, with a counter at the airport (© or fax 1/296-5970), offers the Volkswagen Polo for $19 per day (insurance included) and 19¢ per kilometer.

Fox Auto Rental, III. Hajógyári sziget 130, 1033 Budapest (✆ **1/457-1150;** fax 1/457-1151), rents the Fiat Seicento for $40 per day for a rental of 1 to 3 days, $34 per day for a rental of 4 to 6 days, and $199 for a week, insurance and mileage included. They also require a deposit of 100,000 Ft ($360) on a credit card. Though located far from the city center, Fox will deliver the car to you at your hotel without charge.

DRIVING TIPS

DRIVING REGULATIONS   The speed limit in Hungary is 50kmph (30 mph) in built-up areas, 90kmph (50 mph) on main roads, and 130kmph (75 mph) on motorways. Safety belts must be worn in the front seat and, when available, in the backseat; children under 6 may not sit in the front seat and may not travel without a safety belt. Horns may not be used in built-up areas, except in an emergency. Headlights must be on at all times on all intercity roads and highways. Drunk-driving laws are strictly enforced; any alcohol content in the driver's blood is illegal.

Cars are required to have in them at all times a first-aid kit and a reflective warning triangle. A decal indicating country of registration is also required. These items should be included in all rental cars. If you're driving a rental car from Bulgaria, France, Greece, Israel, Poland, Italy, Romania, or the former USSR, make sure you have the so-called green card (proof of international insurance), not automatically given by all rental agencies. Hungarian police set up random checkpoints, where cars are pulled over and drivers made to present their papers. If all your papers are in order, you'll have no trouble. Still, foreigners residing in Budapest and driving cars with foreign plates report being routinely stopped by police and fined for rather ridiculous infractions. Hungarian police are no longer allowed to impose on-the-spot fines for driving violations, a favorite and much abused practice of years gone by, but instead now issue written tickets for infractions.

There are plenty of gas stations along major routes. Newly built sections of the major highways outside Budapest require payment of a toll.

BREAKDOWN SERVICES   The **Hungarian Auto Club** (Magyar Autóklub) operates a 24-hour free emergency breakdown service: Call ✆ **188** (note, however, that not all operators speak English).

The Autóklub also has an **International Aid Service Center,** at II. Rómer Flóris u. 4/a (✆ **1/345-1744**), established specifically for foreign motorists. (Stay on the line, you will be connected.) Services provided include emergency aid, towing, and technical advice.

PARKING   Parking is very difficult in central Pest and parts of central Buda, but little problem elsewhere in the city. People have always parked virtually anywhere that a car would fit—on the sidewalk, in crosswalks, etc, but the recent introduction of awkward posts lined up along the curb in inner Pest has made this much more difficult in this part of the city. Cars are regularly towed from illegal spots (and brought to Szent István Park). If your car has been towed, ask a Hungarian to help you call ✆ **1/383-0700** (no English spoken), or ask Tourinform or Vista for help. On practically all central streets, a *fizető* sign indicates that there's a fee for parking in that area. Purchase a ticket from the machine and leave the ticket on the dashboard (visible from the window). In some cases, the parking fee is collected by an agent who approaches you as you park. Fees vary with the centrality of location from 80 Ft to 300 Ft (30¢–$1.10) per hour. Some neighborhoods, notably Buda's Castle District, allow vehicular access only to cars with special resident permits. There are numerous parking garages in the Inner City, including those at V. Aránykéz u. 4–6, V. Szervita tér 8, and VII. Nyár u. 20. Many vacant lots on Pest's Inner City side streets now house makeshift parking lots; prices are lower than those at garages, but the lots are not always as secure.

BY BIKE

Budapest is not a bicycle-friendly city by any stretch of the imagination, though an effort to incorporate bike lanes into the city streets is now underway. The project is far from complete, but eventually Budapest may be a nice place for a bike ride. As it currently stands, we do not recommend biking in the city for safety reasons. This said, the brave and undaunted can rent bikes from several places. **Charles Apartment House,** I. Hegyalja út 23 (© **1/201-1796**), will rent you a bike for 2,000 Ft ($7.20) per day. A 20,000 Ft ($72) security deposit is required, and you must present your passport for identification. **Bringóhintó,** XIII. Hajós A. sétány (© **1/329-2746**), on Margaret Island, also rents bikes. Incidentally, Margaret Island is closed to cars and, thus, is ideal for casual bike riding. Look for the map titled *"Kerékpárral Budapesten"* ("Budapest on Bike"), which shows biking trails and streets with bike lanes.

Inquire about organized bike tours at **Vista Visitor Center** (© **1/267-8603**), where you can also pick up a Hungary bike tour map. Another welcome new development for cyclists are the bike paths along Lake Balaton (see chapter 11, "The Lake Balaton Region").

FAST FACTS: **Budapest**

Airport See "Getting There," in chapter 2, "Planning Your Trip to Budapest."

American Express Budapest's only American Express office is between Vörösmarty tér and Deák tér in central Pest, at V. Deák Ferenc u. 10, 1052 Budapest (© **1/235-4330** or 235-4300; fax 1/267-2028). In summer, it's open Monday through Saturday from 9am to 7:30pm, Sunday from 9am to 2pm. In winter, it's open 9am to 5:30pm Monday through Saturday, and 9am to 2pm on Sunday. There's an American Express cash ATM on the street in front. Depending on whether your account allows it, these ATMs dispense either cash (forints only) or traveler's checks (U.S. dollars only). Check with American Express beforehand if you wish to use these ATMs abroad.

For lost traveler's checks, come to the office as soon as you can and they will assist you. If you do not want to wait that long, use a 20-Ft coin to initiate a call to England; the call (© **00-800-11128**) is otherwise toll-free. For a lost credit card, make a local call to © **1/235-4310** during business hours or to © **1/460-5233** after hours. If this is unsuccessful, try calling England at © **00-44-181-551-1111** (or dial © **00/800-04411** for the U.K. direct operator, and ask to call collect).

Area Code The country code for Hungary is 36; the city code for Budapest is 1.

Babysitters **Ficuka Baby Hotel,** V. Váci u. 11b, I em. 9 (© **1/338-2836** or 1/483-0713 (ask for Livia Nagy), will send an English speaking babysitter to your hotel for 850 Ft ($3) per hour for one child, or 950 Ft ($3.40) per hour for two children. For four or more children, two babysitters are sent. Babysitters are trained in first aid and early childhood learning. Often they are university students. Reserve a babysitter by phone between 10am and 6pm, Monday through Friday.

For longer stays in Budapest, we recommend **Korompay Family Day Care,** XI. Menesi út 19 (© **1/466-5740** or 06-30/921-7820; fax 1/466-5095), for children 2 to 4 years. Mrs. Katalin Korompay and her assistant Sylvia are both former kindergarten teachers. The Korompay house, a 5-minute walk from Buda's Móricz Zsigmond körtér, is spacious and clean with plenty of toys and kid-size furniture. There is a large garden with a sand-box. Mrs. Korompay cooks vegetarian meals for lunch. A warm, whole-some place. A full day (8:30am to 4:30pm) costs 1,800 Ft ($6.50).

Bookstores See "Bookstores," in chapter 8, "Budapest Shopping."

Business Hours Most **stores** are open Monday through Friday from 10am to 6pm and on Saturday from 9 or 10am to 1 or 2pm. Some shops close for an hour at lunchtime, and most stores are closed Sunday, except those in the central tourist areas. Some shop owners and restaurateurs also close for 2 weeks in August. On weekdays, food stores open early, at around 6 or 7am, and close at around 6 or 7pm. Certain grocery stores, called "nonstops," are open 24 hours (however, a growing number of shops call themselves "non-stop" even if they shut for the night at 10 or 11 pm). **Banks** are usually open Monday through Thursday from 8am to 3pm and on Friday from 8am to 1pm. **Museums** in Budapest are usually open Tuesday through Sunday from 10am to 6pm.

Climate See "When to Go," in chapter 2, "Planning Your Trip to Budapest."

Currency See "Money," in chapter 2, "Planning Your Trip to Budapest."

Currency Exchange See "Changing Money," in chapter 2, "Planning Your Trip to Budapest."

Doctors & Dentists We recommend the **American Clinic,** I. Hattyu u. 14 (© **1/224-9090**), a newly opened private outpatient clinic with two U.S. board–certified physicians and several English-speaking Hungarian doctors. There is an OB-GYN on staff, and an ultrasound machine on the premises; referrals are available for specialists. Payment is expected at time of service (credit cards accepted), but they will provide coded invoices in English in a form acceptable to most insurance carriers. The clinic is located in a modern building across the street from the Mammut shopping center, just a few minutes by foot from Moszkva tér (Red metro). Check with Vista Visitor Center for discount coupons. Another suitable facility is **IMS,** a private outpatient clinic at XIII. Váci út 202 (© **1/350-0733**) with English-speaking doctors; it's reached via the Blue metro line (Gyöngyös utca). The same drill applies with respect to pay-ment and insurance claims. IMS also operates an emergency service after hours and on weekends, III. Vihar u. 29 (© **1/388-8257**).

For dental work, we recommend **Dr. Susan Linder,** who has an office at II. Vihorlat u. 23 (© **1/335-5245**) (by foot from Pasaréti tér, which is reached by bus 5 or 29). Dr. Linder is the dentist for the U.S. and British embassies. Her hours are Monday, Tuesday, and Thursday from 8am to 6pm; she is also available for emergencies, except on weekends. In a pinch, you can also try **S.O.S. Dent Kft,** a 24-hour emergency dental clinic at VII. Király u. 14 (© **1/269-6010**), just a few minutes by foot from Deák tér (all three metro lines); look for the red cross on the building. The dentists on staff do not all speak English. One more useful medical emergency number is the **Anonymous AIDS Advisory Service** (© **1/466-9283**).

Driving Rules See "Getting Around," earlier in this chapter.

Drugstores See "Pharmacies," below.

Electricity Hungarian electricity is 220 volts, AC. If you plan to bring any North American electrical appliances, you'll need a 110–220 volt transformer/converter. Transformers are available at electrical supply stores throughout the city. We recommend **Trakis-Hetra Ltd.,** at VII. Nefelejcs u. 45 (© **1/342-5338** or 322-1459). The nearest metro station is Keleti pu. (Red line). If there is a transformer built into the adapter of the appliance, as in many laptop computers, you will need only a small adapter to fit the North American flat plugs into the round holes in the wall. This adapter may be hard to find in Budapest.

Embassies The embassy of **Australia** is at XII. Királyhágó tér 8–9 (© **1/457-9777**); the embassy of **Canada,** at XII. Budakeszi út 32 (© **1/392-3360**); the embassy of the **Republic of Ireland,** at V. Szabadság tér 7 (© **1/302-9600**); the embassy of the **United Kingdom,** at V. Harmincad u. 6 (© **1/266-2888**); and the embassy of the **United States,** at V. Szabadság tér 12 (© **1/475-4400**). New Zealand does not have an embassy, but the U.K. embassy handles matters for New Zealand citizens.

Emergencies Dial © **104** for an ambulance, © **105** for the fire department, or © **107** for the police.

Eyeglasses *Optika* or *ofotért* is the Hungarian name for an optometrist's shop. The word for eyeglasses is *szemüveg.*

Fax Faxes can be sent from any post office ("Posta"), where a one-page fax costs 1,250 Ft ($4.50), and a two-page fax costs 1,900 Ft ($6.85). It is also possible to send a fax from any of several **MATÁV** (the Hungarian telephone company) offices: MATÁV Pont Orion Oktogon, VI. Teréz krt. 24; MATÁV Pont Mammut, I. Széna tér; and MATÁV Pont Budai Skála, XI. Október 23 utca. The main telecommunications office, at Petőfi Sándor u. 17 (near Deák tér), also provides fax service. You can also send a fax from **Vista Visitor Center** at V. Paulay Ede u. 7 (© **1/267-8603**). Luxury hotels also often have fax service.

Internet Access We generally use **Vista Visitor Center,** at V. Paulay Ede u. 7 (© **1/267-8603**) (Metro: Deák tér, all three metro lines), which has about 10 terminals in a small mezzanine area. The cost is 11 Ft (4¢) per minute; but the wait is sometimes pretty long. It's open Monday through Friday from 9am to 8pm, and Saturday and Sunday from 10am to 6pm. Another option, with less of a wait, is **Internet Café,** V. Kecskeméti u. 5 (© **1/328-0292**), near Kálvin tér (Blue line). This drab space has about 20 terminals in a basement room, and the cost is 700 Ft ($2.50) per hour, with pricing by 30-minute intervals (except 10 minutes or less, which costs 150 Ft/55¢). Internet access is also available at any MATÁV offices (see "Fax," above. You may also want to try **AMI Internet Café** at V. Váci u. 40, ((© **36/1-267-1644;** www.amicoffee. hu) open daily from 9am to 2am, which has a good high speed connection. But do not confuse this place with a neighbor; **Netvillage,** at V. Váci u. 19-21 (in the basement of the recently opened "Millennium Center"), has poor service and a staff that is more interested in serving drinks than in helping customers with internet problems.

Language Hungarian (*Magyar*), a member of the Finno-Ugric family of languages, is unrelated to any of the languages of Hungary's neighboring countries. By and large, Hungarians accept the obscurity of their language and welcome and encourage any attempts made by foreigners to communicate. Many Hungarians speak German and/or English. Particularly in Budapest, you shouldn't have much problem making yourself understood. Everyone involved in tourism speaks at least a little English.

Colloquial Hungarian (published by Routledge, Chapman, Hall) is a good phrase book and comes with a cassette. Also, see "Appendix B: Help with a Tough Tongue," in the back of this book.

Laundry & Dry Cleaning Self-service launderettes (*patyolat*) are scarce in Budapest. As far as we know, the city's only centrally located Laundromat is at V. Vármegye u. 1, on the corner of Városház utca (Metro: Ferenciek tere, Blue line), open Monday through Friday 7am to 7pm, and Saturday 8am to 1pm. The Mister Minit chain, a locksmith and shoe repair service found in large shopping centers now offers a laundry services as well. The chain **A Házimosoda** ("The Home Laundry"), with locations throughout Buda (but none in Pest) ((© **1/275-6008**), is a full-service laundry and dry cleaning business that also offers a convenient pickup and delivery service (provided you have the patience to wait for an answer to your call). Many hotels and pensions also provide laundry services. Private room hosts, as well, usually are happy to make a little extra money doing laundry. For 1-hour dry cleaning, try **Ruhatisztító Top Clean,** at the Nyugati Skála Metro department store (across the street from Nyugati train station; no phone); they are open Monday through Friday from 7am to 7pm, and Saturday from 9am to 2pm.

Libraries The **United States Information Service (USIS)** has a public reference center in the Central Bank building, at V. Szabadság tér 7–9 ((© **1/302-6200** or 1/302-0426). The USIS reference center holdings include a large CD-ROM database of recent newspapers and magazines, as well as a variety of reference texts. The former USIS book collection is now a part of the library of the **Faculty of the Arts at ELTE University,** XIV. Ajtósi Dürer sor 19–20 ((© **1/343-0148,** ext. 4435). Known as the "American Library," it is open to the public. Hours reflect the university's calendar, so call ahead. It's open Monday through and Friday from 9am to 5pm (except opening at noon on Wednesday).

The **British Council library** is at VII. Benczúr u. 26 ((© **1/478-4700**). It's open Monday through Friday from 11am to 6:45pm (closed in summer).

Lost Property The **BKV (Budapest Transportation Authority)** lost-and-found office is at VII. Akácfa u. 18 ((© **1/267-5299**). For items lost on a train or in a train station, call (© **1/312-0213.** For items lost on an intercity bus (not on a local BKV bus), call (© **1/318-2122.** Good luck.

Luggage Storage There are left-luggage offices (*csomagmegőrző,* or *poggyász*) and lockers at all three major railroad stations. At Keleti, the office is in the main waiting room alongside Track 6. It's open 4am to midnight, and the daily cost is 160 Ft (60¢) for "normal" parcels and 320 Ft ($1.15) for "bulky" parcels, assessed for any part of a calendar day (thus overnight storage counts as 2 days). The lockers are in the same general area, and require 200 Ft (70¢) (two 100 Ft coins needed); instructions in English are posted on every tenth locker or so. At Nyugati, the office is in the waiting room behind the international ticket office and is open 24 hours. The cost is the same as at Keleti. The lockers are nearby, and the cost is also the same as at Keleti. Déli Station has a new highly automated locker system in operation in the main ticket-purchasing area; the lockers are very large, and directions for use are provided by a multilingual computer. The cost is 250 Ft (90¢) per day.

Mail/Post Office Mail can be received by clients at American Express (see "American Express," above); a single AMEX traveler's check is sufficient to prove that you're a client. Others can receive mail ℅ Poste Restante, Magyar Posta, Petőfi Sándor u. 17–19, 1052 Budapest, Hungary (© **36/ 1-318-3947** or 487-1100). This confusing office (open Monday through Friday from 8am to 8pm and on Saturday from 8am to 2pm), not far from Deák tér (all metro lines), is the city's main post office. There are also post offices near Keleti and Nyugati stations. The post office near Keleti is at VIII. Baross tér 11/c (© 36/1-322-9013), and is open Monday to Saturday, 7am to 9pm. The post office near Nyugati is at VI. Teréz krt. 51 (© 36/ 1-312-1480), and is open Monday to Saturday, 7am to 9pm and Sunday 8am to 8pm.

At press time, an airmail postcard costs 100 Ft (36¢); an airmail letter, 150 Ft (55¢) and up, depending on size of envelope and weight.

Maps See "City Layout" under "Orientation," earlier in this chapter.

Names Hungarians write their names with the family name first, followed by the given name. When mentioning Hungarian names in this book we have employed the international form of given name followed by family name. The only exception is with street names, where we have used the Hungarian style: hence Ferenc Deák (the man) but Deák Ferenc utca (the street).

Newspapers & Magazines The International Herald Tribune, USA Today, The Guardian, The Guardian Weekly, The Financial Times, The Times of London, The European, Newsweek, and Time are all commonly found in luxury hotels and at kiosks and bookstores in the central Pest neighborhood around Váci utca. At larger newsstands you can also find People, Vogue, Harpers, and, once in a blue moon, The New York Times. On any given day at **Sajtó Térkép,** with locations at V. Kálvin tér 3 (Blue line) and V. Városház u. 3–5 (Ferenciek tere, Blue line), you might also find such periodicals as Barrons, The Nation, The Economist, GQ, Architectural Digest, or House and Garden. Pick up the Budapest Sun, an English-language weekly, with articles on current events and politics in Hungary. The monthly Look provides monthly listings of cultural events, similar to Pesti Est, another monthly publication that is trilingual. Both are free of charge and widely available.

Pharmacies The Hungarian word is *gyógyszertár,* or occasionally, *patika.* Generally, pharmacies carry only prescription drugs. Some hotels advertise "drugstores," but these are just shops with soap, perfume, aspirin, and other nonprescription items. There are a number of 24-hour pharmacies in the city—every pharmacy posts the address of the nearest one in its window. If necessary, ask for a specific address at Tourinform. Your best bet for 24-hour service throughout the year is Oktogon Patika on Teréz körút, next to Hotel Radisson (off Oktogon square, trams no. 4, 6).

Religious Services in English Roman Catholic masses are held at 5pm on Saturday in the **Jesuit Church of the Sacred Heart,** VII. Mária u. 25 (© 1/ 318-3479). Nondenominational services are given on Sunday at 10:30am at the **Óbuda Community Center,** III. Kiskorona u. 7 (© 1/250-0288). Presbyterian and Anglican services are held on Sunday at 11am at VI. Vörösmarty u. 40 (© 1/302-3917). The **Christian Science Society** is located at II. Kútvölgyi út 20–22. Although not in English, services are held at the **main synagogue,** VII. Dohány u. 2–8 (© 1/342-8949), on Friday at 6pm and Saturday at 9am.

Restrooms The word for toilet in Hungarian is *WC* (pronounced vay-tsay). *Női* means "women's"; *férfi* means "men's." For free and generally clean, well-stocked toilets, try any of Budapest's ubiquitous McDonald's or Burger Kings (but avoid the Burger King at Astoria).

Safety By U.S. standards, Budapest is a relatively safe city—muggings and violent attacks are rare. Nevertheless, foreigners are always prime targets. Although they are clearly less of a threat now than a few years ago, teams of professional pickpockets still plague Budapest. They operate on crowded trams, metros, and buses. Be particularly careful on bus no. 26 (Margaret Island) and trams no. 4 and 6 or in any other crowded setting. The pickpockets' basic trick is to create a distraction to take your attention away from yourself and your own security. Avoid being victimized by wearing a money belt under your clothes instead of wearing a fanny pack or carrying a wallet or purse. No valuables should be kept in the outer pockets of a knapsack.

Sadly, people of color need to be wary of racist gangs, who, though small in number, have made some highly publicized attacks in the past few years. Such crimes are usually committed late at night.

Shoe Repair The Hungarian word is for cobbler is *cipész* or *cipő javítás,* and scarcely a neighborhood in the city is without one. Or you can try a Mister Minit shop (a chain of mini shops found in many major shopping areas) if all you need is something quick and professionally less demanding. Ask your hotel reception for the nearest one.

Smoking Smoking is forbidden in all public places (including all public transport), except most restaurants and pubs, where smoking is considered to be an indispensible part of the ambience. Although a 1999 law requires all restaurants to post a nonsmoking section, the fact is that most barely comply. Expect restaurants to be smoky places. *Tilos a dohányzás* or *Dohányozni tilos* means "No Smoking."

Taxes Taxes are included in restaurant and hotel rates, and shop purchases. Foreigners are entitled, upon leaving the country, to a refund of the 25% VAT on certain purchases. See chapter 8, "Budapest Shopping," for details.

Taxis See "Getting Around," earlier in this chapter.

Telephone The Hungarian phone company MATÁV provides much better service than in the past, but it still falls significantly short of Western standards. For best results, dial slowly and don't be too quick to trust a busy signal; rather, try again.

The **area code** for Budapest is 1, and all phone numbers in Budapest (except mobile phones) have seven digits. Phone numbers in this book are printed with the area code. Most other towns in Hungary have a two-digit area code and six-digit telephone numbers. To make a call from one Hungary area code to another, first dial 06; when you hear a tone, dial the area code and number. Numbers that begin with 06-20, 06-30, or 06-70 followed by a seven-digit number, are **mobile phone numbers.** If the mobile number you've been given has only six digits, it is incorrect; add a 9 before the other six digits. Mobile phones are extremely popular and some of the listings in this book are mobile phone numbers. Be aware that all phone calls, regardless of location, made to a mobile phone are charged as long distance calls. Budapest telephone numbers are constantly changing as MATÁV continues to upgrade its system. (You should note, for instance, that any Budapest number beginning with a "1" has been changed; try replacing the 1 with a 3 or a 4.) Usually, if the number you are dialing has recently changed, you will get a recording first in Hungarian and than in English, indicating the new number. If further information is needed, dial ℂ **198** for **local directory assistance.**

Public **pay phones** charge varying amounts for local calls depending on the time of day that you place your call. It's apparently cheapest to call late in the evenings and on weekends. Public phones operate with 20-Ft coins or with phonecards (in 50 or 120 units) which can be purchased from post offices, tobacco shops, supermarkets, travel agencies, and any MATÁV customer service office (MATÁV Pont).

Hotels typically add a surcharge to all calls (although some allow unlimited free local calls).

For international calls, there are several options. Our preferred method these days is to make all international calls from abroad through a U.S.-based "callback" service. These services allow you to gain access to a U.S. dial tone from abroad, typically by means of dialing in to a computer in the U.S. which then automatically calls you back with the dial tone. International calls made in this manner are billed at competitive U.S. calling rates, which are still significantly cheaper than Hungarian international rates. These services generally charge an activation fee and a monthly maintenance fee, as well as other fees, so you ought to make a judgment as to whether you are likely to be making enough calls for it to be worthwhile. A company called **Kallback** seems to offer the best package; call ℂ **800/959-5255** or 800/516-9992; www.kallback.com.

Alternatively, you can use a phonecard and access the international operator through a public phone, though older phones are less reliable; again, a 20-Ft coin is required to start the call. You can also place an international call at the post office at VI. Teréz krt. 51 (near Nyugati railway station), as well as from these MATÁV offices: MATÁV Pont in West End City Center near Nyugati station, MATÁV Pont in Mammut at I. Széna tér and MATÁV Pont Budai Skála at XI. Október 23 u. The main telecommunications office, at Petőfi Sándor u. 17 (near Deák tér), also provides telephone service.

The above-mentioned phonecard will allow you to call the U.S. and Canada for 94 Ft (34¢) per minute, 24 hours a day, 7 days a week. There is a 450 Ft ($1.60) connecting fee. Purchase either 50-unit (800 Ft/$2.90) or 120-unit (1,800 Ft/$6.50) cards.

Hungarian telephone books list the numbers of all countries that can be directly dialed. MATÁV also publishes a useful English-language pamphlet on international calling that includes country codes. Failing either of these resources, dial **199** for international directory assistance. Direct dial to the **United States** and **Canada** is 00/1; to the **U.K.,** 00/44; to **Australia,** 00/61; and to the **Republic of Ireland,** 00/353.

You can reach the **AT&T** operator at ℂ **00/800-01111,** the **MCI** operator at ℂ **00/800-01411,** and the **Sprint operator** at ℂ **00/800-01877.**

Other country direct access numbers connect you to operators in the country you're calling, with whom you can arrange your preferred billing. **Australia Direct** is ℂ **00/800-06111, Canada Direct** is ℂ **00/800-01211, New Zealand Direct** is ℂ **00/800-06411,** and **U.K. Direct** is ℂ **00/800-04411** (BT) or 00/800-04412 (Mercury).

To make **a call to Hungary from abroad,** dial the appropriate numbers to get an international dial tone (011 from the U.S.), then dial 36 (Hungary country code), followed by the appropriate city code (for Budapest, 1), followed by the six- or seven-digit telephone number.

Time Zone Hungary is on Central European time, 2 hours ahead of Greenwich mean time and 6 hours ahead of eastern standard time from March 26 to October 26; from October 27 to March 25 (during the equivalent of daylight saving time), the difference is 1 hour and 5 hours, respectively.

Tipping The tipping rate is generally 10%. Among those who welcome tips are waiters, taxi drivers, hotel employees, barbers, cloakroom attendants, toilet attendants, masseuses, and tour guides. If a restaurant bill includes a service fee, as most restaurants have traditionally done, there is no need to tip. However, there is a new trend of not including a service charge in the newer, trendy restaurants; waiters are likely to remind you if this is the case. See "The Check, Please: Tips on Tipping," in chapter 5, "Where to Dine in Budapest," for more information.

Water Tap water in Budapest is generally considered safe for drinking. Mineral water, which many Hungarians prefer to tap water, is called *ásványvíz*. Purified bottled water (*szénsav mentes*) is sold in delicatessens and groceries in the tourist areas; all brands have a pink label for identification.

4

Where to Stay in Budapest

Budapest's hotels range from beautiful, historic turn-of-the-century gems to drab, utilitarian establishments typical of the city's Socialist period. Although the most notable establishments—among them the stunning Art Nouveau Hotel Gellért, the "thermal" Hotel Béke Radisson, and Castle Hill's distinctive Hilton Hotel—are among the city's priciest, accommodation rates in Budapest remain among the lowest of any European capital.

Despite the number of new hotels and pensions that have opened in recent years, Budapest retains its reputation as a city without enough guest beds. Indeed, in high season it can be quite difficult to secure a hotel, pension room, or hostel bed (although private rooms are always available), so make reservations and get written confirmation well ahead if possible.

When booking, keep in mind that if you want a room with a double bed, it should be specifically requested; otherwise, you are likely to get a room with twin beds. Single rooms are generally available, as are extra beds or cots. Hungarian hotels often use the word "apartment" to describe connected rooms without a kitchen. In these listings, we have referred to such rooms as suites, reserving the term "apartment" for accommodations with kitchen facilities.

BUDGET LODGINGS Although there is an unfortunate dearth of recommendable budget hotels in Budapest, travelers can take advantage of the wealth of good alternative accommodations. Small pensions, rooms in private homes, and a number of good youth hostels make the city inviting to travelers on any budget. Remember that location plays a significant role in cost, with inflated prices for centrally located accommodations the norm. Budapest's efficient public transportation means that reaching downtown from points outside will not be as difficult as you might expect; if you're on a budget, consider staying outside the center in a room removed from the din and smog (and prices) of inner Pest. Pensions in the Buda Hills are far cheaper than downtown hotel rooms; what's more, they are generally located in quiet residential neighborhoods, and most have lovely gardens. We have selected what we consider to be the nicest of the many pensions in the Buda Hills. We also urge you to consider booking a room in Buda's sleepy, but centrally located, Watertown neighborhood, home to a number of recommended hotels.

ACCOMMODATIONS AGENCIES
Most accommodations agencies can secure private room rentals, help reserve hotel and pension rooms, and book you into a youth hostel. The most established agencies are the former state-owned travel agents Ibusz, Cooptourist, MÁV Tours, and Budapest Tourist. Although newer, private agencies have proliferated, the older ones tend to have the greatest number of rooms listed. There are agencies at the airport, in all three major train stations, throughout central Pest, and along the main roads into Budapest for travelers arriving by car.

The main **Ibusz reservations office** is at Ferenciek tere 10 (© **1/485-2700;** fax 1/318-2805), reached by the Blue metro line (open in summer Monday through Friday 8:15am to 6pm; in the off-season, Monday through Friday to 5pm). All major credit and charge cards are accepted. **Cooptourist,** Nyugati Station (© **36/1-458-6200**), is open 9am to 4:30pm Monday through Friday and does not accept credit cards. **Budapest Tourist,** Nyugati Station (© **36/1-318-6552**), is open 9am to 5:30pm Monday through Friday, 9am to 12:30pm Saturday, and does not accept credit cards. **MAV Tours,** Keleti Station (© **36/1-382-9011**), is open 9am to 5pm Monday through Friday and does not accept credit cards.

Be aware that tourists have reported that agents may urge them to take a more expensive room than they wanted. Stick to your guns—the agent will eventually help you reserve a room you desire.

SEASONS Most hotels and pensions in Budapest divide the year into three seasons. **High season** is roughly from March or April through September or October. The week between Christmas and New Year's, Easter week, and the period of the Budapest Spring Festival are also considered high season. (The weekend of the Grand Prix, second weekend in August, is especially tight.) **Mid-season** is usually considered the months of March

and October and/or November. **Low season** is roughly November through February, except Christmas week. Some hotels discount as much as 50% in low season, while others offer no winter discount; be sure to inquire.

PRICE CATEGORIES Many hotels and pensions in Budapest list their prices in euros; a few list them in U.S. dollars. The hard currency price rates are solely intended as a hedge against forint inflation. All hotels in Budapest accept payment in Hungarian forints as well as foreign currencies. Where prices are quoted in euros, we based our dollar conversions on exchange rates of 1.10€ to $1, the rates at press time. As these exchange rates fluctuate over time, of course, the price of a room in dollars will fluctuate along with them.

All hotels are required to charge a 12% value-added tax (VAT). Some build the tax into their rates whereas others tack it on top of their rates. When booking a room, ask whether the VAT is included in the quoted price. Unless otherwise indicated, prices in this book include the VAT.

Hotels in Hungary are rated by the international five-star system. The ratings, however, are in our view somewhat arbitrary and are not included in our entries for that reason.

Note: We have found that the websites of hotels are frequently inaccurate with respect to rates, so make sure to call the hotel and confirm.

1 The Inner City & Central Pest
VERY EXPENSIVE
Budapest Marriott ★★ A massive cement edifice from the outside, but measuring up to international standards of luxury on the inside, the Marriott is a clean and efficient option with few surprises. Accessible to Pest's main shopping and business areas, it hugs the Danube promenade between the Erzsébet and Chain bridges. Rooms, all of which look out to the river (most have balconies), are comfortable, having been renovated after the Marriott chain took over the hotel in 1993 (from the Inter-Continental chain). Nonsmoking rooms and others equipped for guests with disabilities are available.

Budapest Accommodations

Ananda Youth Hostel **27**

Aquincum
  Corinthia Hotel **2**

Best Hostel **33**

Best Western Hotel Art **19**

Budapest Marriott **15**

Carlton Budapest **10**

Caterina Youth Hostel **30**

Charles Apartment House **12**

City Panzió Ring **35**

City Panzió Pilvax **22**

Club Hotel Ambra **28**

Danubius Grand Hotel
  Margitsziget **3**

Family Hotel **36**

Hilton Budapest **6**

Hotel Astra Vendégház **7**

Hotel Béke Radisson **32**

Hotel Andrássy **39**

Hotel Citadella **16**

Hotel Délibáb **38**

Hotel Erzsébet **21**

Hotel Express **11**

Hotel Gellért **17**

Hotel Ibis Centrum **20**

Hotel Kulturinnov **5**

Hotel Liget **37**

Hotel MEDOSZ **31**

Hotel Orion **13**

Hotel Papillon **1**

Hotel Victoria **9**

International
  Apartment House **8**

K & K Hotel Opera **29**

Kempinski Hotel Corvinus **23**

King's Hotel **24**

Marco Polo Hostel **25**

Mercure Hotel Budapest
  Nemzeti **26**

Peregrinus ELTE Hotel **18**

Radio Inn **40**

Thermal Hotel Helia **4**

Yellow Submarine Lotus
  Youth Hostel **34**

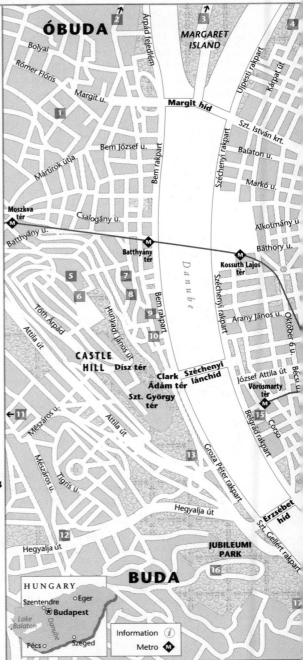

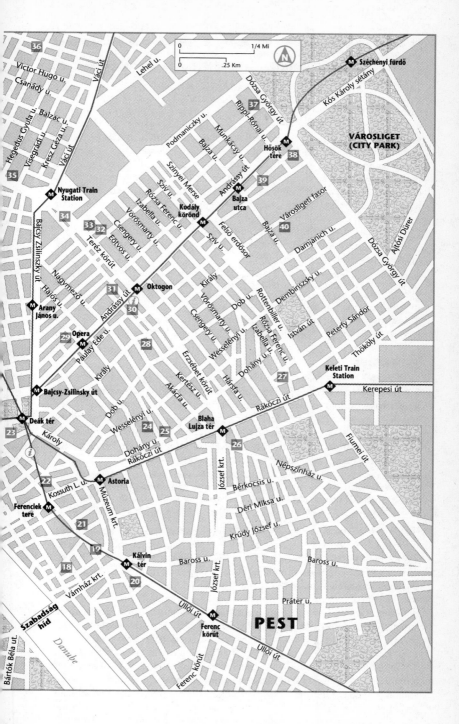

0   1/4 Mi

0   .25 Km

36

Victor Hugo u.

Csanády u.

Hegedüs Gyula u.

Visegrádi u.

Balzac u.

Kresz Géza u.

Váci út

Váci út

Lehel u.

Dózsa György út

Rippl-Rónai u.

37

Széchényi fürdő

Kós Károly sétány

Munkácsy u.

Podmaniczky u.

Bajza u.

Hősök tére

38

**VÁROSLIGET
(CITY PARK)**

35

**Nyugati Train
Station**

Szinyei Merse

Andrássy út

39

Alfösi Dürer

Bajcsy Zsilinszky út

34

Szív u.

Rózsa Ferenc u.

Kodály
körönd

Bajza
utca

Városligeti fasor

Bajza u.

40

Dózsa György út

33 **32**

Izabella u.

Csengery u.

Vörösmarty u.

Eötvös u.

Felso erdősor

Szív u.

Damjanich u.

Nagymező u.

Teréz körút

Hajós u.

Andrássy út

31

Oktogon

30

Király

Dob u.

Rottenbiller u.

Dembinszky u.

István út

Petery Sándor

**Arany
János u.**

Vörösmarty u.

Csengery u.

Rózsa Ferenc u.

Thököly út

29

Opera

28

Paulay Ede u.

Wesselényi u.

Izabella u.

Dohány u.

27

**Keleti Train
Station**

Király

Erzsébet körút

Kertész u.

Harsfa u.

Rákóczi út

Kerepesi út

Flumei út

Bajcsy-Zsilinszky út

Dob u.

Akácfa u.

**Blaha
Lujza tér**

Deák tér

23

Károly

Wesselényi u.

24

25

26

Dohány u.

Rákóczi út

József krt.

Népszínház u.

22

Astoria

Kossuth L. u.

Múzeum krt.

Bérkocsis u.

**Ferenciek
tere**

Déri Miksa u.

21

Krúdy József u.

19

**Kálvin
tér**

Baross u.

József krt.

Baross u.

18

20

Vámház krt.

Üllöi út

Práter u.

**Szabadság
hid**

Bartók Béla út.

Danube

PEST

**Ferenc
körút**

Üllöi út

Ferenc körút

59

V. Apáczai Csere János u. 4, 1052 Budapest. ✆ **1/266-7000.** Fax 1/266-5000. www.marriott.com. 362 units. 206€–236€ ($185–$212) double. Lower weekend rates available. VAT not included. AE, DC, MC, V. Parking available in indoor garage for 5000Ft ($18) per day and for 4000Ft ($14.40) in outdoor guarded space. Metro: Deák tér (all lines). **Amenities:** Restaurants (3); swimming pool; fitness center; sauna; 24-hour room service; massage; babysitting; laundry service; currency exchange; squash court; solarium. *In room:* A/C, TV, minibar, safe.

Kempinski Hotel Corvinus 🏠 Located in the heart of Pest, just off Deák tér, this slick German-run hotel, opened in 1993, has quickly earned a reputation as the hotel of choice for corporate visitors (and also musicians—Madonna, the Rolling Stones, Michael Jackson) to Budapest. One thing is for sure: The Kempinski is far and away the most expensive place in town ($1,840 a night for a suite, not including room service!). The building itself is, at least from the outside, a cement behemoth, one of a number of ugly new buildings marring this neighborhood. From the inside, however, everything is quietly and unmistakably luxurious. The rooms are as well appointed as one might expect from such a hotel, and soundproof windows shield guests from the noise of the busy traffic below.

The hotel has a number of excellent restaurants and its American-style buffet breakfast has received rave reviews.

V. Erzsébet tér, 1051 Budapest. ✆ **800/426-3135** in North America, 0088/426-3135-8588 in Britain, or 1/429-3777. Fax 1/429-4777. www.kempinski-budapest.com. 398 units. 304€ ($276) double; 482€–2,031€ ($437–$1,840) suite. VAT not included. Children 11 and under stay free in parents' room. Breakfast 20€ ($17.95) extra. AE, MC, V. Parking 5,000Ft ($18) per day. Metro: Deák tér (all lines). **Amenities:** Restaurants (3), bars (2); swimming pool; sauna; solarium; fitness room; massage; salon; barbershop; 24-hr. room service; concierge; car rental desk; business center; laundry service; dry cleaning (weekdays only). *In room:* A/C, TV, minibar.

EXPENSIVE

Club Hotel Ambra 🏠🏠 The Hungarian-owned and operated Club Hotel Ambra opened for business in 1998, and attracts a mostly business clientele. The hotel houses 16 fully equipped apartments (with bedroom, bathroom, kitchen, and living room) and five standard double rooms. Several of the apartments have terraces that look out over an interior courtyard. The skylit breakfast room and bar area are particularly inviting. It's a good place for those who want to stay close to central Pest, but want some relative peace and quiet.

VII. Kisdiófa u. 13, 1077 Budapest. ✆ and fax **1/321-1533.** www.hotelambra.hu. 16 apts, 5 rooms $75–$145 (depending on the number of beds in the quarters, which have 1–4 beds). Rates include breakfast. Rates 20% lower in low season. AE, MC, V. Parking in hotel garage for $7. Metro: Oktogon (Yellow line). **Amenities:** Jacuzzi; sauna; pay-per-use solarium. *In room:* A/C, TV, minibar, full kitchen (apartments only).

Hotel Béke Radisson 🏠🏠 The Béke Radisson, situated not far from Nyugati railway station on Pest's Outer Ring (Nagykörút), carries on a long tradition. In 1913, the Hotel Brittania opened on the same spot. An art nouveau gem, it was one of the most modern Budapest hotels of its time. Unfortunately, the hotel was badly damaged in World War II, and it was not until 1955 that it was reopened under the hopeful name Béke (meaning "peace"). The hotel underwent renovations again in the 1980s, reopening in 1985 after a reconstruction that respected the hotel's original design. Rooms are smartly furnished in dark wood, although the soundproof windows don't exactly muffle all the noise from the busy boulevard below. Nonsmoking rooms are available.

The hotel has a noteworthy collection of restaurants. The Shakespeare Restaurant serves breakfast and lunch in a bright, cheerful room with a skylight and Shakespearean frescoes by Jenő Haranghy, preserved from the original Hotel Brittania. The elegant Szondi Restaurant (named after a Hungarian hero who fought the Turks) serves Hungarian/international dinners accompanied by

Gypsy music. The restaurant is decorated with Turkish weaponry and frescoes and stained-glass windows (also from the original hotel) depicting scenes from Szondi's life. László Héjja, the longtime chef, has an excellent reputation. In the Zsolnay Cafe, delicious pastries are served on hand-painted Zsolnay porcelain. The decor here is also carefully chosen and pays respect to the original hotel: Venetian mirrors, chandeliers, a grand piano. There is also a casino just off the lobby.

VI. Teréz krt. 43, 1067 Budapest. ☎ 1/301-1611. Fax 1/301-1615. www.radisson.com. 247 units. 147€–168€ ($133–$152) double; 305€ ($276) suite. VAT is not included. In low season the rates are 10% less. Breakfast 14.25€ ($12.90) extra. AE, MC, V. Parking 3,900Ft ($14) per day. Metro: Nyugati pu. (Blue line) or Oktogon (Yellow line). **Amenities:** Restaurants (3); swimming pool; fitness center; sauna; tour desk; car rental; business center; salon; 24-hr. room service; massage; babysitting; laundry service; dry cleaning; drugstore; solarium. *In room:* A/C, TV, minibar, safe, hair dryer.

Hotel Erzsébet ✩   Originally built in 1872, the Erzsébet Hotel took as its namesake the queen of Austria-Hungary. The present hotel is the result of a total reconstruction in 1985 and some minor renovations in 2000. Its central Pest location is unbeatable: just a few minutes' walk from the southern end of Váci utca. Rooms are smartly furnished, with many features of a luxury hotel. If you want a modern, centrally located hotel at slightly lower prices, this could be the place for you; though you should be prepared for a less knowledgeable staff at the reception desk.

V. Károlyi Mihály u. 11–15, 1053 Budapest. ☎ 1/328-5700. Fax 1/328-5763. www.danubiusgroup.com. 123 units. 140€ ($126) double. Rates include breakfast. Rates 20% lower in low season. Discounts for groups of 10 or more. AE, MC, V. Free parking available for 12 cars. Metro: Ferenciek tere (Blue line). **Amenities:** Restaurant; car rental; babysitting on request; laundry service; dry cleaning on request; garden. *In room:* A/C, TV, minibar.

K & K Hotel Opera ✩✩✩ *Value*   Operated by the Austrian K & K hotel chain, this tasteful, elegant establishment opened in 1994 and expanded in 1997. Directly across the street from the Opera House in central Pest, the hotel building blends nicely with the surrounding architecture. And the soundproofed windows in the guest rooms do a good job of keeping out street noise. The interior design is equally pleasing. The staff is uniformly friendly and helpful. This hotel is within close proximity not just of the Opera House, but of Budapest's theater district as well.

VI. Révay u. 24, 1065 Budapest. ☎ 1/269-0222. Fax 1/269-0230. www.kkhotels.com. 205 units. 143€ ($129) double and 122€ ($110) single. Rates 5% lower in low season. Rates include breakfast. AE, DC, MC, V. Parking 1,920Ft ($6.90). Metro: Opera (Yellow line). **Amenities:** Fitness room; sauna; business center; nonsmoking rooms. *In room:* A/C, TV, minibar, safe.

Mercure Hotel Budapest Nemzeti ✩✩✩ *Finds*   This turn-of-the-20th-century Hotel Nemzeti, just off Blaha Lujza Square, underwent a 1987 restoration that returned much of its original art nouveau splendor. This is perhaps Pest's most handsome and historic hotel. Its biggest drawback is its location; though very centrally located, the hotel directly overlooks what is perhaps the busiest square of the Outer Ring. Half the rooms face the heavily trafficked street (and those rooms' soundproofing does not mask the noise), while the other half face into a lovely interior courtyard (request one of the latter). The rooms were recently renovated with modern furnishings and new carpeting. Rooms have wonderful high ceilings and spacious bathrooms. The rooms on the top (fifth) floor are most interesting, with slanted ceilings and funky windows (there is an elevator). There is also a nonsmoking floor.

In addition to the lobby pub, the hotel has a restaurant, recently restored to its formal elegance as one of Budapest's most fashionable eateries.

VIII. József krt. 4, 1088 Budapest. © **1/477-2000**. Fax 1/477-2001. www.mercure-nemzeti.hu. 76 units. 112€ ($101) double. Rates include breakfast. Rates 20% lower in low season. AE, DC, MC, V. Parking available in neighborhood garage for 2,500Ft ($9) per day. Metro: Blaha Lujza tér (Red line). **Amenities:** Restaurant (1); car rental desk; 24-hr. room service; laundry service. *In room:* A/C, TV, minibar, safe, hair dryer.

MODERATE

City Panzió Pilvax ☆   Opened in 1997, this is one of three new Inner City pensions owned by the Taverna Hotel group, which also owns the large Hotel Taverna on Váci utca. The staff is friendly, the rooms are clean and efficient, but the place clearly lacks the charm found in many of the pensions in the Buda Hills. It costs a bit more, too, but the location is obviously what you are paying for. The pension is on a narrow, quiet street just a few minutes by foot from the hubbub of central Pest.

V. Pilvax köz 1–3, 1052 Budapest. © **1/266-7660**. Fax 1/317-6396. www.taverna.hu. 32 units. 90€ ($81) double; 70€ ($63) single. Rates 10% lower in low season. Rates include breakfast. AE, DC, MC, V. Parking 35€ ($31); garage is at nearby Hotel Taverna. Metro: Ferenciek tere (Blue line). **Amenities:** Restaurants (2); bar; bicycle rental; business center; laundry service. *In room:* TV, minibar, hair dryer.

City Panzió Ring ☆   Opened in 1997, this is another of three new central Pest pensions owned by the Taverna Hotel group. This pension is located on Pest's bustling Outer Ring boulevard (hence the name), on the fringes of the fashionable Újlipótváros neighborhood. It is just a block away from Nyugati railway station and a 10-minute walk to the Danube embankment and to Margaret Island, the city's loveliest park. The small rooms are clean but without character. It is a perfectly adequate place, but if you are looking for a pension with Old-World charm, you'll have to stray farther from the center of the city. A Japanese tearoom is schedule to open here in the spring of 2002.

XIII. Szent István krt. 22, 1137 Budapest. © **1/340-5450**. Fax 1/340-4884. www.taverna.hu. 39 units. 84€ ($75) double; 65€ ($58.50) single. Rates 30% lower in low season. Rates include breakfast. AE, DC, MC, V. Limited parking available for 2,500Ft ($9) per day. Metro: Nyugati pu (Blue line). **Amenities:** Restaurant, bar; bicycle rental; business center; laundry service. *In room:* TV, minibar.

Hotel Ibis Centrum ☆☆   Located just a few steps from bustling Kálvin tér, the relatively new Hotel Ibis Centrum—it opened in 1998—is a good downtown option. Comfortable, neat as a pin, and reasonably priced, the hotel has three nonsmoking floors (a feature otherwise unheard of in this price category), and a few rooms are equipped for travelers with disabilities. There's also a roof garden and lobby bar.

IX. Ráday u. 6, 1092 Budapest. © **1/215-8585**. Fax 1/215-8787. 126 units. $100 double. Rates include breakfast. Rates 20% lower in low season. MC, V. Parking available for 2,600Ft ($9.35) per day. Metro: Kálvin tér (Blue line). **Amenities:** Bar; nonsmoking rooms. *In room:* A/C, TV, dataports.

King's Hotel ☆☆ *(Finds)*   The King's Hotel opened for business in 1995 in a beautifully renovated and restored fin-de-siècle building in the heart of Pest's Jewish district. Despite the somewhat drab modern furnishings, the rooms retain a 19th-century atmosphere, many with small balconies overlooking the quiet residential street. Most, but not all of the rooms have a private bathroom. The reception is uniformly friendly and helpful. The hotel restaurant is strictly kosher, the only of its kind in Budapest. It is open for breakfast, lunch, and dinner; food is prepared under the observation of Rabbi Hoffman. *Note:* Meals are served on weekends and Jewish holidays in the hotel's restaurant by prior arrangement only.

Tips **Euros & Dollars**

Several hotels and pensions in Budapest list their prices in U.S. dollars and many list them in euros, the new currency of the European Union. This is done solely as a hedge against forint inflation, as Hungary is not actually a member of the European Union. All hotels in Budapest accept payment in Hungarian forints as well as foreign currencies. We have converted prices given in euros into dollars based on an exchange rate of 1.1€=$1, the rate at press time. As these exchange rates fluctuate over time, of course, the price of a room in dollars will fluctuate along with them.

VII. Nagydiófa u. 25–27 Budapest. ℂ and fax **1/352-7675**. 80 units. $60–$80 double; ($140) suite. Rates include breakfast. AE, DC, MC, V. Parking available on street for $5 per day. Metro: Astoria (Red line). **Amenities:** Restaurant (Kosher). *In room:* A/C, TV.

Peregrinus ELTE Hotel ★★ *Value*   Peregrinus ELTE Hotel is ideally located in the heart of the Inner City of Pest, across the street from a historic Serbian Church on a small side street half a block from Váci utca, the popular pedestrian-only street. This is the guesthouse of Pest's ELTE University. While many guests are affiliated with the university, the hotel is open to the public as well. You should reserve well in advance. The building dates from the turn of the 20th century and was renovated when it was opened in 1994. The rooms are simple but comfortable. Payment must be in cash in Hungarian forints.

V. Szerb u. 3, 1056 Budapest. ℂ **1/266-4911**. Fax 1/266-4913. 26 units. 19,623ft ($69) double; 15,700ft ($55) in low season. Rates include breakfast. No credit cards. No parking. Metro: Kálvin tér (Blue line). *In room:* TV, minibar.

INEXPENSIVE

Hotel MEDOSZ ★ *Value*   The MEDOSZ was formerly a trade-union hotel for agricultural workers. It is located on sleepy Jókai tér, in the heart of Pest's theater district, just across the street from the bustling Liszt Ferenc tér, Pest's most recent center of night life, a couple of blocks from the Opera House. This is as good as it gets off the river in central Pest. Although the hotel has not been renovated since privatization, it remains a great value given its location. The rooms are simple but clean. Next door to Hotel MEDOSZ is one of Budapest's special treats for children: a puppet theater (*bábszínház*).

VI. Jókai tér 9, 1061 Budapest. ℂ **1/374-3000**. Fax 1/332-4316. 68 units. 49€ ($43.70) double; 36€ ($32.65) single. Rates are 20% lower in low season. Rates include breakfast. No credit cards. Metered parking difficult in neighborhood. Metro: Oktogon (Yellow line). **Amenities:** Restaurant, bar; laundry service; solarium. *In room:* TV.

2 Central Buda

VERY EXPENSIVE

Hotel Gellért ★★★ *Kids*   First opened in 1918, this splendid, sprawling art nouveau hotel has not seen any renovation since 1970. It's pretty run-down now, but still one of the most charming hotels in Budapest. Located at the base of Gellért Hill in Buda, on the bank of the Danube, the Gellért is one of several thermal hotels in Budapest managed or owned by Danubius Hotels. The circular hotel lobby has marble columns and a mezzanine level. The quality and size of the rooms vary greatly—it seems to be hit or miss. Only 29 rooms have air-conditioning. Some rooms with balconies offer great views over the Danube, but these can be noisy since the hotel fronts loud and busy Gellért Square.

While the majority of guests don't come for the official spa treatment, there are a number of spa-related facilities that all guests can use free of charge: 2 pools (one indoors, one with child-pleasing artificial waves), a steam room, and the art nouveau Gellért Baths, perhaps the most popular of Budapest's thermal baths (most tourists visit them at least once during their stay). If you come in the summer, a nighttime plunge under the stars is definitely a must.

XI. Gellért tér 1, 1111 Budapest. ℂ **1/385-2200.** Fax 1/466-6631. www.danubiusgroup.com. 233 units. 179€–192€ ($161–$173) double; 238€–256€ ($214–$230) suite. Rates include breakfast. Spa packages available. AE, DC, MC, V. Free parking. Tram: 47 or 49 from Deák tér. **Amenities:** Restaurants (3); bar; swimming pools (2); tour desk; business center; 24-hr. room service; babysitting; laundry service. *In room:* A/C (some rooms), TV, minibar.

EXPENSIVE

Best Western Hotel Art ★★   This hotel, opened in a fully restored and renovated turn-of-the-century building in 1994, is brilliantly located on a quiet side street in the southern end of Pest's Inner City. The reception is a bit stuffy and overly formal for a hotel of this size and quality, but the rooms are clean and comfortable and come with air conditioning, a rare amenity in the dry heat of the summer.

V. Királyi Pál u. 12, 1053 Budapest. ℂ **1/266-2166.** Fax 1/266-2170. hotelart@mail.matav.hu. 32 units. 102€ ($92) double. Rates include buffet breakfast. AE, MC, V, DC. Parking available for 3,400Ft ($12.25) per day at the nearby Hotel Corona. Metro: Kálvin tér (Blue line). **Amenities:** Restaurant (1); exercise room; sauna; laundry service. *In room:* A/C, TV, dataport, minibar.

Carlton Budapest ★★ *(Finds)*   Formerly the Alba Hotel (built in 1990), this hotel was fully renovated in 1999–2000 (a bit soon after construction, no?) and reopened under the name Carlton Budapest in February 2000. The hotel belongs to a Swiss chain, and the Swiss influence is pervasive—from the buffet breakfast that features half a dozen kinds of muesli to the antiseptically clean rooms. The hotel is nestled in a tiny cobblestone alley in Buda's Watertown, directly beneath Buda Castle. It has seven floors, but only rooms on the top floor have views; the two best are no. 706, which has a view of the castle, and no. 707, which overlooks Matthias Church. Other seventh-floor rooms offer a pleasing vista of red-tiled Buda rooftops.

I. Apor Péter u. 3, 1011 Budapest. ℂ **1/224-0999.** Fax 1/224-0990. www.carltonhotel.hu. 95 units. 82€–102€ ($75–$92) double. Rates include breakfast. Rates 15% lower in low season. AE, DC, MC, V. Parking 11.25€ ($10) per day. Many buses run to Clark Ádám tér, including no. 16 from Deák tér. **Amenities:** Bar; limited room service; car-rental desk; babysitting; laundry service. *In room:* A/C, TV w/pay movies, dataport, minibar, hair dryer, safe.

Hotel Astra Vendégház ★★ *(Finds)*   This little gem of a hotel opened in 1996 inside a renovated 300-year-old building on a quiet side street in Buda's lovely Watertown neighborhood. The rooms are large, with wood floors and classic Hungarian-style furniture; the overall effect is a far more homey and pleasant space than that found in most Budapest hotel rooms. Indeed, the hotel is tasteful through and through, and the staff are friendly. Some rooms overlook the inner courtyard, while others face the street.

There is a dark cellar bar with a pool table, and a simple, unadorned breakfast room.

I. Vám u. 6, 1011 Budapest. ℂ **1/214-1906.** Fax 1/214-1907. astra112@kiwwi.hu. 12 units. All rooms are double and cost 97€ ($87) for two people and 82€ ($74) for one. Rates include breakfast. Rates 10% lower in low season. Free parking available on street. Metro: Batthyány tér (Red line). **Amenities:** Restaurant, bar; car-rental desk; babysitting (on request). *In room:* A/C, TV, minibar.

Hotel Budapest ⭐ A metallic-looking 1960s Socialist-style cylinder from the outside, the Hotel Budapest recently refurbished its interiors in response to guests' criticism. It now sports newly upholstered furniture, new carpeting, and bright white (instead of drab gray) paint—the result is a clean modern look.

The hotel soars above the neighborhood and offers numerous views; each room boasts a full wall of windows. Your room may overlook the Danube or face up into the hills of Buda. Request a room on a high floor. The vista over the city from the roof garden is simply breathtaking at night. All rooms have air-conditioning. The hotel is within walking distance of Moszkva tér, Buda's central transportation hub, and just across the street from the base of the cogwheel railway, which takes you straight up into the Buda Hills. Locals love to hate the Hotel Budapest, and while it's somewhat of a blight on the landscape, it's also an intriguing place.

II. Szilágyi Erzsébet fasor 47, 1026 Budapest. ℡ 1/202-0044. Fax 1/212-2729. www.danubiusgroup.com. 289 units. 148€ ($133) double; 128€ ($115) single; 189€ ($170) suite. Rates include breakfast. Rates 15% lower in low season. AE, DC, DISC, MC, V. Parking 7€ ($6.20) per day. Tram: 56 from Moszkva tér to Fogaskerekú Vasút. **Amenities:** Restaurants (2); bar; exercise room; sauna; car-rental desk; small business center; salon; 24-hour room service; babysitting; laundry service. *In room:* A/C, TV, minibar.

Hotel Victoria ⭐⭐ The Hotel Victoria, located in Buda's lovely Watertown district, is separated from the Danube bank only by the busy road that runs alongside the river. It's situated in a narrow building, with only three rooms on each of its nine floors. This design makes two-thirds of the accommodations corner rooms with large double windows providing great views over the river to Pest's skyline beyond. The rooms are quite large, with spacious bathrooms. The middle rooms, though smaller than the corner rooms, also have windows facing the river. Unfortunately, noise from the street beneath your window may disturb your rest. The hotel is just minutes by foot from both Batthyány tér and Clark Ádám tér, with dozens of metro, tram, and bus connections.

I. Bem rakpart 11, 1011 Budapest. ℡ 1/457-8080. Fax 1/457-8088. www.victoria.hu. 27 units. 102€ ($100) double; 97€ ($95) single. Rates include breakfast. Rates 25% lower in low season. AE, DC, MC, V. Parking in garage 8.70€ ($7.80). Tram: 19 from Batthyány tér to the 1st stop. **Amenities:** Bar; sauna; limited room service; laundry service. *In room:* A/C, TV, dataport, minibar, hair dryer, safe.

International Apartment House ⭐⭐⭐ *Value* This unique establishment, opened in 1994, is located in a lovely apartment building in Buda's Watertown district. The owner, a German art collector, purchased 12 apartments in the building, renovated them, and installed an elevator for his guests. There is no sign on the street, just a bell with the name "International Apartment House." Reception is on the fourth floor. The place is a 5-minute walk from the metro station, on a quiet street in the upper part of Watertown. The apartments are all quite different from one another, both in terms of size and in terms of facilities and decor (hence a huge disparity in prices). Each apartment is decorated with original artwork and outfitted with a different design and modern furniture. Some apartments have balconies, others have decks; some have glorious views. All apartments enjoy fully equipped kitchens with microwave, toaster, etc. In addition, all the apartments have a CD player (each with an eclectic CD collection), a VCR (free videos available for borrowing), an answering machine, and a fax machine. Two apartments have air-conditioning, and several have built-in Jacuzzis. A place to come home to—this is the perfect choice for business travelers who are spending more than a few days in Budapest.

Meal and shopping services are available for a fee.

I. Donáti u. 53, 1015 Budapest. ℂ 1/356-7198. Fax 1/214-3660. www.inapho.com. 12 units. $120–$220 apartments (reduced rates for long-term stays). Breakfast is $5 extra for continental and $10 extra for cooked breakfast. No credit cards—cash only. Parking available on street. Metro: Battyhány tér (Red line). **Amenities:** Fully-staffed business center; laundry service. In room: TV/VCR, fax, dataport, kitchen, minibar, coffeemaker.

MODERATE

Hotel Orion ☆ Conveniently located in Buda's Watertown neighborhood, between Castle Hill and the Danube, this small five-story hotel is tucked away on a relatively quiet street near many of the city's best sights. Though the rooms are bright and cheerful enough, and five have balconies, they unfortunately enjoy neither castle nor river views. Döbrentei tér, a messy but convenient transportation hub, is a few minutes away by foot.

I. Döbrentei u. 13, 1013 Budapest. ℂ 1/356-8933 or 1/356-8583. Fax 1/375-5418. www.hotels.hu/orion. 30 units. 100€–107€ ($90–$97) double. Rates include breakfast. Rates lower in low season. AE, DC, MC, V. Free parking on street. Tram: 19 from Battyhány tér to Döbrentei tér. **Amenities:** Restaurant; sauna; tour desk; car-rental desk; limited room service; nonsmoking rooms. In room: A/C, TV, dataport, minibar.

INEXPENSIVE

Charles Apartment House ☆ (Value) This is one of the better housing deals in Budapest. Owner Károly Szombati has amassed 50 apartments in a group of apartment buildings in a dull but convenient Buda neighborhood (near the Hotel Novotel). It is a 30-minute walk to downtown Pest, or a 5-minute bus ride. All accommodations are ordinary Budapest flats in ordinary residential buildings. The furnishings are comfortable and clean, and all apartments have full bathrooms and kitchens. Hegyalja út is a very busy street, but only two apartments face out onto it; the rest are in the interior or on the side of the building. A nearby park has tennis courts and a track. There is a new restaurant in the guesthouse, and a pub and grocery store nearby. The friendly, English-speaking reception is open 24 hours. Laundry service is available, as is bike rental.

I. Hegyalja út 23, 1016 Budapest. ℂ 1/212-9169. Fax 1/202-2984. www.charleshotel.hu. 50 units. 44€–104€ ($41–$91.50) apt for 1–4. Rates include breakfast. Rates 5%–20% lower in low season. AE, DC, MC, V. Parking 5.10€ ($4.60) per day or for free on a nearby side street. Bus: 78 from Keleti pu. to Mészáros utca. **Amenities:** Restaurant; bar; bicycle rental; tour desk; business center; babysitting; laundry service. In room: A/C, TV, kitchen, minibar, hair dryer, safe.

Hotel Papillon ☆ The Hotel Papillon, opened in 1992 as a joint Hungarian-German venture, is a pleasing Mediterranean-style white building on a quiet Buda side street. It is located in the area where central Buda begins to give way to the greenery of the Buda Hills, but is still an easy bus ride to the center of the cit. A Mediterranean feeling pervades the interior and the spare pink guest rooms. Seven rooms have terraces; all have refrigerators. In summer, the hotel's restaurant serves meals on a pleasant outdoor terrace. Laundry service is available.

II. Rózsahegy u. 3/b, 1024 Budapest. ℂ and fax 1/212-4003 or 1/212-4750. www.hotels.hu/papillon. 20 units. 56€ ($51) double. Rates include breakfast. Rates 20%–25% lower in low season. AE, MC, V. 4 free spaces in secure hotel lot. Bus: 91 from Nyugati pu. to Zivatar utca. **Amenities:** Restaurant; bar; small outdoor pool; car-rental desk; limited room service; babysitting; laundry service. In room: TV, refrigerator.

3 The Castle District

VERY EXPENSIVE

Hilton Budapest ★★★   One of only two hotels in Buda's elegant Castle District (the other is Hotel Kulturinnov), the Hilton, built in 1977, is widely considered the city's classiest hotel. Its location, on Hess András tér, next door to Matthias Church and the Fisherman's Bastion, is no less than spectacular. The hotel's award-winning design incorporates both the ruins of a 13th-century Dominican church (the church tower rises above the hotel) and the baroque facade of a 17th-century Jesuit college (the hotel's main entrance). The ruins were carefully restored during the hotel's construction, and the results are uniformly magnificent. Although the building is clearly modern, its tasteful exterior blends in fairly well with the surrounding Castle District architecture. More expensive rooms have views over the Danube, with a full Pest skyline; rooms on the other side of the hotel overlook the delightful streets of the Castle District. All rooms are handsomely furnished and are equipped with such amenities as two-line telephones and bathrobes.

The luxurious Dominican Restaurant has an international menu; dinner is accompanied by piano music. The colorful Kalocsa Restaurant has a Hungarian menu and nightly Gypsy music. The Margareeta Cafe, with outdoor tables behind the hotel by the Fisherman's Bastion, has coffee and pastries, in addition to afternoon barbecue lunches in the summertime. Drinks are served in the Faust Wine Cellar and the Lobby Bar, and there's also a sushi bar. There's a casino in the hotel, and the lovely Dominican Courtyard is the site of summer concerts.

I. Hess András tér 1–3, 1014 Budapest. ✆ 1/488-6600. Fax 1/488-6644. www.hilton.com. 322 units. 215€–312€ ($193–$281) double; 383€–562€ ($345–$506) suite. Children stay free in parents' rm. Breakfast 17€ ($15.65) extra. AE, DC, MC, V. Parking for 5,600 Ft ($20) per day in garage. Bus: "Várbusz" from Moszkva tér or 16 from Deák tér. **Amenities:** Restaurants (3), bars (3), lounge; fitness room; concierge; tour desk; free airport minibus; full business center salon; 24-hr. room service; babysitting; laundry service; doctor/dentist on call; nonsmoking rooms. *In room:* A/C, TV w/pay movies, dataport, minibar, hair dryer, safe.

MODERATE

Hotel Kulturinnov ★★ *Finds*   This guesthouse is run by the Hungarian Culture Foundation, a foundation dedicated to forging ties with ethnic Hungarians in neighboring countries. Although it is open to the public, few travelers seem to know about it. There are three reasons to stay here: location, location, location. Hotel Kulturinnov is right in the middle of Buda's lovely Castle District; your only other accommodation choice up here is the Hilton, at three or four times the cost. Rooms at the guesthouse are clean and simple. Although a reader reported a problem with insects in her room, we haven't received any other negative reports or have had any problems ourselves. Each room is equipped with a refrigerator. The hotel is located directly across the street from Matthias Church and the Plague Column, but the entrance is unassuming and practically unmarked. Go through the iron grille gateway and pass through an exhibition hall, continuing up the grandiose red-carpeted staircase to the right.

I. Szentháromság tér 6, 1014 Budapest. ✆ 1/355-0122 or 1/375-1651. Fax 1/375-1886. 16 units. 71€ ($64) double. Rates almost 50% lower in low season. Rates include breakfast. AE, DC, MC, V. Parking 2,500 Ft ($9) per night. Bus: "Várbusz" from Moszkva tér or 16 from Deák tér. **Amenities:** Restaurants (2), bars (2). *In room:* Refrigerator.

4 Outer Pest

VERY EXPENSIVE

Thermal Hotel Helia ★★ *Kids*   The Thermal Hotel Helia is one of several so-called thermal hotels in Budapest now managed and owned by Danubius Hotels. The hotel originally opened in 1990 as a Hungarian-Finnish joint venture. Despite the change in ownership, it continues to provide all the spa and sauna related amenities of the two cultures. While the majority of guests do not come for the official spa treatment, there are a number of spa-related facilities that all guests can use free of charge: swimming pool, sauna, thermal bath, Jacuzzi, steam bath, and fitness room.

The bright, sunny guest rooms sport tall windows. Some rooms have balconies, and four suites have private saunas. A few rooms are equipped for visitors with disabilities.

The Restaurant Saturnus, open for dinner only, offers international cuisine with live music. The adjoining Restaurant Jupiter, open for both lunch and dinner, has a fixed-price buffet table with a well-stocked salad bar.

XIII. Kárpát u. 62–64, 1133 Budapest. ⓒ 1/452-5800. Fax 1/452-5801. www.danubiusgroup.com. 262 units (5 with wheelchair access). 174€ ($156) double; 251€–358€ ($225–$322) suite. Rates include breakfast and spa facilities. AE, DC, MC, V. Free parking. Trolleybus: 79 from Keleti Station. **Amenities:** Restaurants (2); indoor pool; health club & spa; business center; salon/barber; room service (6am–10:30pm); massage; babysitting; same-day laundry service; dry cleaning; nonsmoking rooms; safe-deposit boxes. *In room:* A/C, TV, dataports (in some rooms), minibar.

EXPENSIVE

Hotel Liget ★ *Kids*   Although unabashedly modern and somewhat out of sync with the surrounding architecture, the Hotel Liget is well located just off Pest's Heroes' Square and across the street from the Fine Arts Museum and the City Zoo (a boon for families with young kids). It is a 30-minute walk to the center of Pest, but the Yellow metro line whisks you into the center in no time at all. The rooms are comfortable and modern, if unimaginatively furnished.

VI. Dózsa György út 106, 1068 Budapest. ⓒ 1/269-5300. Fax 1/269-5329. 139 units. www.liget.hu. 112€ ($101) double. Rates include breakfast. Rates 25% lower in low season. AE, MC, V. Parking 8.20€ ($7.35) per day in garage. Metro: Hósök tere (Yellow line). **Amenities:** Restaurant, bar; exercise room; sauna; tour desk; 24-hr. room service; massage; laundry service; dry cleaning; nonsmoking rooms. *In room:* A/C, TV, minibar.

MODERATE

Family Hotel ★★ *Kids*   A charming, elegant little place opened in 1991, the Family Hotel stands 2 blocks from the Danube in a quiet, mostly residential neighborhood in the Újlipótváros (New Leopold Town), just north of the Inner City of Pest. Szent István Park, an unassuming neighborhood park, is only 5 minutes away by foot. Perhaps the nicest thing about this hotel is the low-key atmosphere; it has only one bar (in the Hungarian/international restaurant) and there's very little for sale elsewhere. The suites—all duplexes—are among the nicest rooms in the city, with skylights over the upstairs bedrooms and enormous floor-to-ceiling windows. All rooms in the hotel are spacious, with simple wood furniture and large bathrooms. The wonderfully big suites are suitable for families.

XIII. Ipoly u. 8/b, 1133 Budapest. ⓒ 1/320-1284. Fax 1/329-1620. 92€ ($83) double; 123€ ($110) suite. Rates include breakfast. Rates 20% lower in low season. AE, DC, MC, V. Parking available on the street for $5 per day. Trolleybus: 79 from Keleti pu. to Ipoly utca. **Amenities:** Restaurant, bar; sauna. *In room:* A/C, TV, minibar.

Hotel Andrássy ★★ *Finds*   Formerly known as Hotel Centrál, the Hotel Andrássy was reopened after an ambitious extension and renovation in September

2001. The Andrássy is a little gem of a hotel, located in an exclusive embassy neighborhood just off Pest's Andrássy út, a minute's journey from Heroes' Square and the City Park, and a 25-minute walk from the center of Pest. The lobby is spacious and tasteful, with marble columns. The enormous suites are marvelous and feature luxuriously large double beds and spacious bathrooms, with massage showers, as well as vintage Hungarian furniture, carpets, and prints. There's a safe in each suite and at the reception desk. The standard rooms, although quite nice, can't compare to the suites, so a splurge is recommended here. Half of the guest rooms come with a terrace.

VI. Munkácsy Mihály u. 5–7, 1063 Budapest. ✆ 1/321-2000. Fax 1/322-9445. www.andrassyhotel.com. 71 units (including 8 luxury suites). 110€–150€ ($99–$135) double; 200€–250€ ($180–$225) suite. Rates include sauna and fitness facilities but do not include breakfast and the 3% tourist tax. Breakfast 13€ ($11.70) extra. AE, MC, V. Parking 2,500 Ft ($9) per day. Metro: Bajza utca (Yellow line). **Amenities:** Restaurant; swimming pool (not until 2003); exercise room; sauna; concierge; limousine service; 24-hr. business center; 24-hr. room service. *In room:* TV/VCR, dataport, minibar, safe.

INEXPENSIVE

Hotel Délibáb   The ancient Hotel Délibáb enjoys a wonderful location across the street from Heroes' Square and City Park, in an exclusive Pest neighborhood that's home to most of the city's embassies. It's a 30-minute walk to the center of Pest, or a 5-minute ride on the Yellow metro line. Rooms here are surprisingly spacious and have nice wood floors; the fixtures are old, but everything works and is clean.

VI. Délibáb u. 35, 1062 Budapest. ✆ 1/342-9301 or 1/322-8763. Fax 1/342-8153. 34 units. 57€ ($52) single; 71€ ($63) double. 25% lower in low season. Rates include breakfast. Major credit cards accepted. Parking in neighborhood difficult. Parking in the hotel's yard is 2,500Ft ($9) per day. Metro: Hősök tere (Yellow line). **Amenities:** Restaurant, bar; laundry service; nonsmoking rooms. *In room:* TV, refrigerator (in some rooms).

Radio Inn ★★ *(Value* As the official guesthouse of Hungarian National Radio, the Radio Inn houses many visiting dignitaries, and also offers apartments to individual tourists. The inn is in an exclusive embassy neighborhood (next door to the embassy of the People's Republic of China), a stone's throw from City Park, and a block from Pest's grand Andrássy út. The metro's Yellow line takes you into the center of Pest in 5 minutes; alternatively, it's a 30-minute walk. Behind the building, there's an enormous private courtyard full of flowers. The huge apartments (all with fully equipped, spacious kitchens) are comfortably furnished and painstakingly clean. Note that the toilets and bathrooms are separate, European style. The management is somewhat old-system (read: begrudging with information, slightly suspicious of foreigners), yet cordial enough. Make sure you reserve well ahead of arrival. The restaurant housed in the same building is a superb place for dinner.

VI. Benczúr u. 19, 1068 Budapest. ✆ 1/342-8347 or 1/322-8284. Fax 1/322-8284. www.hotels.hu/radio_inn_budapest. 32 units. 10,000 Ft–22,000 Ft ($36–$79) apt for 1 to 3. Breakfast 1,200 Ft ($4.30) extra. MC, AE, MC, V. Parking available on street. Metro: Bajza utca (Yellow line). Amenities: Restaurant, bar; 24-hr. room service; laundry service; nonsmoking rooms. *In room:* TV, kitchen (apartments only), minibar.

Richter Panzió ★★ *(Finds* Across the street from the towering Honvéd Hotel, the Richter Panzió sits in a busy part of Pest's Zugló neighborhood, just 5 minutes by bus from Keleti Station (on a night-bus route). The pension, opened in 1991 by the famous Hungarian circus family of the same name, is managed by a friendly staff. The guest rooms are delightful, with light-wood floors and huge windows. Most rooms have double beds; the six rear rooms have terraces. There's a small bar in the cozy lobby and an outdoor deck, plus a whirlpool, sauna, and a pool table.

XIV. Thököly út 111, 1145 Budapest. ✆ **1/363-5735** or 1/363-5761. Fax 1/363-3956. 29 units. 67€ ($59.40) double. Rates include breakfast. Rates 15%–20% lower in low season. MC, V. Free parking. Bus: 7 (Black) from Keleti pu. to Kolumbusz (or Columbus) utca. **Amenities:** Bar; whirlpool; sauna; laundry service. *In room:* TV.

5 Óbuda

VERY EXPENSIVE

Aquincum Corinthia Hotel ★★ *(Kids)* Located on the banks of the Danube, just minutes from Óbuda's lovely Old City center, the Aquincum Corinthia Hotel was opened in 1991. This is a "thermal" hotel, though not all guests come for the spa facilities. Spa-related facilities that all guests can use free of charge include a swimming pool, sauna, thermal baths, Jacuzzi, steam bath, Scottish shower, and fitness room. This delightful, modern hotel is built on the site of a supposed Roman spa; hence its Roman theme. The rooms are cheerful, with soundproof windows and complimentary bathrobes.

The Restaurant Apicius serves both lunch and dinner, with a salad bar and buffet lunch. There's live piano music nightly. The Iris Bar has live music and— here's a new one—a magician!

III. Árpád fejedelem utja 94, 1036 Budapest. ✆ **1/436-4100.** Fax 1/436-4759. www.corinthiahotels.com. 310 units. 200€ ($179) double; 256€ ($230) suite. Rates include breakfast and spa facilities usage. DC, MC, V. Parking available for 3,900Ft ($14) in garage. Train: HÉV suburban railway from Batthyány tér to Árpád híd. **Amenities:** Restaurant, bars (2), nightclub; indoor pool; exercise room & spa; bicycle rental; car-rental desk; business center; room service; babysitting; laundry service; dry cleaning; executive rooms. *In room:* A/C, TV, dataport, minibar, hair dryer.

INEXPENSIVE

Hotel Római ★ *(Finds)* A former resort for minor Communist party officials, this hotel is a bit off the beaten track, but its location in the Római Fürdő section of Óbuda, on the banks of the Danube, is refreshingly peaceful. The lobby is spacious and comfortable, equipped with pool tables and a bar. The rooms were recently renovated and refurbished, though they no particular design to them. Each has a balcony. There's an outdoor swimming pool and a large garden. It takes a while to get here from the center of Budapest (especially if you do not have a car), but you will feel as if you are staying in the countryside.

III. Szent János u. 16, 1039 Budapest. ✆ and fax **1/388-6167.** www.mivo.hu. 24 units; 16 apts. 56.25€ ($50) double; 82€ ($74) apt (sleeps 4). Breakfast included. All major credit cards accepted. Free parking. Train: Suburban HÉV line from Batthyány tér to Római Fürdő; then bus no. 34 to Szent János utca. **Amenities:** Restaurant, bar; outdoor pool; car-rental desk. *In room:* TV, refrigerator.

San Marco Guest House ★★ *(Finds)* Paul and Eva Stenczinger, with assistance from daughter Andrea, run this small pension on the top floor of their house. They speak fluent English and will help guests with restaurant reservations, theater tickets, taxis, train tickets, and other matters. They will also point out the best neighborhood restaurants for a quiet and delicious dinner. The house is comfortable and homey but unassuming—much like the residential Óbuda neighborhood it's located in. Three rooms face the back, where there's a flower-filled garden (breakfast is served here in summer). All rooms have slanted ceilings and good windows. Most of the Stenczingers' business consists of returning guests and personal referrals from former guests.

III. San Marco u. 6, 1034 Budapest. ✆ **1/388-9997** or 1/388-8964. Fax 1/388-9997. saiban@elender.hu. 5 units (2 with shared shower and toilet). 10,000 Ft–12,000 Ft ($36–$43) double. Rates include breakfast. Rates 10%–15% lower in low season. AE, MC, V. Parking available on street or for a fee in a nearby garage. Tram: 17 from Margit híd (Buda side) to Nagyszombat utca. Bus: 6 or 60 from Nyugati station to Timár utca. *In room:* A/C, TV.

6 The Buda Hills

EXPENSIVE

Petneházy Club Hotel ★★ *Kids*   The word "bungalow" does not do justice to the easy elegance of the wood cabins of the Petneházy Country Club, which opened in 1991. Luxuriously furnished, each bungalow has a private sauna, kitchen, and porch. Each is spacious, bright, and sparkling clean. Four smaller bungalows are tailored for guests with disabilities. Deep in the Cold Valley (Hűvösvölgy) region of the Buda Hills, Petneházy is more or less beyond the reach of Budapest's public transportation system, so you really need a car to get here. (A City Taxi will take you there from the center for 3,500 Ft/$12.60). Just down the road is the Petneházy Lovasiskola, for horseback riding in the nearby hills (see "Outdoor Activities & Sports," in chapter 6, "Exploring Budapest").

The restaurant has an outdoor barbecue and serves specialties from the grill.

II. Feketefej u. 2–4, 1029 Budapest. ℂ 1/376-5992. Fax 1/376-5738. www.petnehazy.hu. 45 units. 112€ ($101) small bungalow for 2, 143€ ($129) large bungalow for 4. Rates include breakfast. Weekly rates available. Rates 10% lower in low season. AE, DC, DISC, MC, V. Free parking. Drive or take a cab. **Amenities:** Restaurant, bar; swimming pool; sauna; golf driving range; tennis; bike rental; horseback riding; Ping-Pong; babysitting. *In room:* TV, kitchen, minibar, safe.

MODERATE

Budai Hotel   A 15-minute winding walk from the tram station, the Budai sits high in a quiet section of the Wolf Meadow (Farkasrét) district of the Buda Hills. The rooms are simply furnished; all have private bathrooms, some have terraces. The rooms on the top floor have the best views of the surrounding hills. The view from the hotel's terrace restaurant is also grand. *Note:* The receptionist speaks little English.

XII. Rácz Aladár u. 45–47, 1121 Budapest. ℂ and fax 1/249-0208. www.hotels.hu/budaihotel. 23 units. 64€ ($57.50) double; 77€ ($69) suite; plus 3% tourist tax. Rates include breakfast. Rates 20% lower in low season. AE, MC, V. Free parking in street opposite the hotel, or in secure garage for 3.10€ ($2.75). Tram: 59 from Moszkva tér to the last stop. **Amenities:** Restaurant, bar; exercise room; 24-hr. room service; massage; babysitting; dry cleaning. *In room:* TV, minibar.

Gizella Panzió ★   This fine pension in the Buda Hills is a 10-minute walk from the tram station. Built on the side of a hill, it has a lovely view and a series of terraced gardens leading down to the swimming pool. The pension also features a solarium. Guest rooms are all unique but uniformly quaint and sunny. Owner Gizella Varga has good taste. A sightseeing car and driver can be arranged for guests upon request. Gizella Panzió also rents fully furnished flats in the center of town for 56€ to 92€ ($51 to $83), depending on the number of people.

XII. Arató u. 42/b, 1121 Budapest. ℂ and fax 1/249-2281. 9 units. 56.25€ ($51) double; 66.50€ ($60) suite. Rates include breakfast. Rates lower in low season. MC, V. Free parking. Tram: 59 from Moszkva tér to the last stop. **Amenities:** Bar; outdoor pool; exercise room; sauna; laundry service. *In room:* TV, minibar.

Hotel Panda   Opened in 1990, the Hotel Panda is on Pasaréti Square, in a pleasant neighborhood in the Buda Hills. There's a grocery store and several other businesses in the busy little square. The hotel reception is friendly and efficient, however, the desirability of the rooms varies greatly. Rooms facing the front (10 in all) have terraces, with southern exposure and nice views. Rooms elsewhere in the hotel, with smaller windows and without terraces, can get a bit stuffy. Most bathrooms have a window; all have a bidet. While the larger suites are quite big, the smaller ones are identical in size to normal double rooms. The hotel has a sauna (600 Ft/$2.15 for 30 min.) and a restaurant which serves international/Hungarian cuisine. There is a terrace for summer dining. Note that the Budapest Atlas incorrectly identifies the hotel, placing it much lower down on Pasaréti út, at no. 33.

II. Pasaréti út 133, 1026 Budapest. ℂ **1/275-0133** or 1/275-0134. Fax 1/394-1002. www.budapesthotelpanda. com. 28 units. 61.35€ ($55) double; 71.50€ ($64) suite. Rates include breakfast. Rates 15% lower in low season. AE, MC, V. Limited free parking. Bus: 5 from Marcius 15 tér or Moszkva tér to Pasaréti tér (the last stop). **Amenities:** Restaurant; sauna; massage. *In room:* TV, minibar.

INEXPENSIVE

Beatrix Panzió The Beatrix Panzió, situated in the Buda Hills and opened in 1991, is an agreeable, modern place, with smart, comfortable rooms. The suites have private balconies and full kitchens. A sundeck is available for guests' use and the landscaped garden has a goldfish pond; in good weather, breakfast is served in the garden. Management, if requested, cooks up a traditional Hungarian barbecue (hearty gulyás over an open fire); price negotiable. The staff will assist you with making touring plans. Széher út is a small but heavily traveled road, not a back street, like those most pensions are found on, but the guest rooms are not noisy. A well-stocked grocery store is conveniently located down the street.

II. Széher út 3, 1021 Budapest. ℂ and fax **1/275-0550.** www.beatrixhotel.hu. 15 units. $55 double; $90 suite. Rates include breakfast. Rates 20% lower in low season. No credit cards. Free parking in secured lot. Tram: 56 from Moszkva tér to the 7th stop. **Amenities:** Restaurant; sauna; 24-hr. room service; laundry service (limited). *In room:* TV, minibar, safe, kitchens (suites only).

G.G. Panoráma Panzió ★ *Finds* G.G. are the initials of Mrs. Gábor Gubacsi, the friendly English-speaking owner of this small guesthouse. All guest rooms are on the top floor of the Gubacsi home, located on a steep quiet street in the elegant Rose Hill (Rózsadomb) section of the Buda Hills. Several bus lines from different parts of the center converge on the neighborhood, making it a fairly convenient place to stay. The rooms are small, but tastefully furnished; they share a common balcony, which has a great view of the hills. There's also a common kitchen and dining area for the guests, with full facilities (including a minibar), as well as garden space for picnics, reading, and relaxing. It's a casual but classy place, and the Gubacsis take good care of their guests.

7 Fullánk str, 2nd district, H-1026 Budapest Hungary. ℂ +36-1-394-6034 or +36-1-394-4718 fax. E-mail: panzio@ggpanorama.hu. Website: www.ggpanorama.hu. 4 units. 829 Ft ($50) double. Breakfast $3 extra. No credit cards. Parking available on street. Bus: 11 from Batthyány tér to Majális utca or 91 from Nyugati pu. *In room:* TV, kitchen, shared telephone.

Hotel Queen Mary ★ Opened in 1992, this hotel is situated high up in the hills in a tranquil, affluent neighborhood. The rooms are modern and efficient, but might be said to lack character. Each room has a terrace; those on the ground floor share the terrace with adjacent rooms. Unfortunately, the hotel has less garden space than most Buda pensions. There are, however, a solarium and a restaurant (serving only dinner) with outdoor dining in summer.

XII. Béla király út 47, 1121 Budapest. ℂ and fax 1/395-8377 or 1/274-4000. www.budapest. nethotels.com/queenmary. 22 units. 67€ ($59.40) double; 64€–77€ ($57.50–$69) suite. Rates include breakfast. Rates 20% lower in low season. MC, V. Free parking. Bus: 28 from Moszkva tér to Béla király út. **Amenities:** Restaurant; bar; sauna; limited room service; laundry service; dry cleaning. *In room:* TV, minibar.

St. Christoph Villa ★ *Value* Opened in 1991, St. Christoph Villa is a small family-run pension in a pleasant but remote neighborhood of the Buda Hills. The bright rooms have large windows and solid blond-wood furniture. Each room is different—nos. 4 and 5 are the nicest. The common indoor space is unimpressive, but the garden is lovely. Breakfast is served outside in nice weather. If the owners take to you, they're likely to treat you to a traditional gulyás party one evening in the garden.

II. Galóca u. 20, 1028 Budapest. ☎ and fax **1/275-8903** or 1/275-8907. 5 units. 41€ ($37) double. Rates include breakfast. Rates 15% lower in low season. No credit cards. Free parking. Bus: 56 from Moszkva tér to the last stop, then 64 to Kossuth Lajos utca. *In room:* TV.

Siesta Villa   Deep in the heart of a fashionable section of the Buda Hills, this lovely property's major drawback is that it's a hearty 10-minute walk from the bus stop. There are three guest rooms, each with a spacious bathroom and large windows. In summer, breakfast is served in the garden, and budget travelers will appreciate that the drinks in the common self-service minibar cost supermarket prices. The owner, Dr. Ágota Borbás, speaks adequate English and lives on the premises. She has just added a small separate guesthouse with kitchen, suitable for a family. *Note:* If you arrive on a Sunday, make sure you do not arrive after 9pm.

II. Madár u. 8/a, 1025 Budapest. ☎ and fax **1/275-1318**. www.hotels.hu/siesta_villa. 3 units. 11,000Ft ($40) for 1 person; 14,000Ft ($50) for 2 people; 18,000Ft ($65) for three people. Rates include breakfast. Rates 10% lower in low season. No credit cards. Free parking on the street. Bus: 11 from Batthyány tér to the last stop; then a 10-min. walk. **Amenities:** Massage; laundry service; dry cleaning. *In room:* TV.

Vadvirág Panzió 🏠🏠 ⟨*Value*⟩   A good 10-minute walk from the bus stop, the Vadvirág (its name means wildflower) is in a gorgeous part of the Buda Hills just a few blocks behind the Béla Bartók Memorial House. Sloping gardens and terraces surround the pension. Inside, the hallways are decorated with prints by the late Hungarian-born op artist Victor Vasarely. The rooms are all different; most are small but tastefully furnished. Half the rooms have balconies; some have refrigerators. Room 2 is the best in the house: It's a small suite with a balcony. There's a sauna (8.10€/$6.90 per hr.) and a small restaurant with plenty of outdoor seating.

II. Nagybányai út 18, 1025 Budapest. ☎ **1/275-0200**. Fax 1/394-4292. www.hotels.hu/hotelvadvirag. 15 units. 51€ ($46) double; 71.50€–87€ ($64–$78) suite. Rates include breakfast. MC, V. Parking available in private garage for 5.10€ ($4.60) per day or for free on street. Bus: 5 from Március 15 tér or Moszkva tér to Pasaréti tér (the last stop). **Amenities:** Bar; sauna; laundry service. *In room:* TV, minibar, safe.

7 Margaret Island

EXPENSIVE

Danubius Grand Hotel Margitsziget 🏠   On the northern tip of lovely Margaret Island, in the middle of the Danube, this hotel was originally built in 1873. Destroyed in World War II, it was restored and reopened in 1987. It is connected by an underground tunnel to the adjacent Thermal Hotel Margitsziget. While the majority of guests don't come for the official spa treatment, a number of spa-related facilities of the Thermal Hotel can be used free of charge: swimming pool, sauna, and thermal bath. The rooms are standard for a four-star hotel, and the fitness room, sauna and pools have just been modernized to meet the highest standards.

This is one of only two hotels on Margaret Island, Budapest's most popular park. Though two bridges connect the island with the rest of the city, vehicular traffic (except one city bus) is forbidden except for access to the hotels.

The Széchenyi Restaurant serves international/Hungarian cuisine, including special dietetic dishes and kosher meals on request; there is terrace dining. There are several other dining and drinking options and guests have access to Thermal Hotel Margitsziget's Thermal Star Night Club, with live shows nightly.

XIII. Margitsziget, 1138 Budapest. ☎ **1/452-6200**. Fax 1/452-6264. www.danubiusgroup.com. 164 units. 164€–184€ ($147–$166) double. Breakfast is 10.20€ ($9.20) extra. Rates 20% lower in the low season. Spa facilities usage also included in the rate. AE, DC, MC, V. Parking 2,000 Ft ($7.20) per day. **Amenities:** Restaurant, bar (3), lounge; access to nearby spa and salon; business center; 24-hr. room service; babysitting; laundry service; valet service. *In room:* AC, TV, dataport, minibar, coffeemaker, safe.

Value Staying in Private Rooms

Private rooms have long been considered the best option for budget travelers in Hungary. When you book a private room, you get a room in someone's apartment; usually you share the bathroom either with the hosts or other guests. Breakfast is not officially included, but the host will often offer a continental spread (bread, butter, jam, coffee or tea) for around 550 Ft to 850 Ft ($2.50 to $3.90). You may have limited kitchen privileges (ask in advance to be sure). Some landlords will greet you when you arrive, give you a key, and seemingly disappear; others will want to befriend you, change money, show you around, and cook for you.

Most rooms are quite adequate, some even memorable, but any number of reasons may cause you to dislike your accommodations: Noisy neighborhoods, tiny bathrooms, and wretched coffee are among the complaints we've heard from the occasional displeased traveler. The great majority of guests, though, are satisfied; certainly, staying in a private room provides a window into everyday Hungarian life that would be missed otherwise (except, perhaps, in some of the family-run pensions).

You can book rooms through accommodation agencies (see the information at the beginning of this chapter). Prices vary slightly between agencies, but, generally speaking, an average room will cost about 4,500 Ft to 6,000 Ft ($16 to $21.60) for two people, or 3,800 Ft ($13.70) for a single, plus a 3% tourism tax (though high-end rooms in fashionable neighborhoods can cost significantly more). Most agencies add a 30% surcharge (to the first night only) for stays of less than 4 nights. When booking a room, make sure you know its exact location on a map and how to get there before leaving. There's scarcely an address in Budapest that cannot be reached by some form of public transportation, so regard with skepticism anyone who tells you that you must take a taxi. In peak season you may need to shop around a bit for the location you want, but you can always find a room somewhere. Arriving at an agency early in the day will afford the best selection.

In Keleti Station, where most international trains arrive, you are likely to be approached by all sorts of people offering you private rooms. Many are honest folks trying to drum up some business personally, though the more aggressive ones can be intimidating if not downright annoying; dismiss them out of hand. But keep in mind that when the middleman (the agency) is eliminated, prices tend to be slightly better, so you might consider taking a room from one of these people, especially if you arrive late at night when the agencies are closed or long lines at the agencies drive you to despair. Trust your judgment and don't let anyone pressure you. Feel free to haggle over prices.

8 Youth Hostels

There is intense competition in Budapest between rival youth hostel companies, on the one hand, and between these companies and privately run hostels on the other hand. The two leading companies are **Travellers' Youth Way Youth**

Hostels, also known as "Mellow Mood Ltd."(© **1/340-8585** or 1/329-8644; fax 1/320-8425; www.hostels.hu), and **Universum Youth Hostels** (© or fax **1/275-7046**). Travellers' runs one year-round hostel (Diáksport) and seven summer-only hostels, while Universum Youth Hostels operates one year-round hostel (Marco Polo) and four summer-only hostels.

International trains arriving in Budapest are usually met by young representatives of these companies and some of the privately run youth hostels. (The larger companies even have their agents board Budapest-bound international trains at the Hungarian border crossing to work the backpacking crowd before the train reaches Budapest.) Your best bet is to book a bed in advance at one of our recommended hostels; if you haven't, you can make phone calls on your arrival and try to secure a hostel bed or you can try your luck with these hawkers. Since they make a commission on every customer they bring in, they tend to be pushy and say whatever they think you want to hear about their hostel. Shop around and don't let yourself be pressured. Most hostels that solicit at the station also have a van parked outside. The ride to the hostel is usually free, but you may have to wait a while until the van is full.

Travellers' operates a youth hostel placement office at Keleti Station (© **1/343-0748**), off to the side of track 9 and track 6 near the international waiting room. This office, open daily 7am to 8pm, can help you book a bed in one of Travellers' hostels or in other hostels.

In July and August, a number of university dormitories and other empty student housing are converted into hostels, many managed by Travellers'. Their locations (as well as their condition) have been known to change from year to year, so we haven't reviewed any of them in this guide. The youth hostels and budget lodgings listed below are all open year-round.

The main office of the **Hungarian Youth Hostel Federation** (Magyar Ifjúsági Szállások Szövetsége) is located on the fourth floor of VII. Almássy tér 6 (near Blaha Lujza tér, Red line; © **1/352-1572**, ext. 203—just press 203). They can provide you with a full listing of youth hostels in Hungary, including those in Budapest. You can also pick up an IYHF card (no photo required) for 1,400 Ft ($5). There is also a useful youth travel agency called **Mellow Mood Ltd.,** located at VII. Baross tér 15 (© **1/331-6393;** Baross utca on tram 4,6). It's open Monday through Friday from 8am to 4pm.

INNER CITY & CENTRAL PEST

Best Hostel *Value*   Located on the first floor (remember, European first floor) of a residential apartment building just around the corner from Nyugati train station, this year-round hostel, opened in 1997, puts you within walking distance of all the sites of central Pest. Rooms are tightly furnished and a bit worn looking, but fairly clean. The rooms sleep different numbers of people (anywhere from 2 to 9). Each guest gets a locker with key. The common room, with TV and breakfast tables, has large windows and a cheerful, sunny feeling. One shortcoming is the three toilets and three showers in a hostel that sleeps up to 29 people. There is also a common bulletin/message board with lots of interesting information and commentary. Reception is open daily from 9am to 11pm. Internet access costs 10 to 25 Ft (3¢ to 9¢) per minute, depending on time of day. There's no curfew and no lockout. *Note:* Rooms are not sex-segregated.

VI. Podmaniczky u. 27 I/11 & 12 (doorbell no. 33). © 1/332-4934. Fax 1/269-2926. www.besthostel.hu. 2,500Ft ($9) flat rate per person. Discount of 150 Ft (55¢) for IYHF members. Rates include breakfast. No credit cards. No parking available. Metro: Nyugati pu. (Blue line). **Amenities:** Communal kitchen.

Caterina Youth Hostel   The dominant feature of this perfectly located year-round youth hostel is its namesake Caterina, the 50-ish gruff, overly maternal, and very energetic proprietor. Caterina, who lives in an apartment next door, has been operating the youth hostel since 1991. She speaks very little English but doesn't let that stop her from trying. Caterina runs a tight ship; the hostel is immaculately clean (she evicts all guests from 10am to noon, when she personally scours the place). The hostel has shared toilets and bathrooms. Each guest gets a key; there is no curfew. Caterina also takes in laundry service from guests, which she does in her own apartment.

VI. Andrássy út 47 III/18 (doorbell no. 11). ℂ **1/342-0804.** ℂ and fax 1/352-6147. www.extra.hu/caterina. One 5-bed rm, one 6-bed rm, one 3-bed rms, two 2-bed rms and two apartments. Beds cost 2,500Ft ($9) in all rooms and 3,500Ft ($12.60) in apartments. No discount for IYHF members. Rates do not include breakfast. No credit cards. No parking available. Metro: Oktogon (Yellow line). **Amenities:** Laundry service; communal kitchen.

Marco Polo Hostel *(Value)*   Although this place calls itself a youth hostel, it is really more in the nature of a budget hotel. On a recent visit here, we noticed that most of the guests were well-dressed middle-aged Europeans; this is no backpackers' haunt. Given the central location and the clean, modern rooms (opened in 1997), it appears to be a very good deal. There is no curfew and no lockout. Open year-round, it is operated by Universum Youth Hostels. *Note:* Some rooms are equipped for travelers with disabilities.

VII. Nyár u. 6, 1072 Budapest. ℂ **1/344-5367.** Fax 1/342-9589. www.hostelmarcopolo.com. 36 double rms, 5 quad rms, five 12-bed rms (all with shower and toilet). 7,500Ft ($27) per person in double rm, 5,500Ft ($20) per person in quad, 3,600Ft ($13) per person in 12-bed rm. Rates include breakfast. 10% discount for IYHF members. No credit cards. Parking available for a fee. Metro: Blaha Lujza tér (Red line). **Amenities:** Laundry service; communal kitchen.

Yellow Submarine Lotus Youth Hostel ★★   This private hostel, open year-round, is centrally located across the street from Nyugati train station, on the very busy Teréz körút. It is within walking distance of all central Pest attractions. The hostel is on the third floor of a residential building. There is nothing more than a small sign downstairs by the mailbox to let you know you are in the right place. Ring the bell, and you will be buzzed in. You need not repeat this ritual more than once, as all guests are given keys. There is no curfew. The reception desk is manned by a dry-witted and multilingual Russian fellow named Ollie, who spends his days happily dispensing free advice about Budapest and about travel in Hungary and in Eastern Europe (he knows the latest visa requirements for all countries in the region). The rooms are clean and spacious, but the bathrooms can get a bit grimy. Rooms are mixed sex. Each guest gets a locker; locks are provided with a deposit. Guests are expected to be quiet after 10pm. English-language newspapers are provided daily.

VI. Teréz krt. 56 (3rd floor), 1066 Budapest. ℂ and fax **1/331-9896.** www.yellowsubmarinehostel.com. Three 10-bed rms, two 2–4 bed rms. 2,400Ft ($8.65) for bed in 10-bed rm, 3,500Ft ($12.60) for bed in 3- or 4-bed rm, 7,000Ft ($25) for bed in 2-bed rm. 5%–10% discount for IYHF members. Rates include breakfast. AE, MC, V. No parking available. Metro: Nyugati pu. (Blue line). **Amenities:** Laundry service; communal kitchen.

CENTRAL BUDA

Hotel Citadella *(Overrated)*   Budapest's most famous (or at least its oldest) budget hotel, this tired old establishment is located inside the Citadella, the 19th-century Habsburg garrison that commands a panoramic view over the city from the top of Gellért Hill. The rooms, luxuriously large, are well-worn but clean, with high ceilings and remarkable views. The public bathrooms are merely passable. Nearby you'll find an expensive restaurant, a nightclub, and a casino.

XI. Citadella sétány, 1118 Budapest. (C) **1/466-5794.** Fax 1/386-0505. 5 dorm rms (some with toilet and shower, some without), 15 quad rms (some with shower). 10,300 Ft ($37) for a double room; 14,800 Ft ($53) for a quad room; 1,840 Ft ($6.60) for dorm bed. Breakfast 500 Ft ($1.80) extra. No credit cards. Free parking. Bus: 27 from Móricz Zsigmond körtér to the Citadella.

OUTER PEST

Ananda Youth Hostel ★★ *Value* This hostel is run by an interesting South American fellow named Jairo Bustos (who has operated at least two other hostels of the same name in Budapest earlier in the 1990s). It's well located just a few minutes by foot from Keleti railway station (where most international trains arrive), on the corner of Alsóerdósor utca and Péterfy Sándor utca. Like most other centrally located, privately run youth hostels in town, Ananda is located in a residential building (a classic Pest apartment house), and there is little evidence from the street of its existence within (just a small buzzer that says "hostel"). This year-round hostel has extremely clean rooms (mixed sex) and a friendly, engaging staff. Guests are given large lockers in which to store gear. The hostel is frequented in equal parts by tired rail travelers arriving at Keleti station and by meditation-vegetarian types who have been drawn by Mr. Bustos, a magnetic personality who is somewhat famous among certain circles of locals and Euro travelers.

VII. Alsóerdósor u. 12 (2nd floor). (C) and fax **1/322-0502.** anandayh@freemail.c3.hu. 10 beds in 3 rms. 2,000Ft–2,500Ft ($7.20–$9), depending on the number of beds in a room. No credit cards. No parking available. Metro: Keleti pu (Red line). **Amenities:** Laundry service; communal kitchen.

Diáksport Party Hostel ★★ Located in a barren, dreary part of Pest, this year-round hostel, now operated by Travellers' Youth Way Youth Hostels, has long been one of the most crowded and popular youth hostels in Budapest. After years of neglect, it was renovated in 1999 and expanded a bit in 2000. The rooms are still tiny cubicles and the bathrooms are still overcrowded, but at least the place is clean and can sleep more travelers. The guests tend to be overwhelmingly young and rowdy; the 24-hour on-premises bar is never empty. Live music in the bar, 2 to 3 nights per week in summer, draws large crowds. Don't come to this hostel looking for a good night's sleep or a quiet place to read. Internet access is available for 550 Ft ($2) per half-hour.

XIII. Dózsa György út 152 (enter from side street, Angyalföld út). (C) **1/340-8585** or 1/329-8644. Fax 1/320-8425. www.travellers-hostels.com. 11 single rms, 28 double rms, 5 rms with 3–4 beds, and 9 dorm rms. 3,200 Ft–4,600 Ft ($11.50–$16.55) per bed (depending on rm.). 10% discount for IYHF members. Breakfast 300 Ft ($1.10). No credit cards. Parking available in the neighborhood. Metro: Dózsa György út (Blue line). **Amenities:** Bar; laundry service; communal kitchen.

Station Guesthouse ★★ *Finds* Opened in 1997 in a large house in a drab neighborhood in outer Pest (on the train tracks just minutes from the suburban Zugló railway station), this year-round hostel proudly boasts a nonstop party atmosphere. Don't come here for a quiet place to stay. For many guests, the time spent at this hostel is a principal part of the time spent in Budapest. The hostel is not run by a hostel chain, and the informative staff is fiercely proud of its independence—they treat you as guests in their house. The rooms (mixed-sex) are standard dorm rooms. The well-stocked bar is open—and in use—24 hours a day. The common room has a pool table (free use) and walls filled with murals and other creations of the guests. There is live music (rock, blues, jazz), principally performed by hostel guests. The hostel has a fully equipped kitchen (grocery store nearby), and the facilities are surprisingly clean given the somewhat hedonistic atmosphere. Internet access is available at 20 Ft (7¢) per minute.

XIV. Mexikói út 36/b. © **1/221-8864.** Fax 1/383-4034. www.hotels.hu/station. Attic floor space 1,500 Ft ($5.40) per mattress for the first night with a 100Ft (35¢) discount per night for additional nights (in summer only); three 8-bed rms, 2,200 Ft ($7.90) per bed, with additional night discounts going down as low as 1,800Ft ($6.50); one 6-bed rm, 2,200 Ft ($7.90) per bed, with additional night discounts going down as low as 1,800Ft ($6.50); one 4-bed rm, 2,500 Ft ($9) per bed, with additional night discounts going down as low as 2,100 Ft ($7.55); three 3-bed rms, 3,000 Ft ($10.80) per bed, with additional night discounts going down as low as 2,600 Ft ($9.35); two 2-bed rms 3,000 Ft($10.80) per bed, with additional night discounts going down as low as 2,600 Ft ($9.35). No discount for IYHF members. Breakfast for 400 Ft ($1.45). No credit cards. Plenty of parking available on street and in the yard. Bus: No. 7 (Red) from Keleti station to Hungaria krt.; walk under railway embankment, and turn right on Mexikói út. **Amenities:** Bar; laundry service; communal kitchen.

5

Where to Dine in Budapest

Budapest features an increasingly diverse range of restaurants to go along with those older (read: formerly state-owned) and more traditional eateries that have stood the test of time. Ethnic restaurants have appeared on the scene in the last decade; you'll find Asian, Korean, Indian, Middle Eastern, Greek, Mexican, and Thai restaurants in the city. Of course, most tourists understandably want to sample authentic Hungarian food while in Budapest. In this city, traditional fare runs the gamut from greasy to gourmet. There are few palates that can't be pleased here. Budapest is gaining a reputation for good dining at reasonable prices, so live it up.

WHERE TO EAT *Étterem* is the most common Hungarian word for restaurant and is applied to everything from cafeteria-style eateries to first-class restaurants. A *vendéglő*, or guest house, is a smaller, more intimate restaurant (literally an "inn"), often with a Hungarian folk motif; a *csárda* is a countryside *vendéglő* (often built on major motorways and around Lake Balaton and other holiday areas). An *étkezde* is an informal lunchroom open only in the daytime. *önkiszolgáló* means self-service cafeteria; these are typically open only for lunch. Stand-up *büfés* (snack counters) are often found in bus stations and near busy transportation hubs. A *cukrászda* or *kávéház* is a classic Central European coffeehouse, where lingering over a beverage or pastry has developed into an art form.

There are also a number of types of establishments that, though primarily for drinking, also serve meals. A *borozó* is a wine bar; these are often found in cellars (they are likely to include in their name the word *pince* [cellar] or *barlang* [cave]), and generally feature a house wine. A *söröző* is a beer bar; these places, too, are often found in cellars. Sandwiches are usually available in borozós and sörözős. Finally, a *kocsma* is a sort of roadside tavern. Kocsmas are found on side streets, in residential neighborhoods; the Buda Hills are filled with them. Most kocsmas serve a full dinner, but the kitchens close early.

MUSIC Live Gypsy music is a feature in many Hungarian restaurants, although primarily in the ones catering to tourists. Generally speaking, what you find in restaurants is not authentic Gypsy music, but an ersatz pop variety. If a member of the band plays a number at your table, good manners dictate that you give a tip; the appropriate amount varies with the price category of the restaurant itself (500 Ft to 1,000 Ft/$1.80 to $3.60 is a fair starting point). You may, however, politely decline his or her offer to play for you.

RESTAURANT REVIEWS *The Budapest Sun* regularly reviews new restaurants in town. You can also look for recommendations online at **www.virtualhungary.com/catalog/restaura.htm**.

PRICE CATEGORIES For purposes of this book, we classified

> ### *Tips* The Check, Please: Tips on Tipping
>
> In restaurants in Budapest, the customer has to initiate the paying ritual. You may find that your waiter has disappeared by the time you're ready to settle up. Call over any restaurant employee and ask to pay. The waiter whose job it is to collect payment (maybe your waiter, maybe not) will eventually (don't hold your breath) be sent to your table with the bill, which is usually nestled in a small booklet. Occasionally you'll be asked to confirm what you ordered. If you think the bill is mistaken, don't be embarrassed to call it into question; locals will commonly do this. Waiters readily correct the bill when challenged. In most restaurants, after handing over the bill the waiter will disappear. Though most restaurants build in a service charge, tipping is the norm; the tip (generally about 10%) should be included in the amount you place in the booklet, which you may leave on the table. If you want to split your bill, the waiters are happy to do so, provided you have let them know in advance while ordering your meal.
>
> In smaller, less formal lunchroom-type places, waiters will often remain at your table after delivering the bill, waiting patiently for payment. In these face-to-face encounters, state the full amount you are paying (bill plus tip), and the waiter will make change on the spot.
>
> A developing trend among some new restaurants is to dispense with adding a service charge. In these instances, a more robust tip is expected. As many Hungarians and foreigners alike expect that a service charge is already added to the bill, you may find that waiters are not shy about reminding diners of "appropriate" tipping manners.

restaurants as follows. A restaurant is Very Expensive if a main course costs more than $10; Expensive, between $7 and $10, Moderate, $3 to $7; and Inexpensive, $3 and under. Remember that all things are relative—a Very Expensive meal in Budapest may cost less than a cup of coffee with a pastry in Rome.

In the listings below, few restaurants outside the "Very Expensive" and "Expensive" categories accept credit or charge cards, and even some in these two categories don't accept them. You can assume that English-language menus are available in all "Very Expensive" and "Expensive" restaurants and in most "Moderate" restaurants.

Sometimes waiters will mention "specials" that don't appear on the menu, and in some of the more expensive new establishments they are proudly willing to adjust their menu in accordance with your taste. It is customary to ask the price before ordering such a special. Also, some restaurants don't list drinks on the menu, while others list them but omit the prices. Again, feel free to inquire about the price before ordering.

WARNING The U.S. Embassy circulates a list of restaurants that engage in "unethical business practices" such as "excessive billing," using "physical intimidation" to compel payment of excessive bills, and "assaulting customers" for nonpayment of excessive bills. If you don't want to encounter the restaurant mafia, avoid these places: **Mephisto Café,** V. Váci utca;

Muskátli Espresso, V. Váci u. 11;
Fontana Cabaret, V. Váci u. 11a;
Arany Bárány Restaurant, V.

Harmincad u. 4; **Tropical Bar,** V.
Galamb utca; **Art Café,** V. Váci utca;
and **Pigál Bar,** VIII. Kiss József u. 1.

1 Restaurants by Cuisine

ASIAN

Marquis de Salade, ✪✪✪ (The
Inner City & Central Pest, $$,
p. 87)

COFFEEHOUSES

Angelika Cukrászda ✪✪✪
(Central Buda, p. 98)
Central Kávéház ✪ (The Inner
City & Central Pest, p. 97)
Gerbeaud's ✪ (The Inner City &
Central Pest, p. 97)
Lukács Cukrászda ✪ (The Inner
City & Central Pest, p. 98)
Művész Kávéház ✪✪ (The Inner
City & Central Pest, p. 98)
Ruszwurm Cukrászda ✪ (The
Castle District, p. 98)

CREPERIE

Korona Passage ✪✪ (The Inner
City & Central Pest, $, p. 89)

CZECH/SLOVAK

Prágai Svejk Vendéglő ✪ (The
Inner City & Central Pest, $$,
p. 88)

FRENCH

Le Jardin de Paris ✪✪ (Central
Buda, $$$, p. 91)
Lou Lou ✪ (The Inner City &
Central Pest, $$$, p. 83)

GREEK

Taverna Dionysos ✪ (The Inner
City & Central Pest, $$, p. 88)
Taverna Ressaikos ✪✪ (Central
Buda, $$, p. 94)

HUNGARIAN

Alabárdos ✪ (The Castle District,
$$$$, p. 94)
Alföldi Kisvendéglő ✪ (The Inner
City & Central Pest, $$, p. 86)
Antique Restaurant ✪✪ (The
Inner City & Central Pest,
$$$$, p. 82)

Aranyszarvas ✪✪ (Central Buda,
$$, p. 91)
Bagolyvár ✪ (Beyond Central Pest,
$$$, p. 90)
Csarnok Vendéglő ✪ (The Inner
City & Central Pest, $, p. 88)
Csendes Étterem ✪ (The Inner
City & Central Pest, $, p. 88)
Fészek ✪✪ (The Inner City &
Central Pest, $$, p. 86)
Gundel ✪✪ (Beyond Central Pest,
$$$$, p. 90)
Horgásztanya Vendéglő ✪ (Central
Buda, $$, p. 91)
Kacsa Vendéglő ✪ (Central Buda,
$$$, p. 91)
Kádár Étkezde ✪ (The Inner City
& Central Pest, $, p. 89)
Kéhli Vendéglő ✪ (Northern Buda
& Óbuda, $$$$, p. 96)
Kis Buda Gyöngye ✪✪ (Northern
Buda & Óbuda, $$$, p. 96)
Kisharang Étkezde ✪ (The Inner
City & Central Pest, $, p. 89)
Kiskacsa Vendéglő ✪✪ (The Inner
City & Central Pest, $, p. 89)
Kispipa Vendéglő ✪✪ (The Inner
City & Central Pest, $$, p. 87)
Légrádi & Társa Vendéglő ✪✪
(The Inner City & Central Pest,
$$$$, p. 82)
Makkhetes Vendéglő ✪✪ (The
Buda Hills, $, p. 95)
Malomtó Étterem ✪✪ (Northern
Buda & Óbuda, $$, p. 96)
Náncsi Néni Vendéglője ✪✪ (The
Buda Hills, $$, p. 95)
Önkiszolgáló ✪ (The Castle Dis-
trict, $, p. 94)
Szeged Vendéglő (Central Buda,
$$, p. 92)
Szép Ilona ✪✪ (The Buda Hills,
$$, p. 95)
Udvarház a Hármashatárhegyen ✪
(The Buda Hills, $$$$, p. 95)

Új Sipos Halászkert ✯ (Northern Buda & Óbuda, $$, p. 96)

INDIAN
Govinda ✯✯ (The Inner City & Central Pest, $$, p. 87)

INTERNATIONAL
Articsóka ✯✯ (The Inner City & Central Pest, $$$, p. 83)
Gundel ✯✯ (Beyond Central Pest, $$$$, p. 90)
Kis Buda Gyöngye ✯✯ (Northern Buda & Óbuda, $$$, p. 96)

ITALIAN
Pizzeria Pink Cadillac ✯ (The Inner City & Central Pest, $, p. 89)

KOREAN
Senara ✯ (The Inner City & Central Pest, $$$, p. 86)

MEXICAN
Iguana Bar & Grill ✯ (The Inner City & Central Pest, $$, p. 87)

MIDDLE EASTERN
Marquis de Salade ✯✯✯ (The Inner City & Central Pest, $$, p. 87)

Semiramis ✯✯ (The Inner City & Central Pest, $, p. 90)

PIZZA
Marxim ✯ (Central Buda, $, p. 94)
Pizzeria Pink Cadillac ✯ (The Inner City & Central Pest, $, p. 89)

SALAD BAR
Korona Passage ✯✯ (The Inner City & Central Pest, $, p. 89)

SEAFOOD
Horgásztanya Vendéglő ✯ (Central Buda, $$, p. 91)
Új Sipos Halászkert ✯ (Northern Buda & Óbuda, $$, p. 96)

THAI
Bangkok House ✯ (The Inner City & Central Pest, $$$, p. 83)

VEGETARIAN
Gandhi Vegeteriánus Étterem ✯ (The Inner City & Central Pest, $, p. 86)
Govinda ✯✯ (The Inner City & Central Pest, $$, p. 87)

2 The Inner City & Central Pest

VERY EXPENSIVE

Antique Restaurant ✯✯ HUNGARIAN   This new establishment has a fantastic location in the heart of Pest. Run by an ambitious female member of the Légrádi family, it is in fact a combination of an antique shop on the ground floor and a stylish restaurant in the basement. The place can sit only 30 people in the elegant dining area. There is live Hungarian music every evening to accompany the delicious dishes always made from fresh organic ingredients. The house is so confident of its cuisine that there is a standing offer to cook up any exquisite meal to satisfy even the most sophisticated connoisseur's palate.

V. Bárczy István u. 3-5. ☎ 1/266-4993. Reservations recommended. Soups: 900 Ft–1,200 Ft ($3.25–$4.30), main dishes 2,500 Ft–7,000 Ft ($9–$25.20). AE, MC, V. (Cash is "preferred"). Mon–Fri noon–3 pm, 7pm–midnight; Sat 7pm–midnight. Closed Sun. Metro: Deák tér (all lines).

Légrádi & Társa Vendéglő ✯✯ HUNGARIAN   A very small (just nine tables) and inconspicuously marked restaurant on a surprisingly sleepy side street in the southern part of the Inner City, Légrádi & Partner is one of Budapest's most elegant and formal restaurants. The food is served on Herend china, the cutlery is sterling, and an excellent string trio livens the atmosphere with its repertoire of Hungarian classics. If you're on a budget, pass on the initial, pre-menu offer of hors d'oeuvres, which costs 1,500 Ft ($5.40). The cream of asparagus soup is a fine interpretation of a Hungarian favorite. The chicken paprika served with cheese dumplings seasoned with fresh dill will surpass any you've tried elsewhere, and the veal cavalier, smothered in a cauliflower-cheese sauce, is equally sumptuous.

V. Magyar u. 23. ⑦ 1/318-6804. Reservations highly recommended. Soup 600 Ft–700 Ft ($2.15–$2.50); main courses 2,000 Ft–3,500 Ft ($7.20–$12.60). AE, MC, V. Mon–Sat 6pm–midnight. Metro: Kálvin tér (Blue line).

EXPENSIVE

Articsóka ✹✹ INTERNATIONAL   An exceptionally well-designed establishment, this is a welcome new addition to classy Budapest's nightlife and a favorite of Hungarian show biz and media celebrities. It is actually a complex consisting of a restaurant, cafe, roof terrace, art gallery, and theater. The Moorish interior exhibits a careful harmonious design in every detail, from the quality of paper of the menu to the type of lighting. The restaurant offers an exceptional combination of excellent food, a spectacular design, a polite staff, and entertainment. The menu (in three languages; English, German, Italian) is selected with great care; the variety is impressive, including Hungarian as well as vegetarian and international delicacies. Try the cold goose liver with celery-and-apple salad or the roasted goose liver in an apple-walnut calvados sauce. If you feel like something lighter your choice may be fillet of salmon with creamed spinach. Whatever your choice for a main course, you should not leave without tasting the divine French chocolate cake, definitely the best in town (and a very affordable 790 Ft/$2.85).

Note: On Friday evenings there is a free theater performance of excellent quality; check out on the program in advance at **www.articsoka.hu**.

VI. Zichy Jenő u. 17. ⑦ 1/302-7757. Reservations especially for the roof terrace are recommended. Appetizers 680 Ft–1,890 Ft ($2.45–$6.80); soup 540 Ft–600 Ft ($1.95–$2.15); main courses 990 Ft–4,300 Ft ($3.55–$15.50). MC, V. Daily 11am–midnight. Metro: Opera (yellow line).

Bangkok House ✹ THAI   A welcome addition to Budapest's ever-evolving restaurant scene, Bangkok Restaurant features exotic and original Thai cuisine in a rich and lively setting. There are folk dance performances on Friday and Saturday evenings to accompany the extensive and overwhelming menu. Either stick to Thai dishes you already know or solicit suggestions from your waiter. Each dish appears lovingly prepared with the freshest ingredients. Duck soup with bamboo shoots and wild mushrooms makes a nice appetizer, as do the spring rolls. For a main course, you might try the Mekong catfish soup (a complete meal in itself) or the grilled shark with wild lemongrass and chili sauce. Service is gracious. Despite a recent change in management and name, the place has maintained the excellent reputation among the city's burgeoning Asian population that the previous restaurant, Chan Chan, enjoyed on the same premises.

V. Só u. 3. ⑦ 1/266-0584. Reservations recommended. Soup 600 Ft–1,100 Ft ($2.15–$4); main courses 1,100 Ft–4,000 Ft ($4–$14.40). AE, MC, V. Daily noon–11pm. Metro: Ferenciek tere (Blue line).

Lou Lou ✹ FRENCH   Located on a quiet side street not far from Parliament in the financial district, this is a handsome addition to the Budapest dining scene. Károly Rudits, who formerly manned the kitchen at the Kempinski hotel, opened this small (just eight tables), candlelit cellar space in 1996. The decor is rustic and tasteful, with Roman yellow walls and a vaulted ceiling.

The lengthy menu is in English. If you want to splurge, opt for the grilled prawns or veal. Fresh fish dishes are the specialty of the house. Lou Lou also features an extensive wine list (which is framed on the wall and will be pulled down

Budapest Dining

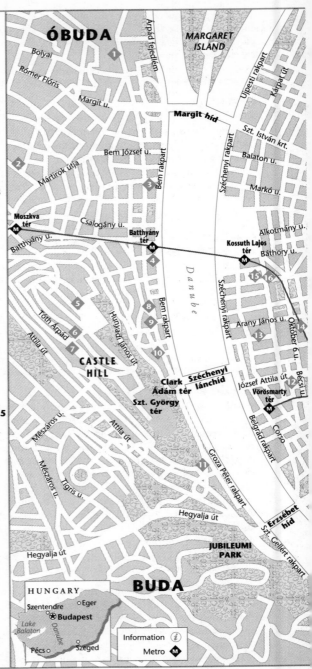

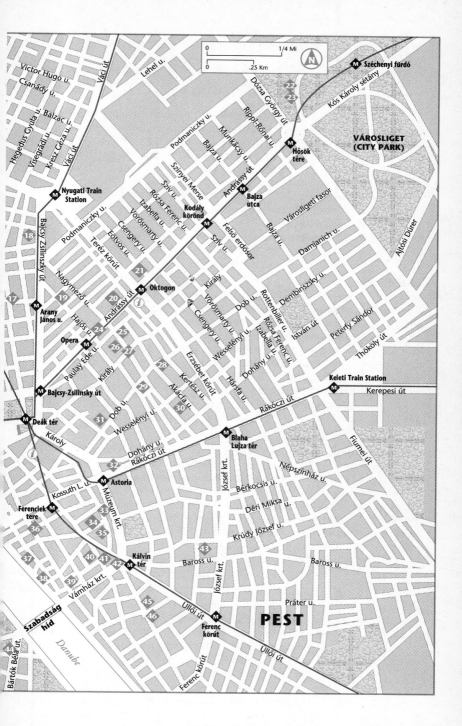

Victor Hugo u.
Csanády u.
Hegedüs Gyula u.
Visegrádi u.
Kresz Géza u.
Balzac u.
Váci út
Váci út
Lehel u.
Dózsa György út
Rippl-Rónai u.
M Széchenyi fürdő
Kós Károly sétány

22
23

Podmaniczky u.
Munkácsy u.
Bajza u.

**VÁROSLIGET
(CITY PARK)**

M Nyugati Train
Station

Szinyei Merse

Andrássy út

M Hősök
tére

M Bajza
utca

Szív u.
Rózsa Ferenc u.
Izabella u.
**Kodály
körönd**
Felső erdősor
Szív u.

Városligeti fasor

Bajza u.
Damjanich u.

Ajtósi Dürer

Bajcsy Zsilinszky út

18

Podmaniczky u.
Vörösmarty u.
Csengery u.
Eötvös u.
Teréz körút

21

Király

Vörösmarty u.
Csengery u.
Dob u.
Rottenbiller u.
Rózsa Ferenc u.
Izabella u.
Dembinszky u.
István út
Péterfy Sándor

17

Nagymező u.
Andrássy út
20
M Oktogon
(i)

19

M Arany
János u.
Hajós u.
24
25

26 27

Opera
M

Wesselényi u.
Dohány u.
Thököly út

Paulay Ede u.
Király
28
Erzsébet körút
Kertész u.
Akácfa u.

M Keleti Train Station
Kerepesi út

M Bajcsy-Zsilinsky út
29
30

Dob u.
Wesselényi u.
Rákóczi út
Fiumei út

M Deák tér
31

Károly
(i)

Dohány u.
Rákóczi út
32

M Blaha
Lujza tér

Népszínház u.

M Astoria
Kossuth L. u.
Múzeum krt.
33

József krt.
Bérkocsis u.
Déri Miksa u.
Krúdy József u.

**Ferenciek
tére** **M**
36
34
35

43

40 41
42
M **Kálvin
tér**
Baross u.
Baross u.

37
38
39

Vámház krt.
45
46

József krt.

**Szabadság
híd**

Bártók Béla út
44

Danube

Üllői út
M **Ferenc
körút**
Üllői út

Ferenc körút

Práter u.

PEST

for you to study), ranging to 12,500 Ft ($45) a bottle. A House wine is also available and is a good choice.

Vigyázó F. u. 4. ☎ **1/312-4505.** Reservations recommended. Appetizers 900 Ft–2,000 Ft ($3.25–$7.20); main courses 1,500 Ft–3,000 Ft ($5.40–$10.80). AE, MC, V. Mon–Fri noon–3pm and 7pm–midnight; Sat 7pm–midnight. Closed Sun. Metro: Deák tér (all lines) or Kossuth tér (Red line).

Senara ⭐ KOREAN   Senara offers top-flight Korean fare in air-conditioned comfort in the heart of Pest. The tables, divided by tasteful wood latticework, offer considerable privacy. Korean music plays softly in the background. Many of the meat meals are cooked on a grill sunk into the middle of each table. The menu, though available in English, is complicated and arcane. Your best bet is one of the special menu meals, which come with soup, salad, rice, kimchee, and a main course. The delightful *Pulkogi* menu is a beef-and-chicken combination: You cook the thin strips of meat at your table, dip them in soy sauce, and eat them with rice—delicious!

VII. Dohány u. 5. ☎ **1/269-6549.** Reservations recommended. Main courses 1,200 Ft–2,600 Ft ($4.30–$9.35); menu meals 1,540 Ft–3,780 Ft ($5.55–$13.60). AE, MC, V. Mon–Sat 11:30am–2:30pm and 6–11pm. Metro: Astoria (Red line).

MODERATE

Alföldi Kisvendéglő ⭐ HUNGARIAN   The spicy, paprika-laced tastes of the Hungarian Plain are well presented in this time-tested Pest eatery. Prix fixe menu meals come with two courses (500 Ft/$1.80) or three (600 Ft/$2.15); the entrees change daily, and unfortunately are not posted in English. Nevertheless, they are a great bargain. The comprehensive menu is otherwise in English (but with lots of funny mistakes). Choose between a rustic interior with air-conditioning or sidewalk tables on a busy road. The waiters are overly formal and can be a bit old school (that is, rude).

V. Kecskeméti u. 4. ☎ **1/317-4404.** Soup 350 Ft–630 Ft ($1.25–$2.25); main courses 680 Ft–1,500 Ft ($2.45–$5.40); menu meals 500 Ft–600 Ft ($1.80–$2.15) (served daily 11am–3pm). No credit cards. Daily 11am–midnight. Metro: Kálvin tér (Blue line).

Fészek ⭐⭐ *Value* HUNGARIAN   Owned by the same folks who own the better-known Kispipa Vendéglő (see below), Fészek is located in the quiet, interior courtyard of a building at the corner of Dob utca and Kertész utca. A small, easy-to-miss sign on the street is the only advertisement. Pass through a dim lobby to enter the restaurant. Savory wild game and freshwater fish dishes are the house specialties. The outdoor dining experience here is without equal in the busy center of Pest. Be sure to reserve ahead of time since Fészek is invariably crowded.

VII. Kertész u. 36. ☎ **1/322-6043.** Reservations recommended. Soup 180 Ft–480 Ft (65¢–$1.75); main courses 500 Ft–2,000 Ft ($1.80–$7.20); menu meals (four courses) 1,920 Ft ($6.90). AE, MC, V. Daily noon–1am. Tram: 4 or 6 to Király utca.

Gandhi Vegetariánus Étterem ⭐ VEGETARIAN   A friendly, New Age-style restaurant, it serves interesting vegetarian food in a tranquil, smoke-free atmosphere. Choose from two daily menu options written (in Hungarian and English) on a blackboard. For instance, stuffed squash with Indian ragout and brown rice; or potato pumpkin casserole with garlic Roquefort sauce, steamed cabbage, and spinach soufflé. Or you can simply order soup (cream of cauliflower perhaps, or lentil) and the salad bar, though the salads lack variety. Seating is plentiful. There is a browsing bookshelf stocked with New Age and Eastern literature. Photographs of Gandhi hang on the walls.

V. Vigyázó Ferenc u. 4. ☎ **1/269-1625.** Soup 380 Ft ($1.35); small menu meal 980 Ft ($3.50); large menu meal 1,680 Ft ($6). V, MC. Daily noon–10:30pm. Metro: Deák tér (all lines).

Govinda ★★ *Value* INDIAN/VEGETARIAN   This tiny restaurant, owned and operated by Hare Krishnas, features exceptional Indian vegetarian cuisine. There is no proselytizing; just a bit of incense, traditional Indian music, and friendly (English-speaking) waiters. The chef, trained in India, prepares authentic and exotic offerings for a different menu each day. You choose either a large or small menu meal. The meal includes soup, fresh-baked Indian bread, main dish (an assortment of interesting, savory smaller dishes), a strange and wonderful drink (such as spicy ginger ale or lemonade with rosewater), and a dessert. Everything is lovingly prepared. On a hot day, sit upstairs, where it is air-conditioned.

V. Belgrád rakpart 18. ℂ 1/318-1144. Small menu meal 1,000 Ft ($3.60); large menu meal 1,300 Ft ($4.70). Daily noon–9pm. Metro: Ferenciek tere (Blue line).

Iguana Bar & Grill ★ MEXICAN   This classy Mexican restaurant opened to immediate success in summer 1997. The restaurant boasts a spacious, beautifully designed interior with a bi-level dining area. Still, it can be difficult to find a table—especially on weekends. When you do manage to get seated, crispy home-made tortilla chips and salsa are waiting for you. One of the Czech Republic's best beers, *Budvar,* makes the perfect accompaniment. You might also try the *Iguana Beer,* made especially for the restaurant by a small Csepel Island brewery. Though the chef is Hungarian, he trained in the American Southwest, so the flavors are indeed authentic. Fiery souls should start off with the Jalapeño Poppers, breaded jalapeño peppers stuffed with cheese and rolled in matzoh crumbs. For an entree, consider one of the daily specials (posted on a blackboard). Beef burritos or Chicken à la Mo also make excellent choices.

V. Zoltán u. 16. ℂ 1/331-4352 or 1/302-7556. Reservations recommended. Appetizers 600 Ft–1,200 Ft ($2.15–$4.30); main courses 900 Ft–2,600 Ft ($3.25–$9.35). AE, MC, V. Sun–Thurs 11:30am–midnight, Fri–Sat 11:30am–1am. Metro: Kossuth tér (Red line).

Kispipa Vendéglő ★★ *Value* HUNGARIAN   Unobtrusively located on a residential street in Erzsébetváros, behind the old Jewish district, Kispipa (Little Pipe) is a well-lit, medium-size establishment. Unfortunately, it is closed in July and August, but if you are here any other time of year it is worth a visit. The cream-colored walls are lined with vintage Hungarian poster advertisements, and piano music contributes to the relaxed atmosphere. The menu is extensive; wild-game dishes are the house specialty. Five "complete menu" deals offer soup, main course, and dessert for a very reasonable price. Kispipa, formerly one of Budapest's only private restaurants, has played a small part in modern Hungarian history: The political party FIDESZ (Young Democrats), now the ruling party, was founded (illegally, no less) here in 1988.

VII. Akácfa u. 38. ℂ 1/342-2587. Reservations recommended. Main courses 500 Ft–2,000 Ft ($1.80–$7.20); menu meal 1,920 Ft ($6.90). AE, DISC, MC, V. Mon–Sat noon–1am. Closed July and Aug. Metro: Oktogon (Yellow line).

Marquis de Salade ★★★ ASIAN/MIDDLE EASTERN   Vegetarians will jump for joy here. This recently renovated restaurant turns out an amazing assortment of exceptional dishes from a number of cuisines. Located on the edge of Pest's theater district, it is a favorite luncheon spot of Hungarian actors. The connection between the delightful Eastern cuisine and the theater is rooted in the marriage of the owner, an Azeri woman, to Péter Halász, an outstanding member of the ELTE University Theater (whose radical initiatives forced him to leave Hungary in the 1960s, before returning again in 1989 to become a central figure in Budapest's alternative-theater scene). Additionally, the restaurant employs an eclectic mix of eight cooks from seven different areas (Russia,

Bangladesh, Hungary, China, Italy, and the Caucasus Mountains). The sophisticated yet earthy offerings reflect this diversity. A nonsmoking area is available. Tablecloths and other tapestries are for sale.

VI. Hajós u. 43. ℭ 1/302-4086. Appetizers 750 Ft–2,500 Ft ($2.70–$9); main courses 1,200 Ft–2,800 Ft ($4.30–$10.10). V. Daily 11am–midnight. Metro: Arany János u. (Blue line).

Prágai Svejk Vendéglő ℛ CZECH/SLOVAK   Hankering for a taste of the neighboring regions? Svejk restaurant offers fine examples, including plump, delicious potato dumplings *(sztrapacska* in Hungarian or *knedli* in Czech*)* served with sheep cheese and bacon. Heartier appetites might order the ragout with steamed knedli. Eight different types of unsurpassable Czech beer are available here. Service is uniformly friendly and quick. The walls feature quotes and illustrations from Jaroslav Hasek's famous novel about the clumsy, overweight, ever-failing Svejk, a soldier in the Austro-Hungarian army. Live piano music is featured.

VII. Király u. 59/b (enter on side street, Kürt u.). ℭ 1/322-3278. Soup 400 Ft ($1.45); main courses 1,200 Ft–2,000 Ft ($4.30–$7.20). AE, V. Daily noon–11pm. Tram: 4 or 6 from Nyugati pu.

Taverna Dionysos ℛ GREEK   This faithful rendition of a Greek tavern on Pest's Danube embankment is an early arrival in a new and trendy restaurant neighborhood in the pleasant southern end of the Inner City, not far from the central market hall. (This part of the river embankment is also gradually turning into the center of gay nightlife in Budapest; see "Gay and Lesbian Bars" in chapter 9, "Budapest After Dark.") Authentic Greek fare, at reasonable prices, in the center of the city make this place a plus. Weather permitting, sidewalk dining is available.

V. Belgrád rakpart 16. ℭ 1/318-1222. Appetizers 240 Ft–460 Ft (85¢–$1.65); main courses 1,190 Ft–2,100 Ft ($4.30–$7.55). Reservations recommended. AE, MC, V. Daily noon–midnight. Metro: Ferenciek tere (Blue line).

INEXPENSIVE

Csarnok Vendéglő ℛ *Finds* HUNGARIAN   On the Inner City's quiet Hold utca (Moon Street), the Csarnok Vendéglő is located between Szabadság tér and Bajcsy-Zsilinszky út, not far from the United States Embassy. Its name comes from the wonderful turn-of-the-20th-century market hall *(csarnok)* next door. One of the few restaurants in this part of the Inner City, it's even more notable for its uniformly low prices. The menu (in English translation) features typical Hungarian Vendéglő fare, heavy as usual on meat dishes. Outdoor seating is available on the sidewalk, but sit inside for the full effect.

V. Hold u. 11. ℭ 1/269-4906. Main courses 550 Ft–1,000 Ft ($2–$3.60). No credit cards. Mon–Sat 9am–midnight, Sun noon–10pm. Metro: Arany János utca (Blue line).

Csendes Étterem ℛ HUNGARIAN   Located on the Múzeum körút section of Pest's Inner Ring boulevard, just a few minutes' walk from the main tourist area around Váci utca, the Csendes Étterem ("Quiet Restaurant") features inexpensive Hungarian, Slovak, and Transylvanian dishes. The restaurant has a decidedly rustic look, with exposed wooden rafters, wooden booths, and tasteful horse posters decorating the walls. The English-language menu is full of amusing errors. Csendes is a student hangout; ELTE University is just down the street.

V. Múzeum krt. 13 (enter from side street, Ferenczy István utca). ℭ 1/267-0218. Soup 210 Ft–540 Ft (75¢–$1.95); main courses 650 Ft–1,300 Ft ($2.35–$4.70). No credit cards. Mon–Sat noon–10pm. Metro: Astoria (Red line) or Kálvin tér (Blue line).

Kádár Étkezde ⭐ *Finds* HUNGARIAN   By 11:45am, Uncle Kádár's, in the heart of the historic Jewish district, is filled with a steady stream of lunchtime regulars—from paint-spattered workers to elderly Jewish couples. Uncle Kádár, a neighborhood legend, personally greets them as they file in. From the outside, the only sign of the place is a small red sign saying "Kádár Étkezde." And, to be sure, the place is no more than a lunchroom, but it has a wonderful atmosphere. Photographs (many autographed) of actors and athletes adorn the walls, and old-fashioned seltzer bottles decorate every table. The food is simple but hearty, and the service is fast and friendly. The menu is only in Hungarian, but if you see something you like on someone else's table you can always point. Try the soup, regardless. Served in a deep bowl, with bread, it's practically a meal in itself. Table sharing is the norm here. Customers pay at the front, then return to hand the waitress a tip.

VII. Klauzál tér 9. ℂ **1/321-3622.** Soup 240 Ft (85¢); main courses 460 Ft–750 Ft ($1.65–$2.70). No credit cards. Tues–Sat 11:30am–3:30pm. Metro: Astoria (Red line) or Deák tér (all lines).

Kisharang Étkezde ⭐ *Finds* HUNGARIAN   This is a tiny (five or six tables; and a stand-by shelf along the side wall) and inexpensive eatery, whose name means "little bell". The food is basic, hearty Hungarian fare; the menu is posted on the wall. An English-language menu is available upon request. Most customers are white-collar workers from the surrounding neighborhood of government office buildings and the Central European University, a center of learning endowed by the financier and ex-patriate Hungarian György Soros. Table sharing is the norm.

V. Oktober 6 u. 17. No phone. Dishes 350 Ft–780 Ft ($1.25–$2.80). No credit cards. Mon–Fri 11am–3pm (lunch only). Metro: Arany János utca (Blue line) or Kossuth tér (Red line).

Kiskacsa Vendéglő ⭐⭐ *Value* HUNGARIAN   A small restaurant with rustic furnishings and red-and-white-checked tablecloths, Kiskacsa ("Little Duck") is our current favorite little neighborhood eatery. The food is exceptional for the price range, and the menu incredibly deep. Try the *csirkemell szatmári módra*, chicken breast with dumplings wrapped in bacon and dressed with a creamed carrot sauce. Vegetarians might try *kertész palacsinta*, a crêpe stuffed with steamed veggies, served in a cheese sauce. The service can be lackadaisical. With your bill, the waiter brings a cup with dice. If you roll three sixes, your meal is on the house.

VII. Dob u. 26 (corner of Kazinczy utca). ℂ **1/322-6208.** Main courses 700 Ft–1,100 Ft ($2.50–$3.95). Sun, 10% off for families. Daily noon–midnight. Metro: Astoria (Red line).

Korona Passage ⭐⭐ *Kids* CREPERIE/SALAD BAR   This is a great place for lunch in Central Pest. The prices are incredibly low, especially considering that it's in the Mercure Korona luxury hotel. Giant crêpes are made to order—fillings range from cheese to sweet walnut purée—and are delicious. Skip the self-service salad bar, which is never well stocked. The long, arcade-style restaurant, with a skylight and thriving plants, is bright, clean, air-conditioned, and smoke free. High chairs are available for the little ones. The Hotel Mercure Korona was built at the spot where the original medieval Pest city wall once stood, and a piece of it remains in the restaurant.

In the Mercure Korona Hotel, V. Kecskeméti u. 14. ℂ **1/317-4111.** Crêpes 470 Ft–620 Ft ($1.70–$2.25); salad bar 500 Ft ($1.80). AE, DC, MC, V. Daily 10am–10pm. Metro: Kálvin tér (Blue line).

Pizzeria Pink Cadillac ⭐ *Value* PIZZA/ITALIAN   An early arrival on Ráday utca, one of Central Pest's up-and-coming streets—just recently turned into a pedestrian-only area with bars, cafes, and restaurants lined up on both sides—this glitzy little pizzeria offers some of the city's best pizza. Lasagna and other pasta dishes are also served. Ingredients are fresh and everything is tasty. Free delivery is available.

IX. Ráday u. 22. ✆ **1/216-1412** or 1/317-4111. Pizzas 595 Ft–1,450 Ft ($2.15–$5.20); pasta 580 Ft–995 Ft ($2.10–$3.60). Mon–Fri 11am–1am, Sat–Sun noon–1am. Metro: Kálvin tér (Blue line).

Semiramis ★★ *Finds* MIDDLE EASTERN   Located just a block from Parliament and a few blocks from Nyugati Station, this little eatery is best suited for lunch since it tends to run out of the more popular dishes by evening. Seating is primarily upstairs in a small and cozy loft decorated with Middle Eastern tapestries and colorful straw trivets. The waiters are uniformly friendly, and all speak English. This was the first dining place with a Middle Eastern menu in town and it has managed to maintain its reputation for good and reliable service over the past fifteen years. Everything is delicious, including the house specialty, chicken breast with spinach (*spenótos csirkemell*), which consists of far more spinach than chicken. Vegetarians can easily build a meal out of several appetizers; try the yogurt-cucumber salad (*yogurtos saláta*) and the *fül* (a zesty garlic and fava bean dish). Scrumptious *shwarma* sandwiches are also available.

V. Alkotmány u. 20. ✆ **1/311-7627**. Main courses 749 Ft–990 Ft ($2.70–$3.55). No credit cards. Mon–Sat noon–9pm. Metro: Kossuth tér (Red line).

3 Beyond Central Pest
VERY EXPENSIVE
Gundel ★★ *Moments* HUNGARIAN/INTERNATIONAL   Budapest's fanciest and most famous restaurant, Gundel was reopened in 1992 by the well-known restaurateur George Lang, owner of New York's Café des Artistes. The Hungarian-born Lang, author of *The Cuisine of Hungary*, along with his partner Ronald Lauder, son of Estée Lauder and a one-time New York gubernatorial candidate, has spared no effort in attempting to re-create the original splendor for which Gundel, founded in 1894, achieved its international reputation.

Located in City Park, Gundel has an opulent dining room and a large, carefully groomed garden. The kitchen prides itself on preparing traditional dishes in an innovative fashion. Lamb and wild-game entrees are house specialties. The menu also tends to highlight fruits and vegetables in season. In late spring, for instance, don't miss out on the asparagus served in hollandaise with grilled salmon. Gundel has perhaps the most extensive wine list in town, and the waiters are well versed in its offerings. The homemade fruit ice cream served in the shape of the fruit makes for a delectable dessert, as does the famous Gundel torta, a decadently rich chocolate layer cake. Budget-minded travelers should consider eating at Bagolyvár, the less fancy "home-style" restaurant next door, also owned by George Lang (see below).

XIV. Állatkerti út 2. ✆ **1/322-1002** or 1/321-3550. www.gundel.hu. Reservations highly recommended. Soup 1,000 Ft ($3.60); main courses 3,600 Ft–6,900 Ft ($13–$24.85). AE, DC, MC, V. Daily noon–4pm and 7pm–midnight. Metro: Hősök tere (Yellow line).

EXPENSIVE
Bagolyvár ★ *Kids* HUNGARIAN   Bagolyvár (Owl Castle) offers something unique to the budget traveler—a taste of Gundel, Budapest's most famous (and most expensive) restaurant, at less than wallet-flattening prices. George Lang, the well-known owner of Gundel, wanted to offer Hungarian "home-style" cooking to the general public at a reasonable price, and thus was born his second

Budapest eatery, located just next door to Gundel in City Park. The Bagolyvár menu is limited to half a dozen main courses (supplemented by daily specials), which include roast veal with green beans as well as layered Savoy cabbage. Delicious desserts include chocolate poppy-seed cake and fresh fruit salad. The food is carefully prepared and presented. The decor and ambience are pleasant and unpretentious. The building is itself a nice example of art-nouveau by the outstanding architect of the time, Károly Kós, whose other excellent project is the Budapest Zoo next door. Highchairs are available for young children. Outdoor dining is available in the restaurant's garden, next to a small pond.

XIV. Állatkerti út 2. € 1/321-3550. Reservations recommended. Soup 300 Ft–440 Ft ($1.10–$1.60); main courses 1,300 Ft–3,500 Ft ($4.70–$12.60). AE, MC, V. Daily 11am–11pm. Metro: Hősök tere (Yellow line).

4 Central Buda

EXPENSIVE

Aranyszarvas ★★ HUNGARIAN   The Golden Stag is located in a historic building in central Buda's Tabán district, just below and to the south of Castle Hill. There's indoor seating in a dining room with a restrained wild-game motif, but on pleasant nights customers dine on the outdoor terrace. A string trio is available to serenade, but must be requested in advance. As the name and decor suggest, this restaurant serves wild game, and the menu lists a variety of reasonably priced dishes, such as hunter's saddle of hare, Serbian wild boar, and venison stew. The desserts are worth sampling as well, particularly the mixed strudel, prepared with seasonal fruit.

I. Szarvas tér 1. € 1/375-6451. Reservations recommended. Soup 450 Ft ($1.60); main courses 1,600 Ft–2,900 Ft ($5.75–$10.45). AE, DC, MC, V. May–September, daily noon–11pm; Oct–April, daily 4–11pm. Bus: A number of buses serve Döbrentei tér, including no. 8 from Március 15 tér.

Kacsa Vendéglő ★ HUNGARIAN   Kacsa (meaning "duck") is located on the main street of Watertown, the Buda neighborhood that lies between Castle Hill and the Danube. Here you'll find an intimate, elegant, and understated dining atmosphere. A string trio is appealing, but the service seems overly attentive and ceremonious. Enticing main courses include roast duck with morello cherries, haunch of venison with grapes, and pike served Russian style. The vegetarian plate is the best we've had anywhere. For dessert, sample the assorted strudels, prepared with fruits in season.

Fő u. 75. € 1/201-9992. Reservations recommended. Soup 400 Ft–500 Ft ($1.45–$1.80); main courses 1,900 Ft–3,000 Ft ($6.85–$10.80). MC, V. Daily 6pm–1am. Metro: Batthyány tér (Red line).

Le Jardin de Paris ★★ FRENCH   In the heart of Buda's Watertown, just across the street from the hideous Institut Français, is this wonderful little French bistro. A cozy cellar space, it is decorated with an eclectic collection of graphic arts. A jazz trio entertains diners from 7pm to 11pm. The menu features a variety of nouvelle French specialties, and the wine list offers French as well as Hungarian vintages. Presentation is impeccable, and the waiters are not overbearing. There's outdoor seating in a garden area in summer.

I. Fő u. 20. € 1/201-0047. Reservations recommended. Soup 590 Ft–890 Ft ($2.10–$3.20); appetizers 850 Ft–2,000 Ft ($3.05–$7.20); main courses 1,500 Ft–2,500 Ft ($5.40–$9) AE, DC, MC, V. Daily noon–midnight. Metro: Batthyány tér (Red line).

MODERATE

Horgásztanya Vendéglő ★ HUNGARIAN/SEAFOOD   Just a short block from the Danube, in Buda's Watertown (Víziváros), the Horgásztanya Vendéglő is a family-style fish restaurant of reliable quality and modest prices for this part

Snacks on the Run

Budapest is a great place for snacking. There are kiosks and *bufes* turning out impromptu meals near every major transportation hub. Below are our favorites—good alternatives to the international fast-food joints proliferating in Budapest. Generally, you can pick up a meal on the run for 500 Ft ($1.80) or less.

Astoria Directly across the street from Pizza Hut, you'll find a tiny hole in the wall called **Pizza Kucko.** This place was here long before Pizza Hut arrived on the scene, and guess what? Their pizza is better!

Bajcsy-Zsilinszky út Rétes Cukrászda, at VI. Bajcsy-Zsilinszky út 15 (Metro: Arany János utca, on the Blue line), offers delightful *meggyes rétes* (sour cherry strudel) and *meggyes pite* (a variation on the same). Buy by the dozen.

Blaha Lujza tér Next door to the Hotel Mercure Nemzeti, at VIII. József krt. 2, you'll find **Hot Pot Forró Krumpli,** a little place with all sorts of baked potatoes for sale.

Deák tér In the Inner City's Deák tér neighborhood, we recommend the small open-faced sandwiches available at **Duran Szendvics** (another chain of sandwich places in town), VI. Bajcsy-Zsilinszky út 7. Three or four of these colorfully displayed sandwiches would make a meal. Another good place is **Quint Büfé,** just down the street from the Tourinform office and across the street from the Jet gas station on Barczy István utca. Here you can get large portions of upscale cafeteria food (but not at upscale prices).

Déli railway station Try the **Gyros Bufe** in the upper level of the station (enter from Alkotás út). Delicious gyros sandwiches, made from turkey, are sold here.

Keleti railway station Time to kill before catching your train? Try **El Fayoumi Étterem,** at VIII. Nefelejcs u. 5. Delicious gyros and falafels are dispensed here. In the mood for something sweet? The unnamed **pastry trailer** permanently parked at the head of Nefelejcs utca, in front of the Kentucky Fried Chicken outlet, offers a soft, flaky *kakaos csiga* (chocolate snail) and equally fresh brioche.

Kossuth tér A good snack can be hard to find in this neighborhood full of government buildings (e.g., Parliament) and other offices. If you need a little something here, try **McKiwan's Sendvics** (a chain with

of town. Don't worry, non–fish eaters can enjoy dining here too; the extensive menu (in English) lists a variety of Hungarian specialties. The decor is traditional Hungarian, catering to tourists.

I. Fő u. 27. ✆ 1/212-3780. Soup 290 Ft–1,550 Ft ($1.05–$5.60); main courses 900 Ft–2,250 Ft ($3.25–$8.10). No credit cards. Daily noon–11pm. Metro: Battyhány tér (Red line).

Szeged Vendéglő HUNGARIAN Come to this classic Vendéglő for a taste of Szeged, the southern Hungarian city admired for its zesty cuisine (see several other stores in the city), where you can pick up a few open-faced sandwiches (from a very wide selection). Always fresh.

Móricz Zsigmond körtér   This busy Buda transportation hub has the single most delicious sweet snack available in this entire city full of sweets. We refer, of course, to the *kürtőskalács* sold in the little kiosk in the triangle in front of McDonald's. This is a delicious Transylvanian honey bread quite unlike anything else you've ever tasted. Traditionally the dough is wrapped around a bottle and baked in an extremely hot oven. Here it is baked on a metal pipe, and served delightfully fresh. The kiosk is open every day, but closes at 7:30pm.

Moszkva tér   Hungarian-style fast-food sandwiches are available 24 hours a day from the rather grungy **Gyorsbüfé** (Fast Buffet) kiosk. As you emerge from the metro (Red line), it's to the left of the clock; look for the line of people. The menu changes daily, but usually two or three types of hot sandwiches are available: *Húsos meleg szendvics* is meat sauce and melted cheese on half a baguette; hamburger is, well, a Hungarian variation on the tradition (*sajtos* is with cheese). *Hamburger hús nélkül* has no burger; it is a bun stuffed with fixings, the best choice for vegetarians. Ice cream is also available.

Nyugati railway station   In the underpass beneath Nyugati railway station (beneath the *Skala Metro* department store), you will find an unnamed stand selling deep-fried chicken sandwiches. They make a great snack. Not far away, at IV. Visegrádi u. 1, is **Ramen House Miyako,** considered by many to be Budapest's best Japanese noodle house. It's open daily until 1am. The excellent Turkish bakery, **Török Pékség** ★★, just down the street toward the Danube, at IV. Szent István krt. 13, sells freshly baked pita bread and a broad selection of baklava and other lovely pastries (but avoid the bad Turkish-Chinese restaurant next door to the bakery).

Outer Ring Boulevard (from Oktogon to Blaha Lujza tér)   This stretch of the Outer Ring Boulevard boasts the two best Turkish kebab stands in the city. At Erzsébet körút 5, you'll find **Abbas Basha** ★★, and at Erzsébet körút 17 is **Gül Baba Török Büfé**. Both offer a variety of mouthwatering kebab sandwiches and other dishes, along with racks of sweet baklava. Kebab eaters: in Hungary, "doner" is lamb, while "gyros" is either turkey or pork (if this distinction matters to you, make sure you ask before buying); both are delicious. Vegetarian sandwiches are available on request.

"Szeged: Hungary's Spice Capital" in chapter 13, Southern Hungary: The Great Plain & the Mecsek Hills," for information on trips to Szeged). The house specialties are spicy fish dishes, including the famous fish soup, *Szeged halászlé*. The restaurant is a touch old school, but the food is good and hearty. Ersatz Gypsy music is performed nightly. The restaurant is just down the street from the Hotel Gellért, not far from Buda's Móricz Zsigmond körtér.

XI. Bartók Béla út 1. ✆ **1/466-6503** or 1/209-1668. Soup 500 Ft ($1.80); main courses 1,200 Ft–1,800 Ft ($4.30–$6.50). V. Daily noon–11pm. Tram: 47 or 49 from Deák tér to Hotel Gellért.

Taverna Ressaikos ★★ GREEK   Located in the heart of Buda's Watertown (Víziváros), just next door to the Hotel Carlton Budapest, the Taverna Ressaikos features carefully prepared food at reasonable prices. Portions are generous. Try the calamari or the sumptuous lamb in wine. The menu also features a number of interesting goat dishes. Vegetarians can easily make a meal out of appetizers such as stuffed tomatoes, spanakopita, and tsatsiki. The live guitar music (Thursday through Saturday) can get a bit too loud, and the service, while attentive, is definitely on the slow side.

I. Apor Péter u. 1. ✆ 1/212-1612. Reservations recommended. Soup and appetizers 300 Ft–800 Ft ($1.10–$2.90); main courses 750 Ft–1,300 Ft ($2.70–$4.70). V, MC. Daily noon–midnight. Bus or tram: Any to Clark Ádám tér, including bus no. 16 from Deák tér.

INEXPENSIVE

Marxim ★ *Kids* PIZZA   On a gritty industrial street near Moszkva tér, Marxim's chief appeal lies not in its cuisine but in its décor, which teenagers seem to enjoy. The motif is Marxist nostalgia; the entrance is marked by a small neon red flag. The cellar space is a museum of barbed wire, red flags, banners, posters, and cartoons recalling Hungary's dark past. Amazingly, this is one of very few places in Budapest where you can still see this kind of stuff, so thoroughly have symbols of the Communist period been erased. (Another place, of course, is *Szoborpark* [Statue Park]; see "Where Have All the Statues Gone" in chapter 6, "Exploring Budapest," for details.) Several years ago, Marxim was unsuccessfully prosecuted under a controversial law banning the display of the symbols of "hateful" political organizations. The loud, very smoky cellar space is more bar than restaurant. A number of draft beers are available on tap.

II. Kisrókus u. 23. ✆ 1/316-0231. Pizza 440 Ft–990 Ft ($1.60–$3.55); pasta 450 Ft–650 Ft ($1.60–$2.35). No credit cards. Mon–Thurs noon–1am, Fri–Sat noon–2am, Sun 6pm–1am. Metro: Moszkva tér (Red line).

5 The Castle District
VERY EXPENSIVE

Alabárdos ★ HUNGARIAN   In the heart of the Castle District, Alabárdos offers Hungarian-style nouvelle cuisine in an intimate, elegant setting. The historic building it's housed in has several medieval details; 15th-century arches can be seen in the courtyard. The atmosphere inside is hushed and elegant, although slightly pretentious. The walls are judiciously decorated in a medieval motif. A guitarist performs unobtrusively. Meals are served on Zsolnay porcelain, from Pécs. The menu is extensive. Weather permitting, outdoor dining is available in the courtyard.

I. Országház u. 2. ✆ 1/356-0851. www.alabardos.hu. Reservations required. Soup 1,200 Ft–1,500 Ft ($4.30–$5.40); main courses 3,000 Ft–9,000 Ft ($10.80–$32.40). AE, DC, DISC, MC, V. Mon–Sat noon–4pm and 7pm–11pm. Bus: Várbusz from Moszkva tér or 16 from Deák tér to Castle Hill. Funicular: From Clark Ádám tér to Castle Hill.

INEXPENSIVE

Önkiszolgáló ★ *Value* HUNGARIAN   Located directly across the street from the Hilton Hotel, in the Fortuna Courtyard (where the bookstore Litea is located; see p. 159 in chapter 8, "Budapest Shopping"), this humble self-service cafeteria offers a rare commodity: cheap and hearty meals in the Castle District. The entrance is the second door on the left inside the archway, up one flight of stairs; it's marked only by a small sign posting the open hours. Just follow the stream of locals at lunchtime. Point out your selections, share a table, and bus your own tray when you finish.

I. Hess András tér 4 (first floor in the Fortuna Courtyard). No phone. Soup 240 Ft (85¢); main courses 220 Ft–540 Ft (80¢–$1.95). Mon–Fri 11:30am–2:30pm. Bus: Várbusz from Moszkva tér or 16 from Deák tér to Castle Hill. Funicular: From Clark Ádám tér to Castle Hill

6 The Buda Hills

EXPENSIVE

Udvarház a Hármashatárhegyen ★ *Kids* HUNGARIAN This lovely restaurant high in the Buda Hills boasts several elegant dining rooms, in addition to tables on the terrace with a great panoramic view of the surrounding hills. Dinner here makes for a full evening; in the courtyard there's a folklore show, with music and dance. The menu features a large variety of Hungarian specialties, particularly fish and game. Other than by taxi, the only way to get here is by taking bus no. 65 to the last stop (note that the last bus heads back at 10pm).

I. Hármashatárhegyi út 2. © 1/388-8780. Reservations recommended. Soup 400 Ft–550 Ft ($1.45–$2); main courses 1,500 Ft–3,100 Ft ($5.40–$11.15). AE, DC, DISC, MC, V. Apr–Nov, Tues–Sun 11am–11pm; Dec–March, daily 6pm–11pm. Bus: 65 from Kolosy tér in Óbuda to the last stop.

MODERATE

Náncsi Néni Vendéglője ★★ *Finds* HUNGARIAN Decorated with photographs of turn-of-the-20th-century Budapest, this popular but remote restaurant is located high in the Buda Hills. There's outdoor garden dining in the summer, with live accordion music at night. The menu features typical Hungarian dishes, prepared with great care. In our opinion, their cottage cheese dumplings are the very best in town. The restaurant is near St. Christoph Villa and the Petneházy Country Club, recommended hotels.

II. ördögárok út 80. © 1/397-2742. Reservations recommended for dinner. Soup 500 Ft–550 Ft ($1.80–$2); main courses 1,200 Ft–2,000 Ft ($4.30–$7.20). MC, V. Daily noon–11pm. Tram: 56 from Moszkva tér to the last stop, then change to bus No. 63 to Széchenyi utca.

Szép Ilona ★★ HUNGARIAN This cheerful, unassuming restaurant serves a mostly local clientele. There's a good selection of Hungarian specialties; try the *borjúpaprikás galuskával* (veal paprika) served with *galuska* (a typical Central European style of dumpling) or smoked pork with risotto. There's a small sidewalk-side garden for summer dining. The Szép Ilona is located in a pleasant Buda neighborhood; after your meal, take a stroll through the tree-lined streets.

II. Budakeszi út 1–3. © 1/275-1392. Soup 290 Ft–610 Ft ($1.05–$2.20); main courses 780 Ft–2,300 Ft ($2.80–$8.30). No credit cards. Daily 11:30am–10pm. Bus: 158 from Moszkva tér (departs from Csaba utca, at the top of the stairs, near the stop from which the Várbusz departs for the Castle District).

INEXPENSIVE

Makkhetes Vendéglő ★★ *Finds* HUNGARIAN In the lower part of the Buda Hills, Makkhetes (the name means "7 of Acorns," a Hungarian playing card) is a rustic little neighborhood eatery. The crude wood paneling and absence of ornamentation give it a distinctly country atmosphere. The regulars (the waiters seem to know everyone who enters) start filing in at 11:30am for lunch. The food is good and the portions large. You won't go wrong with the *paprika csirke galuskával* (chicken paprika with dumplings). Outdoor dining is available.

XII. Némethvölgyi út 56. © 1/355-7330. Soup 250 Ft–550 Ft ($90¢–$2); main courses 500 Ft–1,500 Ft ($1.80–$5.40). No credit cards. Daily 11am–10pm. Tram: 59 from Moszkva tér to Kiss János altábornagy utca stop (then walk up hill to the right on Kiss János altábornagy utca).

7 Northern Buda & Óbuda

VERY EXPENSIVE

Kéhli Vendéglő ★ HUNGARIAN   Housed in a historic Óbuda building, Kéhli is an upscale traditional Hungarian restaurant with a cozy dining room and an enclosed garden. Located behind the Aquincum Corinthia Hotel in Óbuda's old city, the restaurant can be a bit difficult to find—ask a local when you get in the general vicinity. One of the house specialties is Szinbád's Favorite, named for the famous pirate introduced to Hungary by the early 20th-century novelist Gyula Krúdy; the dish consists of pork stuffed with chicken liver rolled in bacon and served in a paprika-and-mushroom sauce. The restaurant used to be frequented by the novelist, who is famous for his appetizing descriptions of hedonistic meals he enjoyed on the premises. Another dish worth sampling is the roast goose liver with garlic. For the real adventurous, try the beef bone marrow served with pepper and paprika on slices of toast for an appetizer. Dinner is accompanied by live gypsy music.

III. Mókus u. 22. ✆ 1/250-4241. Reservations recommended. Soup 550 Ft–980 Ft ($2–$3.50); main courses 1,400 Ft–3,900 Ft ($5.05–$14.05). AE, MC, V. Mon–Fri 5pm–midnight, Sat–Sun noon–midnight. Train: HÉV suburban railway from Batthyány tér to Árpád híd.

EXPENSIVE

Kis Buda Gyöngye ★★ *Finds* HUNGARIAN/INTERNATIONAL   On a quiet side street in a residential Óbuda neighborhood, Kis Buda Gyöngye (Little Pearl of Buda) is a favorite of Hungarians and visitors alike. This lively, cheerful restaurant features an interior garden shaded by a wonderful old gnarly tree. Inside, an eccentric violin player entertains diners. The standard Hungarian fare is prepared with great care. Consider the goose plate, a rich combination platter including roast goose leg, goose cracklings, and goose liver. Service can be slow.

III. Kenyeres u. 34. ✆ 1/368-6402 or 1/368-9246. Reservations highly recommended. Soup 680 Ft–780 Ft ($2.45–$2.80); main courses 1,800 Ft–3,200 Ft ($6.50–$11.50). AE, DC, MC, V. Mon–Sat noon–midnight. Closed Sun. Tram: 17 from Margit híd (Buda side).

MODERATE

Malomtó Étterem ★★ HUNGARIAN   Right across the street from the Lukács thermal baths, the Malomtó (named for the nearby Mill Pond) sits at the base of a hill. There are two outdoor terraces, well shaded from the road, and live guitar music nightly. The menu features a good variety of Hungarian wild game specialties and seafood dishes, in addition to the standard Hungarian specialties. You might notice that the menu posted outside differs from the one distributed at the tables, though this seems to be related more to mismanagement than to any attempt at deception. Since the main courses are huge, you may want to bypass soup and salad. The *Bélszín kedvesi módra* (beef and goose liver in a creamy mushroom sauce) is sumptuous. On a recent visit, we tried the *sztrapacska oldalassal* (pork ribs with ewe cheese dumplings) and found it delightful. Service can be on the slow side.

II. Frankel Leó u. 48. ✆ 1/326-2847. Reservations recommended for dinner. Soup 220 Ft–320 Ft (75¢–$1.15); main courses 800 Ft–2,000 Ft ($2.90–$7.20). AE, DC, MC, V. Daily noon–midnight. Tram: 4 or 6 to Margit híd (Buda side), then walk along Frankel Leó utca to the Lukács Baths (Lukács Fürdő).

Új Sipos Halászkert ★ HUNGARIAN/SEAFOOD   In its own handsome building on Óbuda's dignified main square, this restaurant consists of several rooms with a comfortable air of worn elegance. Though the exterior of the restaurant has received a fresh paint job and the addition of the word "Új" (new) to its name, the inside is, to our eyes, unchanged. The menu specializes in Hungarian seafood dishes. A string trio enhances the atmosphere, and there is a small interior garden area.

III. Fő tér 6. ℭ **1/250-1064** (public phone in lobby). Reservations recommended. Soup 350 Ft–660 Ft ($1.25–$2.40); main courses 850 Ft–1,800 Ft ($3.05–$6.50). 10% service charge added to the bill. AE, DC, DISC, MC, V. Daily noon–midnight. Train: Suburban HÉV line to Árpád híd.

8 Traditional Coffeehouses

Like Vienna, imperial Budapest was famous for its coffeehouse culture. Literary movements and political circles alike were identified in large part by which coffeehouse they met in. Sándor Petőfi, the revolutionary poet of 1848 fame, is said to have instructed his friend János Arany, another leading Hungarian poet of the day, to write to him in care of the Pilvax Coffee House, as he spent more time there than at home. Although Communism managed to dull this cherished institution, a handful of classic coffeehouses miraculously survived the tangled tragedies of the 20th century, and, with just a few exceptions, all have been carefully restored to their original splendor.

All the classic coffeehouses offer delicious pastries and coffee in an atmosphere of luxurious—if occasionally faded—splendor. Many offer small sandwiches, some serve ice cream, and some feature bar drinks. Pastries are displayed in a glass case and generally cost between 300 Ft and 600 Ft ($1.10 and $2.15); coffee costs 250 Ft (90¢) and up. Table sharing is common, and lingering for hours over a single cup of coffee or pastry is perfectly acceptable, and is in fact encouraged by the free daily papers provided by the house.

THE INNER CITY & CENTRAL PEST

Central Kávéház ★   This latest addition to the Viennese coffee house culture in Budapest is a perfect replica of the original establishment that stood on the premises from 1887. The reopening is exceptional in that the house is run by a civil society of local patriots whose main sponsor is Hungary's own home-grown successful businessman, Imre Somody—one of the very few of the new millionaires who seems willing to recycle his profits by reinvesting in the country's general wealth. The place is perfectly located in the inner city, always busy with an interesting mix of the local university crowd from ELTE and CEU as well as celebrity intellectuals, in addition to the ever present tourists, who have taken to the place immediately. Although on the gallery there is a superb restaurant as well, the place is still more like a coffeehouse, offering the best flavors of coffee in the area in an amazingly affordable price range of 280 Ft to 950 Ft ($1–$3.40). You can enter its calm green interior to check out the free copies of the *Budapest Sun* and *Budapest Business Journal* over a coffee and a fresh croissant as early as 8 am in the morning; it's the only place open at this time of the day in the area.

V. Károlyi Mihály u. 9.ℭ **1/266-2110.** Sun–Thurs 8am–midnight; Fri–Sat 8am–1am. Metro: Ferenciek tere (Blue line).

Gerbeaud's ★ (Kids)   Gerbeaud's is probably Budapest's most famous coffeehouse. Founded in 1858, it has stood on its current spot since 1870. Whether you sit inside amid the splendor of turn-of-the-20th-century furnishings or outside on one of Pest's liveliest squares, you will be sure to enjoy the fine pastries that have made the name Gerbeaud famous; we especially recommend their moist plum pies (*szilvás lepény*). Its reputation and location ensure that it's filled to capacity throughout the year; good luck getting a table in the late afternoon.

In good weather, try getting a table outside on bustling Vörösmarty tér and watch your kids play around (and on) the square's fountain.

V. Vörösmarty tér 7. (€) 1/429-9000. Daily 9am–9pm. Metro: Vörösmarty tér (Yellow line).

Lukács Cukrászda 🍷   A faithful reproduction of a vintage coffeehouse, this large, airy establishment was recently resurrected decades after a coffeehouse of the same name closed its door. It represents a major part of the recent efforts to bring back the lively coffee shop life of the capital. It is just a few minutes' walk from Oktogon. The local crowds that fill Művész Kávéház just down the street have not yet befriended this place. Perhaps the idea of sharing the entrance with a bank is not bohemian enough for the demanding local crowd. Nevertheless, it is a great place to sit in air-conditioned splendor and write postcards over a long cup of joe.

VI. Andrássy út 70. (€) 36/1-302-8747. Mon–Fri 9am–8pm, Sat–Sun 10am–8pm. Metro: Opera (Yellow line).

Művész Kávéház 🍷🍷   Just across Andrássy út from the Opera House, Művész (Artist) is one of Budapest's finest traditional coffeehouses; it was around even in the communist times. The lush interior includes marble table tops, crystal chandeliers, and mirrored walls. Despite its Old-World grandeur, Művész retains a casual atmosphere. There are tables on the street, but sit inside for the full coffeehouse effect. Decaffeinated cappuccino is available, still a rarity in Budapest. Elaborate ice-cream sundaes seem to be a favorite with locals and tourists alike.

VI. Andrássy út 29. (€) 1/352-1337 or 1/351-3942. Daily 9am–midnight. Metro: Opera (Yellow line).

CENTRAL BUDA

Angelika Cukrászda 🍷🍷🍷   The Angelika Cukrászda is housed in a historic building next to St. Anne's Church on Buda's Batthyány tér. The sunken rooms of this cavernous cafe provide the perfect retreat on a hot summer day. The place was recently extended to include a grill restaurant outside and a complex of terraces on three levels. Now you will find a perfect view of the Parliament building and the Chain Bridge. The stained-glass windows and marble floors contrast beautifully with the off-white canvas upholstery and cast iron furniture. You can choose from among a selection of excellent pastries and teas (a rarity in Budapest, a city of serious coffee addicts). There is also a small gallery inside the coffeehouse, where artworks are displayed.

I. Batthyány tér 7. (€) 1/201-4847 or 1/212-3784. Daily 9am–2pm. Metro: Batthyány tér (Red line).

THE CASTLE DISTRICT

Ruszwurm Cukrászda 🍷 *Kids*   More than a century old, the Ruszwurm is an utterly charming little place, with two rooms outfitted with small tables and chairs, and wall shelves lined with antiques. It is owned by the Szamos dynasty of pastry and marzipan chefs (you can also visit their museum in Szentendre, see "Szentendre" in chapter 10, "The Danube Bend"). It can be very difficult to find

---

Impressions

The cafes are never empty here . . . Everyone loiters on the Corso, for no one is in a hurry in Budapest. If a cool breeze comes up, the waiters bring small steamer rugs for their patrons.

—Grace Humphrey, American memoirist, 1936

Our Favorite Sweets

Hungary is a land of sweet teeth. The country's confections will satisfy even the most rabid cravings.

Found only in Hungary, **Dobos Torta** is a light chocolate layer cake with a caramelized frosting. **Ischler** is a delightful Viennese specialty—two shortbread cookies with apricot jam filling, double-dipped in dark chocolate. **Meggyes Rétes**, a sour cherry strudel, is a traditional favorite. And just when you thought the sour cherry strudel was unbeatable, along comes this heavenly poppy-seed strudel, **Mákos Rétes.**

Kakaós Csiga is a chocolate snail: Buttery and flaky rolled pastry sprinkled with chocolate. They're available in bakeries everywhere (but not cafes). A *kifli* is a cross between a croissant and a roll. The *Szegedi* variety (named for Szeged, the southeastern city from whence it comes) has a sweet almond glaze. It's available at cafes or bakeries, but you might have to travel to Szeged for an authentic taste.

Sold from kiosks that sell nothing else, *kürtőskalács* is a delicious, melt-in-your-mouth honey bread quite unlike anything else you've ever tasted. It is traditionally made with dough wrapped around a bottle and baked in an extremely hot oven. It's not available in regular shops or cafes.

It is a mystery why Ben and Jerry haven't figured this one out yet. Hungarian **cinnamon ice cream** (*fahej*) is to die for. And if you come across the rarest of its varieties, cinnamon rice ice cream (*fahejes rizs*), by all means, try it.

a free table, and the four out front on the sidewalk seem forever occupied. You must try the unsurpassable *krémes*, a two-layered ever-crisp pastry confection with vanilla cream filling. Another favorite here is the *Dobos torta,* a multi-layered cake with a thin caramel crust on top;

I. Szentháromság u. 7. ✆ 1/375-5284. Daily 10am–7pm. Bus: Várbusz from Moszkva tér or 16 from Deák tér to Castle Hill. Funicular: From Clark Ádám tér to Castle Hill.

9 Cafes & Bistros

Cafe Incognito   Sophisticated but informal, Incognito opens far out onto the street in summer. There's a full bar.

VI. Liszt Ferenc tér 3. ✆ 1/342-1471. Mon–Fri 10am–midnight, Sat–Sun noon–midnight. Metro: Oktogon (yellow line).

Darshan Cafe and Udvar   Darshan is a small, always crowded hangout with a groovy Indian ambience. Pass through a gate strung with bells to reach the complex of shops, cafes and dance places in the small courtyard. You may want to look around in the Indigo Record shop (alternative music) or browse over the impressive Hungarian artsy T-shirt collections while waiting for your beer to arrive; at 300 Ft to 650 Ft ($1.10 to $2.35) for half a liter on tap, this is definitely a bargain on a hot summer day. Featured on the menu is an eastern variation on a traditional Hungarian dish known as *főzelek*—part casserole, part stew, and entirely vegetarian. Enjoy.

Krúdy Gyula u. 7. ℂ **1/266-5541.** Mon–Wed 10:30am–1am; Thurs–Fri 10:30am–2pm; Sat 6pm–2am; Sun 6pm–midnight.

Két Szerecsen ⭐⭐   A refined, artsy place in the theater district (Jókai tér), the recently opened Két Szerecsen already enjoys a loyal following. The warm orange walls display prints of turn-of-the-20th-century coffee advertisements (including some with overtly racist images). The kitchen serves up an assortment of Mediterranean dishes, including a delicious *tapas* assortment. Don't miss the lemon soup. This is also a good place to come for breakfast, which is served weekdays until 11am. Két Szerecsen features a full bar. In winter, stop in for a mug of mulled wine.

VI. Nagymező u. 14. ℂ **1/343-1984.** Mon–Fri 8am–1am, weekends 11am–1am. Metro: Opera or Oktogon (Yellow line).

Old Amsterdam ⭐⭐   A great success off the inner ring, Old Amsterdam is a favorite of everyone from foreign business types to young, hip travelers. The establishment has a genuine Dutch cafe quality with its extensive selection of the best beers in Europe, including Belgian fruit beers of all kinds, and a menu offering an assortment of Dutch cheeses.

Király Pál u. 14. ℂ **1/266-3649.** Mon–Sat noon–2am, Sun 6pm–1am. Metro: Kálvin tér (Blue line).

Paris, Texas ⭐⭐   A cozy place to eat, drink, and talk through the night, Paris, Texas is very popular with the city's university students. The walls of three adjacent rooms are lined with old photographs, providing a window into the local culture of the 1910s and '20s. In the summer, there is outdoor seating. Once a week Paris, Texas features a "beer day," when it serves draft beer at a 30% discount.

IX. Ráday u. 22. ℂ **1/217-7737.** Mon–Fri 10am–3am, Sat–Sun 4pm–3am. Metro: Kálvin tér (Blue line).

6

Exploring Budapest

Historic Budapest is surprisingly small, and many sights listed in the following pages can be reached by foot from the city center. Take the time to stroll from one place to the next; you'll find yourself passing magnificent, if often run-down, examples of the city's distinctive architecture.

SUGGESTED ITINERARIES

If You Have 1 Day

Spend a few hours in the morning exploring the **Inner City** and **Central Pest.** Walk the length of Váci útca, the city's trendiest shopping street, to Vörösmarty tér. Stop for cappuccino and a slice of apple strudel (almás rétes) at the sumptuous Gerbeaud coffeehouse. Stroll along the Danube as far as the neo-Gothic **Parliament** building, noting along the way the **Chain Bridge** and the **Gresham Palace.** Lunch with the locals at Kisharang Étterem on Október 6 utca. Save the whole afternoon for visiting the major sites of **Castle Hill** and exploring the cobblestone streets of the **Castle District.**

If You Have 2 Days

On your first day, see **Pest,** as above, saving the Castle District for day 2. Walk the **Outer Ring Boulevard,** noting Nyugati Railway Station and the **New York Palace,** grand examples of turn-of-the-20th-century architecture. Stop for coffee and a slice of *dobos torta* (layer cake) in the newly renovated Lukács Cukrászda, just a block away from Oktogon on grand Andrássy út. Later, head to Buda's Gellért Hotel and unwind in its medicinal **spa** waters. Refreshed,

hike up the stairs of Gellért Hill to see the **Liberation Monument** and an unparalleled panorama of the city.

Devote most of your second day to the **Castle District,** as above. Visit some smaller museums as well, like the **Music History Museum** (check for a recital) or the **Military History Museum.** Head back to Pest later to see **Heroes' Square** and **City Park.** Splurge on dinner at Gundel, where visiting royalty dined in turn-of-the-20th-century Budapest. Afterward, stroll the length of grand **Andrássy út** back toward the center of Pest.

If You Have 3 Days

Spend Days 1 and 2 as suggested above. Spend one evening attending a concert at the **Ferenc Liszt Music Academy,** Budapest's finest hall.

On the third day, take a boat up the Danube to **Szentendre,** a charming riverside town, home to a flourishing artist's colony. Don't miss the **Margit Kovács Museum,** where the work of Hungary's most innovative ceramic artist can be seen. Return in time for a final dinner at elegant Kacsa Vendéglő in Budapest's Watertown.

If You Have 4 or 5 Days

In the morning of Day 4, visit central Pest sights you may have missed, such as the **Opera House** or **St. Stephen's Basilica.** After lunch, cross the **Chain Bridge** to Watertown, Buda's historic riverside neighborhood. See **St. Anne's Church,** the **Capuchin Church,** and the **Király Baths,** one of the only remaining examples of 16th century Turkish architecture in Budapest. Later, take a ride through the scenic Buda Hills on the **Children's Railroad.**

On the fifth day, first thing in the morning, visit one of Pest's authentic **indoor market halls** and sample Hungary's scrumptious fruit in season. Head to the **Ethnographical Museum** or the **Applied Arts Museum,** treasure troves of the rich Hungarian culture. After lunch, get away from the hustle and bustle of the city on **Margaret Island.** Stroll through the rose gardens, rent a bike, or just sunbathe in this peaceful setting. Later, as the sun is setting, return to the Castle District for a final look.

1 The Top Attractions

PEST
MUSEUMS

Museums are closed on Mondays, except where noted. Most museums offer substantial student and senior discounts. Many also offer a family rate. Inquire at the ticket window.

Nemzeti Múzeum (Hungarian National Museum) ★   The Hungarian National Museum, an enormous neoclassical structure built in 1837–47, was one of the great projects of the early–19th-century Age of Reform, a period that also saw the construction of the Chain Bridge and the National Theater (no longer standing), as well as the development of the modern Hungarian national identity. The museum was a major site in the beginning of the Hungarian Revolution of 1848–49; on its wide steps on March 15, 1848, the poet Sándor Petőfi and other young radicals are said to have exhorted the people of Pest to revolt against the Habsburgs. The very presence of such an imposing structure in the capital, and its exhibits proudly detailing the accomplishments of the Magyars, played a significant role in the development of 19th-century Hungarian nationalism.

The museum's main attraction is the replica of the so-called crown of St. Stephen (King Stephen ruled 1000–38). The original was moved to its new location, the Parliament building, as part of Hungary's second millenium celebrations in 2000. The crown was ceremoniously returned by former U.S. Secretary of State Cyrus Vance to Hungary in 1978 from the United States, where it had been stored since the end of World War II. Few Hungarians would assert, however, that the two-tiered crown on display ever actually rested on Stephen's head: Its lower part was evidently a gift to King Géza I (1074–77), and its upper part was built for Stephen V, almost 250 years after the first Stephen's death. The two main museum exhibits on view are "The History of the Peoples of Hungary from the Paleolithic Age to the Magyar Conquest" and "The History of the Hungarian People from the Magyar Conquest to 1989" ★. "The Hungarian Royal Insignia" is another permanent exhibit.

VIII. Múzeum krt. 14. ✆ 1/338-2122. Admission 400 Ft ($1.70). Tues–Sun 10am–6pm (to 5pm in winter). Metro: Kálvin tér (Blue line).

Néprajzi Múzeum (Ethnographical Museum)   Directly across Kossuth tér from the House of Parliament, the vast Ethnographical Museum is located in the stately neo-Renaissance/eclectic former Hungarian Supreme Court building. The ornate interior rivals that of the Opera House. A ceiling fresco of Justitia, the goddess of justice, by the well-known artist Károly Lotz, dominates the lobby. Although a third of the museum's holdings are from outside Hungary, concentrate on the items from Hungarian ethnography. The fascinating permanent exhibition, "From Ancient Times to Civilization," features everything from drinking jugs to razor cases to chairs to clothing.

V. Kossuth tér 12. (℗ 1/473-2440. Admission 500 Ft ($1.80). Tues–Sun 10am–6pm (5pm in winter). Metro: Kossuth tér (Red line).

Szépművészeti Múzeum (Museum of Fine Arts)   Planned at the time of the 1896 millennial celebration of the Magyar Conquest, the Museum of Fine Arts opened 10 years later in this neoclassical behemoth on Heroes' Square, at the edge of City Park, on the left side of the huge square. Do not mistake it for the other building of the same period, on the right side of the square, Műcsarnok (Exhibition Hall), the busy venue of contemporary art events, performances, and debates, most of which are unfortunately not particularly accessible to non-speakers of Hungarian. The museum is the main repository in Hungary of foreign art; as such, it ranks among Central Europe's major collections. A significant part of the collection was acquired in 1871 from the Esterházys, an enormously wealthy noble family which had spent centuries amassing great art. There are eight departments: Egyptian Art, Antiquities, Baroque Sculpture, Old Masters, Drawings and Prints, 19th- and 20th-century Masters, and Modern Sculpture. Most great names associated with the old masters—Tiepolo, Tintoretto, Veronese, Titian, Raphael, van Dyck, Brueghel, Rembrandt, Rubens, Hals, Hogarth, Dürer, Cranach, Holbein, Goya, Velázquez, El Greco, and others—are represented here. The 19th-century French artists best represented in the museum are Delacroix, Corot, and Manet. It has been said, though, that while the museum suffers no shortage of works by the old masters, it can boast precious few outright masterpieces.

XIV. Hősök tere. (℗ 1/343-9759. Admission 500 Ft ($1.80). Tues–Sun 10am–5:30pm. Metro: Hősök tere (Yellow line).

HISTORIC SQUARES & BUILDINGS

Hősök tere (Heroes' Square) ★★ (Kids)   Situated at the end of Pest's great boulevard, Andrássy út, and at the entrance to its most famous park, City Park (Városliget), the wide open plaza of Hősök tere (Heroes' Square) is one of the symbols of the city. During the country's Communist era, Socialist holidays were invariably celebrated with huge military reviews in the square. In 1989, a rally here on the day of the reburial of Imre Nagy (executed after the 1956 uprising against the Soviet-backed regime) attracted 300,000 people to the square.

The square, like the park beyond it, was laid out for the 1896 Magyar Conquest millennial celebration. In its center stands the 118-foot-high Millennial Column; arrayed around the base of the column are equestrian statues of Árpád and the six other Magyar tribal leaders who led the conquest. Behind the column, arrayed along a colonnade, are 14 heroes of Hungarian history, including King Stephen I, the country's first Christian king (first on left); King Matthias Corvinus, who presided over Buda's Golden Age in the 15th century (sixth from right); and Lajos Kossuth, leader of the 1848–49 War of Independence (first on

Budapest Attractions

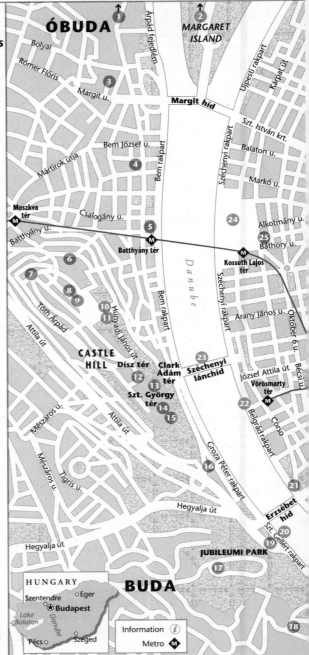

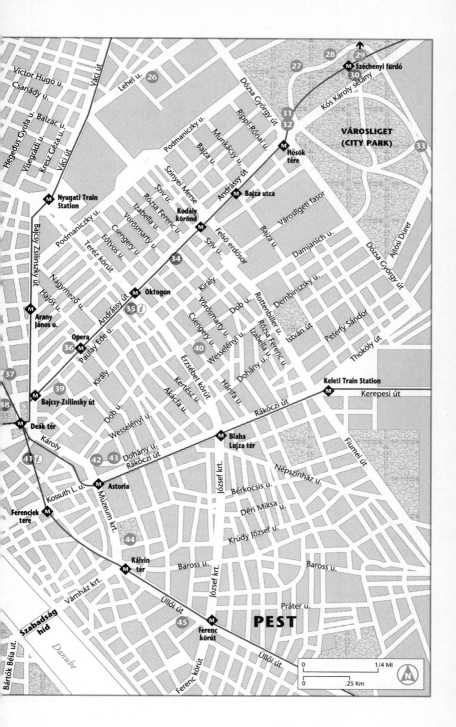

Victor Hugo u.
Csanády u.
Hegedüs Gyula u.
Balzac u.
Visegrádi u.
Krez Géza u.
Váci út
Lehel u.
26
Váci út
Podmaniczky u.
Bajza u.
Munkácsy u.
Rippl-Rónai u.
Dózsa György út
27
28
29
30
M Széchenyi fürdő
Kós Károly sétány
**VÁROSLIGET
(CITY PARK)**
31
32
33
M Hősök tére
Szinyei Merse
Szív u.
Rózsa Ferenc u.
Izabella u.
Vörösmarty u.
Andrássy út
M Bajza utca
Kodály körönd
Felső erdősor
Szív u.
Városliget fasor
Bajza u.
Damjanich u.
Ajtósi Durer
Dózsa György út
M Nyugati Train Station
Bajcsy Zsilinszky út
Podmaniczky u.
Teréz körút
Eötvös u.
Csengery u.
Nagymező u.
Hajós u.
Andrássy út
34
Király
Vörösmarty u.
Csengery u.
Dob u.
Rottenbiller u.
Dembinszky u.
István út
Peterfy Sándor
Thököly út
35 i
M Oktogon
M Arany János u.
36
M Opera
Paulay Ede u.
Király
Dob u.
Wesselényi u.
40
Erzsébet körút
Kertész u.
Akácfa u.
Wesselényi u.
Izabella u.
Rózsa Ferenc u.
Dohány u.
Hársfa u.
Keleti Train Station
Kerepesi út
37
38
39
M Bajcsy-Zsilinsky út
Dob u.
Wesselényi u.
Rákóczi út
M Deák tér
Károly
41 i
42 43
Dohány u.
Rákóczi út
M Blaha Lujza tér
Flumei út
Népszinház u.
M Astoria
Kossuth L. u.
Múzeum krt.
József krt.
Bérkocsis u.
Ferenciek tere
Déri Miksa u.
44
Krúdy József u.
Baross u.
Baross u.
Kálvin tér
Várnház krt.
Üllői út
József krt.
Práter u.
PEST
Szabadság hid
Bártók Béla út.
Danube
45
Ferenc körút
Ferenc körút
Üllői út

0   1/4 Mi
0   .25 Km
N

105

> **Fun Fact Striking a Sour Note**
>
> A political scandal marked the Hungarian State Opera House's opening
> performance in 1884. Ferenc Liszt had written a piece to be performed
> especially for the event, but when it was discovered that he had incorpo-
> rated elements of the Rákóczi March, a patriotic (and anti-Habsburg)
> Hungarian melody, he was prevented from playing it.

right). The statues were restored in 1996, in honor of the 1,100th anniversary
of the Magyar Conquest. Kids, especially young boys, adore looking at the
equestrian statues, and the square is close to many kid-friendly activities. Flank-
ing Heroes' Square are two of Budapest's major museums: the Museum of Fine
Arts and the Exhibition Hall.

Take the metro to Hősök tere (Yellow line).

Magyar Állami Operaház (Hungarian State Opera House) ★★ Completed in 1884, the Opera House, on Pest's elegant Andrássy út, is the crowning
achievement of famous Hungarian architect Miklós Ybl's. Budapest's most
celebrated performance hall, it boasts a fantastically ornate interior featuring
frescoes by two of the best-known Hungarian artists of the day, Bertalan Székely
and Károly Lotz. Both inside and outside are dozens of statues of such greats as
Beethoven, Mozart, Verdi, Wagner, Smetana, Tchaikovsky, and Monteverdi.

Home to both the State Opera and the State Ballet, the Opera House has a
rich and evocative history. Well-known directors of the Opera House have
included Gustav Mahler and Ferenc Erkel. See "The Performing Arts," in chapter 9, for information on performances.

VI. Andrássy út 22. © 1/331-2550. Admission (only on guided tours) 600 Ft ($2.15). Tours given daily at 3
and 4pm (available in English). Metro: Opera (Yellow line).

Parliament Budapest's great Parliament building, completed in 1902, was
built to the eclectic design of Imre Steindl. It mixes a predominant neo-Gothic
style with a neo-Renaissance dome. Standing proudly on the Danube bank, visible from almost any riverside vantage point, it has been from the outset one of
Budapest's symbols, though until 1989 a democratically elected government had
convened here exactly once (just after World War II, before the Communist
takeover). Built at a time of extreme optimism and national purpose, the
building was self-consciously intended to be one of the world's great houses of
Parliament, and it remains one of the largest state buildings in Europe. The main
cupola is decorated with statutes of Hungarian kings.

On either side of the cupola are waiting rooms leading into the respective
houses of Parliament. Here the members of Parliament are said to gather during
breaks in the session to smoke and chat—note the cigar holders on the side of
the doors. The waiting room on the Senate side (blue carpet) is adorned with
statues of farmers, peasants, tradesmen, and workers. The statues that decorate
the waiting room on the representatives' side (red carpet) are of sailors, soldiers,
postal officials, etc. The interior decor is predominantly neo-Gothic. The ceiling
frescoes are by Károly Lotz, Hungary's best-known artist of that genre. Note the
purportedly largest handmade carpet in Europe, from the small Hungarian
village of Békésszentandrás. The Parliament is also home to the legendary crown
jewels of St. Stephen, which were moved here from the National Museum in
2000, as part of the Hungarian millenium celebration.

V. Kossuth tér. (℅) 1/441-4415. Admission (by guided tour only): 30-min. tour in English, 1,500 Ft ($5.40). Tickets are available at gate X, enter at gate XII. Tours are given daily 10am and 2pm, but not on days in which Parliament is in session. Metro: Kossuth tér (Red line).

CHURCHES & SYNAGOGUES

Bazilika (St. Stephen's Church) ★ Although not a basilica in the technical sense of the word, Hungarians like to call St. Stephen's "The Basilica" in honor of its sheer size: It's the largest church in the country. The Basilica took over 50 years to build (the collapse of the dome in 1868 caused significant delay); three leading architects, two of whom (József Hild and Miklós Ybl) died before work was finished, presided over its construction. It was finally completed in 1906, but during its long construction Pest had undergone radical growth; strangely, while the front of the church dominates sleepy Szent István tér, the rear faces out onto the far busier Inner Ring boulevard. The bust above the main entrance is of King Stephen, Hungary's first Christian king. Inside the church, in the Chapel of the Holy Right (Szent Jobb Kápolna), you can see Hungarian Catholicism's most cherished—and bizarre—holy relic: Stephen's preserved right hand. The church was considered so sturdy that it was used to store important documents and artworks during World War II bombing. If a church ever needed a good spring cleaning, this is it. Organ concerts are held here at 7pm on Monday evenings from July through October; tickets cost 800 Ft ($2.90). Daily mass is held at 8am, 5:30 and 6pm; Sunday mass at 8, 9, and 10am, noon, 6 and 7:30pm.

V. Szent István tér 33. (℅) 1/317-2859. Church, free; treasury, 150 Ft (55¢); tower, 400 Ft ($1.45). Church, daily 7am–7pm, except during services; treasury, daily 9am–5pm (10am–4pm in winter); Szent Jobb Chapel, Mon–Sat 9am–5pm (10am–4pm in winter) and Sun 1–5pm; tower, Apr–Oct 10am–6pm, (closed Nov–Mar). Metro: Arany János utca (Blue line) or Bajcsy-Zsilinszky út (Yellow line).

Belvárosi Plébániatemplom (Inner City Parish Church) ★ The Inner City Parish Church, standing flush against the Erzsébet Bridge in Pest, is one of the city's great architectural monuments, and the oldest building in Pest. The 12th-century Romanesque church first built on this spot was constructed inside the remains of the walls of the Roman fortress of Contra-Aquincum. In the early 14th century, a Gothic church was built, and this medieval church, with numerous additions and reconstructions reflecting the architectural trends of the time, stands today. Both Gothic and baroque elements can be observed on the exterior. Inside are niches built in both styles, as well as a *mihrab* (prayer niche) dating from the Turkish occupation, evidence of its conversion in those years to a mosque. The painting on the altar is the work of the 20th-century artist Pál Molnár (his work can also be seen in St. Anne's Church). The church was almost torn down when the Erzsébet Bridge was built in the late 19th century. Fortunately, an alternative plan won out, calling for the new bridge to wind around the church in a serpentine fashion (this interesting construction is best viewed from Gellért Hill). Daily mass is held at 6:30am and 6pm; Sunday mass at 9am, 10am, noon, and 6pm.

V. Március 15 tér. (℅) 1/318-3108. Free admission. Mon–Sat 6am–7pm, Sun 8am–7pm. Metro: Ferenciek tere (Blue line).

Moments **A Heavenly View**

The tower of St. Stephen's Church offers great views of the city. The climb is not recommended for the weak of knees or lungs, but a newly installed elevator will whisk you up in no time.

Dohány Synagogue ✿ Built in 1859, this is the world's second-largest synagogue (and the largest in Europe). Budapest's Jewish community still uses it. The architecture has striking Byzantine and Moorish elements; the interior is vast and ornate, with two balconies, and the unusual presence of an organ.

The synagogue has a rich but tragic history. Adolf Eichmann arrived with the occupying Nazi forces in March 1944 to supervise the establishment of the Jewish ghetto and the subsequent deportations. Up to 20,000 Jews took refuge inside the synagogue complex, of whom 7,000 did not survive the bleak winter of 1944–45. They're buried in the courtyard, where you can also see a transported piece of the original brick ghetto wall. An ambitious restoration was recently completed, funded in large part by a foundation set up by the American actor Tony Curtis, who is of Hungarian-Jewish descent. The building's original splendor is now apparent. The National Jewish Museum is inside the Synagogue complex (see "More Museums & Sights," below).

VII. Dohány u. 2–8. ✆ 1/342-8949. Admission by donation. Officially open Tues–Thurs 10am–5pm, Fri 10am–3pm, Sun 10am–1pm. Metro: Astoria (Red line) or Deák tér (all lines).

BUDA
MUSEUMS

Budapesti Történeti Múzeum (Budapest History Museum) ✿ This museum, also known as the Castle Museum, is the best place to get a sense of the once-great medieval Buda. It might be worth it to splurge for a guided tour; even though the museum's descriptions are written in English, the history of the palace's repeated construction and destruction is so confusing and arcane that it's difficult to understand what you're really seeing.

"The Medieval Royal Palace and its Gothic Statues" exhibit consists almost entirely of rooms and artifacts uncovered during the post–World War II excavation and rebuilding of the palace. A visit here is more notable perhaps for the rooms and halls themselves than for the fragments and occasional undamaged pieces of statues, stone carvings, earthenware, and the like. The recently opened "History of Budapest Since 1686" exhibit is notable for its photographs.

I. In Buda Palace, Wing E, on Castle Hill. ✆ 1/225-7815. Admission 500 Ft ($1.80). Guided tours by qualified staff in English for serious history buffs, price negotiable, are available upon advance request. May 15–Sept 15, Wed–Mon 10am–6pm; Sept 16–May 14, Wed–Mon 10am–5pm. Bus: Várbusz from Moszkva tér or 16 from Deák tér to Castle Hill. Funicular: From Clark Ádám tér to Castle Hill.

Nemzeti Galéria (Hungarian National Gallery) ✿ A repository of Hungarian art from medieval times to the 20th century, the Hungarian National Gallery is an enormous museum whose entire collection you couldn't possibly view during a single visit. The museum was founded during the great reform period of the mid-19th century and moved to its present location in Buda Palace in 1975. Few people outside Hungary are familiar with even the country's best-known artists. Nevertheless, Hungary has produced some fine artists, particularly in the late 19th century, and this is the place to view their work. The giants of the time are the brilliant Mihály Munkácsy ✿✿, whose masterpieces include *The Lintmakers, Condemned Cell,* and *Woman Carrying Wood;* László Paál, a painter of village scenes, including *Village Road in Berzova, Path in the Forest at Fontainbleau,* and *Depth of the Forest;* Károly Ferenczy ✿✿, whose mastery of light is seen in *Morning Sunshine* and *Evening in March;* and Pál Szinyei Merse, the plein air artist, whose own development paralleled that of the early French impressionists (see *Picnic in May*). Some other artists to look for are Gyula Benczœr, who painted grand historical scenes; Károly Lotz, best known as a

Impressions

When I got tired of the noisy streets of Pest and the artificial gay life there, I loved to wander about quaint silent Buda, where everything and everybody seemed to have stood still a couple of centuries ago.
—Elizabeth Keith Morris, English memoirist, 1931

fresco painter (*Opera House, Matthias Church*), here represented by a number of nudes and several fine thunderstorm paintings; and Bertalan Székely, a painter of historical scenes and landscapes. József Rippl-Rónai's canvases are premier examples of Hungarian postimpressionism and art nouveau (see *Father and Uncle Piacsek Drinking Red Wine and Grandmother*), while Tivadar Csontváry Kosztka, the "Rousseau of the Danube," is considered by some critics to be a genius of early modern art.

I. In Buda Palace, Wings B, C, and D, on Castle Hill. © 1/375-5567. Admission 500 Ft ($1.80). Mar 16–Nov 14, Tues–Sun 10am–6pm; Nov 15–Mar 15, Tues–Sun 10am–4pm. Bus: Várbusz from Moszkva tér or 16 from Deák tér to Castle Hill. Funicular: From Clark Ádám tér to Castle Hill.

A FAMOUS CHURCH

Mátyás Templom (Matthias Church) Officially named the Church of Our Lady, this symbol of Buda's Castle District is popularly known as Matthias Church after the much-loved 15th-century renaissance king, the main donor of the building, who was twice married here. Although the structure dates to the mid-13th century, like other old churches in Budapest it has an interesting history of destruction and reconstruction, always being refashioned in the architectural style of the time. The last two Hungarian kings (Habsburgs) were crowned in the church: Franz Joseph in 1867 (Liszt wrote and performed his *Coronation Mass*) and Charles IV in 1916. The church interior is decorated with works of two outstanding 19th-century Hungarian painters, Károly Lotz and Bertalan Székely. Organ concerts are held here every other Friday evening in July and August at 8pm. Daily mass is held at 8:30am, 12:30pm, and 6pm; Sunday mass at 8:30am, 9:30am, noon, and 6pm.

I. Szentháromság tér 2. © 1/355-5657. Church, free; exhibition rooms beneath the altar, 200 Ft (70¢). Daily 9:30am–6pm. Bus: Várbusz from Moszkva tér or 16 from Deák tér Castle Hill. Funicular: From Clark Ádám tér to Castle Hill.

SPECTACULAR VIEWS

Gellért Hegy (Gellért Hill) *Moments* Gellért Hill, towering 230m above the Danube, offers the single best panorama of the city. The hill is named after the iron-fisted Italian Bishop Gellért, who assisted Hungary's first Christian king, Stephen I, in converting the Magyars. Gellért became a martyr when vengeful pagans rolled him in a barrel to his death from the side of the hill on which this enormous statue now stands. The bishop defiantly holds a cross in his outstretched hand.

On top of Gellért Hill you'll find the **Liberation Monument,** built in 1947, supposedly to commemorate the Red Army's liberation of Budapest from Nazi occupation, though many believe that Admiral Horthy, Hungary's wartime leader, had planned the statue prior to the liberation to honor his fighter-pilot son, who was killed in the war. A mammoth statue, it's one of the last Socialist realist memorials you'll find in Hungary. The statue's centerpiece, a giant female figure holding a leaf aloft, is affectionately known as *Kiflis Zsuzsa* (*kifli* is a crescent-shaped roll eaten daily by many Hungarians, while Zsuzsa, or Susie, is a common girl's name). Hungarian children like to call the smaller flame-holding figure on her side *Fagylaltos fiú* (the boy with the ice-cream cone).

Also atop Gellért Hill is the **Citadella** (*©* **1/365-6076**), a symbol of power built by the Austrians in 1851 for military control, shortly after they crushed the Hungarian War of Independence of 1848–49. It costs 300 Ft ($1.10) to enter the Citadella, open daily from 9am to 7pm. Although there's not much inside, the view is great. To get here, take bus no. 27 from Móricz Zsigmond körtér or hike up on any of the various paved pathways that originate at the base of the hill.

Halászbástya (Fisherman's Bastion) *Overrated*   The neo-Romanesque Fisherman's Bastion, perched on the edge of Buda's Castle District near Matthias Church and the Hilton Hotel, affords a marvelous panorama of Pest. Built at the turn of the last century, it was intended mainly for decorative purposes, despite its military appearance. Looking out over the Danube to Pest, you can see (from left to right): Margaret Island and the Margaret Bridge, Parliament, St. Stephen's Basilica, the Chain Bridge with the Hungarian Academy of Sciences and the Gresham Palace behind it, the Vigadó Concert Hall, the Inner City Parish Church, the Erzsébet Bridge, and the Szabadság Bridge. To get to the Halászbástya, take the Várbusz from Moszkva tér or bus no. 16 from Deák tér, or funicular from Clark Ádám tér to Castle Hill.

ÓBUDA
ROMAN RUINS

The **ruins of Aquincum** *★*, the once-bustling capital of the Roman province of Pannonia, are spread throughout the southern part of Óbuda. The various sites are far enough away from each other, and the layout of modern Óbuda sufficiently anti-pedestrian, that it's difficult to see everything. The main Budapest-Szentendre highway cuts through Óbuda, causing no small amount of pedestrian frustration. Fortunately, two major sites are right across the road from each other, near the Aquincum station of the suburban HÉV railroad. The ruined **Amphitheater of the Civilian Town** is directly beside the HÉV station. It's open all the time and you're free to wander through (you should be aware, though, that homeless people may live inside its walls). Across the highway from the amphitheater stand the ruins of the Civilian Town. Everything is visible from the roadside, except for the collection of the **Aquincum Museum,** at III. Szentendrei u. 139 (*©* **1/368-8241**). This neoclassical structure was built at the end of the 19th century in harmony with its surroundings. The museum exhibits coins, utensils, jewelry, and pottery from Roman times. Its most unique exhibit is the portable water organ from A.D. 228 Entry is 400 Ft ($1.45). It's open from May to September, Tuesday through Sunday from 9am to 6pm; and from Oct to Apr, Tuesday through Sunday 9am to 5pm. Take the HÉV suburban railroad from Batthyány tér to Aquincum.

BRIDGING PEST & BUDA

Széchenyi Lánchíd (The Chain Bridge) *Moments*   The Chain Bridge is, along with Parliament and the Castle, one of the dominant symbols of Budapest. As the first permanent bridge across the Danube (1849), it paved the way for the union of Buda, Óbuda, and Pest into a single city. Prior to 1849, people relied on a pontoon bridge that had to be dismantled when ships passed and could be swept away in stormy weather. The initiative for the Chain Bridge came from the indefatigable Count István Széchenyi, the leading figure of Hungarian society during the mid–19th-century Age of Reform. The Scotsman Adam

Impressions

*How much beauty there is in the Chain Bridge, what elegant silence,
haughty humility, charming lightness, and archaic melancholy!*
                         —Antal Szerb, 20th-century Hungarian writer

Clark, for whom the square on the Buda side of the bridge is named, came to
Budapest to supervise the massive project; he chose to remain in the city until
his death many years later. The bridge was blown up by the retreating Nazis in
World War II, but was rebuilt immediately after the war. Located in the heart of
the city, it's best admired at night, when it's lit up like a chandelier (until midnight). It's an easy walk across if you're heading to Castle Hill—or merely want
a mid-river view of the city.

2 More Museums & Sights

PEST

Bélyegmúzeum (Postal Stamp Museum)   This may seem like an attraction of decidedly limited appeal, but generations of philatelists the world over
have admired the artistic creations of Magyar Posta. This wonderful little
museum has rack after rack of the country's finest stamps. The mistakenly
printed upside-down "Madonna with Child" in Rack 49 is Hungary's most
valuable stamp. The stamps of **Rack 65** abjectly demonstrate how the worst
inflation the world has ever seen devastated Hungary in the 1940s. Variations on
Lenin and Stalin can be seen in **Racks 68 to 77,** and **Racks 70 to 80** contain numerous brilliant examples of Socialist realism. You don't have to be a
stamp collector to enjoy a visit to the Postal Stamp Museum. The staff is
extremely friendly and well informed.

VII. Hársfa u. 47. ✆ 1/341-5526. Admission 100 Ft (35¢). April–Oct, Tues–Sun 10am–6pm; Nov–March,
Tues–Sun 10am–5:30pm. Tram: 4 or 6 to Wesselényi utca.

Iparművészeti Múzeum (Museum of Applied Arts)   It's worth a trip to
the Museum of Applied Arts just to see the marvelous building it's housed in,
designed by Ödön Lechner in the 1890s. Lechner, whose most famous creation
is the Town Hall in the Great Plain city of Kecskemét (see p. 210), is the
architect who was most adventurous in combining traditional Hungarian folk
elements with the art nouveau style of his time. The building's ceramic decora-
tion comes from the famous Zsolnay factory in Pécs. If you're impressed by this
structure, pay a visit to the former Post Office Savings Bank on Hold utca,
another fine example of Lechner's work (see "Walking Tour 3: Leopold Town &
Theresa Town," in chapter 7, "Strolling Around Budapest"). The museum's permanent exhibits are divided into five sections: furniture; textiles; metalwork;
ceramics, porcelain, and glass; and an eclectic display of books, leather, and
ivory. Much of the museum's space is given to temporary exhibitions.

IX. üllői út 33–37. ✆ 1/217-5222. Admission 300 Ft (85¢). Open April–Nov, Tues–Sun 10am–6pm, and
Dec–March 10am–4pm. Metro: Ferenc körút (Blue line).

**Nemzeti Zsidó Múzeum és Levéltár (National Jewish Museum and
Archives)**   The museum is located in the Dohány Synagogue complex; a
tablet outside informs visitors that Theodor Herzl, the founder of Zionism, was
born on this spot. The four-room museum is devoted to the long history of Jews
in Hungary. Displays include Sabbath and holiday items (including some

Where Have All the Statues Gone?

Ever wonder where all the vanished Communist statues went after the fall? Just a decade ago Budapest, and the rest of Hungary for that matter, was filled with memorials to Lenin, to Marx and Engels, to the Red Army, and to the many lesser-known figures of Hungarian and international Communism. Torn rudely from their pedestals in the aftermath of 1989, they sat for a few years in warehouses gathering dust, until a controversial plan for a **Socialist Statue Park** (Szoborpark Múzeum) was realized. The park's inconvenient location and the relatively small number of statues on display (reflecting nothing of their former ubiquitousness) make it less than it could be. Moreover, the best examples of the genre, dating from the Stalinist period of the late 1940s and 1950s, were removed from public view long before 1989 and have presumably long since been destroyed.

Located in the XXII district (extreme southern Buda) on Balatoni út (℡ **1/227-7446**), the museum park is a memorial to an era, to despotism, and to bad taste. The museum gift shop sells all sorts of Communist-era memorabilia, such as T-shirts, medals, and cassettes of Red Army marching songs. Admission is 300 Ft ($1.10). The park is open March 16 to November 13 daily, from 10am to dusk (November 14 to March 15 to 4pmonly). To get there, take the black-lettered bus no. 7 from Ferenciek tere to Kosztolányi Dezsó tér. Board a yellow Volán bus (to Érd) at Platform 6 for a 20-minute ride to the park.

gorgeous examples of Herend Passover plates) and ritual and everyday artifacts. The last room contains a small but moving exhibit on the Holocaust in Hungary.

VII. Dohány u. 2–8. ℡ 1/342-8949. Admission 500 Ft ($1.80). Guided tours in English 1,000 Ft ($3.60). Mon–Thurs 10am–5pm, Fri 10am–3pm, Sun 10am–1pm. Closed Sat. Metro: Astoria (Red line) or Deák tér (all lines).

Postamúzeum (Post Office Museum) ✰ *Finds*   The exhibits here are of limited interest, but the building itself and the apartment in which the museum is situated—the opulently furnished former Sexlehner family flat—are simply dazzling. Chandeliers dangle from the frescoed ceilings, and intricately carved wood moldings trim the walls.

VI. Andrássy út 3. ℡ 1/269-6838. Admission 50 Ft (20¢). Tues–Sun 10am–6pm. (In winter closing at 4pm) Metro: Bajcsy-Zsilinszky út (Yellow line) or Deák tér (all lines).

A JEWISH CEMETERY

Kozma Cemetery *Finds*   The city's main Jewish cemetery is in the eastern end of the Kőbánya district, a long tram ride from the center of town. An estimated half-million people are buried here. A vast, peaceful place, it's still in use today. Ornate art deco tombs stand proudly near the main entrance, their faded grandeur a testament both to the former status of those buried beneath them and to the steady passage of time. The cemetery is also the site of Hungary's most moving Holocaust memorial, a set of nine walls with the names of victims etched in. About 6,500 names appear, of the 600,000 Hungarian Jews estimated to have perished in the war. Survivors and relatives have penciled in hundreds of additional names.

X. Kozma u. 6. © **1/342-1335**. Free admission. Mon–Thurs 8am–4pm, Fri and Sun 8am–2pm. Tram: 37 from Blaha Lujza tér to the next to last stop.

BUDA

Hadtörténeti Múzeum (Museum of the History of Warfare)   Housed in a former barracks in the northwestern corner of the Castle District, this museum has exhibits from the time of the Turkish occupation to the 20th century. Uniforms, decorations, models, weapons, maps, and photographs are unfortunately accompanied only by Hungarian text. The Turkish weaponry display is particularly interesting, but the highlight is undoubtedly the room devoted to the 1956 Hungarian Uprising. Here, consecutive panels of large, mounted photographs detail the 13 chaotic days. Artifacts round out the display, in particular a Soviet flag with the center cut out (where the hammer and sickle were), and the legendary hand of Stalin, the only known surviving piece of the giant statue of the Soviet dictator whose public destruction was one of the failed uprising's most cherished moments. Toy soldiers ⭐ are available in the gift shop.

I. Tóth Árpád sétány 40. © **1/356-9522**. Admission 250 Ft (90¢). Apr through Sept Tues–Sun 10am–6pm, Oct trough March 10am to 4pm. Bus: Várbusz from Moszkva tér or 16 from Deák tér to Castle Hill. Funicular: From Clark Ádám tér to Castle Hill.

Kereskedelmi és Vendéglátóipari Múzeum (Museum of Commerce and Catering)   These are two separate but related exhibits located on opposite sides of a courtyard in the Castle District; a single ticket entitles you to entry to both. The prime attraction of the catering exhibit is the antique baking equipment: pie tins, cookie molds, and utensils. The commerce exhibit has a wider appeal, with assorted (somewhat randomly assembled) vintage items: cigar boxes, advertisements, liquor bottles, fountain pens, sewing equipment, and ration books, all evoking that wonder turn-of-the-century Pest atmosphere. A "Gyula Meinl" display shows that the still ubiquitous Austrian grocery chain had an early presence in Hungary. Two fascinating photos (why they're here is inexplicable) show the World War II destruction of the Chain Bridge and the Erzsébet Bridge.

I. Fortuna u. 4. © **1/375-6249**. Admission 100 Ft (35¢). Wed and Thurs 10am–5pm; Sat and Sun 10am–6pm. Bus: Várbusz from Moszkva tér or 16 from Deák tér to Castle Hill. Funicular: From Clark Ádám tér to Castle Hill.

Kőzépkori Zsidó Imaház (Medieval Jewish Prayer House) *Finds*   This tiny, medieval Sephardic synagogue was unexpectedly discovered in the 1960s during general excavation work in the Castle District. It dates to approximately 1364, when Jews were allowed to return to the Castle District, from which they had been expelled four years earlier by King Lajos. But after the massacre of Buda's Jews in the late 17th century (following the defeat of the occupying Turks by a Habsburg-led Christian army), the synagogue was turned into an apartment and, over the ensuing centuries, forgotten. A nearby excavation unearthed the ruins of another, much larger, synagogue dating from 1461; all that remains of it are a keystone, on display now inside this synagogue, and three stone columns standing in the courtyard here. Some Hebrew gravestones are also on display behind a grate in the entryway; the small one in the center of the front row dates from the 3rd century A.D. The English-speaking caretaker will give you a free informal tour if you express an interest.

I. Táncsics Mihály u. 26. © **1/355-8849**. Admission 100 Ft (35¢). May–Oct Tues–Sun 10am–6pm. Bus: Várbusz from Moszkva tér or 16 from Deák tér to Castle Hill. Funicular: From Clark Ádám tér to Castle Hill.

Ludwig Museum   In the northern end of the Buda Palace, this was formerly the Museum of the Hungarian Worker's Movement. Now converted to a more politically correct purpose, it houses a less-than-inspiring permanent exhibition of contemporary Hungarian and international art.

I. In Buda Palace, Wing A, on Castle Hill. © 1/375-9175. Admission 300 Ft ($1.10); free Tues. Tues–Sun 10am–6pm. Bus: Várbusz from Moszkva tér or 16 from Deák tér to Castle Hill. Funicular: From Clark Ádám tér to Castle Hill.

Semmelweis Orvostörténeti Múzeum (Semmelweis Museum of Medical History)   This museum, which traces the history of medicine from ancient times to the modern era, is located in the former home of Ignác Semmelweis, Hungary's leading 19th-century physician. Semmelweis is hailed as the "savior of mothers" for his role in identifying the cause of puerperal (childbed) fever and preventing it by advocating that physicians wash their hands between patients, an uncommon practice of the time. The museum, spread over four rooms, displays everything from early medical instruments to anatomical models to old medical textbooks. There's also a faithfully reconstructed 19th-century pharmacy. Descriptions are only in Hungarian, but many exhibits are self-explanatory. In the Semmelweis Memorial Room, two bookcases display the eminent scholar's collection of medical texts. Keen eyes might notice the seven volumes of Osler's Modern Medicine, written long after Semmelweis's death; they were a gift from former U.S. President George Bush to the late József Antall, who became the prime minister of Hungary after the first democratic elections in 1990. Antall had previously been director of the Semmelweis Museum.

I. Apród u. 1–3. © 1/375-3533. Admission 200 Ft (70¢). Tues–Sun 10:30am–5:30pm. Take any bus or tram to Döbrentei tér (for example, bus no. 8 from Március 15 tér).

A MUSLIM SHRINE

Gül Baba Türbéje (Tomb of Gül Baba) ⭐ *Finds*   The unfortunate Turkish dervish Gül Baba died at dinner. It was no ordinary meal either, but a 1541 gala in Matthias Church celebrating the conquest of Buda. Gül Baba was a member of a Turkish order involved in horticulture, specifically in the development of new species of roses; today his tomb, located in a wonderfully steep, twisting neighborhood at the beginning of the Hill of Roses (Rózsadomb) district, is maintained as a Muslim shrine by the Turkish government. The descriptions are in Hungarian and Turkish, but an English-language pamphlet is available on request. The tomb, set in a park and surrounded by lovely rose gardens, is the northernmost Muslim shrine in Europe. The recently restored museum was reopened in 1997 in an official ceremony attended by Turkey's President Demirel.

II. Mecset u. 14. © 1/355-8764. Admission 200 Ft (70¢). Tues–Sun 10am–6pm. Tram: 4 or 6 to the Buda side of Margaret Bridge; the most direct route to Gül Baba tér is via Mecset utca, off Margaret utca.

Impressions

There is no other town of the land of the faithful, and perhaps in all the world which gushes forth in such wonderful abundance its springs to cure all ills, as Buda.

—Evlia Chelebi, Turkish traveler, 16th century

> **_Fun Fact_ Did You Know?**
>
> • A network consisting of 6 miles (10 km) of tunnels, built in the Middle Ages for military purposes, lies underneath Buda's Castle District.
>
> • Budapest was the site of the European continent's first underground metro line, which you can still ride today (the Yellow line).
>
> • Budapest did not become a unified city until 1873, when Pest, Buda, and Óbuda merged.
>
> • All of Budapest's bridges were blown up by the retreating Nazis in the final days of World War II.
>
> • The Red Army liberated Pest from Nazi occupation on January 18, 1945, but did not manage to liberate Buda until February 13.
>
> • The Swedish diplomat Raoul Wallenberg, stationed in Budapest, saved thousands of Jews from Nazi deportation by issuing fake passports and setting up "safe houses," only to disappear himself into the Soviet gulag after the city's liberation.
>
> • Budapest's Jewish population (about 80,000) is the largest of any European city outside Russia.
>
> • Budapest is home to the northernmost Turkish shrine in Europe, the tomb of Gúl Baba.
>
> • The elusive chess champion Bobby Fischer is rumored to be living somewhere in Budapest.

ÓBUDA

Lakásmúzeum (Zsigmond Kun Folk Art Museum) ★★ *Finds*   Here in Mr. Zsigmond Kun's former apartment you can admire his wonderful collection of Hungarian folk art. For almost a century he traveled around Hungary collecting and documenting folk art. On display are ceramics and brandy flasks, tapestries and chairs, sheep bells, shepherds' hats, and hundreds of other examples of Hungarian folk art. Mr. Kun died at the age of 107 on January 2. 2000; his life spanned three centuries. The museum staff speaks with great fondness of "Zsigmond Bácsi" (Uncle Zsigmond). The museum is currently under renovation, and is expected to re-open by Christmas 2002.

III. Fő tér 4. ℭ **1/368-3811**. Admission 100 Ft (35¢); English-language guidebook 50 Ft (20¢). Tues–Sun 2–6pm. Train: HÉV suburban railroad from Batthyány tér to Árpád híd.

Varga Imre Gyűjtemény (Imre Varga Collection) ★★ *Finds*   Imre Varga is Hungary's best-known contemporary sculptor. This small museum, just off Óbuda's Fő tér, shows a good cross section of his sensitive, piercing work. Historical subjects on display inside the museum range from the pudgy, balding figure of Imre Nagy, reluctant hero of the 1956 Hungarian Uprising, to the dapper, capped Béla Bartók. The museum also has a garden where Varga's sad, broken figures stand forlornly or sit on benches resting their weary feet; live cats prance around in the garden, enhancing the atmosphere. For an example of the sculptor's work in a public context, see the recently installed statue of Imre Nagy near Parliament.

III. Laktanya u. 7. ℭ **1/250-0274**. Admission 250 Ft (70¢). Tues–Sun 10am–6pm. Train: HÉV suburban railroad from Batthyány tér to Árpád híd.

Victor Vasarely Museum This museum, devoted to the works of the Hungarian-born founder of op art, was opened in 1987 after the artist donated some 400 works to the Hungarian state. A huge, airy place, it extends over two floors. On display is a full range of the late artist's colorful, geometric art.

III. Szentlelek tér 1. 🕐 1/250-1540. Admission 200 Ft (70¢); free Wed. Apr–Oct Tues–Sun 10am–6pm, Nov–Mar 10am–5pm. Train: HÉV suburban railroad from Batthyány tér to Árpád híd.

AN ARCHITECTURAL WONDER

Leo Frankel Synagogue 🌟 Still in use today, the Leo Frankel Synagogue is about as bizarre an architectural creation as Budapest has to offer. This seemingly normal apartment building looks no different from its neighbors—until you notice the Star of David and the menorah carved into its facade. But that's just the beginning: The synagogue is lodged inside and completely fills the interior courtyard. The Synagogue was built in 1887–88. In 1928, it was surrounded by a six-story apartment house. This was done both to protect the Synagogue from anti-Semitic violence and to provide accommodation for 51 Jewish families, including the families of the synagogue's rabbis and cantors. During the Second World War, the Nazi invaders abused the Synagogue as a stable, and made it absolutely unusable. Since the 1990 regime change, the Synagogue has been restored twice, most recently in 2000.

Insider Tip: The whole scene is best viewed from above; climb the stairs, or take the elevator. An official tour of the synagogue is available through Chosen Tours (see "Specialty Tours," later in this chapter).

II. Frankel Léo u. 49. 🕐 1/326-1445. Open Mon–Fri 9am–1pm, by prior arrangement. Services Fri nights and Sat mornings. Admission: 550 Ft ($2) suggested, but any donations gratefully accepted. Tram: 17 from the Buda side of Margaret Bridge (2 stops).

3 Parks, Gardens & Playgrounds

Hungarians love a stroll in the park, and on weekends and summer afternoons, it seems as if the whole of Budapest is out enjoying what Hungarians lovingly refer to as "the nature."

Popular **Margaret Island (Margit-sziget)** 🌟🌟 has been a public park since 1908. The long, narrow island, connected to both Buda and Pest via the Margaret and Árpád bridges, is barred to most vehicular traffic. In addition to three important ruins—the Dominican Convent, a 13th- to 14th-century Franciscan church, and a 12th-century Premonstratensian chapel—facilities on the island include the Palatinus Strand open-air baths (see "Spa Bathing & Swimming: Budapest's Most Popular Thermal Baths," below), which draw upon the famous thermal waters under Margaret Island; the Alfréd Hajós Sport Pool; and the Open Air Theater. Sunbathers line the steep embankments along the river, and bikes are available for rent. (See "Getting Around by Bike," in chapter 3, "Getting to Know Budapest.") There are also several snack bars and open-air restaurants. Despite all this, Margaret Island remains a quiet, tranquil place. In any direction off the main road you can find well-tended gardens or a patch of grass under the shade of a willow tree for a private picnic. Margaret Island is best reached by bus no. 26 from Nyugati tér, which runs the length of the island, or tram no. 4 or 6, which stops at the entrance to the island midway across the Margaret Bridge. *Warning:* These are popular lines for pickpockets. See "Safety" in "Fast Facts: Budapest," in chapter 3, "Getting to Know Budapest."

City Park (Városliget) 🌟 is an equally popular place to spend a summer day, and families are everywhere in evidence. Heroes' Square, at the end of Andrássy

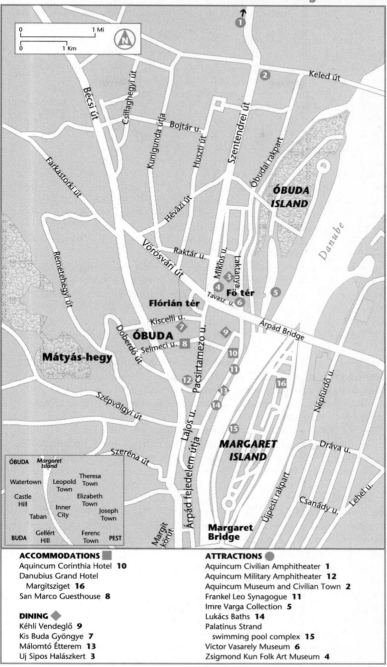

út, is the most logical starting point for a walk in City Park. Built in 1896 as part of the Hungarian millennial celebrations, it has been the site of some important moments in Hungarian history. The lake behind the square is used for boating in summer and for ice-skating in winter. The Vajdahunyad Castle by the lake was built as a temporary structure in 1896 for the millennial celebration to demonstrate the different architectural styles in Hungary; it was so popular that a permanent structure was eventually designed to replace it. It is now the home of the **Agricultural Museum,** the largest of its kind in Europe (200 Ft (70¢) admission; open Tue to Sun 10am to 6pm, in winter 5pm; Metro: Széchenyi Fürdő Yellow line). The park's **Animal Garden Boulevard** (Allatkerti körút), the favorite street of generations of Hungarian children, is where the zoo, the circus, and the amusement park are all found (see "Especially for Kids," below). Gundel, Budapest's most famous restaurant, is also here, as are the Széchenyi Baths, with a splendid outdoor pool. The southern end of City Park is considerably less crowded, with fewer buildings. The **Transport Museum** is among the few sights here, while the nearby Petőfi Csarnok is the venue for a variety of popular cultural events, concerts and flea market fairs.

The Yellow metro line makes stops at Hősök tere (Heroes' Square), at the edge of the park, and Széchenyi Fürdő, in the middle of it.

There are numerous parks and nature reserves in the **Buda Hills.** You can ride the Children's Railroad through the hills or the János Hill chairlift to its highest point (see "Especially for Kids," below). The Buda Hills are a great place to explore on your own; you'll hardly ever stray too far from a bus or tram line, and yet you'll feel as if you're in the countryside, far from a bustling capital city. Moszkva tér is the best place to start an excursion into the hills. Pick up tram no. 56 or bus no. 21, 22, or 28; get off when you see an area you like.

Our son, Aryeh, spent several months with us in Budapest and served as our consultant on **playgrounds.** You can depend on his recommendations. The Hungarian word for playground is *játszótér* (or játszó kert).

Károly kert ★★, a wonderful little enclosed park in the southern half of the Inner City, is bordered by Ferenczy István utca, Magyar utca, and Henszlmann Imre utca. Enter the park through a wrought-iron gate. Once inside, you'll find swings and seesaws, an enclosed miniature soccer field, a sandbox with a slide emptying into it, and a nice stretch of green grass to run on. In the middle of all this is a fountain surrounded by flowers. The equipment is not as modern as at some of the city's other playgrounds, but the park has a distinct Old-World charm. Indeed, it once belonged to the adjacent Károlyi mansion. The home of Mihály Károlyi, who served briefly as Hungarian Prime Minister in 1918, was recently restored to its old splendor and continues to function as the venue for the Museum of Hungarian Literature. Its location in the Inner City makes it a convenient destination.

Another fine playground is located not far from Buda's busy transportation hub, Móricz Zsigmond körtér. At the intersection of Villányi út and Tas Vezér utca (directly across the street from the Hotel Flamenco), this playground is entirely self-enclosed (no dogs allowed), very large, and has lots of modern equipment. The park is clean and well maintained.

Pest's **City Park** (see above) has a large, shaded playground called Iskolás játszókert. It is in the southwest corner of the park, near the intersection of Dózsa György út and Ajtósi Dürer sor. This narrow, rectangular shaped playground has an excellent wooden climbing structure and innovative swings.

Jugglers, dancers and an assortment of acrobats fill the street.

She shoots you a wide-eyed look as a seven-foot cartoon character approaches.

What brought you here was wanting the kids

to see something magical while they still believed in magic.

America Online Keyword: Travel

With 700 airlines, 50,000 hotels and over 5,000 cruise and vacation getaways, you can now go places you've always dreamed of.

Travelocity.com
A Sabre Company
Go Virtually Anywhere.

"WORLD'S LEADING TRAVEL WEB SITE 5 YEARS IN A ROW" WORLD TRAVEL AWARDS

I HAVE TO CALL THE TRAVEL AGENCY AGAIN. DARN, OUT TO LUNCH. NOW I HAVE TO CALL THE AIRLINE. I HATE CALLING THE AIRLINES. I GOT PUT ON HOLD AGAIN. "INSTRUMENTAL TOP-40" ... LOVELY. I HATE GETTING PUT ON HOLD. TICKET PRICES ARE ALL OVER THE MAP. HOW DO I DIAL INTERNATIONALLY? OH SHOOT, FORGOT THE RENTAL CAR. I'M STILL ON HOLD. THIS MUSIC IS GIVING ME A HEADACHE. I WONDER IF SOMEONE ELSE HAS CHEAPER FLIGHTS. FORGET IT, CAN'T TAKE IT ANYMORE ... I'M HANGING UP.

YAHOO! TRAVEL
100% MUZAK-FREE

Booking your trip online at Yahoo! Travel is simple. You compare the best prices. You click. You go have fun. Tickets, hotels, rental cars, cruises & more. Sorry, no muzak.

YAHOO!®
Travel
travel.yahoo.com

Other good playgrounds can be found in VII. Almássy tér, between Blaha Lujza tér and Oktogon, and at Hild tér, in a small park near the Pest side of the Chain Bridge.

Margaret Island, for all its charm, lacks a decent playground. The best it has to offer is just off the main road to the left after you pass the stadium at the head of the island.

If you find yourself in Buda's Watertown district (perhaps on our Watertown walking tour, see p. 148), and you need to make a little play stop, there is a small, colorful neighborhood playground on Franklin utca, between Donáti utca and Iskola utca. It is a quiet, residential area.

Another neighborhood playground is found in **Pillangó Park,** just across the street from the Pillangó utca metro station (Red line). This playground is situated in the midst of a huge Socialist-era housing development in outer Pest. The architecture is not pretty, but this is how most people live in Budapest; it's worth a look. The playground features a manually operated merry-go-round for the little ones, and another nearby playground has a cable swing for bigger kids.

Rainy day desperation? Take the kids to the Moszkva tér McDonald's or to IKEA (Red line metro to örs vezér tere), both of which have decent indoor play spaces.

4 Especially for Kids

The following attractions are for kids of all ages, since just about everyone loves a train ride in the hills, a Ferris wheel, or a good puppet show. Three attractions here—the zoo, the amusement park, and the circus—are located in City Park (Városliget), along the famed Animal Garden Boulevard (Állatkerti körút). You could easily spend a whole child-oriented day here.

See also later in this chapter for information on the Palatinus Strand outdoor swimming pool complex and horse and pony riding in the Buda Hills.

MUSEUMS

Csodák Palotája (Palace of Wonders) *Kids*   Opened in 1997, and sponsored in part by the Soros Foundation, Csodák Palotája is an interactive science center featuring dozens of fun, educational exhibits—for instance, lasers, optical puzzles, and mazes—in one large room. It's best for kids over 3 years old.

XIII. Váci út 19. (℃ **1/350-6397** or 1/350-6398. Admission 450 Ft ($1.60) adults, 400 Ft ($1.45) children 3 and over, free for children under 3. Tues–Fri 9am–5pm; Sat–Sun 10am–6pm. Closed in Aug. Metro: Lehel tér (Blue line). From the metro station, walk north on Váci út (in direction of Bulcsu utca and Déval utca).

Természettudományi Múzeum (Museum of Natural History) *Kids*
Using the natural history of the Carpathian Basin, the exhibitions here trace human development from the earliest times to the emergence of civilized society. The museum features a large "discovery room" on the first floor, in which all the exhibits are interactive. Participation is both educational and fun. The museum is nicely situated next to Orczy Kert (Orczy Garden), a large park featuring over 100 different species of trees and a small lake. Until after World War II, the park belonged to the Ludoviceum, the Hungarian Military School, which now houses the museum.

VIII. Ludovika tér 2. (℃ **1/313-5015** or 1/333-0655. Admission 240 Ft (85¢) adults, 120 Ft (45¢) children. Open Wed–Mon, 10am–6pm, closing 1 hr. earlier in winter. Metro: Nagyvárad tér (Blue line).

Impressions

The last time we were here we happened to see the breaking of the winter's ice, and it was a wondrous sight to behold the great blocks borne down by the swift current, heave and struggle and beat against each other, and then clash headlong against the massive stonework of the Chain Bridge, with a crash like that of a volley of musketry.
                                        —Nina Elizabeth Mazuchalli, English traveler, 1881

FAMILY FUN IN CITY PARK

Allatkert (Zoo) *Kids*   Opened in 1866, the zoo is located near the circus and the amusement park on City Park's famous Animal Garden Boulevard, a favorite spot of Hungarian youngsters for 130 years. Although the zoo has been modernized several times, it still retains the sad flavor of an old-style, fairly inhumane zoo. Nice attractions here are the pony rides and two important examples of art nouveau architecture: the main entrance gate and the elephant house. Two recently renovated greenhouses, the largest of their kind in Central Europe, contain spectacular tropical plants.

XIV. Allatkerti krt. 6–12. ℭ **1/343-6075.** Admission 450 Ft ($1.60) adults, 400 Ft ($1.45) children 14 and under. Daily 9am–7pm (to 5pm in winter). Metro: Hősök tere or Széchenyi fürdő (Yellow line).

Közlekedési Múzeum (Transport Museum) *Kids*   Located near the Petőfi Csarnok in the little touristed southeastern corner of City Park, this wonderful museum, which just celebrated its 100th anniversary in 1999, features large-scale 1:5 models of various kinds of historic vehicles, especially trains. The museum also features vintage motorcycles and bicycles, early model cars, and antique horse buggies. A model train set runs every 15 minutes on the mezzanine level; follow the crowds. On weekends, a film on aviation history is shown at 11am. The gift shop features all sorts of transportation-related trinkets. The aviation exhibit is housed in the Petőfi Csarnok, an all-purpose community center nearby; a single entrance ticket is valid for both exhibitions.

XIV. Városligeti krt. 11. ℭ **1/343-0565.** Admission 200 Ft (70¢), adults; 70Ft (25¢) children. Tues–Fri 10am–5pm, Sat–Sun 10am–6pm. Trolleybus: 74 from Károly körút (pick it up on Dohány utca, across the street from Dohány Synagogue) or 72 from Podmaniczky utca, near Nyugati Station.

Vidám Park (Amusement Park) *Kids*   Much frequented by Hungarian families, Vidám Park (literally "Happy Park"), unlike Disneyland or Copenhagen's Tivoli, is eminently affordable. Two rides in particular are not to be missed. The 100-year-old **Merry-Go-Round** (*Körhinta*) , constructed almost entirely of wood, was recently restored to its original, delightful grandeur. The riders must actively pump to keep the horses rocking. Authentic Wurlitzer music plays. As the carousel spins round and round, it creaks mightily. The **Ferris wheel** (*óriáskerék*) is also wonderful, although it has little in common with the rambunctious Ferris wheels of the modern age. A gangly, bright-yellow structure, it rotates at a liltingly slow pace, gently lifting you high into the sky for a remarkable view. The Vidám Park also features Europe's longest wooden roller coaster.

Note: Parents must pay for a ticket when accompanying young children, even if the child is too young to go on a ride by him- or herself.

Next door is a toddlers' amusement park (Kis Vidám Park), although several rides in the Vidám Park are also suitable for toddlers.

XIV. Állatkerti krt. 14–16. ℂ **1/343-0996**. Admission 300 Ft ($1.10) adults, 100 Ft (35¢) children; rides 200 Ft–600 Ft (70¢–$2.15). Apr–Sept, daily 10am–8pm; Oct–Mar, 10am–7pm. Metro: Széchenyi fürdő (Yellow line).

A RAILROAD & CHAIRLIFT

Gyermekvasút (Children's Railroad) ★★ *Kids*   Hungarian children, specially trained and under adult supervision, run this scenic narrow-gauge railway, making it especially exciting for youngsters. The youthful engineers are dressed in miniature versions of the official MÁV (Hungarian State Railways) uniforms, with all the appropriate paraphernalia. The railway was built in the late 1940s and was formerly run by the Young Pioneers, the youth movement of the Communist party, although these days it has no political affiliation. The train winds its 7 miles (11km) long way slowly through the Buda Hills, providing numerous panoramas along the way.

You can board at either terminus, or anywhere along the way. To get to the Hűvösvölgy terminus, take tram no. 56 from Moszkva tér to the last stop. To get to the Széchenyi-hegy terminus, take the same no. 56 tram from Moszkva tér two stations to the cogwheel railway (fogaskerekű vasút) (the cogwheel station is called Városmajor, and it is across the street from the Hotel Budapest, on Szilágyi Erzsébet fasor in Buda; see "By Cogwheel Railway & Funicular" under "Getting Around," in chapter 3, "Getting to Know Budapest"). One-way travel time is 45 minutes; call the Széchenyi hegy terminus (ℂ **1/395-5420**) for more information.

A one-way trip costs 140 Ft (50¢) for adults and 50 Ft (18¢) for children ages 4 to 14; a round-trip ticket is 260 Ft (95¢) and 90 Ft (32¢). Trains run every hour or so Mon–Fri 10am–5pm; and every 45 minutes or so on Sat and Sun 10am–6pm. No trains run on Mon Sept–Mar.

János-Hegy Libegő (János Hill Chairlift) ★ *Kids*   This somewhat primitive chairlift takes you up János Hill to within a steep 10-minute walk of Budapest's highest point. At the top is the neo-Romanesque *Erzsébet Kilátó* (Lookout Tower), built in 1910. It costs 150 Ft (55¢) to climb the tower (well worth it for the view); you'll find a nondescript snack bar there. The tower is open daily from 8am to 5pm. You can ride the chair back down, hike back down to the no. 158 bus, or, if you have a map of the Buda Hills, hike out to any number of other bus connections. Call Tourinform (ℂ **1/317-9800**) for more information.

XII. Zugligeti út 93. ℂ **1/394-3764**. A one-way chairlift trip costs 300 Ft ($1.10) for adults, 150 Ft (55¢) for children; a round-trip ticket is 500 Ft ($1.80) for adults, 250 Ft (90¢) for children. The lift operates Apr 1–Sept 15 9am–6pm; Sept 16–Mar 31 9am–4pm. Closed every 2nd Mon. Take bus no. 158 from Moszkva tér to the last stop.

ENTERTAINMENT: THE CIRCUS, PUPPET THEATERS & FOLK DANCING

Nagy Cirkusz (Great Circus) *Kids*   It's not the Big Apple Circus or Cirque du Soleil, but kids love it just the same. Budapest has a long circus tradition, though most Hungarian circus stars still opt for the more glamorous and financially rewarding circus life abroad. When buying tickets it's helpful to know that *porond* means ring level and *erkély* means balcony. The box office is open from 10am to 7pm.

XIV. Állatkerti krt. 7. ℂ **1/343-9630**. Tickets 600 Ft–1,000 Ft ($2.15–$3.60); children under 4 free. Performances one on weekdays, 3 on Sat and 2 on Sun afternoons. Metro: Hősök tere or Széchenyi fürdő (Yellow line).

IN-LINE SKATING & ICE SKATING

Görzenál Roller Blading *Kids*   If your kids enjoy in-line skating, skateboarding, and trampolining, this is the place for them. Rental skates are available for 400 Ft ($1.45). You can spend the day here on one admission price.

Kids Bábszínházak (Puppet Theaters)

Kids from all countries love Hungarian puppet theater ⚹. The shows are all in Hungarian, but with such standard fare as Cinderella, Peter and the Wolf, and Snow White, no one has trouble following the plot. The audience is an important part of the show: Hungarian children shriek "*Rossz farkas!*" ("Bad wolf!"), for instance, at every appearance of the villain in Peter and the Wolf.

Budapest has two puppet theaters, with the season running from September to mid-June. Tickets are extremely cheap, usually in the 300 Ft to 500 Ft ($1.10 to $1.80) range. The **Budapest Puppet Theater** (Budapesti Bábszínház) is at VI. Andrássy út 69 (☎ 1/321-5200); the nearest metro station is Oktogon (Yellow line). The **Kolibri Puppet Theater** (Kolibri Bábszínház) is at VI. Jókai tér 10 (☎ 1/353-4633); Jókai tér is halfway between the Oktogon and Opera stations of the Yellow metro line. Shows start at various times throughout the day, and tickets are available all day at the box offices.

III. Árpád fejedelem út 2000. ☎ 1/250-4800. Admission 500 Ft ($1.80). Sun–Thur 9am–8pm, Fri and Sat 9am–9pm. Bus: 6 from Nyugati pu. Train: HÉV suburban railway from Battyhány tér to Árpád fejedelem.

Jégpálya (Ice Ring) Pólus Center *Kids*   Pólus Center rink is a decent-sized rink in this shopping mall. Your other option for ice skating is in Vidámpark (see above). The fee is 390 Ft ($1.40) for half an hour. You can rent skates for 100 Ft (35¢), and can receive some basic training for 300 Ft ($1.10).

XV. Szentmihályi u. 131. ☎ 1/419-4070. Admission 200 Ft (70¢) for 1 hr. 200 Ft (70¢) to rent skates. Trolley bus: 6 from Keleti station.

5 For the Music Lover

Three museums in Budapest celebrate the contributions that great Hungarian artists have made in the realm of music.

The greatest Hungarian composer of the 19th century, and one of the country's most famous sons, was undoubtedly **Ferenc (Franz) Liszt** (1811–96). Although Liszt spent most of his life abroad, he maintained a deep interest in Hungarian culture and musical traditions, as evidenced by his well-known "Hungarian Rhapsodies." He also was one of the great virtuoso pianists of his century. Liszt created the symphonic poem with his *Les Preludes* (1848). He served as the first president of Budapest's Academy of Music, which is named after him.

If Liszt was the towering figure of 19th-century Hungarian music, **Béla Bartók** (1881–1945) and **Zoltán Kodály** (1882–1967) were the giants of the early 20th century. The founders of Hungarian ethnomusicology, Bartók and Kodály traveled the back roads of the country in the early 1900s, systematically recording not only Hungarian and Gypsy folk music but also music of the whole Carpathian Basin region. Peasant folk music had for hundreds of years been an important part of the rural culture in the region, but by the turn of the century it was in danger of being lost. In addition to saving an enormous wealth of music from oblivion, Bartók and Kodály made some important discoveries in their research, noting both the differences and the interrelationships between Hungarian and other folk music traditions (especially Gypsy music), which had over time fused considerably. Both men were composers, and the influence of the folk music they so cherished can be readily heard in their work. Kodály established the internationally acclaimed Kodály method of musical education and lived to become the grand old man of Hungarian music, while Bartók died relatively young in the United States, an impoverished, embittered refugee from fascism.

Regularly scheduled concerts are given at the museums below; see the listings for details. For complete schedule information, check Budapest's free bimonthly *Koncert Kalendárium,* available at the Central Philharmonic Ticket Office on Vörösmarty tér.

Bartók Béla Emlékház (Béla Bartók Memorial House)
High in the Buda Hills, this little museum is housed in Béla Bartók's final Hungarian home. Every year on September 26th, the date of Bartók's death, the Bartók String Quartet performs in the museum. Concerts are also performed on Friday evenings in spring and autumn.

II. Csalán u. 29. (✆ 1/394-2100. Museum, 300 Ft ($1.10); concerts, 800 Ft ($2.90). Open Tues–Sun 10am–5pm. Bus: 5 from Március 15 tér or Moszkva tér to Pasaréti tér (the last stop).

Liszt Ferenc Emlékmúzeum (Ferenc Liszt Memorial Museum)
Located in the apartment in which Liszt spent his last years, this modest museum features several of the composer's pianos, including a child's Bachmann and two Chickering & Sons grand pianos. Also noteworthy are the many portraits of Liszt done by the leading Austrian and Hungarian artists of his time, including two busts by the Hungarian sculptor Alajos Stróbl. Concerts are performed here on Saturdays at 11am.

VI. Vörösmarty u. 35. (✆ 1/322-9804. Admission 250 Ft (90¢). Guided group tours in English, 6,000 Ft ($21.60), if arranged in advance. Mon–Fri 10am–6pm, Sat 9am–5pm. Closed 1st 3 weeks of Aug. Metro: Vörösmarty utca (Yellow line).

Zenetörténeti Múzeum (Museum of Music History)
Various instruments and manuscripts are displayed in this museum, housed in a historic building in Buda's Castle District. You'll find a reproduction of Béla Bartók's workshop as well as the Bartók Archives. For lack of sponsorship, this gorgeous concert venue has been silent since mid-2000, to the deep regret of local music afficionados. Perhaps by the time you arrive, the museum will again be hosting concerts.

I. Táncsics M. u. 7. (✆ 1/214-6770 (ext. 250). Admission 300 Ft ($1.10). Tues–Sun 10am–6pm. Bus: Várbusz from Moszkva tér or 16 from Deák tér to Castle Hill. Funicular: From Clark Ádám tér to Castle Hill.

6 Organized Tours

BUS TOURS

Ibusz *Overrated* (✆ 1/485-2700 or fax 1/318-2805), with decades of experience, sets the standard for organized tours. Ibusz offers 11 different boat and bus tours, ranging from basic city tours to special folklore-oriented tours. Ibusz operates all year, with an abbreviated schedule in the off-season. All buses are air-conditioned, and all guides speak English. Some sample offerings are a 3-hour **Budapest City Tour** for 5,500 Ft ($19.80) (children under 12 are free), and a 2-hour Parliament Tour (inside the building for 2 hours) for 7,500 Ft ($27). Bus tours leave from the Erzsébet tér bus station, near Deák tér (all metro lines). There's also a free hotel pickup service 30 minutes before departure time. For a full list of tours, pick up the Ibusz "Budapest Sightseeing" catalog, available at all Ibusz offices, Tourinform, and most hotels. Tours can be booked at any Ibusz office and at most major hotels, or by calling Ibusz directly at © **1/485-2700.** All major credit cards are accepted.

BOAT TOURS

A boat tour is a great way to absorb the scope and scale of the Hungarian capital, and a majority of the city's grand sights can be seen from the river. The Hungarian state company **MAHART** operates daily sightseeing cruises on the Danube. The Budapest office of MAHART is at V. Belgrád rakpart (© **1/318-1704** or 1/489-4013). Boats depart frequently from Vigadó tér (on the Pest waterfront, between the Erzsébet Bridge and the Chain Bridge and near the Budapest Marriott hotel) on weekends and holidays in the spring and every day in summer. Additionally, MAHART offers chartered boat tours (for large groups) up and down the Tisza River in eastern Hungary from April 1 to October 15. These tours are booked through separate agencies in the towns of departure (Tokaj, Kisköre, Tiszacsege, Szolnok, Szeged, and many others along the river). Ask at MAHART for further information and the telephone numbers necessary for booking.

Legenda, at XI. Fraknó u. 4 (© **1/317-2203** or fax 1/266-4190, www.legenda.hu), a private company founded in 1990, offers several boat tours on the Danube. The daytime tour, called "Duna Bella," operates twice daily and includes a stop at Margaret Island. Tickets cost 3,200 Ft ($11.50). The nighttime tour is called "Danube Legend" and is more than a bit hokey, but worth it for the view of the city all lit up. "Danube Legend" tickets cost 3,700 Ft ($13.30), which includes refreshments. The one hour long tours run from mid-April to mid-October; all boats leave from the Vigadó tér port, Pier 7. Tickets are available through most major hotels, at the dock, or through the Legenda office. Look for their brochure at Tourinform.

WALKING TOURS

Several new companies offer walking tours of historic Budapest. We recommend "The Absolute Walking Tour in Budapest" offered by **Image Advantage** ★ (© **06-30/211-8861;** www.budapestours.com). The tour, conducted by knowledgeable and personable guides, start at pick-up point 1 outside the Evangelical Church in Deák tér (all metro lines) at 9:30 and at 1:30pm or at pick-up point 2 on the front steps of the Műcsarnok at Hősök tere (yellow line) at 10am and 2pm; from mid-May through September. From October through mid-December and February through mid-May, tours start daily at 10:30am and 11am only. Tickets are 2,990 Ft ($10.75); children under 12 are free. Show this book (or the company's flyer, on display at many tourist haunts) and you'll get a 500 Ft ($1.80) discount. Buy your ticket from the tour guide at the start of the tour. Tours last anywhere from 3½ to 5 hours, depending on the mood of the group, and take you throughout both central Pest and central Buda.

Budapest Walks (© **1/340-4232**) is another company offering walking tours. It offers two tours, one of Pest and one of the Castle District. Tours are conducted daily from May through September only. The Castle Hill tour starts at 2pm, and meets in front of the Matthias Church in Buda's Castle District; the Pest tour starts at 10am and meets in front of Café Gerbeaud, in Pest's Vörösmarty tér. Both tours last 2½ hours; the Pest tour is 3,200 Ft ($11.50), with a tour of Parliament included it costs 4,500 Ft ($16.20); the Buda tour is 3,800 Ft ($13.70).

Another outfit offering walking tours of the Castle District is **Castle Walks** (© **1/488-0453**). These tours, which cost 1,500 Ft ($5.40), start in front of the Matthias Church, daily at 11am and 3:30pm from mid-June through mid-September; Saturdays and Sundays only from mid-September through mid-October. Tickets are available at various hotel receptions or on the spot.

SPECIALTY TOURS

Chosen Tours (© and fax **1/355-2202**) specializes in tours related to Jewish life and heritage in Budapest. The 1½- to 2-hour guided walking tour of Pest's historic Jewish Quarter is a good introduction to that fascinating neighborhood. Tours are conducted from April through October and run Monday through Friday and Sunday beginning at 10am in front of the Dohány Synagogue, on Dohány utca. The walking tour costs $11. You should reserve a place ahead of time (Chosen Tours offers a free pickup service from select hotel locations). Chosen Tours also offers an additional 1-hour, air-conditioned bus tour of Jewish sights in Buda. Called "Budapest Through Jewish Eyes," the combination tour ticket costs $17. Reserve a place beforehand. Other tours, available for private bookings, include a tour of Jewish art and a tour to Szentendre, as well as tours catering to individual needs and interests (such as "roots" tours).

7 Spa Bathing & Swimming: Budapest's Most Popular Thermal Baths

Hungarians are great believers in the medicinal powers of thermal bathing, and few can deny that time spent in thermal baths is enjoyable and relaxing. The baths of Budapest have a long and proud history, stretching back to Roman times. Under Turkish occupation, the bath culture flourished, and several still-functioning bathhouses—Király, Rudas, and Rácz—are among the architectural relics of the Turkish period. In the late 19th and early 20th centuries—Budapest's "golden age"—several fabulous bathhouses were built: the extravagant eclectic Széchenyi Baths in City Park, the splendid art nouveau Gellért Baths, and the solid neoclassical Lukács Baths. All are still in use and are worth a look even for nonbathers.

Gellért Baths   Budapest's most spectacular bathhouse, the Gellért Baths are located in Buda's Hotel Gellért, the oldest Hungarian spa hotel and an art nouveau jewel. Enter the baths through the side entrance.

The exterior is in need of restoration, but once inside the lobby, you'll be delighted by the details. The unisex indoor pool is without question one of Europe's finest, with marble columns, majolica tiles, and stone lion heads spouting water. The segregated Turkish-style thermal baths, one off to each side of the pool through badly marked doors, are also glorious though in need of restoration. The outdoor roof pool attracts great attention for 10 minutes every hour on the hour, when the artificial wave machine is turned on. There are separate nude sunbathing decks for men and women, but you'll have to figure out where they are. In general, you need patience here.

XI. Kelenhegyi út 4. © **1/466-6166.** Take tram no. 47 or 49 from Deák tér to Szent Gellért tér. Admission to the thermal bath costs 1,100 Ft ($3.95); 15-minute massage is 1,300 Ft ($4.70) plus tip. Lockers are free; a cabin can be rented for 400 Ft ($1.45). Admission to all pools and bath 1,600 Ft ($5.75) adults, 800 Ft ($2.90) children. Prices and the lengthy list of services are posted in English. The thermal baths are open daily, in summer 6am–7pm; in winter Mon–Fri 6am–7pm, on weekends 6am–2pm, with the last entrance an hour before closing. In the summer you can come and enjoy the bathing facilities at night on Fri and Sat 8pm–midnight.

Tips Taking in the Waters

Thermal bathing is an activity steeped in ritual. For this reason, and because bathhouse employees tend to be unfriendly relics of the old system, many foreigners find a trip to the baths stressful or confusing at first. As with any ritualistic activity, it helps to spend some time observing before joining in. Even then, you are likely not to know what to do or where to go. The best advice is to try and enjoy the for- eignness of the experience—why else do we leave home? The most confusing step may well be the first: the ticket window with its endless list of prices for different facilities and services, often without English translations. Chances are you're coming to use one of these facilities or services: *uszoda*, pool; *termál*, thermal pool; *fürdő*, bath; *gőzfürdő*, steam bath; massage; and sauna. There is no particular order in which people move from one to the next; do whatever feels most comfort- able. Towel rental is *törülköző* or *lepedő*. An entry ticket generally entitles you to a free locker in the locker room (*öltöző*); or, at some bathhouses, you can opt to pay an additional fee for a private cabin (*kabin*). At the Király, everyone gets a private dressing room and an employee locks and unlocks the rooms (see below).

Remember to pack a bathing suit—and a bathing cap, if you wish to swim in the pools—so you won't have to rent vintage-1970 models. In the single sex baths, nude bathing is the custom and the norm. Towels are provided, but usually as you reenter the locker area after bathing. You may want to bring your own towel with you into the bathing areas if this makes you uncomfortable. Flipflops are also a good idea. Soap and shampoo are only allowed in the showers, but should be brought out to the bath area to avoid having to return to the com- paratively cold locker room prematurely. You will, most likely, want to wash your hair after soaking in the sulphuric waters. Long hair must be tied back when bathing. Leave your eyeglasses in the locker as they will be irremediably fogged up in the baths.

Generally, extra services (massage, pedicure) are received after a bath. Tipping is tricky; locker room attendants do not expect (except perhaps at the Gellért) but would welcome a tip in the 100 Ft to 200 Ft range (35¢ to 70¢), while masseurs and manicurists expect a tip in the 200 Ft to 500 Ft range (75¢ to $1.45).

Although there are drinking fountains in the bath areas, it's a good idea to drink plenty of water before a bath. And don't bathe on an empty stomach; the hot water and steam take a toll on the unfortified body. Most bathhouses have snack bars in the lobbies where you can pick up a cold juice or sandwich on your way out. After the baths, you will be thirsty and hungry. Be sure to replenish yourself.

Király Baths The Király Baths are one of Budapest's most important architectural monuments to Turkish rule, and a place where Hungarian culture meets the Eastern culture that influenced it.

The bath itself, built in the late 16th century, is housed under an octagonal domed roof. Sunlight filters through small round windows in the ceiling. The water glows. The effect is perfectly tranquil. In addition to the thermal baths, there are sauna and steam room facilities. Bring a towel, if you like, since you will not receive one until the end of your treatment. Upon exiting the baths, help yourself to a cotton sheet from the pile near the base of the stairs. Wrap yourself up and lounge with a cup of tea in the relaxation room. Here, you can also order a pedicure or massage.

Men can use the baths on Monday, Wednesday, and Friday from 9am to 6pm. Women are welcome on Tuesday and Thursday from 6:30am to 7pm and on Saturday from 6:30am to noon.

I. Fő u. 84. ℰ 1/202-3688. Admission to baths 600 Ft ($2.15). Metro: Batthyány tér (Red line).

Rudas Baths ★★   Near the Erzsébet Bridge on the Buda side is another of Budapest's classic Turkish baths. The baths are for men only (both sexes are admitted to the swimming pool). Before 9am, the crowd is predominantly composed of older men, and according to local lore, these baths become something of a pickup spot after 9am.

The first baths were built on this site in the 14th century, although the Rudas Bathhouse dates to the late 16th century. It boasts an octagonal pool and domed roof; some of the small window holes in the cupola have stained glass, while others are open to the sky, allowing diffuse light to stream in. You'll find most of the same services and facilities as at the Király: thermal bath, sauna, and steam bath.

I. Döbrentei tér 9. ℰ 1/358-1322. Admission to thermal baths 800 Ft ($2.90), swimming pool 600 Ft ($2.15). Hours: weekdays 6:30am–6pm, weekends 6am–1pm. Bus: 7; get off at the Buda side of the Erzsébet Bridge, turn left, and venture down to the riverside. Or walk; it's just across the river.

Széchenyi Baths   Part of an immense health spa located in the City Park, the Széchenyi Baths are perhaps second only to the Gellért Baths in terms of facilities and popular appeal.

Ivy climbs the walls of the sprawling pool complex here. On a nice day, crowds of bathers, including many families and tourists, visit the palatial unisex outdoor swimming pool. Look for the older gentlemen concentrating intently on their chess games, half-immersed in the steaming pool. Turkish-style thermal baths are segregated and located off to the side of the pool.

Admission to the thermal baths is 1,500 Ft ($5.40); massage and dressing cabins are extra. Individual prices are posted in English. The thermal baths and swimming pool are open daily from 6am to 7pm.

XIV. Állatkerti út 11–14, in City Park. ℰ 1/321-0310. Admission to thermal baths 1,500 Ft ($5.40); massage and dressing cabins are extra. Individual prices are posted in English. Open daily 6am–7pm. Metro: Széchenyi fürdő (Yellow line).

OTHER CHOICES

Rácz bathhouse is located at I. Hadnagy u. 8–10 (ℰ **1/375-8373**), near the Erzsébet Bridge in Buda. It's open from 6:30am to 7pm. The entrance fee is 500 Ft ($1.80). Women bathe on Monday, Wednesday, and Friday; and men on Tuesday, Thursday, and Saturday.

Lukács bath and swimming pool, at II. Frankel Leo u. 25–29 (ℰ **1/326-1695**), is open daily from 6am to 7pm. The entrance fee is 800 Ft ($2.90). Take tram 4 or 6 to the Buda side of the Margaret Bridge; walk from there.

More modern spa facilities are available at the two Thermal Hotels: **Helia** and **Aquincum Corinthia** (see chapter 4, "Where to Stay in Budapest").

AN OUTDOOR POOL COMPLEX

Palatinus Strand *★★ Finds*   In the middle of Margaret Island is Budapest's best located strand (literally "beach," but better translated, in this context, as "outdoor pool complex"). It's a fantastic place, fed by the Margaret Island thermal springs. There are three thermal pools, a vast swimming pool, a smaller artificial wave pool, a water slide, segregated nude sunbathing decks, and large, grassy grounds. The waters of the thermal pools are as relaxing as at any of the bathhouses, but the experience here is not as memorable as it is at the older indoor bathhouses. Facilities include Ping-Pong tables, pool tables, trampolines, and dozens of snack bars: in other words, a typical Hungarian strand. *Warning:* Beware of pickpockets on the bus to the complex.

XIII. Margit-sziget. (© 1/340-4505. Admission to all pools 600 Ft ($2.15) adults, 500 Ft ($1.80) children and teenagers; 400 Ft ($1.45) adults after 5pm Mon–Fri. Hours: May to mid-Sep daily 8am–7pm. Last entry at 6pm. Take bus no. 26 from Nyugati pu.

8 Outdoor Activities & Sports

BIKING   Although we don't recommend biking in Budapest, see "Getting Around," in chapter 3, "Getting to Know Budapest," for some biking options.

GOLF   For information, contact the **Hungarian Golf Club,** V. Bécsi út 5 (© 1/317-6025). The nearest golf course is located on Szentendre Island, 25 minutes north of Budapest by car. Call the course directly at © 26/392-463, or send a fax to 26/392-465. For putting practice, the **19th Hole Golf Driving Range** is located at II. Adyliget, Feketefej u. 6. (© 06-30/944-1185).

HORSEBACK RIDING   Riding is a popular activity in Hungary. A good place to mount up is the **Petneházy Lovasiskola** (Riding School), at II. Feketefej u. 2 (© 1/397-5048). As far out in the Buda Hills as you can go without leaving the city limits, the school is located in open country, with trails in the hills. The weekday hourly prices are as follows: Riding on the track with a trainer costs 1,200 Ft ($4.30) for 30 minutes; open riding with a guide is 2,500 Ft ($9). There are also pony rides for children at 700 Ft ($2.50) for 1/4 hour, and horse-cart rides at 3,000 Ft ($10.80) for 30 minutes. (Note that rates are about 70% more expensive on the weekend.) The Petneházy Country Club is down the road. At the stable is a great little *csárda*, recently renovated; you might want to have lunch here. The stable is open year-round, weekdays 9am to noon and 2 to 4pm; weekends 9am to 5pm. Take bus no. 56 (56E is fastest) from Moszkva tér to the last stop, then bus no. 63 to Feketefej utca, followed by a 10-minute walk.

Vista Visitor Center, at VI. Paulay Ede u. 7 (see "Information," in chapter 3, "Getting to Know Budapest"), sponsors overnight horseback riding adventures beyond Budapest. The **Hungarian Equestrian Tourism Association,** located at V. Ferenciek tere 4 (© 1/317-1644; fax 1/267-0171), might also serve your riding interests.

IN-LINE SKATING & ICE-SKATING   There are several options for both in Budapest. While at least one of the ice rinks is more appropriate for children, adults can rent in-line and ice skates elsewhere in the city. See "Especially for Kids," earlier in this chapter.

SQUASH   City Squash Courts (Országos Fallabda Központ), at II. Marczibányi tér 13 (© 1/325-0082), has four courts. An easy walk from Moszkva tér (Red metro line), their hourly rates—per court—are 3,600 Ft ($12.95) for 1 hour of play during peak hours (Monday through Friday, 5 to 10pm) and 2,800

Ft ($10.10) for 1 hour of play at other times. Racquets can be rented for 500 Ft ($1.80); balls can be purchased. It's open daily from 7am to midnight. The **Hotel Marriott Squash Court,** at V. Apáczai Csere J. u. 4 (© 1/266-4290), also rents out court time for 3,500 Ft ($12.60) per hour. Racquets rent for 500 Ft ($1.80).

TENNIS   If you plan to play tennis in Budapest, bring your own racquet along since most courts don't rent equipment; when it is available, it's usually primitive.

Many of Budapest's luxury hotels, particularly those removed from the city center, have tennis courts that nonguests can rent. The **MTK Sport Complex,** in Buda at XI. Bartók Béla út 63 (© **1/209-1595**), boasts 13 outdoor clay courts. The fee is 700 Ft ($2.50) per hour during the day or 1,200 Ft ($4.30) per hour at night, under floodlights. Three outdoor courts are covered by a tent year-round; from October through April all courts are covered and the price of play throughout the day is 2,200 Ft ($7.90) per hour (again to cover the cost of lighting). Equipment is not available for rental. It's open daily from 6am to 10pm. Móricz Zsigmond körtér, a transportation hub served by countless buses and trams, is only 5 minutes from the center by foot.

7

Strolling Around Budapest

Budapest is a city to see by foot. The following walking tours are intended to introduce you to the texture and color of the city. Many of the city's top attractions—the Buda Palace and Parliament, the National Gallery, and the National Museum among them—are included on these tours, but dozens of minor sites—vintage pharmacies and quiet courtyards, market halls and medieval walls—are visited as well. On these walking tours, special attention is paid to the hidden Budapest, the glorious details that taken together make this the memorable city that it is.

WALKING TOUR 1   PEST'S INNER CITY

Start:	Deák tér.
Finish:	Danube Promenade.
Time:	3 to 4 hours (excluding museum stops).
Best Times:	Tuesday through Saturday.
Worst Times:	Monday, when museums are closed, and Sunday, when stores are closed.

The city of Pest, like most medieval cities, was surrounded by a protective wall. The wall is long gone, though some remnants remain, which we'll see on this tour. The historic center of the city, inside the walled area, is still known as the Belváros, or Inner City. The Erzsébet Bridge divides the Inner City into two parts: The busier northern half features luxury hotels along the Danube Promenade (Dunakorzó) and the boutiques and shops of the pedestrian-only Váci utca; the quieter southern half, meanwhile, is largely residential, but is also home to the main buildings of Eötvös Loránd University and a number of lovely churches. This sleepy southern half is undergoing a revitalization since the 1996 extension of pedestrian-only Váci utca. Pest's Inner Ring boulevard (Kiskörút) wraps around both halves, tracing the line of the former medieval city wall. This walking tour spends equal time in each half of the Inner City, visiting museums, churches, stores, courtyards, and a great market hall en route. We'll end with a leisurely stroll down the Danube Promenade.

Begin at Deák tér, where all three metro lines converge. If you have any questions about theater tickets, activities, or excursions, now would be a good time to pop into:

❶ Tourinform

At V. Sütő u. 4. Budapest's main tourist information bureau has helpful information on lodging, cultural programs, and excursions.

Alternatively, you could start with a visit to the:

❷ Underground Railway Museum

Located in the underground passage beneath Deák tér. Here, you can see a beautifully preserved train from the European continent's first underground system, built in Budapest in 1896.

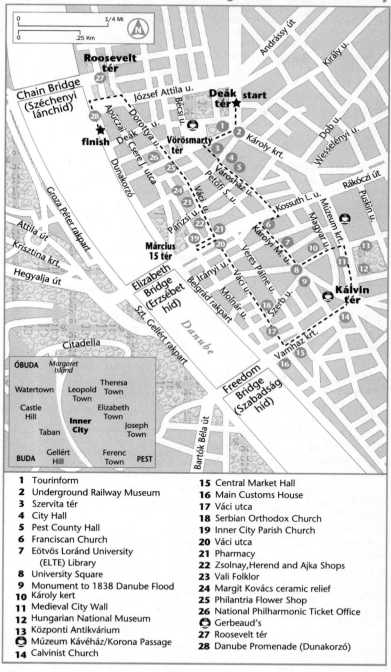

1 Tourinform
2 Underground Railway Museum
3 Szervita tér
4 City Hall
5 Pest County Hall
6 Franciscan Church
7 Eötvös Loránd University
  (ELTE) Library
8 University Square
9 Monument to 1838 Danube Flood
10 Károly kert
11 Medieval City Wall
12 Hungarian National Museum
13 Központi Antikvárium
🗘 Múzeum Kávéház/Korona Passage
14 Calvinist Church

15 Central Market Hall
16 Main Customs House
17 Váci utca
18 Serbian Orthodox Church
19 Inner City Parish Church
20 Váci utca
21 Pharmacy
22 Zsolnay,Herend and Ajka Shops
23 Vali Folklor
24 Margit Kovács ceramic relief
25 Philantria Flower Shop
26 National Philharmonic Ticket Office
🗘 Gerbeaud's
27 Roosevelt tér
28 Danube Promenade (Dunakorzó)

From nearby Szomory Dezső tér, head down Fehérhajó utca toward Szervita tér, formerly Martinelli tér. Ahead of you, you'll notice Váci utca, the crowded pedestrian street. The tour will return there later; for now, turn left into:

❸ Szervita tér

This is the site of the early 18th-century baroque Servite Church, the column of the Virgin Mary, and the former Török Banking House with its colorful Secessionist mosaic.

Continue now on Városház utca (City Hall Street), which begins to the left of the church. Dominating this street is the 18th-century:

❹ City Hall

The largest baroque edifice in Budapest, it was originally designed as a hospital by Anton Martinelli.

The lime-green neoclassical building at Városház u. 7 is the 19th-century:

❺ Pest County Hall

After a visit to the inner courtyards, you will see, as you emerge onto busy Kossuth Lajos utca, the Erzsébet Bridge to your right, with the northern slope of Gellért Hill behind it.

Directly across the street (reached via the underpass) is the:

❻ Franciscan Church

A church stood here as early as the 13th century, but the present church dates from the 18th century. The relief on the building's side depicts Miklós Wesselényi's heroic rescue effort during the awful Danube flood of 1838. Next door, a shop sells religious artifacts, including hand-painted icons from Bulgaria, Ukraine, and Russia. The name of the shop is **Ecclesia,** at V. Ferenciek tere 7–8 (🕾 **1/317-3754**), and it is open Monday through Friday, 9:30am to 5:30pm, and Saturday 9:30am to 1pm.

Continuing south on Ferenciek tere, the striking neoclassical building with the colorful dome is the:

❼ Eötvös Loránd University (ELTE) Library

Continuing straight on Károlyi Mihály utca, the next big square is:

❽ University Square (Egyetem tér)

Site of the ELTE Law School; the baroque University Church, with a copy of the *Black Madonna* of Czestochowa above the altar; and the Sándor Petőfi Literary Museum, a veritable shrine to Hungarian literary heroes (almost all are largely unknown outside Hungary).

At the far end of the square:

❾ A small monument to the 1838 Danube flood

This can be seen on the wall at the corner of Szerb utca and Király Pál utca; a map shows the extent of the flooding. Notice that the entire Inner City was underwater!

Returning to the top of the square, now turn right onto Henszlmann Imre utca. After half a block, you will see:

❿ Károly kert

On your left. This beautifully maintained neighborhood park has benches in the shade, swings, a miniature soccer field, and a lovely fountain with begonias growing around it. The park is filled with children all day long.

Exit the park onto Magyar utca and turn left, then right onto Ferenczi István utca. Emerge onto busy Múzeum körút, and turn right again. Take a quick detour into the quiet courtyard of Múzeum körút 21, where you will find a well-preserved section of:

⓫ Pest's medieval city wall

Most of the city wall is long gone, but this part is in good shape and dates back to the 15th century.

Back out on Múzeum körút, you will note, across the street, the massive neoclassical:

⓬ Hungarian National Museum

Legend has it that the fiery poet Sándor Petőfi recited his incendiary "National Song" on the museum steps on the first day of the 1848 anti-Habsburg Hungarian Revolution. The museum's most famous exhibit, the legendary Hungarian crown jewels of King Stephen were moved to the House of Parliament as part of the Millenium frenzy; in the museum you can see a replica of the regalia. The jewels have an astonishing history nonetheless: complex tales of theft, subterfuge, and rescue. Spirited out of Hungary before the Soviet liberation of 1945, they ended up in U.S. government hands. President Carter's secretary of state, Cyrus Vance, ceremoniously returned them to the Hungarian government in 1978. The National Museum is one of those museums where, depending on your interest, you can spend 10 minutes or 10 hours.

This part of Múzeum körút has long been known for its *antikvária,* stores selling rare books and maps. At Múzeum krt. 13–15, you'll find the:

⑬ Központi Antikvárium

Another antikvárium, called Honterus, is ahead at Múzeum krt. 35.

☕ TAKE A BREAK
Choose between the **Múzeum Kávéház**, Múzeum krt. 12 (**☎** 1/267-0375), suitable either for a Hungarian lunch or just coffee and pastries, or **Korona Passage**, an airy crêperie/salad bar in the Korona Hotel on nearby Kálvin tér (**☎** 1/317-4111).

Nearby Kálvin tér is named for the 19th-century:

⑭ Calvinist Church

The colorful ceramic tiles that grace the church's roof make it an easily identifiable landmark in the Budapest landscape. Medieval Pest's Kecskeméti Gate stood on Kálvin tér, on the site of the bridge passage between the two buildings of the Hotel Mercure Korona. Turn right at Kálvin tér onto Kecskeméti utca, passing in front of the hotel, and then take your first left

onto tiny Bástya utca. Walk several blocks down this quiet residential street, until it comes to a T-intersection at Veres Pálné utca. On that corner, at the rear of a shabby playground, you will find another fine piece of Pest's medieval town wall. Now turn left onto Veres Pálné utca and return to the körút.

You're now on the Vámház (Customs House) körút section of the Inner Ring. Just ahead of you on the right is the graceful green span of the Szabadság (Freedom) Bridge, with the Gellért Hotel towering over Buda's Danube bank. Now, proceed toward the river to the:

⑮ Central Market Hall (Központi Vásárcsarnok)

This is the largest and most spectacular of Budapest's late 19th-century market halls. Recently renovated and reconstructed, the bright, airy hall houses a wide assortment of fresh-produce vendors, dispensing dairy products, meat and poultry, vegetables, and fruit. Escalators lead to a mezzanine level where traditional folk items are sold. Fast food and drink booths are also upstairs. While the new market hall is clean and extremely pleasant, it clearly lacks the homey grit and verve of a traditional market, such as the outdoor market in Szeged (see chapter 13, "Southern Hungary: The Great Plain & the Meczek Hills").

Next door to the market is the eclectic-style former:

⑯ Main Customs House

Now a university economics building (pop into the lobby to admire the statue of Karl Marx), the house overlooks the Danube—from here, you can admire the full span of the Szabadság Bridge, our favorite of Budapest's seven bridges.

Now take the pedestrian-only:

⑰ Váci utca

All the way back down to the southern end of the Inner City.

Take a short detour at Szerb utca (turn right), named for the lovely 18th-century:

⑱ Serbian Orthodox Church

The church is set off from the street by a small garden. Interestingly, the paintings on the iconostasis reflect the Italian Renaissance instead of the more typical Byzantine style. Return to Váci utca, and continue walking north.

At Szabadsajtó utca, turn left toward the Danube. Passing under the Erzsébet Bridge, you're now back in the northern, more crowded half of the Inner City. Towering above you is the:

⑲ Inner City Parish Church

Built and rebuilt numerous times since the 12th century, the church displays Gothic and baroque elements on the outside, while inside are niches built in both those styles, as well as a *mihrab* (prayer niche) dating from the Turkish occupation.

Pass under the archways of the ELTE Arts Faculty building (walking away from the river), and the next street is:

⑳ Váci utca

Again. This is its more crowded half.

At Váci u. 34, on the corner of Kígyó utca (Snake Street), is a wonderful old:

㉑ Pharmacy

It's furnished with antique wooden cabinets and drawers.

Nearby, on Kígyó utca, you'll find retail shops for:

㉒ Zsolnay and Herend porcelain and Ajka crystal

We are partial to the delightfully gaudy Zsolnay porcelain, from the southern city of Pécs. Even if you don't intend to buy, these shops are worth a peek.

Proceed down Váci utca now. You'll probably make various stops along your way, but one of them should definitely be at:

㉓ Vali Folklor

In the courtyard of Váci u. 23. This tiny shop offers a fine assortment of authentic secondhand Hungarian folk costumes, as well as tapestries, ceramics,

and figurines. Small though it is, this store truly stands tall above all the atrocious neighborhood kitsch. Its extended collection now also features communist era badges, pins and medals from throughout Eastern Europe.

Just down Régiposta utca, across the street from McDonald's, above the door of Régiposta u. 13, is a lovely, but faded:

㉔ Margit Kovács

Ceramic relief of a horse and coach. Kovács was Hungary's greatest ceramic artist. A superb museum dedicated to her work can be visited in the small town of Szentendre, on the Danube Bend (see "Szentendre," in chapter 10, "The Danube Bend").

Look for the art nouveau interior of the:

㉕ Philantria Flower Shop

At Váci u. 9. Note the whimsical carved moldings, as well as wall murals recalling the style of Toulouse-Lautrec.

Váci utca ends in Vörösmarty tér, one of Pest's loveliest squares, which has a number of attractions in addition to the monumental statue of the great Romantic poet Mihály Vörösmarty, author of "The Appeal," Hungary's "second national anthem." Nearby is the:

㉖ National Philharmonic Ticket Office (Nemzeti Filharmónia Jegypénztár)

At Vörösmarty tér 1. Here, you can buy advance tickets for most Budapest performances; no commission is charged.

Across the square, half a block away, at Deák Ferenc u. 10, is the American Express office. But certainly the best-known feature of Vörösmarty tér is its legendary coffeehouse.

TAKE A BREAK
Gerbeaud's, at Vörösmarty tér 7. Founded in 1858, it has been at this site since 1870. The decor and the furnishings are classic turn of the century, while the pastries are among the city's best. In summertime, try any of the fresh fruit strudels (gyümölcs rétes).

Walk down Dorottya utca to the next stop:

㉗ Roosevelt tér

(Described in "Walking Tour 3: Leopold Town & Theresa Town," later in this chapter). The Buda Palace looms on Castle Hill directly across the river, which is spanned here by the Széchenyi Chain Bridge.

Here, where the statue of the great 19th-century educator József Eötvös stands, is the beginning of the fabled:

㉘ Danube Promenade (Dunakorzó)

Gone are the traditional coffeehouses that once lined the length between the Chain Bridge and the Erzsébet Bridge during the late 19th century. In their place rise luxury hotels, the most monstrous of which is the concrete behemoth Budapest Marriott. Nevertheless, all of Budapest still comes to stroll here: Join the throngs, equal parts native and tourist. The glorious unobstructed view of Buda across the river remains as it ever was. Castle Hill towers above the Watertown, whose many steeples pierce the sky. Along the promenade you'll find artists, musicians, vendors, and craftspeople, not to mention various hustlers and lowlifes.

WALKING TOUR 2   THE CASTLE DISTRICT

Start:	Roosevelt tér, Pest side of Chain Bridge.
Finish:	Tóth Árpád sétány, Castle District.
Time:	3 to 4 hours (excluding museum stops).
Best Times:	Tuesday through Sunday.
Worst Time:	Monday, when museums are closed.

A limestone-capped plateau rising impressively above the Danube, Castle Hill was first settled in the 13th century; it remains the spiritual capital of Hungary. The district has been leveled periodically, most recently by the 1945 Soviet shelling of Nazi forces. It was always painstakingly rebuilt in the prevailing style of the day, thus shifting from Gothic to baroque to Renaissance. After World War II, an attempt was made to incorporate various elements of the district's historic appearance into the general restoration. Castle Hill, a UNESCO World Cultural Heritage site, consists of two parts: the Royal Palace itself and the so-called Castle District, a mostly reconstructed medieval city. The Royal Palace now houses a number of museums, including the Hungarian National Gallery. The adjoining Castle District is a compact, narrow neighborhood of cobblestoned lanes and twisting alleys; restrictions on vehicular traffic enhance the Old World feel and tranquillity. Prime examples of every type of Hungarian architecture, from early Gothic to neo-Romanesque, can be seen. A leisurely walk in the Castle District will be a warmly remembered experience.

To get an accurate picture of the dimensions and grandeur of Castle Hill, start the walking tour in Pest's Roosevelt tér, on the:

❶ Széchenyi Chain Bridge

One of the outstanding symbols of Budapest, the first permanent bridge across the Danube was originally built in 1849 and then destroyed by Nazi dynamite during World War II. The 1949 opening ceremony of the reconstructed bridge was held 100 years to the day after its original inauguration.

Arriving in Buda, you're now in:

❷ Clark Ádám tér

This square was named for the Scottish engineer who supervised the building of the bridge and afterward made Budapest his home.

From Clark Ádám tér, take the:

❸ Funicular (sikló)

It will transport you up to the Royal Palace in just a minute or two (see "Getting Around," in chapter 3, "Getting to Know Budapest"). Dating from 1870, it too was destroyed in World War II and was not rebuilt until 1986. You can also walk up the steep stairs to Castle Hill.

Whichever method of ascent you choose, when you arrive at the top, turn and look left at the statue of the:

❹ Turul

The mythical eagle is perched on the wall looking out over the Danube to Pest. The eagle is said to have guided the ancient Magyars in their westward migration.

The main courtyard of the palace, from which the museums are entered, is on the building's far side, but first go down the nearby stairs to see the:

❺ Equestrian Statue of Prince Eugene of Savoy

Prince Eugene was one of the leaders of the united Christian armies that ousted the Turks from Hungary in the late 17th century. Inside the palace are a number of museums. You might want to visit them now or return after the walking tour.

The first is the:

❻ Hungarian National Gallery

The museum houses much of the greatest art ever produced by Hungarians. Don't miss the works of the 19th-century artists Mihály Munkácsy, László Paál, Károly Ferenczy, Pál Szinyei Merse, Gyula Benczúr, and Károly Lotz. Nor should you overlook József Rippl-Rónai, the great art nouveau painter of the turn-of-the-20th-century period.

Proceed to the:

❼ Budapest History Museum

The highlights here are the Gothic rooms and statues uncovered during the post–World War II excavation and rebuilding of the Royal Palace. The rooms and all their contents, dating back as far as the 14th century, were buried for hundreds of years.

Next we have the:

❽ Széchenyi National Library

The library is named for Ferenc Széchenyi (not his more famous son István, after whom the Chain Bridge is named), who founded it in 1802. It now houses the world's greatest collection of "Hungarica," with some four million holdings. In Wing A of the Buda Palace is the:

❾ Ludwig Museum

This repository of contemporary and international art was formerly the Museum of the Hungarian Worker's Movement.

Exiting the palace, pass the new excavations and go through Dísz tér (where bus no. 16 can be caught later). Bearing right at the small grassy triangle with the statue of the swordsman—the famous Hungarian 19th century huszár—emerge onto Tárnok utca. On the left side of the street, you'll find the:

❿ Golden Eagle Pharmacy Museum (Arany Sas Patikamúzeum)

At Tárnok u. 18. Renaissance and baroque pharmacy relics are displayed in this odd and cavernous little museum.

Just ahead on Tárnok utca is:

⓫ Holy Trinity Square (Szentháromság tér)

The central square of the Castle District is where you'll find the Holy Trinity Column, or Plague Column, dating from the early 18th century, and the:

⓬ Matthias Church (Mátyás templom)

Officially called the Church of Our Lady, this symbol of the Castle District is universally known as Matthias Church because the renaissance monarch, Matthias Corvinus, one of Hungary's most revered kings, was the major donor and also got married twice inside it. There's an ecclesiastical

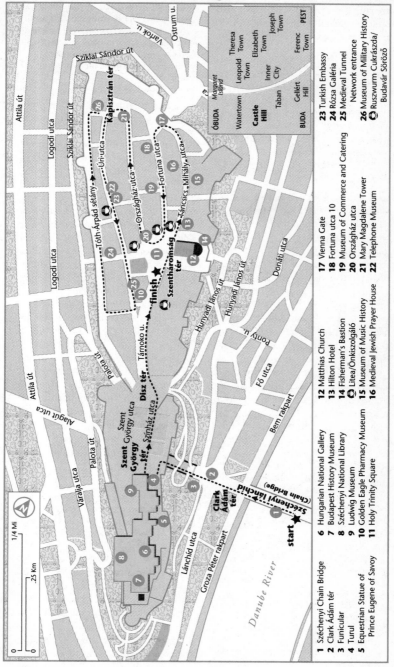

ÓBUDA

Watertown · Leopold Town · Theresa Town · Elizabeth Town · Joseph Town · **PEST**

Margaret Island · **Castle Hill** · Inner City · Ferenc Town

BUDA · Taban · Gellért Hill

Attila út

Logodi utca

Várfok u.

Ostrum u.

Sziklai Sándor út

Kapisztrán tér

Úri utca

Tóth Árpád sétány

Országház utca

Fortuna utca

Táncsics Mihály utca

Szentháromság tér

Szinház utca

Dísz tér

Tárnoko u.

Szent György utca

Szent György tér

Palota út

Attila út

Alagút utca

Palota út

Váralja utca

Lánchid utca

Groza Péter rakpart

Hunyadi János út

Donáti utca

Ponty u.

Fó utca

Bem rakpart

Clark Ádám tér

Széchenyi Lánchid (Chain Bridge)

start

finish

Danube River

1/4 Mi

.25 Km

1 Széchenyi Chain Bridge
2 Clark Ádám tér
3 Funicular
4 Turul
5 Equestrian Statue of Prince Eugene of Savoy
6 Hungarian National Gallery
7 Budapest History Museum
8 Széchenyi National Library
9 Ludwig Museum
10 Golden Eagle Pharmacy Museum
11 Holy Trinity Square
12 Matthias Church
13 Hilton Hotel
14 Fisherman's Bastion
⚓ Litea/Önkiszolgáló
15 Museum of Music History
16 Medieval Jewish Prayer House
17 Vienna Gate
18 Fortuna utca 10
19 Museum of Commerce and Catering
20 Országház utca
21 Mary Magdalene Tower
22 Telephone Museum
23 Turkish Embassy
24 Rózsa Galéria
25 Medieval Tunnel
⚓ Network entrance
26 Museum of Military History
⚓ Ruszwurm Cukrászda/ Budavár Sörözó

art collection inside, and organ concerts are held Friday evenings in the
summer.

Next door to the church is the:

⑬ **Hilton Hotel**
The Castle District's only hotel, the
Hilton tastefully incorporates two
ruins into its award-winning design: a
13th-century Dominican church,
with a tower rising above the hotel,
and the baroque facade of a 17th-
century Jesuit college, the hotel's main
entrance.

Summer concerts are held in the Dominican
Courtyard. Behind the Hilton is the:

⑭ **Fisherman's Bastion
(Halászbástya)**
This sprawling neo-Romanesque
structure was built in 1905 on the site
of an old fish market (hence the name)
affords a marvelous panorama of Pest.
Looking out over the Danube to Pest,
you can see (from left to right):
Margaret Island and the Margaret
Bridge, Parliament, St. Stephen's
Basilica, the Chain Bridge, the Vigadó
Concert Hall, the Inner City Parish
Church, the Erzsébet Bridge, and the
Szabadság Bridge. Avoid the over-
priced restaurant housed inside the
Fisherman's Bastion.

TAKE A BREAK
You may want to stop at
Litea, a bookstore and tearoom located in the Fortuna
Passage, opposite the Hilton. You can
browse, then sit and enjoy a cup of tea
while looking over your selections. If it
is lunch you desire, head to the
Önkiszolgáló in the same Fortuna
Passage. In this self-service cafeteria,
you can get an incredibly cheap and
decent Hungarian lunch. It is open only
on weekdays and only for lunch. The
entrance is marked by a small sign posting the open hours; it is the second door
on the left inside the archway, up one
flight of stairs. Just follow the stream of
Hungarians.

Because the entire length of each of the
Castle District's north-south streets is worth
seeing, the tour will now take you back and
forth between the immediate area of Szentháromság tér and the northern end of the
district. First, head down Táncsics Mihály
utca, to the:

⑮ **Museum of Music History**
At Táncsics Mihály u. 7. Beethoven
stayed here for a spell in 1800, when it
was a private home. It now houses the
archives of the great composer Bartók.
The building next door, at Táncsics
Mihály u. 9, served for many years as
a prison. Among those incarcerated
here were Mihály Táncsics, the 19th-
century champion of free press after
whom the street is named, and Lajos
Kossuth, the leader of the 1848–49
anti-Habsburg revolution. Táncsics
utca was the center of the medieval
Jewish community of Buda. During
general postwar reconstruction work
in the 1960s, the remains of several
synagogues were uncovered. Nearby
is the:

⑯ **Medieval Jewish Prayer House**
At Táncsics Mihály u. 26. The building dates from the 14th century. In
the 15th and 16th centuries, the Jews
of Buda thrived under Turkish rule.
The 1686 Christian reconquest of
Buda was soon followed by a massacre
of Jews. Many survivors fled Buda;
this tiny Sephardic synagogue was
turned into an apartment.

After exiting the synagogue, retrace your
steps about 10 yards back on Táncsics
Mihály utca, turn left onto Babits Mihály
köz, and then turn left onto Babits Mihály
sétány. This path will take you onto the top
of the:

⑰ **Vienna Gate (Bécsi kapu)**
One of the main entrances to the
Castle District. From the top of the
gate, you can look out onto the fashionable Rose Hill (Rózsadomb) neighborhood in the Buda Hills. The
enormous neo-Romanesque building
towering above Bécsi kapu tér houses
the National Archives. Bécsi kapu tér
is also home to a lovely row of houses
(nos. 5–8).

From here, head up Fortuna utca to the house at:

⑱ Fortuna u. 10

This is certainly one of the district's most photographed houses. It dates originally from the 13th century, but has been restored to Louis XVI style. The facade incorporates medieval details.

At Fortuna u. 4, you'll find the charming, unassuming:

⑲ Museum of Commerce and Catering

Mostly food-related artifacts from the turn of the 20th century are lovingly displayed at this unique museum. The museum is open Wednesday to Friday from 10am to 5pm, Saturday and Sunday from 10am to 6pm.

Return to Szentháromság tér and start down:

⑳ Országház utca

This is one of two streets in the Castle District best suited for viewing a mysterious Hungarian contribution to Gothic architecture. Niches of unknown function were built into the entryways of medieval buildings. When uncovered during reconstruction, the niches were either preserved or incorporated into the designs of new, modern structures. Niches can be seen in Országház u. 9 and 20, while number 28 has enormous wooden doors.

Országház utca ends in Kapisztrán tér, site of the:

㉑ Mary Magdalene Tower

Once part of a large 13th-century church, the tower is the only section that survived World War II.

Now take Úri utca back in the direction of the Royal Palace. In a corner of the courtyard of Úri u. 49, a vast former cloister, stands the small:

㉒ Telephone Museum

The museum's prime attraction is the actual telephone exchange (7A1-type rotary system), in use from 1928 to 1985.

In the courtyard is a lovely grassy area where you can sit. Úri u. 45 houses the:

㉓ Turkish Embassy

Ironically, this is the only embassy in the Castle District, which from 1541 to 1686 was the seat of Turkish rule in Hungary. Also on Úri utca are Gothic niches galore, seen in the entryways of nos. 40, 38, 36, 34, 32, and 31. Beautiful gardens fill the courtyards of many buildings on Úri utca. If the entranceways are open, take a peek inside.

No doubt you've noticed the presence in the Castle District of a large number of art galleries. Hungarian naïve and primitive art is on display in:

WINDING DOWN
The **Ruszwurm Cukrászda**, Szentháromság u. 7, has been here since 1827. This little coffeehouse and pastry shop is the only one of its kind in the Castle District. Its pastries are among the city's best. Just down the street, at Úri u. 13, is **Budavár Söröző**, a good spot for a snack, espresso, or beer. It has just two tiny tables inside and three or four outside on the sidewalk.

㉔ Rózsa Galéria

At Szentháromság u. 13. Prices start at about 46,000 Ft ($165).

Úri u. 9 is the entrance to the:

㉕ Medieval Tunnel Network

Which weaves its way through the almost 9 miles (15km) of rock beneath the Castle District. The only part of this network you can actually see is home to the Buda Wax Works, an unimpressive, tacky exhibit on the "legends" of early Hungarian history.

Úri utca ends back in Dísz tér. Take tiny Móra Ferenc utca (to the right) to Tóth Árpád sétány, the promenade that runs the length of the western rampart of the Castle District. This is a shady road with numerous benches. At its northern end, appropriately housed in the former barracks at Tóth Árpád sétány 40, is the:

26 Museum of Military History

To our minds, the highlight of this expansive museum is the room devoted to the 1956 Hungarian Uprising. The 13 chaotic days of the Uprising are detailed in consecutive panels of large mounted photographs. The legendary hand of Stalin is here, too—the only piece known to remain

from the giant statue whose public destruction in the huge parking area behind Műcsarnok (Exhibition Hall) in Heroes' Square was a dramatic moment of the failed Uprising.

The walking tour ends back near Szentháromság tér, where you can catch the Várbusz down to Moszkva tér, or from Dísz tér you can get bus no. 16 to Deák tér.

WALKING TOUR 3   LEOPOLD TOWN & THERESA TOWN

Start:	Kossuth tér, site of Parliament.
Finish:	Múvész Coffeehouse, near the Opera House.
Time:	About 3 hours (excluding museum visits and the Opera House tour).
Best Times:	Tuesday through Sunday. Note that if you want to visit the Parliament building, you should secure your ticket in advance.
Worst Time:	Monday, when museums are closed.

In 1790, the new region developing just to the north of the medieval town walls of Pest was dubbed Leopold Town (Lipótváros) in honor of the emperor, Leopold II. Over the next 100 years or so, the neighborhood developed into an integral part of Pest, housing numerous governmental and commercial buildings; Parliament, government ministries, courthouses, the Stock Exchange, and the National Bank were all built here. This tour will take you through the main squares of Leopold Town. You'll also walk briefly along the Danube and visit a historic market hall. Along the way, you can stop to admire some of Pest's most fabulous examples of art nouveau architecture, as well as the city's largest church. Then you'll cross Pest's Inner Ring boulevard, leaving the Inner City, and head up elegant Andrássy út, on the edge of Theresa Town (Terézváros). There you'll see some wonderful inner courtyards and finish the tour after visiting the dazzling State Opera House (try to arrive here by 3 or 4pm if you'd like to tour the Opera House).

Exiting the Kossuth tér metro (Red line), you'll find yourself on the southern end of:

1 Kossuth tér

Walk toward Parliament, passing the equestrian statue of the Transylvanian prince Ferenc Rákóczi II, hero of an early 18th-century anti-Habsburg revolt. Exiled after the failure of his revolt, Rákóczi wandered from Poland to France and then to Turkey, where he remained until his death. A small monument in front of the statue commemorates the victims of the October 1956 Hungarian uprising, a major part of which played out right in this square.

You can't miss, on your left, one of the symbols of Budapest, the neo-Gothic:

2 House of Parliament

Unless you've only just arrived in Budapest, you certainly will have seen this massive structure hugging the Danube. The Parliament building, designed by Imre Steindl and completed in 1902, had been used only once by a democratically elected government prior to 1989. Since 2000, it has also been home to the fabled Hungarian crown jewels. Unfortunately, you can enter only by guided tour (the half-hour tour is worthwhile for the chance to go inside). See p. 106.

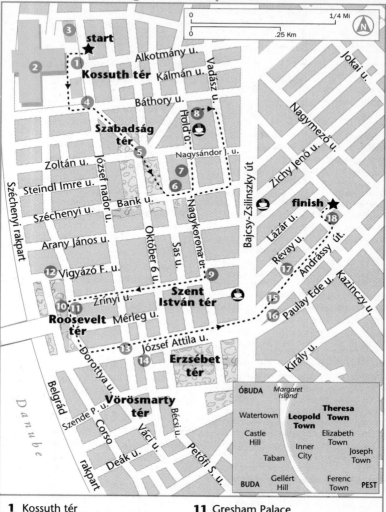

0   1/4 Mi
0   .25 Km

start

Alkotmány u.

Kossuth tér   Kálmán u.

Báthory u.

Szabadság tér

Nagysándor J. u.

Zoltán u.

Steindl Imre u.

Széchenyi u.

Bank u.

Arany János u.

Vigyázó F. u.

Zrínyi u.

Szent István tér

Roosevelt tér   Mérleg u.

József Attila u.

Erzsébet tér

Vörösmarty tér

Deák u.

Vadász u.

Hold u.

Nagykorona u.

Sas u.

Október 6 u.

József nádor u.

Széchenyi rakpart

Belgrád

Szende P. u.

Corso

Váci u.

Bécsi u.

Petőfi S. u.

Dorottya u.

Bajcsy-Zsilinszky út

Zichy Jenő u.

Nagymező u.

Jókai u.

Lázár u.

Révay u.

Andrássy út

Paulay Ede u.

Király u.

Kazinczy u.

finish

D a n u b e

rakpart

ÓBUDA   *Margaret Island*

Watertown   **Leopold Town**   **Theresa Town**

Castle Hill   Elizabeth Town

Inner City   Joseph Town

Taban

BUDA   Gellért Hill   Ferenc Town   **PEST**

1   Kossuth tér
2   House of Parliament
3   Ethnographical Museum
4   Imre Nagy Statue
5   Freedom Square
6   Hungarian National Bank
7   Former Post Office Savings Bank
  Csarnok Vendéglő
8   Inner City Market Hall
9   Szent István tér
10   Roosevelt tér

11   Gresham Palace
12   Hungarian Academy of Sciences
13   József Attila utca
14   Herend Shop
15   Andrássy út
  Rétes Cukrászda/
     Marquis de Salade
16   Post Office Museum
17   Andrássy út 8
18   State Opera House

The grandiose, eclectic-style building across the street from Parliament, the former Supreme Court, now houses the:

❸ Ethnographical Museum

The museum boasts more than 150,000 objects in its collection. The "From Ancient Times to Civilization" exhibition contains many fascinating relics of Hungarian life.

Continue walking in front of Parliament, and walk past the statue of 1848 revolutionary hero Lajos Kossuth; after 45 years in exile, the stubborn Kossuth died in Torino, Italy, but received a hero's burial in Budapest. Notice Kossuth, eyes fixed on the distance, pointing directly toward the Parliament building. Now walk around to the side of Parliament and enter the small park by the Danube at the northern end of Kossuth tér. There's a sensitive Imre Varga statue of Mihály Károlyi, first president of the post–World War I Hungarian Republic. Károlyi, too, died in exile. In 1962, 7 years after his death, his ashes were brought back to his homeland. Across the Danube, to your left, you can see Castle Hill and the church steeples of Watertown (Víziváros) beneath it. The bridge visible to your right is the Margaret Bridge.

Here, you have two options. The more intrepid, and those traveling without children, can turn left, go down the stairs, and scurry across the busy two-lane road to the river embankment. Walk south along the blustery embankment; after completing this circumnavigation of Parliament, cross back and come up the set of stairs. Others can simply circle back to the southern end of Parliament. You'll find a small statue of a seated, somber-looking Attila József, the much-loved interwar working-class poet, whose tragic suicide (by jumping under a train at Lake Balaton) is imitated from time to time in Hungary.

Cross the tram tracks and, walking away from the river, pass the metro entrance and continue through Vértanúk tere ("Square of Martyrs"). Here stands:

❹ Imre Varga's statue of Imre Nagy

Nagy was the reformist communist who led the failed 1956 Hungarian Uprising. He was executed in 1958, two years after the Soviet-led invasion. The statue, *Witnesses to Blood*, was erected in 1996, 7 years after the reburial of Nagy attracted some 300,000 Hungarians to Hősök tere (Heroes' Square). The statue of Nagy crossing a symbolic bridge, like the nearby statue of Kossuth, has his gaze fixed on Parliament in the distance.

Now walk a few blocks down Nádor utca and turn left onto Zoltán utca. The massive yellow building on the right side of Zoltán utca is the Former Stock Exchange, now headquarters of Hungarian Television. There are plans to sell the building and move both television and radio headquarters to a new building somewhere in district IX, a favorite location of the current government for controversial cultural projects, such as the National Theater. The front of the television building is on:

❺ Freedom Square (Szabadság tér)

Directly in front of you is the Soviet Army Memorial, built in 1945 to honor the Soviet-led liberation of Budapest and topped by the last Soviet Star remaining in post-Communist Budapest. The American Embassy is at Szabadság tér 12.

Paying careful attention to the often-unruly traffic here, walk diagonally through the square, aiming for its southeast corner, site of the eclectic:

❻ Hungarian National Bank (Magyar Nemzeti Bank)

Leaving Szabadság tér via Bank utca, you can enter the National Bank through a side entrance. Its well-preserved, ornate lobby reminds one more of an opera house than a bank; its air-conditioned skylit main hall has rows of soft, comfortable chairs where you can take a breather.

Continue on Bank utca, making the first left onto Hold utca (Moon Street), formerly known as Rosenberg házaspár utca, for Ethel and Julius Rosenberg. Next door, to the rear of the National Bank and connected to it by a small footbridge, is the spectacular and newly restored:

❼ Former Post Office Savings Bank (Posta Takarékpénztár)

The bank was built in 1901 to the design of ödön Lechner, the architect who endeavored to fuse Hungarian folk elements with the art nouveau style of his time.

> **TAKE A BREAK**
> On the corner of Hold utca and Nagysándor József utca is **Csarnok** Vendéglő, Hold u. 11. This unassuming little restaurant, visited mainly by neighborhood residents, is good for a typical Hungarian lunch. The restaurant's name is taken from the nearby:

⑧ Inner City Market Hall (Belvárosi Vásárcsarnok)

Built in 1897, this cavernous market hall has been newly restored. The market (which closes at 4pm) is one of the city's liveliest; pick up some fruit in season.

Emerge from the Market Hall onto Vadász utca and turn right. Passing Nagysándor József utca, look right for a great view of the colorful tiled roof of the former Post Office Savings Bank you recently passed. Turn right on Bank utca (the metro station you see on your left is Arany János utca; Blue line) and left on Hercegprímás utca. After a few blocks, you'll find yourself in:

⑨ Szent István tér

This is the site of the famous St. Stephen's Basilica, Budapest's largest church, seating some 8,500 poeple. Built between 1851 and 1905, it is well worth a stop. In the Szent Jobb Kápolna, behind the main altar, you can see an extraordinary and gruesome holy relic: Stephen's preserved right hand, which is paraded around town annually on St. Stephen's Day, August 20th. Monday-night organ concerts are held in the church in summer.

Head down Zrínyi utca, straight across the square from the church entrance. As you pass Október 6 utca, you might want to make a slight detour to Bestsellers, the English-language bookstore owned by the Central European University at no. 11. Bestsellers stocks travel books, especially on Eastern Europe. Alternately, you may want to stop over at the corner of Zrínyi utca and Nádor utca and walk into the building of the

Central European University itself; downstairs you will find their other bookstore, which has a more academic stock of works by Central and East European scholars, including works on the political and economic, cultural changes in the region. Returning now to the Danube, you'll find yourself emerging into:

⑩ Roosevelt tér

This square lies at the head of the famous Chain Bridge. Built in the revolutionary year 1848–49, the bridge was the first permanent span across the Danube.

Roosevelt Square itself is really too full of traffic to be beautiful, but there are several important and lovely buildings here, including:

⑪ The Gresham Palace

Built in 1907, it is one of Budapest's best-known art nouveau buildings. The building is presently scaffolded up in a massive renovation to convert it into a Four Seasons luxury hotel. The plan is to open in its original glory in 2002. This renovation triggered one of the first successful civic protest movements in town since the 1989 change in regime. A group of Green activists chained themselves to the hundred year-old trees in the park in front of the building, defeating a plan to cut them down and transform the graceful park into a parking lot for the hotel. The hotel will instead have an underground garage.

To your right, as you face the river, is the neo-Renaissance facade of the:

⑫ Hungarian Academy of Sciences

Like the Chain Bridge, it was the brainchild of the 19th-century Count István Széchenyi (called "the Greatest Hungarian"), who completed it in 1864. A statue of Széchenyi adorns the square. Guards prevent access beyond the Academy lobby, but it's worth a peek inside. A statue of Ferenc Deák, architect of the 1867 Compromise with Austria, is in a shady grove in the square's southern end by the Atrium Hyatt Hotel.

Turn left away from the river onto bustling:

⑬ József Attila utca

This street was named for the poet whose statue embellishes Kossuth tér. You're now walking along a portion of the Inner Ring (Kiskörüt), which separates the Inner City (Belváros) to your right from Leopold Town (Lipótváros) to your left.

At József nádor tér, you may want to stop in at the:

⑭ Herend Shop

Herend china is perhaps Hungary's most famous product, and this museum-like shop is definitely worth a look.

Continuing up József Attila utca, you'll pass Erzsébet tér, site of Budapest's main bus station, just before reaching Bajcsy-Zsilinszky út. Endre Bajcsy-Zsilinszky, a heroic leader of Hungary's wartime antifascist resistance, was executed by the Arrow Cross (Hungary's Nazi party) on Christmas Eve 1944. Crossing Bajcsy-Zsilinszky út, you'll find yourself at the head of stately:

⑮ Andrássy út

Lined with trees and a wealth of beautiful apartment buildings, this is fin-de-siècle Pest's greatest boulevard. Andrássy út has recently been turned into a lively café and bar scene as well. There are colorful terraces and delicious cakes and ice cream under the shades of the huge trees all the way up to Oktogon.

☕ TAKE A BREAK Walk 1 short block to your left on Bajcsy-Zsilinszky út to **Rétes Cukrászda**, at VI. Bajcsy-Zsilinszky út 15. Try the fabulous meggyes rétes (sour cherry turnover). Or, if you crave a proper meal, drop into **Marquis de Salade**, down Bajcsy-Zsilinskky út at VI. Hajós u. 43, for delightful vegetarian cuisine.

Returning now to Andrássy út, look for no. 3, a building with a stunning entryway, which is the:

⑯ Post Office Museum

Its main attraction is clearly the opulently appointed apartment in which it's located. Imagine: This is how the wealthy of Andrássy út used to live! The frescoes in the entryway are by Károly Lotz, whose frescoes also decorate the Opera House and Matthias Church, in the Castle District.

Cross over to the even-numbered side of Andrássy. Stop to peek into other entryways and courtyards. Be sure to take a look in the vestibule of:

⑰ Andrássy út 8

Here, you'll find more ceiling frescoes and painted glass courtyard doors; the courtyard is typical of this kind of Pest apartment building. Andrássy út 12, is a building that used to belong to the once-feared Interior Ministry, and was the site of torture and other mistreatment of "political criminals." Ironically, given its ugly past, the building has a gorgeous entryway and an inner courtyard with frescoes covering the walls. An officer sometimes guards the entrance; sightseers are usually allowed to poke their heads in.

Continue on Andrássy út until you reach the neo-Renaissance:

⑱ State Opera House.

Designed by Miklós Ybl and built in 1884, the Opera House survived the siege of Budapest at the end of World War II nearly unscathed. In fact, its huge cellars provided shelter for thousands during the bombing. Turning left on Hajós utca, walk around the Opera House. There are a number of music stores on Hajós utca. The street directly behind the Opera House, Lázár utca, affords an unusual view of the Bazilika. And if you are lucky, you can hear performers practicing through open windows on Dalszinház utca. Opera House English-language tours (the only way, short of attending a performance, that you can get a look inside) are daily at 3 and 4pm year-round and start at the front entrance; the cost is 600 Ft ($2.15) per person.

You'll find the Opera station of the Yellow metro line just in front of the Opera House.

Start: Dohány Synagogue.
Finish: Wesselényi utca.
Time: About 2 hours (excluding museum visit).
Best Times: Sunday through Friday.
Worst Time: Saturday, when the museum and most shops are closed.

The Jewish district of Pest has a long and ultimately tragic history. It first sprang up in medieval times just beyond the Pest city wall (which stood where today's Inner Ring boulevard stands), as Jews were forbidden to live inside the town. Later, Pest expanded beyond its walls, and the Jewish district actually became one of the city's more centrally located neighborhoods. The huge synagogues that you'll see on this tour give some idea of its former vitality. Under German occupation in World War II, the district became a walled ghetto, with 220,000 Jews crowded inside; almost half perished during the war. Sadly, the neighborhood is now more or less in a state of decay; buildings are crumbling, garbage is strewn about, and graffiti covers the walls. Nevertheless, this compact little neighborhood is filled with evocative sights.

Halfway between Astoria (Red metro line) and Deák tér (all metro lines) is the:

❶ Dohány Synagogue

This striking Byzantine building, Europe's largest synagogue and the world's second-largest, was built in 1859 and is still used by Budapest's Neolog (Conservative) Jewish community. The synagogue is newly cleaned and restored.

The small freestanding brick wall inside the courtyard, to the left of the synagogue's entrance, is a piece of the original:

❷ Ghetto Wall

The wall kept Budapest's Jews inside this district during World War II. This is not actually where it stood, however; it was situated on Károly körút, the nearby stretch of the Inner Ring boulevard.

To the left of the wall, on the spot marked as the birthplace of Theodor Herzl, the founder of modern Zionism, is the:

❸ National Jewish Museum

On display are ornaments and art from the long history of Hungarian Jewry. The last of the four rooms is given over to a moving exhibit on the Holocaust in Hungary. (Note the

open hours: May through October only, Monday through Thursday from 10am to 5pm, Friday from 10am to 3pm, and Sunday from 10am to 1pm.) The synagogue courtyard can be entered through the rear of the complex on Wesselényi utca.

Inside the courtyard is the still-expanding:

❹ Holocaust Memorial

Designed by Imre Varga, the wonderful contemporary Hungarian sculptor, the memorial is in the form of a weeping willow tree. Thin metal leaves, purchased by survivors and descendants to honor martyred relatives, are slowly filling the many branches. The courtyard behind the memorial is called the Raoul Wallenberg Memorial Park, in honor of the Swiss diplomat who saved thousands of Jewish lives in wartime Budapest. The names of some of Budapest's "righteous Gentiles" are inscribed on four pillars.

Now head down Rumbach utca. On the right, against a cement wall near the corner of Rumbach utca and Dob utca, is the rather bizarre-looking:

⑤ Memorial to Charles Lutz

Lutz was the Swiss consul who aided Wallenberg's heroic attempts to save Budapest's Jews from the Nazi death camps. The inscription from the Talmud reads: "Saving one soul is the same as saving the whole world." Another, rather lonely, memorial to Wallenberg stands irrelevantly on Szilágyi Erzsébet fasor, far away in Buda.

Half a block farther on Rumbach utca is the:

⑥ Rumbach Synagogue

This handsome but decrepit yellow-and-rust–colored building is, in its own way, as impressive as the Dohány Synagogue. Built in 1872 by the Vienna architect Otto Wagner, this Orthodox synagogue is no longer in use. You can't go inside as the building is presently out of use, but the facade itself is worth seeing.

At the corner of Madách út, take a look at the giant archway of:

⑦ Madách tér

In the 1930s, a plan was drawn up for the creation of a great boulevard similar in form and style to Andrássy út. World War II put an end to the ambitious project, and the grand Madách tér leads only to itself now. Looking through the arch on a clear day, you get an unusual view of Gellért Hill, crowned by the Liberation Monument. Several new art galleries can be found on Rumbach utca and Madách út.

Proceed down Rumbach utca and take a right onto Király utca, which forms the northern border of the historic Jewish district. At Király u. 13, head through the long series of:

⑧ Connected courtyards

These emerge onto Dob utca, back in the heart of the Jewish district. This kind of complex—residential buildings connected by a series of courtyards—is typical of the Jewish district. As you can readily see, these courtyards are in extremely poor condition, dirty and

run-down with graffiti-covered walls and abandoned apartments, though the appearance in recent years of several flashy retail shops may presage a general improvement.

TAKE A BREAK
Frohlich Cukrászda, Dob u. 22, is the only functioning kosher cukrászda (sweet shop) left in the district. Here, you can purchase pastries, rolls, or ice cream. (The shop closes for 2 weeks at the end of August.)

Half a block to the left off Dob utca on Kazinczy utca, at no. 41, is the:

⑨ Kosher Salami Workshop (Szalámi és Kolbászáru üzem)

Salami, famous throughout Hungary, is handmade here with ancient machinery. If you make a purchase, be sure to admire the equally ancient cash register in the corner. The sign outside directing you to the entrance is deceptive; simply enter via the doorway in front of you. Open Monday through Thursday from 8am to 4pm, and on Friday from 8am to 1pm.

Back on Kazinczy u., no. 29 is the:

⑩ Orthodox Kazinczy Synagogue

Built in 1913 and still active, this synagogue is being slowly and beautifully restored; it also has a well-maintained and lively courtyard in its center. There are a number of apartments in which members of the community live. While hundreds of tourists a day visit the Dohány Synagogue, far fewer make the trip here.

Go all the way through the courtyard, emerge onto Dob utca, turn right, and head into:

⑪ Klauzál tér

This is the district's largest square and its historic center. A dusty park and renovated playground fill the interior of the square.

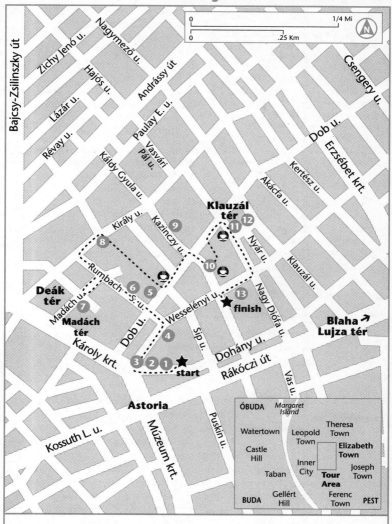

1 Dohány Synagogue
2 Ghetto Wall
3 National Jewish Museum
4 Holocaust Memorial
5 Memorial to Charles Lutz
6 Rumbach Synagogue
7 Madách tér
8 Connected Courtyards

🟢 Frohlich Cukrászda
9 Kosher Salami Workshop
10 Orthodox Kazinczy Synagogue
11 Klauzál tér
12 District Market Hall
🟢 Hanna Kosher/ Kádar Étkezde
13 Judaica Art Gallery

TAKE A BREAK
You have two lunch options in Klauzál tér and its immediate vicinity, each with a markedly different character. **Hanna Kosher Restaurant**, at the Kazinczy Synagogue, the city's only strictly kosher restaurant, is open daily for lunch and offers a somewhat pricey (2,200 Ft/ $7.90) multi-course prix fixe lunch. Buy your ticket at the window and wash your hands at the sink on the way in. Men should keep their heads covered inside. (Note: Meals can't be purchased on Saturdays—they have to be pre-paid the day before). **Kádár Étkezde**, at Klauzál tér 9, is a simple local lunchroom (open only Tuesday through Saturday from 11:30am to 3:30pm) serving a regular clientele, ranging from young paint-spattered workers to elderly Jews.

At Klauzál tér 11, you'll find the:

⑫ District Market Hall (Vásárcsarnok)

One of the half dozen or so great steel-girdered market halls built in Budapest in the 1890s, this one is rather run-down and now houses a Skála grocery store. The entrance area is filled with smaller vendors selling fruit or vegetables.

Now head back out on Nagydiófa utca to Wesselényi utca, where you can end the walking tour at the:

⑬ Judaica Art Gallery, at Wesselényi u. 13

Here you'll find Jewish-oriented books, both new and secondhand (some are in English). Clothing, ceramics, art, and religious articles are also for sale.

WALKING TOUR 5	TABAN & WATERTOWN (VIZIVAROS)

Start: The Pest side of the Erzsébet Bridge.
Finish: The Buda side of the Margaret (Margít) Bridge.
Time: About 2 to 3 hours (excluding museum visits).
Best Time: Any time.

This tour will take you through the narrow, twisting neighborhood along the Buda side of the Danube. Tabán, the area between Gellért Hill and Castle Hill, was once a vibrant but very poor workers' neighborhood. The neighborhood was razed in the early 20th century for "sanitary reasons"; only a handful of Tabán buildings still stand below the green expanse of parks where the rest of Tabán once was. The neighborhood directly beneath Castle Hill, opposite the Inner City of Pest, has been called Víziváros (Watertown) since the Middle Ages. Historically home to fishermen who made a living on the Danube, Víziváros was surrounded by walls in Turkish times. The neighborhood still retains a quiet integrity; above busy Fő utca (Main Street), which runs one street up from and parallel to the river the length of Watertown, you'll wander along aged, peaceful lanes.

Begin the walking tour on the Pest side of the:

① Erzsébet Bridge

The nearest metro stations are Ferenciek tere (Blue line) and Vörösmarty tér (Yellow line). The original Erzsébet Bridge was completed in 1903, but like all the city's bridges was destroyed by the Germans in World War II; the present bridge was constructed in 1964. Note how the bridge skirts around the Inner City Parish Church, which dates to the 12th century. Cross the bridge on the right side with the flow of traffic. In order to do this, you'll need to be in front of the church; there's a staircase opposite, leading up to the bridge.

Walking Tour 5: Tabán & Watertown (Víziváros)

1 Erzsébet Bridge
2 Tabán Parish Church
3 Berlin Wall
4 Semmelweis Medical
  History Museum
5 Ybl Miklós tér
6 Öntőház utca
7 Clark Ádám tér
8 Funicular (sikló)
9 Tunnel
10 Fő utca (Main Street)
11 Jégverem utca
12 Hunyádi János út
13 Institut Français
🛇 Taverna Ressaikos/
  Horgásztanya/
  Le Jardin de Paris
14 Capuchin Church
15 Corvin tér
16 Iskola utca
  (School Street)
17 Bem rakpart
18 Szilágyi Dezső tér
19 Batthyány tér
20 St. Anne's Church
21 The Vasarcsarnok
  (Market Hall)
🛇 Angelika Cukrászda
22 St. Elizabeth's Church
23 Nagy Imre tér
24 Király Baths
25 Chapel of St. Florian
26 Öntödei (Foundry)
  Museum
27 Bem József tér
28 The Buda side of the
  Margaret Bridge

───── Overpass or
       Bridge
┅┅┅┅ Tunnel
▬▬▬▬ Medieval Wall
🛇   Refreshment
       Stop

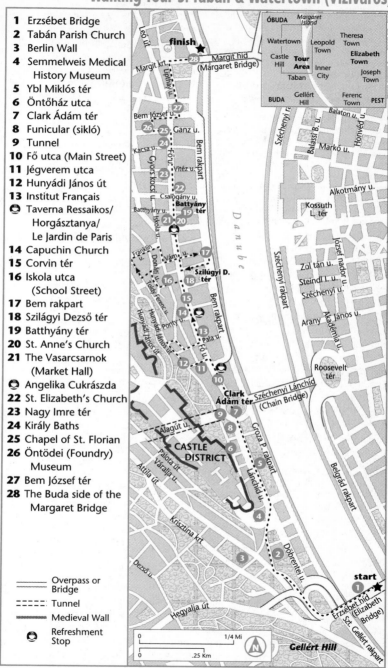

In front of you is Gellért Hill; the statue of Bishop Gellért bears his cross defiantly on the mountainside. From here, the legend goes, vengeful 11th century pagans, recalling the cruelties of the conversion to Christianity, forced the Italian bishop who had aided King Stephen's crusade into a barrel and rolled him to his death in the river far below.

Upon reaching Buda, descend the steps, and, passing the statue of Queen Erzsébet, note the tablet commemorating the antifascists who, on this spot in 1944, blew up a statue of Gyula Gömbös, a leading Hungarian fascist politician of the interwar period. You're now at the bottom of the historic Tabán district. Walk away from the bridge, toward the yellow church whose steeple is visible above the trees. Your first stop here in Buda is the:

❷ Tabán Parish Church

You can enter this church, built in 1736. Inside, you'll find a copy of a 12th-century carving called the *Tabán Christ*. The original is in the Budapest History Museum (inside the Buda Palace). Passing the church, you now see in front of and above you the southern end of the Buda Palace. Watertown is the long, narrow strip of Buda that lies on a slope between Castle Hill and the Danube. Before proceeding to it, note the tile-roofed Stag House on Szarvas tér diagonally across the street. One of Tabán's few remaining buildings, it now houses the Aranyszarvas Restaurant.

If you cross to that side of the street, you can see across busy Attila út (the street that runs behind Castle Hill) two graffiti-covered pillar-like chunks of the:

❸ Berlin Wall

Its presence here recalls the pivotal role Hungary played in the fall of East German communism. Thousands of East German vacationers crossed the border from Hungary into Austria after the "Iron Curtain" was dismantled here in the late summer of 1989. This exodus helped spark the popular movement that led ultimately to the collapse of the East German regime and the breaching of the Berlin Wall.

Continue now down Apród út. The rust-and-white building at Apród út 1–3 is the:

❹ Semmelweis Medical History Museum

Named after one of Hungary's greatest physicians, the museum has exhibits related to a number of medical fields and contains furnishings of the 19th-century Szentlélek Pharmacy.

Proceed to:

❺ Ybl Miklós tér

This narrow square on the Danube is named for Hungary's most celebrated architect. The lovely building at the square's southern end is the former Várkert (Castle Garden) Kiosk; it's now a casino. The patio ceiling is covered with sgraffito. Directly across the street from Miklós Ybl's statue is the Várkert Bazar. It's now in a frightful state of disrepair, but you can still admire the ornate archways and stairs.

Walk the length of the old Bazar to Lánchíd utca, so named because it leads into Clark Ádám tér, the Buda head of the Chain Bridge. Walking away from the river, take the steep set of stairs on your left up to quiet canyonlike:

❻ Öntőház utca

In summer, the terrace gardens of these residential buildings thrive. Flowers, small trees and shrubs, ivy, and grape vines are cultivated with care.

Turn right, winding back down to Lánchíd utca just before it spills into:

❼ Clark Ádám tér

This is a busy traffic circle named for the Scottish engineer who supervised building the Chain Bridge in 1848–49. After completing his assignment, Clark grew so fond of Budapest that he remained here until his death.

Immediately to your left is the:

❽ Funicular (sikló)

It goes up to the Buda Palace. In front of the funicular is the "Zero Kilometer Stone," the marker from which all highway distances to and from Budapest are measured.

Straight across the square from the Chain Bridge is:

⑨ The Tunnel
Built between 1853 and 1857, it connects Watertown with Christina Town (Krisztinaváros) on the other side of Castle Hill. The joke of the day was that the tunnel was built so that the precious Chain Bridge could be placed inside when it rained. Just across the street from the tunnel, a set of stairs marks the beginning of the long climb up to Castle Hill.

Passing straight through the square, you'll find yourself at the head of Watertown's:

⑩ Fő utca (Main Street)
You'll be either on or near this long, straight street for the remainder of this walking tour. As you pass Jégverem utca, make a little detour toward the river to examine the solid wood door at Jégverem u. 2. Note the small door cut out of the larger one, presumably a gatekeeper's door in days gone by, when the main doors were kept closed except for carriages and the like.

Now head left on:

⑪ Jégverem utca
At Kapucinus utca, you get a marvelous view of the steep old tile rooftops down the street.

Proceed up the stairs to the next street:

⑫ Hunyadi János út
Walk through the absurdly tall, narrow doorway of Hunyadi János út 9. Peek into the courtyard to see the crude wooden construction of the inner terrace landings. Hunyadi János út 4, across the street, has a dazzling enclosed atrium interior above the inner courtyard; its timeless beauty is sharply contrasted by the sheer horror of the dungeonlike cellar, clearly visible beneath you.

At the intersection of Szalag utca, turn right and then right again on Szőnyeg utca, back toward Fő utca. Bear left on Pala utca. Crossing Kapucinus utca, continue down the steps. Here are the rooftops you viewed from a distance a short while ago. Emerge onto Fő utca at the site of the monstrous:

⑬ Institut Français.
Note also the reconstructed remains of a medieval house across the street from this French cultural center.

> ☕ **TAKE A BREAK**
> **Taverna Ressaikos,** I. Apor Péter u. 1, serves delicious, carefully prepared Greek cuisine. Other meal options include **Horgásztanya Vendéglő** (The Fisherman's Den), I. Fő u. 29, where Hungarian seafood is served in a rustic setting, and **Le Jardin de Paris,** I. Fő u. 20, a delightful French bistro (see "Central Buda," in chapter 5, "Where to Dine in Budapest").

Across the street from Horgásztanya is the former:

⑭ Capuchin Church
This is the first of several Watertown churches included on this tour. Note the Turkish door and window frames on the church's southern wall.

Just past this church is:

⑮ Corvin tér
Several interesting buildings, including the home of the Hungarian State Folk Ensemble, are located here. If the timing is right, you might hear rehearsal through the open windows. There is presently a major archaeological dig going on at this square. Note also the row of very old baroque houses at the top of the square.

Head above Corvin tér to:

⑯ Iskola utca (School Street)
Turn right on Iskola utca and left up the Donáti lépcső (stairs) to Donáti utca; a clay frieze of two horsemen adorns the residential building to the left, opposite the stair landing. Turn right and walk to the next set of stairs, Toldy lépcső. Turn left up the stairs and right onto Toldy Ferenc utca, a residential street lined with old-fashioned gas lampposts. This street is so tranquil that the only other tourists

are likely to be following this very walking tour. Notice the gorgeous brick secondary school on your right (Toldy Ferenc Gimnázium); a plaque notes *"itt tanított Antall József"* ("József Antall [first post-Communist prime minister] taught here"). Just before Iskola utca is a wonderful little playground, the perfect place to stop if you've been dragging any youngsters along with you.

Now turn right on Iskola utca, then left onto Vám utca. Cross Fő utca, heading to the:

⑰ Bem rakpart

This is the Danube embankment. Directly across the river is Parliament. The next bridge on your left is the Margaret Bridge, where this walking tour will end.

Turn right now and you'll immediately find yourself in:

⑱ Szilágyi Dezsó tér

This neo-Gothic Calvinist Church dates from the end of the 19th century. The composer Béla Bartók lived at Szilágyi Dezsó tér 4 in the 1920s. The Danube bank near this square is the site of a piece of Hungary's darkest history. Here the Arrow Cross (*Nyilas*), the Hungarian Nazis, massacred thousands of Jews in 1944 and 1945, during the last bitter winter of World War II. Many were tied together into small groups and thrown alive into the freezing river.

Returning now to Fő utca, turn right and continue on toward Watertown's main square, Batthyány tér. You may want to stop in at the Herend Village Pottery shop at Bem rakpart 37, on the ground floor of the housing block. You'll find several attractions along:

⑲ Batthyány tér

One of its principal sights is the 18th-century:

⑳ St. Anne's Church

One of Hungary's finest baroque churches, it was almost destroyed in the early 1950s when the Hungarian dictator Mátyás Rákosi (known as "Stalin's most loyal disciple") had the idea that when his mentor visited him at his office in Parliament, Stalin would be loath to look across the Danube at a Buda skyline dominated by churches. Fortunately, Rákosi's demented plan was never realized.

Also on the square is:

㉑ The Vásárcsarnok (Market Hall)

One of several markets built in 1897, it now houses a large, well-stocked grocery store (open on Sunday). The interior might be worth a look. Two doors down is the former White Cross Inn, a rococo building, which, like St. Anne's, dates from the 18th century. The legendary philanderer Casanova is said to have spent a night here, hence the name of the ground-floor nightclub. Next door, at Batthyány tér 3, above the first-floor windows of the building, are several enchanting but shamefully dirty clay friezes.

TAKE A BREAK
Next door to St. Anne's Church in the former presbytery is **Angelika Cukrászda**, I. Batthyány tér 7. This lovely coffeehouse is the perfect place for a little rest. Delicious pastries are served in low-ceilinged, cavernous rooms, clearly designed for ecclesiastical purposes. Or have a cold drink on the newly constructed terraces outside, overlooking the river and the Parliament building on the other bank.

Continuing along Fő utca, the next church on your right is:

㉒ St. Elizabeth's Church

Presently closed for reconstruction, this church has a fine baroque interior. The frescoes date from the 19th century.

You're now approaching the northern border of Watertown; larger streets—such as Batthyány utca and Csalogány utca—now bisect Fő utca. You can no longer see Castle Hill. The next square is:

㉓ Nagy Imre tér

A small park hidden behind a Total gas station, the square is named for the reform Communist leader who played a leading, if slightly reluctant, role in the 1956 Hungarian Revolution. The prisonlike building on the corner is the Military Court of Justice, where Nagy was secretly tried and condemned to death in 1958, thus providing Hungary with yet another martyr. Nagy's rehabilitation and reburial in June 1989 was a moment of great national unity, and a statue of him was recently erected near Parliament (see "Walking Tour 3," earlier in this chapter). The main entrance to the Military Court of Justice is on Fő utca.

Two blocks farther, at Fő u. 82–86, are the:

㉔ Király Baths

This 16th-century bathhouse is now one of the city's major monuments to the period of Turkish rule. Even if you're not going in to bathe, you should take a peek at the gorgeous interior. The baths are open on different days for men and women (see "Spa Bathing & Swimming: Budapest's Most Popular Thermal Baths," in chapter 6, "Exploring Budapest").

Next door, at the corner of Fő utca and Ganz utca, is the baroque:

㉕ Chapel of St. Florian

Today, this is a Greek Orthodox church; it's nice if not spectacular—have a look inside the vestibule.

Turn left on Ganz utca, passing through the small park between the baths and the church. At the end of Ganz utca is the:

㉖ Öntödei (Foundry) Museum

The museum is housed inside the original structure of the famed Abraham Ganz Foundry (founded 1845). From the exterior, painted a creamy yellow with a rusty-red trim, it's hard to imagine the vast barnlike interior. The collection of antique cast-iron stoves is the highlight. This is definitely worth a visit if you're in the neighborhood, although not worth going out of your way to see.

Turn right onto Bem József utca, a street with several small fishing and army-navy-type supply stores, heading back down toward the Danube, where you'll find yourself in:

㉗ Bem József tér

Named after the Polish general who played a heroic role in the 1848–49 Hungarian Revolution. On October 23, 1956, the square hosted a rally in support of the reform efforts in Poland. The rally, and the subsequent march across the Margaret Bridge to Parliament, marked the beginning of the famous 1956 Hungarian Uprising.

Turn left onto Lipthay utca, which is parallel to the river. Admire the buildings on your left along this street before ending the tour at:

㉘ The Buda side of the Margaret Bridge

Here, you can pick up the no. 4 or no. 6 tram and head to either Buda's Moszkva tér (Red metro line) or across the river to Pest's Outer Ring boulevard.

8

Budapest Shopping

Folklore objects are the most popular souvenirs among foreigners visiting Budapest. The chain of Folkart shops (Népművészeti Háziipar) has a great selection of handmade goods at unbeatable prices. Popular items include pillowcases, pottery, porcelain, dolls, dresses, skirts, and sheepskin vests.

Other sources of authentic folk items are the ethnic Hungarian women who come to Budapest with bags full of handmade craftwork from Transylvania, a region of Romania heavily populated with ethnic Hungarians. The police halfheartedly drive them from one neighborhood to the next, and they congregate where they can. Keep your eyes open for these vendors, unmistakable in their characteristic black boots, dark-red skirts, and red or white kerchiefs tied around their heads. Their prices are generally quite reasonable, and bargaining is customary.

PORCELAIN, FOODSTUFFS & MARKETS

Another popular Hungarian item is **porcelain,** particularly from the country's two best-known producers, Herend and Zsolnay. Although both brands are available in the West, here you'll find a better selection and prices up to 50% lower.

Typical **Hungarian foods** also make great gifts. Hungarian salami is world-famous. Connoisseurs generally agree that Pick Salami, produced in the southeastern city of Szeged, is the best brand. Herz Salami, produced locally in Budapest, is a slightly lesser product. You should be aware that some people have reported difficulty in clearing U.S. Customs with salami; bring it home at your own risk. Another typical Hungarian food product is chestnut paste (*gesztenye püré*), available in a tin or block wrapped in foil; it's used primarily as a pastry filling but can also top desserts and ice cream. Paprika paste (*pirosarany*) is something else you'll scarcely find outside Hungary. It comes most commonly in a bright-red tube. Three types are available: hot (*csípős*), deli style (*csemege*), and sweet (*édes*). All these items can be purchased in grocery stores (*élelmiszer*) and delicatessens (*csemege*). Also look for Szamos brand marzipan. **Szamos Confectioners,** a recently reestablished family business originally founded in 1935, is also said to make the best ice cream in the country. They're based in Szentendre, with a shop in Budapest at V. Párisi u. 3, ☎ 1/317-3643.

If you love **open markets,** Budapest is the place for you. There are numerous markets here: flea markets (*használtáru piac*), filled not only with every conceivable kind of junk and the occasional relic of Communism, but also with great quantities of mostly low-quality new items like clothing, cassettes, and shoes; and food markets (*vásárcsarnok, csarnok, or piac*), with row after row of succulent fruits and vegetables, much of it freshly picked and driven in from the surrounding countryside. You can also find saffron and several varieties of dried mushrooms for surprisingly low prices.

1 The Shopping Scene

MAIN SHOPPING STREETS All year long, tourists and locals alike throng the pedestrian-only **Váci utca,** from the stately Vörösmarty tér, the center of Pest, across the roaring Kossuth Lajos utca, all the way to Vámház krt. Váci utca, and most of the pedestrian streets bisecting it, are lined with shops. Boutiques, not visible from the street, fill the courtyards. The prevalence of Euro-fashions is now the trend on Váci utca. "Western-style" prices also prevail. Váci utca was formerly (as recently as the late 1980s) known throughout the country as *the* street for good bookshops. Sadly, only one remains. The street is otherwise largely occupied by the aforementioned clothing boutiques and an overwhelming number of folklore/souvenir shops, as well as cafes and bars.

Another favorite shopping area for tourists is the **Castle District** in Buda, with its abundance of folk-art boutiques and art galleries.

While locals might window-shop in these two neighborhoods, they tend to do their serious shopping elsewhere. One favorite street is Pest's **Outer Ring** (Nagykörút) now extended into **West End Center,** the newest shopping mall—or super-mall might better describe it—in town, just behind to Nyugati railway station; another bustling shopping street is Pest's **Kossuth Lajos utca,** off the Erzsébet Bridge, and its continuation, **Rákóczi út,** which extends all the way out to Keleti Station. **Andrássy út,** from Deák tér to Oktogon, is also a popular, though more upscale shopping street and, in combination with the adjacent **Liszt Ferenc tér,** the most recent hub of night life, with numerous coffee shops, bars and restaurants. In Buda, Hungarian crowds visit the shops of **Margit körút** and the neighborhood of **Móricz Zsigmond körtér,** where the Buda Skála department store is located.

HOURS Most stores are open Monday through Friday from 10am to 6pm and on Saturday from about 9am to about 1pm. Some stores stay open an hour or two later on Thursday or Friday, while some close for an hour at lunchtime. Most shops are closed Sunday, except for those in downtown Pest. Shopping malls are open on weekends, as late as 6pm. Payment by credit or charge card in tourist shopping areas is usually possible.

TAXES & REFUNDS Refunds on the 10% to 25% **value-added tax (VAT),** which is built into all prices, is available for most consumer goods purchases of more than 50,000 Ft ($180) (look for stores with the "Tax-Free" logo in the window). The refund process, however, is elaborate and confusing. In most shops, the salesperson can provide you with the necessary documents: the store receipt, a separate receipt indicating the VAT amount on your purchase, the VAT reclaim form, and the mailing envelope. The salesperson should also be able to help you fill out the paperwork. You must hold on to the full packet until you leave Hungary, at which point you get your forms certified by Customs. Then, mail in your envelope and wait for your refund. Two wrinkles: You must get your forms certified by Customs within 90 days of the purchase, and you must mail in your forms within 183 days of the date of export certification on the refund claim form. Use a separate claim form for each applicable purchase. For further information, contact **Global Refund,** Bég u. 3–5, 1022 Budapest (© **1/212-4019** ext. 518; fax 1/212-4906; www.globalrefund.com).

SHIPPING & CUSTOMS You can ship a box to yourself from any post office, but the rules on packing boxes are as strict as they are arcane. The Hungarian postal authorities prefer that you use one of their official shipping boxes, for sale at all post offices. They're quite flimsy, however, and have been known to break open in transit.

Very few shops will organize shipping for you. Exceptions to this rule include most Herend and Zsolnay porcelain shops, Ajka crystal shops, and certain art galleries, which employ the services of a packing-and-shipping company, Touristpost. Touristpost offers three kinds of delivery: express, air mail, and surface. At the moment, it seems that the service is not available directly to the public but functions only through these particular shops. You may inquire further at **Touristpost,** III. Meggyfa u. 31 (© **1/388-7465;** touristpost@nexus.hu). Though the service is costly (for example, 30,000 Ft/$108 for 60 lbs.), you will still likely save on the price of fine porcelain and crystal purchased in Hungary.

Hungarian Customs regulations do not limit the export of noncommercial quantities of most goods. However, the export of some food staples like coffee (1 kg) is strictly regulated (but rarely enforced). The limit on wine and spirits is 1 liter each, and 500 cigarettes may be exported.

2 Shopping A to Z
ANTIQUES
When shopping for antiques in Budapest, you should know that Hungary forbids the export of many items designated as "cultural treasures." Some purchases come with a certificate allowing export; with other purchases, the responsibility is the buyer's alone to go to the correct office (in the Museum of Applied Arts) and apply for the certificate. Our advice is to buy only from those shops that supply the certificate for you. A journey through Hungarian bureaucracy—like any other—can be a withering experience.

Although it no longer has a monopoly on the sale of antiques, the still state-owned **BÁV (Bizományi Kereskedoház és Záloghitel Rt.)** continues to control the lion's share of the antiques market in Hungary. Here's a partial list of BÁV shops:

- I. Hess András tér 1 (No phone; fax 1/375-0392), in the Castle District, specializing in porcelain and folk art.
- V. Bécsi u. 1 (No phone; fax 1/317-2548), near Deák tér, is the largest of the shops, specializing in antique furniture, chandeliers, carpets, and painting.
- V. Ferenciek tere 5 (© **1/318-3773**), specializing in carpets.
- VI. Andrássy út 27 (© **1/342-5525**), near the Opera House, specializing in antique art, furniture, carpets, porcelain, and silver.
- VII. Dohány u. 16–18 (No phone; fax 1/342-7935), in the historic Jewish neighborhood, specializing in paintings, furniture, and carpets.
- IX. Tűzoltó u. 14 (© **1/215-6657**), specializing in furniture.

Qualitas Antiquitas is a private company with four locations: The store at I. Krisztina krt. 73 (© **1/375-0658**), behind the Castle District, specializes in paintings and furniture; the one at V. Falk Miksa u. 32 (© **1/311-8471**), near Parliament, and the one at Kígyó u. 5 (© **1/318-3246**) specialize in coins, jewelry, and Herend and Zsolnay porcelain. Qualitas Antiquitas also operates an **Auction Hall,** at V. Váci u. 36 (© **1/267-3539**); auctions are on Mondays at 5pm (but no auctions in July and August).

Ecclesia Szövetkezet, at V. Ferenciek tere 7 (© **1/317-3754**), next door to the Franciscan church, has hand-painted icons from Russia, Bulgaria, and Ukraine, starting at around 30,000 Ft ($108); contemporary hand-painted copies start as low as 5,000 Ft ($18).

The **Ecseri Flea Market** (see "Markets," later in this chapter) also deserves mention here, as numerous private antiques dealers operate booths at this one-of-a-kind open-air market.

ART GALLERIES

Budapest is home to a burgeoning—but still fairly unsettled—art gallery scene. The same export rules outlined above regarding antiques apply to all works of art considered to be Hungarian cultural treasures. Before completing a purchase, confirm that you'll be allowed to take the work out of the country; gallery proprietors should have the requisite documentation on hand.

Galleries tend to keep normal store hours (Monday through Friday from 10am to 6pm and Saturday from 10am to 1 or 2pm, sometimes as late as 6pm). They're concentrated in two areas: the Inner City of Pest and Buda's Castle District. An art dealer by the name of Károly Szalóky has an ambitious plan to transform Várfok utca in the Castle District into a street of contemporary Hungarian artists' galleries. He has already opened two new galleries on the street, **Spiritusz** and **XO Gallery** (© 1/214-0373), in addition to his long-standing **Várfok 14 Gallery,** at Várfok u. 14 (© 1/213-5155). Other galleries featuring contemporary Hungarian art include: **Vár Gallery,** I. Táncsics Mihály u. 17 (© 1/355-9802); **Eve Art Gallery,** VI. Király u. 98/b (© 1/322-8466); and **Luttár Gallery,** XIII. Hegedűs Gyula u. 24 (© 1/327-3250).

Artel Gallery, XIII. Pannónia u. 11 (© 1/339-8747), specializes in contemporary paintings from the former Socialist countries of Central and Eastern Europe. **Fortuna 11 Gallery,** I. Fortuna u. 11 (© 1/201-8984), features contemporary painting, and Herend and Zsolnay majolica, glassware, and furniture. **Rózsa Gallery,** I. Szentháromság u. 13 (© 1/355-6866), exhibits Hungarian naïve art. **Studio 1900 Gallery,** XIII. Hegedűs Gyula u. 24/b (© 1/329-5553), and **Chaos Gallery,** VII. Dohány u. 38 (© 1/344-4884), both specialize in 19th- and 20th-century painting. Art students exhibit their work in the **Studio Gallery,** at V. Képíró u. 6 (© 1/267-2033). The **Hologram Gallery,** in the Párizsi Udvar (Paris Passage), off V. Ferenciek tere (© 1/318-3761), is always filled with people; you can even get holographic business cards here.

ART SUPPLIES

Neoart   For the amateur and the professional artist, Neoart offers a wide selection of watercolor, oil, and acrylic paints, as well as brushes, drawing materials, canvas, and paper. Open Monday through Friday 9am to 5pm. VI. Bajcsy köz. 3. © 1/302-7407. Metro: Arany János u. (Blue line).

BOOKSTORES—NEW & SECONDHAND

Bestsellers   Budapest's first English-language bookstore (1992), Bestsellers is a popular meeting spot for English speakers. It's located in the middle of the Inner City, not far from Szabadság tér, site of the American Embassy. The store has a wide selection of fiction, as well as a reasonably good collection of travel books. Newspapers and magazines are also available, including some, like Rolling Stone, that can be hard to find elsewhere. Bestsellers operates a book and CD-ROM ordering service at no extra charge. Open Monday through Saturday 9am to 6:30pm, and Sunday 10am to 4pm. V. Október 6 u. 11. © 1/312-1295. Metro: Arany János utca (Blue line).

Biblioteka Antikvárium   At the head of Andrássy út, near Bajcsy-Zsilinszky út, this is one of central Pest's better antikvária (old- and rare-book shops). They have five bookcases full of English-language books, and a variety of maps and prints. Open Monday through Friday 10am to 6pm, and Saturday 9am to 1pm. VI. Andrássy út 2. ℂ 1/331-5132. Metro: Arany János utca (Blue line) or Deák tér (all lines).

Central European University Bookstore   This store features course books covering a wide variety of disciplines. The selection of books on Central and Eastern European politics and history is particularly notable. The Central European University Press publishes a great variety of books on all topics Central European. Request a copy of their catalog from their U.S. office at 400 W. 59th St., New York, NY 10019 (ℂ 212/547-6932; fax 212/548-4607; mgreenwald@sorosny. org). Open Monday through Friday (except Wed) 9am to 6pm, Wednesday 9am to 6:30pm, and Saturday 10am to 4pm. V. Gerlóczy u. 7. ℂ 1/318-8633. www.cen. ceu.hu/academic_bookstore.html. Metro: Kossuth tér (Red line) or Arany János utca (Blue line).

Corvina Könyvklub (Corvina Book Club)   This store, buried deep in an administrative building in the heart of the Inner City and identified to the public only by the banner hanging in its second-floor window, is the central outlet of the Corvina Press. Corvina, now a privately held company, was founded by the Hungarian state in 1955, charged with the express mission of making Hungarian works available to the world in translation. The press is still serving this useful purpose today. With its discounted prices, this is the shop to come for Hungarian works in translation, though the proprietors, oddly, speak no English. The building entryway is marked "Vigadó Irodaház"; take the marvelous old-fashioned never-stopping lift to the second floor. For a list of titles, contact corvina@mail.matav.hu. Open Monday through Thursday 9am to 4pm, and Friday 9am to 2pm. Vórósmarty tér 1, 2nd floor, Rm. 201. ℂ 1/317-5185. Metro: Vörösmarty tér (Yellow line).

Honterus Antikvárium   Located near the Központi Antikvárium, across the street from the Hungarian National Museum (Nemzeti Múzeum), this shop has more prints and maps on display than any other antikvárium in town. There's a shelf of mostly arcane, out-of-date English-language academic books as well as a stack of National Geographic magazines. Open Monday through Friday 10am to 6pm, and Saturday 10am to 2pm. V. Múzeum krt. 35. ℂ 1/317-3270. Metro: Astoria (Red line) or Kálvin tér (Blue line).

Központi Antikvárium   "Central Antikvárium" is the city's oldest and largest old- and rare-books store. Indeed, it is said to be the largest of its type in all of Central Europe. Opened in 1881 across the street from the Hungarian National Museum on "Antikvárium Row" (Múzeum krt. was the antikvárium street during the pre–World War I era, home to 37 different shops at that time), this shop has books, prints, maps, and a shelf of assorted knickknacks. The "Central Antikvárium" owners have two additional stores nearby: **Mediprint,** V. Múzeum krt. 17 (ℂ 1/317-4948), featuring a unique collection of old medical books; and **Kodály Antikvárium,** V. Múzeum krt. 21 (ℂ 1/317-3347), which sells secondhand sheet music, LPs, and CDs. Open Monday through Friday 10am to 6pm, and Saturday 10am to 2pm. V. Múzeum krt. 13–15. ℂ 1/317-3514. Metro: Astoria (Red line) or Kálvin tér (Blue line).

Libri Studium Könyvesbolt   This is the only bookstore left on Váci utca and a good option for those in search of English-language books (mostly Corvina books) about Budapest or Hungary. Coffee-table books, guidebooks, fiction and poetry in translation, and scholarly works are available. There's also a good selection of maps, including the hard-to-find Cartographia trail map of the Buda Hills (A *Budai Hegység*). Open Monday through Friday 10am to 6:30pm, and weekends 10am to 3pm. V. Váci u. 22. ☏ **1/318-5881.** Metro: Vörösmarty tér (Yellow line) or Deák tér (all lines).

Litea: Literature & Tea Bookshop   Situated in the Fortuna courtyard opposite the Hilton Hotel, this bookshop/teahouse stocks a wide range of books on Hungary; CDs and cassettes of the works of Hungarian composers; and cards, maps, and other quality souvenirs for serious enthusiasts of Hungarian culture. This is one of the few bookshops that sell what we consider the two best architectural guides to Budapest: *Budapest 20th Century Architecture Guide* and *Századeleji Házak Budapesten* (see "Recommended Reading," in chapter 2, "Planning Your Trip to Budapest"). Take your time browsing; order a cup of tea, sit, and have a closer look at the books that interest you. This calm, no-obligation-to-buy atmosphere is a rare find. Open Monday through Saturday 10am to 6pm, and Sunday 1 to 6pm. I. Hess András tér 4. ☏ **1/375-6987.** Bus: Várbusz from Moszkva tér, bus 16 from Deák tér, or funicular from Clark Ádám tér, to Castle Hill.

COINS

Globe Numizmatikai Galéria   This small shop, not far from Deák tér in a quiet part of the Inner City, has a variety of coins and antique paper money for sale. Of particular note are the Roman coins. Open Monday through Thursday 9am to 3pm, and Friday 10am to 2pm. V. Nádor u. 5. ☏ **1/337-7940.** Metro: Deák tér (all lines).

DEPARTMENT STORES & MALLS

Sprawling Örs Vezér tere, the eastern terminus of the Red metro line, is home both to Budapest's branch of the internationally known Swedish **Ikea** chain and to the city's first quasi–American-style mall, **Sugár.** The mall is open Monday through Friday from 9am to 6pm and weekends from 9am to 2pm. Individual shops set their own hours within the mall.

Closer to the center, try the ever-crowded **Skála Metro,** at Nyugati tér across from Nyugati Station, or the equally popular **Buda Skála,** on Október 23 utca, near Móricz Zsigmond körtér. Both are open Monday through Friday from 10am to 6pm and on Saturday from 9am to 1pm.

At Váci utca 16, the **Fontana Department Store** houses the latest in men's and women's international designer fashions. There's also an elegant perfumery and a cafe on the top floor. Fontana is air-conditioned. Open Monday through Friday from 10am to 7pm and on Saturday until 3pm.

Several new American-style malls have sprung up in Budapest over the past few years, and have proven immensely popular to Budapesters. **Duna Plaza,** XII. Váci út 178 (☏ **1/465-1220**), is probably the most popular shopping center/entertainment complex, with 120 different shops (including a Virgin Records Megastore), a nine-screen "Hollywood Cineplex," snack bars and pubs, the best bowling alley in the city. Duna Plaza is open daily 9am to 9pm; the entertainment complex closes later.

⌒ *Tips* Looking for Coins

Coin enthusiasts might also visit the several coin shops across the street from the Dohány utca Synagogue, near Astoria (Red line metro). Sometimes, you can observe a huddle of old men, diehard collectors no doubt, trading old coins with each other on the street in front of these shops.

Polus Center, at XV. Szentmihályi út 131 (℃ **1/419-4028**), is now the second largest shopping mall in the region. It is home to **TESCO,** the British supermarket chain (the only place in town, we believe, where Marmite is sold!), as well as to countless other shops. Wings in the mall have flashy American street names: Rodeo Drive, Sunset Boulevard, Wall Street. Open weekdays 10am to 8pm, weekends 10am to 6pm. A mall shuttle bus or bus 73 (red-lettered) departs for Polus Center from Keleti station.

Mammut, a 1998 construction, was extended in 2001. It is located at II. Lövőház u. 2–6 (℃ **1/345-8024**), next to Fény utca market, near Moszkva tér (Red line metro). Take tram no. 4 or 6. **West End,** the behemoth mall opened in 2000 right behind Nyugati railway station has generated lots of concern about the future of downtown shops and boutiques, and has already led to the demise of numerous small businesses in the immediate area of the Outer Ring boulevard.

FASHION & SHOES

We list just a few options, assuming you'll discover the rest on your own. For discount clothes, see "Markets," below.

Joker Applied Arts   Located just off Blaha Lujza tér, next door to the Hotel Emke, this shop has been in business since the late 1970s (a very long time in ever-changing Budapest). Joker features original handmade goods by local artisans, as well as Asian import items. Clothing, shoes, and accessories are for sale. Proprietor Judit Major is fondly spoken of by her regular customers. Her daughter Andrea now helps her keep shop. Open Monday through Friday 10am to 6pm, and Saturday 10am to 2pm. VII. Akácfa u. 5/a. ℃ **1/341-4281**. Metro: Blaha Lujza tér (Red line).

Náray Tamás   The latest glamorous shop in town is this boutique. Situated in the posh Ybl Palace, across from the Central Kávéház, this elegant and spacious shop sells the creations of Hungary's most celebrated and controversial designer, Tamás Náray. The exquisite taste and cutting-edge status of the collection is also reflected in the extreme price range as well as the trading hours: Monday through Friday noon to 8 pm, and Saturday by appointment only. V. Károlyi M. u. 13. No phone. Metro:

V50 Design Art Studio ✦   Fashion designer Valeria Fazekas has a unique sense for clothes that are both eye-catching and elegant. Her choice of materials is distinctive, her tailoring exquisite. Her hats are works of art. Prices are reasonable, but she does not accept credit cards. She has a second shop at V. Belgrád rakpart 16, where she can often be found working late into the night in the upstairs studio. The first shop is open Monday through Saturday 1 to 6pm; the second shop is open Monday through Friday 10am to 6pm, and Saturday 10am to 1pm. V. Váci u. 50. ℃ **1/337-5320**. Metro: Ferenciek tere (Blue line).

FOR KIDS

Gyerekcipő (Children's Shoes)   This bright, modern shop sells a wide variety of Hungarian and imported toddlers' and kids' shoes. Prices are more or less comparable to American prices, but the colorful selection and the hand-stitched leather make these shoes something special. A casual, kid-friendly atmosphere pervades; Barney or Sesame Street videos play on a TV. Open Monday through Friday 10am to 6pm, and Saturday 10am to 1pm. V. Múzeum krt. 7 (inside the courtyard). ℃ **1/317-8182**. Metro: Astoria (Red line).

Kis Herceg Gyermekdivat (Little Prince Children's Fashion)   Infant and children's clothes and shoes. Bright sunny colors and adorable prints in everything from swimsuits to ski jackets. Open Monday through Friday 9am to 5pm, and Saturday 9am to 1pm. VI. Andrássy u. 55. (©) 1/342-9268. Metro: Oktogon (Yellow line).

FOLK CRAFTS

Except for a few specialty shops like the ones listed below, the stores of the state-owned **Folkart Háziipar** should be your main source for Hungary's justly famous folk items. Almost everything is handmade—from tablecloths to miniature dolls, from ceramic dishes to sheepskin vests. You can shop with the knowledge that all items have been passed by a critical jury. Look for the distinctive label (or sticker) you'll find on all Folkart products: a circle with a bird in the center, surrounded by the words FOLKART/NÉPMŰVÉSZETI HUNGARY. The private folk-art shops lining Váci utca and the streets of the Castle District tend to be much more expensive, and their products, unlike Folkart's, often tend toward the kitschy (though with some notable exceptions). The main store, **Folkart Centrum,** has been relocated to the upper end of the mall at V. Váci u. 58 (© 1/318-5840) and is open daily 10am to 7pm (until 9pm in July and August).

You'll find a second Folkart store at VIII. Rákóci út 32 (© 1/342-0753), with similar offerings at similar prices. It's open Monday to Friday 10am to 6pm, and Saturday 10am to 1pm.

One outstanding private shop on Váci utca is **Vali Folklór,** in the courtyard of Váci u. 23 (© 1/337-6301). This cluttered shop is run by a soft-spoken man named Bálint Ács who travels the villages of Hungary and neighboring countries buying up authentic folk items. He's extremely knowledgeable about the products he sells, and enjoys speaking with customers (in German or English). When he is not around, his elderly mother keeps shop (she speaks no English). The most appealing items here are the traditional women's clothing and the jewelry boxes. From time to time, they also offer marvelous and genuine Russian icons. They have recently extended their collection with a great variety of now hard-to-find Soviet and East European communist-era pins, medals and badges. Prices are fair, and Bálint Ács's mother tailors clothing to size for you in 3 to 4 days. Open Monday through Friday 10am to 6pm, and Saturday and Sunday 10am to 7pm.

Holló Folkart Gallery, at V. Vitkovics Mihály u. 12 (© 1/317-8103), is an unusual gallery selling handcrafted reproductions of original folk-art pieces from various regions of the country. Beautiful carved and painted furniture is for sale, as well as smaller mirrors, decorative boxes, traditional decorative pottery, and wooden candlesticks. Open Monday through Friday 10am to 6pm, and Saturday 10am to 1pm.

GIFTS & HOME DECOR

Interieur Studio   A fragrant potpourri scent greets you as you enter this lovely little shop. You'll find wonderful gift possibilities: exquisite handmade books and photo albums, origami boxes, baskets, natural cosmetics and soaps, hand-dipped candles, a large selection of dried flowers, and beautiful silk-screened papers for gift wrapping. Interieur sells Christmas and Easter decorations in season. Open Monday through Friday 10am to 6pm, and Saturday 10am to 2pm. V. Vitkovics Mihály u. 6. (©) 1/337-7005. Metro: Ferenciek tere (Blue line).

Provence   This shop, featuring furnishings for the home in the spirit of Provence, is one of several wonderful new interior decorating and design shops on Király utca. Provence has ceramic tiles, fabrics, and woven rugs. Open Monday through Friday 10am to 6pm, and Saturday 10am to 1pm. VII. Király u. 21. © 1/352-8449. Metro: Deák tér (all lines).

Vakond Pólóbolt   This tiny shop (barely large enough for two people to stand) features the T-shirts of a whimsical young designer. Colorful designs with fanciful insects, fish, and other animals recall the art of Keith Haring. T-shirts cost 1,500 Ft to 2,900 Ft ($5.40 to $10.45). Open Monday through Friday 10am to 6pm, and Saturday 10am to 1pm. V. Magyar u. 52. No telephone. Metro: Kálvin tér (Blue line).

MARKETS

Markets are very crowded, bustling places. Be wary of pickpockets. Carry your valuables under your clothing in a money belt rather than in a wallet (see "Safety," under "Fast Facts," in chapter 3, "Getting to Know Budapest").

OPEN MARKETS (PIAC)

Ecseri Flea Market   Rows of wooden tables chock-full of old dishes, toys, linens, and bric-a-brac greet you as you enter this market at Nagykórösi út 156. From the tiny cubicles in the narrow corridors, serious dealers market their wares: Herend and Zsolnay porcelain, Bulgarian and Russian icons, silverware, paintings, furniture, clocks, rugs, prewar dolls and stuffed animals, antique clothing, and jewelry. The Ecseri is clearly something more than your average flea market. Antiques buyers beware, though; you'll need permission from the Museum of Applied Arts to take your purchases out of the country. Haggling is standard. Purchases are in cash only. The market runs Monday through Friday 8am to 4pm, and Saturday 6am to 3pm. XIX. Nagykórösi út. © 1/280-8840. Take bus no. 54 from Boráros tér.

Józsefvárosi Piac   The market closest to the city center, the Józsefvárosi piac is informally known as "Four Tigers," an allusion to the tremendous influx of Chinese vendors. The piac, situated on the side of a railroad yard, near the Józsefváros Station, is not really a flea market since most of the goods are not second-hand. But you'll find bargains aplenty: Chinese silk, Turkish dresses, Russian caviar, vodka, the occasional piece of Stalinist memorabilia, toy tanks, Romanian socks, slippers, and chalky-tasting chocolate. Also for sale are dishes, clocks, pens, combs, clothes, tea, and East European condoms. All prices are negotiable. Foreign currency is generally welcomed, though you'll attract far less attention by paying in forints. Dozens of languages are spoken in the tightly packed, crowded lanes of this outdoor market, which operates daily from 7am to 6pm. VIII. Kóbányai út. © 1/459-2100. To get here, take tram no. 28 from Blaha Lujza tér (Red line metro) or no. 36 from Baross tér (Keleti Station, Red line metro), and get off at Orczy tér.

FRUIT & VEGETABLE MARKETS (CSARNOK OR PIAC)

There are five vintage market halls (*vásárcsarnok*) in Budapest. These vast cavernous spaces, architectural wonders of steel and glass, were built in the 1890s in the ambitious grandiose style of the time. Three are still in use as markets and provide a measure of local color you certainly won't find in the grocery store. Hungarian produce in season is sensational, and you'll seldom go wrong with a kilo of strawberries, a cup of raspberries, or a couple of peaches.

The **Központi Vásárcsarnok** (Central Market Hall), on IX. Vámház körút (© 1/217-6067), is the largest and most spectacular market hall. Located on the Inner Ring (Kiskörút), just on the Pest side of the Szabadság Bridge, it was impeccably reconstructed in 1995. This bright, tri-level market hall is a pleasure to visit. Fresh produce, meat, and cheese vendors dominate the space. Keep your eyes open for inexpensive saffron and dried mushrooms, as well. The mezzanine level features folk-art booths, coffee and drink bars, and fast-food booths. The basement level houses fishmongers, pickled goods, a complete selection of spices, and Asian import foods, along with a large grocery store. Open Monday 6am to 5pm, Tuesday through Friday 6am to 6pm, and Saturday 6am to 2pm. The nearest metro station is Kálvin tér (Blue line).

The recently restored **Belvárosi Vásárcsarnok** (Inner City Market Hall), on V. Hold utca (© **1/313-8442**), is located in central Pest in the heart of the Lipótváros (Leopold Town), behind Szabadság tér. It houses a large supermarket and several cheesy discount clothing shops, in addition to a small handful of independent fruit and vegetable vendors. Open Monday 6am to 5pm, Tuesday through Friday 6am to 6pm, and Saturday from 6am to 2pm. Take the metro either to Kossuth tér (Red line) or Arany János utca (Blue line).

The **Rákóczi téri Vásárcsarnok,** on VIII. Rákóczi tér (© **1/313-8442**), badly damaged by fire in 1988, was restored to its original splendor and reopened in 1991. There's only a small area of private vendors; the rest of the hall is filled with retail booths. Open Monday to Friday 6am to 4pm, and Saturday 6am to 1pm. Take the metro to Blaha Lujza tér (Red line) or tram no. 4 or 6 directly to Rákóczi tér.

In addition to these three classic market halls, Budapest has a number of neighborhood produce markets. The **Fehérvári úti Vásárcsarnok,** at XI. Fehérvári út 22 (© **1/381-0355**), in front of the Buda Skála department store, is just a block from the Móricz Zsigmond körtér transportation hub. It's open Monday through Friday from 6am to 6pm. Take tram no. 47 from Deák tér to Fehérvári út, or any tram or bus to Móricz Zsigmond körtér. The **Fény utca Piac,** on II. Fény utca, just off Moszkva tér in Buda, formerly a nondescript neighborhood market, underwent an ambitious reconstruction in 1998 in connection with the building of the Mammut shopping mall, to which it is now attached. Unfortunately, the renovation has meant higher rental fees, which have driven out most of the small independent vendors. Except for a small area on the first floor designated for vendors, the new market retains little of the old atmosphere. Open Monday 6am to 5pm, Tuesday through Friday 6am to 6pm, and Saturday 6:30am to 1pm. Take the metro to Moszkva tér (Red line).

Lehel tér Piac, at VI. Lehel tér, is another neighborhood market, and is currently under reconstruction. We hope the reconstruction will not steal the neighborhood charm we used to love.

MUSIC

Fonó Budai Zeneház Fonó Budai Zeneház entertainment complex is your source for Hungarian folk music. The complex features a folk music store and an auditorium for live folk performances (*táncház*). Weekdays noon to midnight; Saturday 6pm to midnight. I. Sztregova u. 3. © **1/206-5300**. Tram: 47 or 49 from Deák tér (5 stops past Móricz Zsigmond körtér).

Liszt Ferenc Zeneműbolt (Ferenc Liszt Music Shop) Budapest's musical crowd frequents this shop, located near both the State Opera House and the Ferenc Liszt Academy of Music. Sheet music, scores, records, tapes, CDs, and books are available. The store carries an excellent selection of classical music, composed and performed by Hungarian artists. Open Monday through Friday 10am to 6pm, and Saturday 10am to 1pm. VI. Andrássy út 45. © **1/322-4091**. Metro: Oktogon (Yellow line).

Wave   On Révay köz, a small side street off Bajcsy-Zsilinszky út, directly across the street from the rear of St. Stephen's Basilica, Wave is a popular spot among young Hungarians looking for acid rock, rap, techno, and world music. Look for New Age music by Deep Forest, featuring Hungarian singer Márta Sebestyén.

A second music shop, called **Trance,** at VI. Zichy F. út 17 (© **1/302-2927**), specializes in alternative and punk music. They also sell secondhand CDs and LPs. At both stores, concert information is available. Open Monday through Friday noon to 8pm, and Saturday noon to 4pm. VI. Bajcsy-Zsilinszky út 15/d. © **1/ 269-4231.** Metro: Arany János utca (Blue line).

PORCELAIN, POTTERY & CRYSTAL

Herend Shop   Hand-painted Herend porcelain, first produced in 1826 in the town of Herend near Veszprém in western Hungary, is world renowned (check it out at www.herend.com). This shop, the oldest and largest Herend shop in Budapest, has the widest selection in the capital. Unfortunately, they can't arrange shipping. Even if you don't intend to buy, come just to see some gorgeous examples of Hungary's most famous product. The store is located in Pest's Inner City, on quiet József nádor tér, just a few minutes' walk from Vörösmarty tér. Open Monday through Friday from 10am to 6pm and on Saturday from 9am to 1pm. There is also a Herend shop at V. Kigyó u. 5 (© **1/318-3439;** this shop offers shipping. If you're planning a trip to Veszprém or Lake Balaton, don't miss the Herend Museum in the town of Herend (see chapter 11, "The Lake Balaton Region"). V. József nádor tér 11. © **1/317-2622.** Metro: Vörösmarty tér (Yellow line) or Deák tér (all lines).

Herend Village Pottery   If the formal Herend porcelain isn't your style (or in your price range), this delightful, casual pottery might be just the thing. Various patterns and solid colors are available; all are dishwasher and oven safe. Because everything is handcrafted, it's possible to order and reorder particular pieces at a later time. Prices are reasonable here. The owners are very knowledgeable and eager to assist but not pushy. Open Monday through Friday 9am to 5pm, and Saturday 9am to noon.

Another Herend Village Pottery shop (it is an expanding chain) has opened in the Inner City, at V. Váci u. 23 (©**1/318-3240;** fax 1/318-2094). They sell the formal Herend porcelain as well as village pottery. What is more, both shops will arrange shipping (with Touristpost, see above) on large orders. Open Monday to Friday 10am to 6pm, and Saturday 10am to 2pm. II. Fő utca 61 © **1/ 356-7899.** Metro: Batthyány tér (Red line).

Zsolnay Márkabolt   Delightfully gaudy Zsolnay porcelain from the southern city of Pécs is Hungary's second-most-celebrated brand of porcelain, and this shop has Budapest's widest selection. They arrange shipping through Touristpost. Even if you don't intend to buy, come just to see some fabulous examples of Hungary's other internationally known porcelain. (The Zsolnay Museum is in Pécs; see chapter 13, "Southern Hungary: The Great Palin & the Mecsek Hills"). Check it out at www.zsolnayusa.com. Zsolnay shares the store space with Ajka Crystal (which has another shop at V. József Attila u. 7; © **1/317-8133**). Fine stemware and other crystal are available at great prices. Open Monday through Friday 10am to 6pm, and Saturday 10am to 1pm. V. Kígyó u. 4. © **1/318-3712.** Metro: Vörösmarty tér (Yellow line) or Deák tér (all lines).

TEA & COFFEE

Coquan's Kávé   Coquan's imports and roasts high-quality Arabica coffee. It is currently the only shop of its kind in Budapest, opened in 1996 by an American who no doubt saw the need. About 20 different types of coffee are available. You can buy in bulk for 900 Ft to 1,500 Ft ($3.25 to $5.40) per 250 grams (roughly ½ pound) or by the cup. Try an all-butter croissant, a slice of banana bread, or cardamom coffee cake while you're at it. Coquan's has two other shops, at IX. Ráday u. 15 (✆ 1/215-2444) and II. Lövőház u. 12 (✆ 1/345-4275). Shops are open Monday through Friday 8am to 7pm, and Saturday 9am to 5pm. The shops on Ráday utca and Nádor utca are also open Sunday 11am to 5pm. V. Nádor u. 5. ✆ 1/266-9936. Metro: Deák tér (all lines).

1000 TEA   Set back in the courtyard of Váci u. 65 (a teapot-shaped sign points the way), this cozy little shop, with up to 50 different bulk teas available, is a haven for serious tea drinkers, mainly local students and intellectuals. A wall map, stuck with labels from the various teas, indicates their places of origin. Information as to the harvest of individual teas is also posted—in five languages. The owner, Zoltán Buzady, tastes each tea (samples are sent out by the growers to tea buyers in overnight packets) before ordering it for his stock. The shop recently expanded and now features several unique tearooms. In summer, guests are seated in the courtyard, at makeshift tables made of the barrels in which the tea is shipped. Prices range from 500 Ft to 1,000 Ft ($1.80 to $3.60) per pot for several infusions. Open Monday through Saturday noon to 9pm. V. Váci u. 65. ✆ 1/337-8217. Metro: Ferenciek tere (Blue line).

TOYS

Burattino Játék (Burattino Toys)   This is a closet-sized store specializing in handmade wooden toys: trucks, trains, dollhouses, and fancy building blocks. There are also wonderful hand and finger puppets made from felt (the wolf, the fox, and the turtle are particularly special), as well as other original and educational toys. Open Monday through Friday 10am to 6pm, and Saturday 10am to 1pm. IX. Ráday u. 47. ✆ 1/215-5621. Metro: Kálvin tér (Blue line); ascend from underpass to Ráday utca.

Magor Shop   This delightful little shop, inside a small shopping center (about halfway to the rear on the right side), offers a great variety of hand-painted pewter soldiers at cut-rate prices. Kids love them, and so do collectors. Kati, the proprietor, is at work on a tiny table behind the register painting the soldiers. Open Monday through Friday 10am to 6pm, and Saturday 10am to 2pm. V. Kossuth Lajos u. 9–11 (inside the Úttörő Áruház). ✆ 1/266-1119. Metro: Astoria (Red line).

Rokiland   This tiny upstairs shop, just off Blaha Lujza tér, has all sorts of handcrafted pipe-cleaner animals. Prices start at around 350 Ft ($1.25). Several display windows on the street give you an idea of what's available. The best animals here are clearly the monkeys, which one enthusiastic 40-year-old American collector we know has been buying in great quantities since he first came to Hungary more than a decade ago. The snakes are also great; watch the cashier give each one an expert twist before putting it into your bag. Incidentally, we have discovered that these pipe-cleaner animals make great cat toys, too.

There is a second Rokiland store just off Váci utca in central Pest; it is at V. Petőfi Sándor u. 3 (✆ 1/317-3131). Both shops are open Monday through Friday 10am to 6pm, and Saturday 10am to 1pm. VII. Erzsébet krt. 4. ✆ 1/322-2495. Metro: Blaha Lujza tér (Red line).

Toys Anno   Part museum, part specialty shop, Toys Anno might be of more interest to collectors than to kids. The shop sells exact replicas of antique toys from around the world. The tin toys are exceptional, especially the monkeys on bicycles, the lilting Ferris wheel, and the Soviet rocket that prepares for launch by itself. There are also old-fashioned dolls and puzzles. Items are behind glass and tagged with a serial number. Though you have to request prices and ask to see the toys that interest you, the clerk is more than happy to oblige. Open Monday through Friday 10am to 6pm, and Saturday 9am to 1pm. VI. Teréz krt. 54. ✆ 1/302-6234. Metro: Nyugati pu. (Blue line).

WINE & CHEESE

Le Boutique des Vins Sophisticated, classy, welcoming, this wine shop is a cut above the others. It is a great place for learning about and purchasing Hungarian wines. The long-time manager of the shop, Ferenc Hering, speaks excellent English and is extremely well versed in his merchandise. Try the excellent Villány reds (some from the shop's own vineyard) or the fine whites from the Balaton region. You can pick up a fine bottle for 2,000 Ft to 4,000 Ft ($7.20 to $14.40). A wide range of Hungary's famous Tokaj dessert wines, in the general price range of 4,500 Ft to 20,000 Ft ($16.20 to $72), is also available. Shipping can be arranged, but at a steep price. Open Monday through Friday 10am to 6pm, and Saturday 10am to 3pm. V. József Attila u. 12 (behind the Jaguar dealership). ✆ 1/317-5919 or 1/266-4397. Metro: Deák tér (any line).

Okleveles Magyar Borok Háza Okleveles Magyar Borok Háza, the biggest wine cellar in Budapest, sells only international award winners. Several Hungarian labels to look out for: Gál Tibor Eger region reds, Inhauser István Somló region whites, Gere Attila, Tiffan Ede and Bock József Villány region reds and rosés. Open daily 10am to 8pm. Párisi u. 1. ✆ 1/318-2683. Metro: Ferenciek tere (Blue line).

Szega Camembert If you are a lover of cheeses, this vendor at the Fény utca market is worth knowing about. Located on the first floor of the recently renovated market hall (see "Fruit & Vegetable Markets (Csarnok or Piac)," earlier in this chapter), Szega Camembert offers a huge selection of domestic and imported cheeses. You can also buy delicious homemade butter and sour cream here, as well as wholesome breads. Open Monday through Friday 9am to 6pm, and Saturday 8am to noon. II. Fény u. ✆ 1/275-0855. Metro: Moszkva tér (Red line).

T. Nagy Tamás Sajtkereskedése (Thomas T. Nagy's Cheese Shop) Opened in 1994, this shop deals exclusively in cheese, selling more than 300 types of hard and soft cheeses, including Hungarian, as well as imported French, Italian, Dutch, and English varieties. Open Monday through Friday 9am to 6pm, and Saturday 9am to 1pm. V. Gerlóczy u. 3. ✆ 1/327-1000. Metro: Deák tér (all lines).

9

Budapest After Dark

Budapest is blessed with a rich and varied cultural life. And there is no event that is unaffordable to the average tourist. In Budapest, for instance, you can still go to the Opera House, one of Europe's finest, for less than $15 (the most expensive tickets in the house, in the fabulously ornate royal box once used by the Habsburgs, go for less than $35). Almost all of the city's theaters and halls, with the exception of those hosting internationally touring rock groups, offer tickets for $5 to $10. (Of course, you can also get $20 to $30 tickets at the same venue if you wish.) It makes sense in Budapest (as elsewhere, no doubt) to select a performance based as much on the venue as on the program. If, for example, the Great Hall of the Academy of Music is the place, it would be worth your while to consider a program you might not ordinarily be interested in.

The opera, ballet, and theater seasons run from September through May or June, but most theaters and halls also host performances during the summer festivals. A number of lovely churches and stunning halls offer concerts exclusively in the summer. While classical culture has a long and proud tradition in Budapest, jazz, blues, rock, and disco have exploded in the post-Communist era. New clubs and bars have opened up everywhere; the parties start late and last until morning. So put on your dancing shoes or slip your opera glasses into your pocket; whatever your entertainment preference, Budapest nights offer plenty to choose from.

PROGRAM LISTINGS The most complete schedule of mainstream performing arts is found in the free bimonthly *Koncert Kalendárium,* available at the Central Philharmonic Ticket Office in Vörösmarty tér. The *Budapest Sun* and *Look* (see "Fast Facts," in chapter 3, "Getting to Know Budapest") also have comprehensive events calendars; the *Budapest Sun* lists less-publicized events such as modern dance and folk music performances. *Programme in the Hungary Visitors' Guide* and *Budapest Panorama,* free monthly tourist booklets, offer only partial entertainment listings, featuring what their editors consider the monthly highlights.

TICKET OFFICES For opera, ballet, theater, and concert tickets, you're better off going to one of the commission-free state-run ticket offices than to the individual box offices. There are always schedules posted, and you'll have a variety of choices. If none of the cashiers speaks English, find a helpful customer who can translate for you. On the day of the performance, though, you might have better luck at the box office. The **Central Theater Ticket Office** (Színházak Központi Jegyiroda), VI. Andrássy út 18 (✆ 1/276-9523 or 1/267-1267), sells tickets to just about everything, from theater and operetta to sports events and rock concerts. The office is open Monday through Friday 10am to 6pm). For **classical performances,** go to the National Philharmonic Ticket Office (Filharmónia Nemzeti Jegyiroda), V. Vörösmarty tér 1 (✆ **1/318-0281**), open Monday through Friday from 10am to 5:30pm. For **opera and ballet,** go to the Hungarian State Opera Ticket Office (Magyar Állami Opera Jegyiroda), VI. Andrássy út 20 (entrance inside the courtyard; ② 1/ 353-0170),open Monday through Friday 11am to 5pm. For **Spring Festival** events, go to the Festival Ticket Service, V. 1081 Rákóczi út 65 (② 1/ 486-3300), open daily 10am to 6pm before and during the festival. For **rock and jazz concert** tickets, try **Ticket Express,** VI. Jókai u. 40. (② 1/ 353-0692), open daily 9:30am to 9:30pm.

1 The Performing Arts

The major symphony orchestras in Budapest are the Budapest Festival Orchestra, the Philharmonic Society Orchestra, the Hungarian State Symphony Orchestra, the Budapest Symphony Orchestra, and the Hungarian Railway Workers' (MÁV) Symphony Orchestra. The major chamber orchestras include the Hungarian Chamber Orchestra, the Ferenc Liszt Chamber Orchestra, the Budapest String Players, and the newly established Hungarian Virtuosi. Major choirs include the Budapest Chorus, the Hungarian State Choir, the Hungarian Radio and Tele-vision Choir, the Budapest Madrigal Choir, and the University Choir.

Budapest is now on the touring route of dozens of major European ensembles and virtuosos. Keep your eyes open for the performances of well-known visitors.

Note: Most Budapesters tend to dress more formally than casually when attending performances.

OPERA, OPERETTA & BALLET

Budapesti Operettszínház (Budapest Operetta Theater) In the heart of Budapest's theater district, the newly renovated Budapest Operetta Theater is the site not just of operetta, but also of rock opera and musicals. Recent hits have included *The Sound of Music, Hello Dolly,* and *Crazy for You.* The off-season is mid-July to mid-August. The box office is open Monday through Saturday 10am to 7pm. VI. Nagymezó u. 17. ② 1/269-3870. Tickets 800 Ft–2,500 Ft ($2.90–$9). Metro: Opera or Oktogon (Yellow line).

Erkel Színház (Erkel Theater) The Erkel Theater is the second home of the State Opera and Ballet. The largest theater in Hungary, it seats as many as 2,400 people. Though it was built in art nouveau style in 1911, little of its original character shows through the various renovations it has undergone. If you have a choice, go to the Opera House instead (their seasons—mid-September to mid-June—are the same). Chamber orchestra concerts are also performed here. It's open the same hours as the State Opera House, below. VIII. Köztársaság tér 30. ② 1/ 333-0540. Tickets 1,500 Ft–3,000 Ft ($5.40–$10.80). Metro: Keleti pu. (Red line).

Magyar Állami Operaház (Hungarian State Opera House) Completed in 1884, the Opera House is the crowning achievement of the famous Hungarian architect Miklós Ybl. It's easily Budapest's most famous performance hall, and a tourist attraction in its own right. The lobby is adorned with Bertalan Székely's frescoes; the ceiling frescoes in the hall itself are by Károly Lotz. **Guided tours** of the Opera House leave daily at 3 and 4pm; the cost is 1,200 Ft ($4.30).

The splendid Opera House, home to both the State Opera and the State Ballet, possesses a rich history. A political scandal marked the opening performance in 1884: Ferenc Liszt had written a piece to be performed especially for the event, but when it was discovered that he had incorporated elements of the

Rákóczi March, a patriotic Hungarian (and anti-Habsburg) melody, he was prevented from playing it. Gustav Mahler and Ferenc Erkel rank as the Opera House's most famous directors.

Hungarians adore opera, and a large percentage of seats are sold on a subscription basis; buy your tickets a few days ahead of time if you can. The season runs from mid-September to mid-June. Summer visitors, however, can take in the approximately 10 performances (both opera and ballet) of the Summer Operafest, in July or August. Seating capacity is 1,260. The box office is open Monday through Friday from 11am to 6pm. Performances usually start at 7pm, but some longer shows start as early as 5pm. There are occasional weekend matinees. VI. Andrássy út 22. ℂ 1/331-2550. Tickets 3,700 Ft–9,800 Ft ($13.30–$35). Metro: Opera (Yellow line).

CLASSICAL MUSIC

Bartók Béla Emlékház (Béla Bartók Memorial House)   This charming little hall is in Béla Bartók's last Budapest residence, which is also the site of a Bartók museum. A regular Friday concert series is given by the Bartók String Quartet, a prolific group founded in 1957 (they play a lot more than just Bartók). Concerts are performed from the end of September through December. For schedule information, check Budapest's free bimonthly *Koncert Kalendárium.* Performances are on Friday at 6pm, and occasionally other days. II. Csalán út 29. ℂ 1/176-2100. Tickets 1,000 Ft–2,000 Ft ($3.60–$7.20). Bus: 5 from Március 15 tér or Moszkva tér to Pasaréti tér (the last stop).

Budapesti Kongresszusi Központ (Budapest Convention Center)   A large modern hall that's a convention as well as concert site, the Convention Center has established itself in recent years as one of the more important halls in the city. The hall is spacious and comfortable, but lacks the character of the older venues. It's part of the Novotel complex in central Buda. The performance schedule varies. XII. Jagelló út 1–3. ℂ 1/209-4850. Tickets 2,500 Ft–10,000 Ft ($9–$36). Tram: 61 from Moszkva tér or Móricz Zsigmond körtér.

Pesti Vigadó (Pest Concert Hall)   Right in the middle of the famed Danube Promenade (Dunakorzó), the Vigadó is one of the city's oldest music halls, dating to 1864. All sorts of classical performances are held here. Although it's one of the city's best-known halls, Hungarian music lovers rate its acoustics and atmosphere second to the Academy of Music. The concert schedule varies; the box office is always open the day before a performance. V. Vigadó tér 1. ℂ 1/266-6177. Tickets 2,000 Ft–10,000 Ft ($7.20–$36). Metro: Vörösmarty tér (Yellow line) or Deák tér (all lines).

Zeneakadémia (Ferenc Liszt Academy of Music)   The Great Hall (Nagyterem) of the Academy of Music, with a seating capacity of 1,200, is Budapest's premier music hall. Hungary's leading center of musical education, the Academy was built in the early years of the 20th century; the building's interior is decorated in an art nouveau style. The acoustics in the Great Hall are said to be the best of any hall in the city. If you go to only one performance in Budapest, it should be either at the Opera House or here. Unfortunately, the Great Hall is not used in the summer months; the smaller Kisterem, also a fine hall, is used then. In addition to major Hungarian and international performances, you can also attend student recitals (sometimes for free). A weekly schedule is posted outside the Király utca entrance to the Academy. The box office is open Monday through Friday from 2pm to showtime. Performances are frequent. VI. Liszt Ferenc tér 8. ℂ 1/341-4788 or 1/342-0179. Tickets 800 Ft–6,000 Ft ($2.90–$21.60). Metro: Oktogon or Opera (Yellow line).

Music on a Summer's Eve

During the summer, you'll find several special places to enjoy classical music. Tickets for all summer-program venues are available at the **National Philharmonic Ticket Office,** V. Vörösmarty tér 1 (✆ **1/318-0281**), open Monday through Friday 10am to 5:30pm.

The historic outdoor **Dominican Courtyard,** incorporated into the award-winning design of the Castle District's Hilton Hotel, I. Hess András tér 1–3 (✆ **1/488-6600**), is the site for a series of classical recitals during the Budapest Summer Program. The schedule varies each year; recitals are usually in July. Ticket price is 2,800 Ft ($10.10). Take the Várbusz from Moszkva tér or bus no. 16 from Deák tér to Castle Hill.

The Castle District's beautiful **Matthias Church** (Mátyás Templom), I. Szentháromság tér 2, holds a regular Tuesday- and Friday-night series of organ concerts from June through September. Concerts start at 7:30pm. Tickets are either 1,800 Ft or 3,500 Ft ($6.50 or $12.60). You can buy tickets at the National Philharmonic Ticket Office, during the day in the church (9am to 7pm), or just before the performance. Take the Várbusz from Moszkva tér or bus no. 16 from Deák tér to Castle Hill.

Organ concerts are also held Monday evenings at 7pm during July and August at **St. Stephen's Church (Basilica),** Hungary's largest church, V. Szent István tér 33 (✆ **1/317-2859**). Every week features a different organ music program. All tickets cost 1,200 Ft ($4.30) and can be purchased before the performance at the church entry or at the **Central Theater Ticket Office** (Színházak Központi Jegyiroda), VI. Andrássy út 18 (✆ **1/312-0000**).

The **Dohány Synagogue** is the venue for occasional concerts from May through September. Concerts begin at 7pm, but days are not regular. Tickets cost 1,800 Ft to 5,400 Ft ($6.50 to $19.45). For information and tickets, call the Central Theater Ticket Office.

Chamber-music concerts are performed in summer in the auditorium of the **Magyar Tudományos Akadémia,** V. Roosevelt tér 9. The academy building was built in the early 19th century by the Szécheny family (who also sponsored the construction of the Chain Bridge). Concerts are held on Mondays at 7pm in November through December and February through May. Tickets cost 1,300 Ft ($4.70) and include an English-language tour of the building, right before the concert. For information and tickets, contact Zoltán Göllesz at **1/344-7072.**

FOLK PERFORMANCES

Budai Vigadó (Buda Concert Hall)   The Budai Vigadó is the home stage of the Hungarian State Folk Ensemble (Állami Népi Együttes Székháza). The ensemble is the oldest in the country and includes 40 dancers, a 20-member Gypsy orchestra, and a folk orchestra. Under the direction of award-winning choreographer Sándor Timár, the ensemble performs folk dances from all regions of historic Hungary. The *New York Times* called it "a mix of high art and popular tradition . . . Every dance crackled with high speed." Tickets can be reserved by telephone. The box office is open 10am to 6pm daily. Performances usually start at 8pm on Tuesday, Thursday, and Sunday. I. Corvin tér 8. ℰ 1/317-2754. Tickets 5,500 Ft ($19.80). Metro: Batthyány tér (Red line).

Szakszervezetek Fővárosi Művelődési Háza (FMH Cultural House) Another popular folk program venue, the "Folklór Centrum," as some advertisements refer to this theater, features the Budapest Dance Ensemble, the Honvéd Dance Ensemble (the Army's dance troupe), and the Bihari Dance Ensemble. A 10-minute film on Budapest precedes the performance. Tickets can be reserved by telephone. Performance days vary but there is always a show on Mondays and Fridays, May through September. Altogether, there are about 100 performances over the course of the season. XI. Fehérvári út 47. ℰ 1/203-3868. Tickets 3,500 Ft ($12.60); price includes a glass of champagne at intermission. Tram: 47 from Deák tér.

THEATERS

Budapest has an extremely lively theater season from September through June. For productions in English, try the **Merlin Theater,** V. Gerlóczy u. 4 (ℰ **1/317-9338** or 1/266-4632), located on a quiet street in the heart of the Inner City. In 2000, it marked its tenth season of English- and German-language dramatic productions. It's the only primarily foreign-language theater in Budapest, and Hungarian and foreign actors are featured. Tickets cost 1,800 Ft ($6.50); box office hours vary. Take the metro to Astoria (Red line) or Deák tér (all lines).

For musical productions, try the **Madách Theater,** VII. Erzsébet krt. 29–33 (ℰ **1/478-2041**), built in 1961 on the site of the famous Royal Orpheum Theater and beautifully restored in 1999. Ticket prices are 1,050 Ft to 2,050 Ft ($3.80 to $7.40). The box office is open daily from 1 to 7pm; performances are usually at 7pm. Take tram no. 4 or no. 6 to Wesselényi utca. Also staging musical performances is the **Vígszínház (Merry Theater),** XIII. Szent István krt. 14 (ℰ **1/340-4650**), which was recently restored to its original, delightfully gaudy, neo-baroque splendor. Ticket prices are 350 Ft to 1,500 Ft ($1.25 to $5.40). Take the metro to Nyugati pu. (Blue line). In the 1950s, the Vigszínház served as the venue for the Hungarian Communist Party's New Year's Eve balls, hosted by Stalinist-era dictator Mátyás Rákosi.

2 The Club Scene

The club scene in Budapest has found fertile ground since the political changes of 1989, so much so, in fact, that clubs come in and go out of fashion overnight. You'd be wise to check *Pesti Est, Look,* or *Visitors' Guide* (available in tourist offices and at newsstands) or ask a local for the latest club information. There are few specifically jazz or blues clubs in town; most clubs prefer to be recognized for their decidedly eclectic offerings. Performances usually start late, after 9pm. All places serve beer and wine, and many offer mixed drinks as well.

Rigoletto This hip club, closed on Sundays, features a large dance hall. The music varies every night. Live jazz is performed on Tuesdays, Thursday is Latin party night, while Fridays and Saturdays are for the disco fans, mostly with funky, soul and Latin music. An international crowd mixes with local blondes. Open 9pm to 3am. XIII. Visegrádi u. 9; ℰ 1/237-0666; www.rigoletto.hu. No cover. Metro: Nyugati pu. Tram: 4 or 6.

TRAFO An old electric power station renovated and transformed into a cultural center for young, alternative artists, Trafo also hosts the hippest disco in town. The night is Tuesday with DJ Palotai. Discos start at 9pm. IX. Liliom u. 41. ℰ 1/215-1600. Cover: 300 Ft ($1.10). Tram: 4 or 6 to Üllöi út.

Fat Mo's Music Club This is a place that is always crowded. The live jazz band concerts start at 9pm while the dance at 11pm. Your night is definitely Monday with Hot Jazz Band performing in the style of the '20s and '30s. Make sure your book a table if you wish to enjoy their superb food as well. Best succulent beef steaks in town. V. Nyári Pál u. 11, ℂ 1/267-3199. No cover. Metro: Kálvin tér (Blue line).

Fél 10 Jazz Klub A classy, multilevel club, it's one of the few whose dance floor isn't crammed with teenagers. The place features live jazz performances nightly, while techno-free dance parties get going in the wee hours of the morning, Thursday to Saturday. Open Monday through Friday noon to 4am, and Saturday and Sunday 7pm to 4am. VIII. Baross u. 30. No telephone. Cover 500 Ft ($1.80). Metro: Kálvin tér.

Old Man's Take in the best jazz and blues in Hungary, live at Old Man's. The Pege Quartet plays here, as does Hobo and his blues band (incidentally, Hobo was a friend of Alan Ginsberg's and he broke new ground in Hungary by writing his Master's thesis on rock and roll in the 1960s). A very hip spot. Open daily 3pm to 3am. Akácfa u. 13. ℂ 1/322-7645. No cover. Metro: Blaha Luzja tér (Red line).

3 The Bar Scene

Fregatt The first English-style pub in Hungary, though now too crowded and noisy to really feel like one. Hungarians make up the better half of the clientele, but American and other English-speaking ex-pats frequent Fregatt, too. Guinness stout is on draft. Live jazz on Thursday and Sunday. Open Monday through Friday noon to 1am, and Saturday and Sunday 5pm to 1am. V. Molnár u. 26. ℂ 1/118-9997. Metro: Ferenciek tere (Blue line).

Irish Cat Pub This was the first Irish-style pub in Budapest; there's Guinness on tap and a whiskey bar. It's a popular meeting place for ex-pats and travelers. The pub features a full menu. Open Monday through Saturday 10am to 2am, and Sunday 5pm to 2am. V. Múzeum krt. 41. ℂ 1/266-4085. Metro: Kálvin tér (Blue line).

John Bull Pub One in a chain of popular English pubs, the John Bull has comfortable chairs and plush carpeting. The rooms are well ventilated and the service is impeccable. There's occasional live music (Irish, folk, country), but no cover charge.

Look for other John Bull Pubs in Budapest, as well as in smaller cities elsewhere in the country. All are uniformly pleasant places to socialize. Open daily noon to midnight. V. Podmaniczky tér 4. ℂ 1/269-3116. Metro: Arany János utca (Blue line).

Morrison's Music Pub An almost–twenty-something crowd packs this casual pub every night of the week. There's a small dance floor, an eclectic variety of loud live music, and a number of beers on tap. Open Monday through Saturday 8:30pm to 4am. VI. Révay u. 25. ℂ 1/269-4060. Metro: Opera (Yellow line).

4 Gay & Lesbian Bars

As with the fickle dance club scene, "in" bars become "out," or even close down, at a moment's notice. The gay bar scene in Budapest is largely male-oriented at this point, though this, too, is liable to change.

Angel A nondescript basement establishment, with a bar, restaurant, and huge dance floor, Angel has been around for a while now, and is definitely here to stay. The clientele is not exclusively gay, particularly on Friday and Sunday nights, when Angel hosts its now-famous transvestite show, starting at 11:45pm. Open daily 4pm to 4am. VII. Szövetség u. 33. ℂ 1/351-6490. Cover 600 Ft ($2.15). No shows and no cover Thurs. Metro: Blaha Lujza tér (Red line).

Eklektika Café   This cafe is wonderfully appointed with 1950s socialist realist furnishings, and features live jazz on Wednesday, Friday, and Sunday. A quiet, intimate place, Eklektika hosts a women-only night every second Saturday from 10pm on. Open Monday through Friday noon to midnight, and Saturday and Sunday 5pm to dawn. Semmelweis u. 21. ℂ 1/266-3054. No cover. Metro: Deák tér (all lines).

Mystery Bar   This very small but cozy place has a large foreign clientele and is perfect for conversation and meeting new people. Open Monday through Saturday 9pm to 4am. V. Nagysándor József u. 3. ℂ 1/312-1436. No cover. Metro: Arany János utca (Blue line).

5 Hungarian Dance Houses

Although Hungarian folk music no longer survives as a thriving part of rural life (except, perhaps, in Transylvania, now part of Romania), recent years have seen the growth of an urban-centered folk revival movement known as the *táncház* (dance house). An interactive evening of folk music and folk dancing, in a neighborhood community center, might just rank as one of the best and most authentic cultural experiences you can have in Budapest. We've listed a few of the best-known places below. The format usually consists of about an hour of dance-step instruction followed by several hours of dancing accompanied by a live band, which might include some of Hungary's best folk musicians, in an authentic, casual atmosphere. You can come just to watch and listen if you're nervous about not being able to learn the steps.

The leading Hungarian folk band Muzsikás, whose lead singer is the incomparable Márta Sebestyén (they have toured the U.S., playing to great acclaim), hosts a táncház every Thursday (September through June only) at 8pm (300 Ft/$1.10) at the **Marczibányi Square Cultural House (Marczibányi tér Művelődésiház),** II. Marczibányi tér 5/a (ℂ 1/212-0803). Take the Red line metro to Moszkva tér. If you're in town and have an evening to catch a Muzsikás performance, don't miss it. The **FMH Cultural House (Szakszervezetek Fővárosi Művelődési Háza),** XI. Fehérvári út 47 (ℂ 1/203-3868), hosts a táncház for kids every Tuesday (except in July and August), from 5 to 6pm, for 150 Ft (55¢). Folk bands that perform on traditional instruments play every Thursday evening, September through May, for 350 Ft ($1.10). The evening kicks off with a táncház hour for kids, at 5pm. A *csángó táncház,* the oldest and most authentic type of traditional Hungarian folk dance, is held Thursdays 7 to 11pm, for 300 Ft ($1.10). On Fridays you can enjoy the best klezmer bands in town. Tram no. 47 from Deák tér gets you there.

6 More Entertainment

CASINOS   Budapest has about a dozen casinos, mostly in the luxury hotels. Following are some of the more popular casinos: **Casino Budapest Hilton,** I. Hess András tér 1–3 (ℂ 1/375-1333); **Las Vegas Casino,** in the Atrium Hyatt Hotel, V. Roosevelt tér 2 (ℂ 1/266-1234 or 1/317-6022); and **Orfeum Casino,** in the Hotel Béke Radisson, VI. Teréz krt. 43 (ℂ 1/301-1600). Formal dress is required.

MOVIES   A healthy number of English-language movies are always playing in Budapest. The best source of listings and addresses is either the Budapest Sun, Look, or the free weekly, *Pesti Est,* which has an English-language section for movies. Movies labeled *szinkronizált, m.b.,* or *magyarul beszél* mean that the movie has been dubbed into Hungarian; *feliratos* means subtitled. Tickets cost 700 Ft ($2.50). Two cinemas that play daily English-language features are **Művész,** VI. Teréz krt. 30 (© 1/332-6726; tram 4 or 6), and Puskin, V. **Kossuth L.** u. 18 (© 1/429-6080; Red line metro to Astoria).

Video Mania, at VI. Andrássy út 33 (© 1/269-6812), is a multilanguage video rental shop with a good selection (approximately 200 English-language features, including children's videos). A 8,000 Ft ($29) deposit is required for membership (refunded upon return of membership card). New releases cost 690 Ft ($3.8025) for one night, old releases are 650 Ft ($2.35) for two nights, and DVDs are 500 Ft ($1.80) per night. It is open 10am to 10pm every day. Metro: Oktogon (Blue line).

10

The Danube Bend

The Danube Bend (Dunakanyar), a string of small riverside towns just north of Budapest, is a popular excursion spot for foreigners and Hungarians alike. Inasmuch as the name "Danube Bend" suggests a single change in the river's direction, however, it's a misnomer. The Danube, which enters Hungary from the northwest, flows in a southeasterly direction for a time, forming the border with Hungary's northern neighbor, Slovakia. Just after Esztergom, about 25 miles (40km) north of Budapest, the river swings abruptly south. This is the start of the Danube Bend region. The river then swings sharply north again just before Visegrád, and yet again south before Vác. From Vác, it flows more or less directly south, through Budapest and down toward the country's Serbian and Croatian borders.

The delightful towns along the Bend—in particular, Szentendre, Visegrád, and Esztergom—can easily be seen on day trips from Budapest; they're all within a couple of hours. The great natural beauty of the area, where forested hills loom over the river, makes it a welcome departure for those weary of the city. Travelers with more time can even make a long weekend out of the Bend.

1 Exploring the Danube Bend

GETTING THERE

BY BOAT From April to September, boats run between Budapest and the towns of the Danube Bend. In fact, a leisurely boat ride through the countryside is one of the highlights of an excursion. All boats depart Budapest's Vigadó tér boat landing, stopping to pick up passengers 5 minutes later at Buda's Batthyány tér landing, before continuing up the river.

Schedules and towns served are complicated, so contact **MAHART,** the state shipping company, at the Vigadó tér landing (✆ 1/318-1704) for information. You can also get MAHART information from Tourinform.

Round-trip prices are 1,020 Ft ($3.70) to Szentendre, 1,100 Ft ($4) to Visegrád, and 1,155 Ft ($4.15) to Esztergom. Children age 4 to 14 receive a 50% discount.

The approximate travel time from Budapest is 2 hours to Szentendre, 3½ hours to Visegrád, and 5 hours to Esztergom. If time is crucial, you might want to consider taking the train or bus (both of which are also considerably cheaper).

BY TRAIN To Szentendre The HÉV suburban railroad connects Budapest's Batthyány tér with Szentendre. Trains leave daily, year-round, every 20 minutes or so from 4am to 11:30pm. The one-way fare is 300 Ft ($1.10); subtract 100 Ft (36¢) if you have a valid Budapest public transportation pass. The trip takes 45 minutes.

To Visegrád There's no direct train service to Visegrád. Instead, take the train departing from Nyugati Station for Nagymaros. The trip takes 1 hour, and there are 20 daily trains. From Nagymaros, take a ferry across the river to Visegrád. The ferry dock (RÉV) is a 5-minute walk from the train station. A ferry leaves every hour throughout the day. The train ticket to Nagymaros costs 388 Ft ($1.40); the ferry boat ticket to Visegrád costs 150 Ft (55¢). The train-to-ferry trip is much more enjoyable than the long, slow bus ride.

To Esztergom Seventeen trains daily make the run between Budapest's Nyugati Station and Esztergom. The trip takes about 1¼ hours. Train tickets cost 388 Ft ($1.40).

BY BUS Approximately 30 daily buses travel the same interminable route to Szentendre, Visegrád, and Esztergom, departing from Budapest's Árpád híd bus station (at the Blue line metro station of the same name). The one-way fare to Szentendre is 184 Ft (65¢); the trip takes about 30 minutes. The fare to Visegrád is 368 Ft ($1.35), and the trip takes 1¼ hours. To Esztergom, take the bus that travels via a town called Dorog; it costs 414 Ft ($1.50) and takes 1¼ hours. The bus that goes to Esztergom via Visegrád takes 2 hours and costs 610 Ft ($2.20). Keep in mind, of course, that all travel by bus is subject to occasional traffic delays, especially during rush hour.

BY CAR From Budapest, Route 11 hugs the west bank of the Danube, taking you to Szentendre, Visegrád, and Esztergom. Alternatively, you could head "overland" to Esztergom by Route 10, switching to Route 111 at Dorog.

2 Szentendre ★ ★

13 miles (21km) N of Budapest

The center of Szentendre (pronounced *Sen*-ten-dreh) must rank with Pest's Váci utca and Buda's Castle District as the most touristed spots in all Hungary. In the summer, it becomes one huge handcraft and souvenir marketplace. Despite the excess commercialism, Szentendre remains a gorgeous little town. Originally peopled in medieval times by Serbian settlers fleeing Turkish northward expansion, Szentendre counts half a dozen Serbian churches among its rich collection of historical buildings. The town retains a distinctively Mediterranean flavor, rare this far north in Europe.

Since the turn of the century, Szentendre has been home to an artist's colony. About one hundred artists currently live and work here. As a result, it has a wealth of museums and galleries, the best of which are listed below. Surprisingly few people visit the museums, distracted perhaps by the shopping opportunities. You'll appreciate the peace and quiet of the many exhibition halls. In Szentendre, you should explore more than the suffocating tourist scene surrounding the main drag, Fő tér. Hike up the winding cobblestone streets to the Roman Catholic churchyard at the top of the hill for a lovely view of the red-tile rooftops. Wander down side streets. Szentendre is too small for you to get lost in and too beautiful for a less than thorough look around.

ESSENTIALS

For information on getting to Szentendre, see "Exploring the Danube Bend," above. The information office **Tourinform** is at Dumtsa Jenő u. 22 (© **26/ 317-965**), with maps of Szentendre (and the Danube Bend region), as well as concert and exhibition schedules. The office can also provide accommodations information and is open Monday through Friday from 9:30am to 4:40pm and weekends in summer 10am to 2pm. If you arrive by train or bus, you'll come

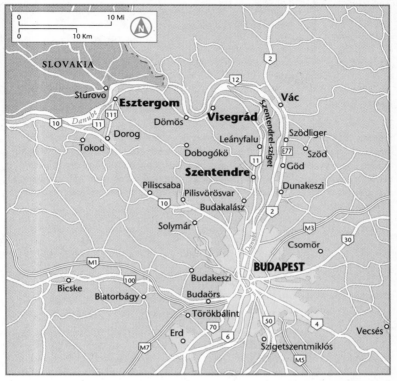

upon this office as you follow the flow of pedestrian traffic into town on Kossuth Lajos utca. If you arrive by boat, you may find the **Ibusz** office sooner, located on the corner of Bogdányi út and Gózhajó utca (© **26/310-181**). It's open April to October, Monday through Friday from 9am to 5pm and weekends 10am to 2pm. From November to March, it's open weekdays only, 9am to 4pm.

Another good source of information, particularly if you are planning to stay in the region more than a day, is **Jági Utazás,** at Kucsera F. u. 15 (© and fax **26/ 310-030**). The staff is extremely knowledgeable and dedicated. From hunting to horseback riding, from helping you find the right pension room to recommending the best *palacsinta* place in town, they seem to know it all. The office is open weekdays, 10am to 6pm in summer and 9am to 5pm in winter.

EXPLORING THE MUSEUMS & CHURCHES

Ámos and Anna Muzeum ★ *Finds*   This exceptional museum was the former home of artist couple Imre Ámos and Margit Anna, whose work represents the beginning of Expressionist painting in Hungary. Opened after Anna's death in 1991, the collection is Szentendre's best-kept secret. Particularly engaging are the drawings Ámos did between periods of forced labor on the Russian front, where he eventually died of typhus. On a lighter note are Anna's wonderful puppets. Ámos's art seems influenced by Chagall, whereas Anna's work invokes Miró and Klee.

Outside the museum in the courtyard is Anna's gravesite, around which visitors have left wishing stones from the garden as tokens of respect.

Bogdányi u. 10. ✆ **26/310-790**. 300 Ft ($1.10). Mon–Sun 10am–6pm, 1pm–5pm in winter.

Barcsay Museum The conservative socialist dictates of the day restricted the work of artist Jenő Barcsay (1900–88). Nevertheless, in his anatomical drawings, etchings, and charcoal and ink drawings, Barcsay's genius shines through. We particularly like his pastel drawings of Szentendre street scenes.

Dumtsa Jenő u. 10. ✆ **26/310-244**. Admission 300 Ft ($1.10). Tue–Sun 10am–6pm.

Blagovestenska Church The Blagovestenska church at Fő tér 4 is the only one of the Serbian Orthodox churches in Szentendre you can be fairly sure to find open. The tiny church, dating from 1752, was built on the site of an earlier wooden church from the Serbian migration of 1690. A rococo iconostasis features paintings of Mihailo Zivkovic. Notice that the eyes of all the icons are upon you.

Fő tér 4. Admission 50 Ft (18¢). Tues–Sun 10am–5pm.

Ferenczy Museum ★★ Next door to the Blagovestenska in Main Square (Fő tér), the Ferenczy Museum is dedicated to the art of the prodigious Ferenczy family. The featured artist is Károly Ferenczy, one of Hungary's leading impressionists; you can see more of his work in Budapest's National Museum. Works of his lesser-known children, Noémi (tapestry maker), Valér (painter), and Beni (sculptor and medallion maker), are also on display.

Fő tér 6. ✆ **26/310-244**. Admission 300 Ft ($1.10). Wed–Sun 10am–5pm.

Margit Kovács Museum ★★★ This expansive museum features the work of Hungary's best-known ceramic artist, Margit Kovács, who died in 1977. Her work may be unlike anything you've ever seen; this museum displays the breadth of her talents. We were especially moved by her sculptures of elderly women and by her folk-art–influenced friezes of village life. When the museum is full, people are required to wait outside before entering.

Vastagh György u. 1. ✆ **26/310-244**. Admission 400 Ft ($1.45). Apr–Oct, Tues–Sun 10am–6pm; Nov–Mar, Tues–Sun 10am–4pm. Walk east from Fő tér on Görög utca.

Serbian Orthodox Museum The Serbian Orthodox Museum is housed next door to the Serbian Orthodox church (services at 10am on Sunday) in one of the buildings of the former episcopate, just north of Fő tér. This collection—one of the most extensive of its kind in predominantly Catholic Hungary—features exceptional 16th- through 19th-century icons, liturgical vessels, scrolls in Arabic from the Ottoman period, and other types of ecclesiastical art. Informative labels are in Hungarian and English.

Pátriárka u. 5. ✆ **26/312-399**. Admission 300 Ft ($1.10). Apr–Oct, Tues–Sun 10am–5pm; Nov–Mar, Fri–Sun 10am–4pm. Walk north from Fő tér on Alkotmány utca.

SIGHTS OUTSIDE TOWN

Golf & Tennis Country Club Located in the northern corner of Szentendre Island, just outside the village of Kisoroszi, this country club features an 18-hole golf course with tree-lined fairways. The course is open March 1 to November 15. Greens fees per day run 4,500 Ft to 6,500 Ft ($16 to $23) in winter, 8,000 Ft to 10,000 Ft ($29 to $36) in summer; higher fees are for weekend play. Clubs are available for rent. Call or fax to reserve a tee time. The country club also has a driving range and tennis courts.

Szentendre Island. ✆ and fax **26/392-465**.

Szentendre

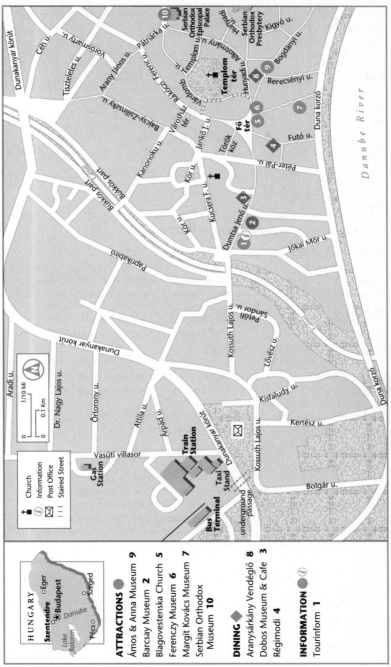

HUNGARY

Eger
Szentendre ○ ● Budapest
Danube
Pécs ○ ○ Szeged
Lake Balaton

ATTRACTIONS ●

Ámos & Anna Museum **9**
Barcsay Museum **2**
Blagovestenska Church **5**
Ferenczy Museum **6**
Margit Kovács Museum **7**
Serbian Orthodox
Museum **10**

DINING ◆

Aranysárkány Vendéglő **8**
Dobos Museum & Cafe **3**
Régimodi **4**

INFORMATION ⓘ

Tourinform **1**

Church
Information
Post Office
Stairled Street

Pap-sziget (Priest's Island)   This island at the northern end of town provides a place to rest and relax, with thermal waters in the outdoor bathing pools. Bring a suit and towel or rent them there.

Facilities include basic locker rooms. No entrance fee. Buses for Leányfalu and Visegrád pass the bridge to Pap-sziget.

Skanzen (Open-Air Ethnographical Museum) *Kids*   About 2 miles (3 km) northwest of Szentendre is one of Hungary's better *skanzens,* or reproduction peasant villages. This ambitious skanzen, the largest in the country, represents rural life from all regions of the country. There are several reconstructed 18th- and 19th-century villages, with thatch-roofed houses, blacksmith and weaving shops, working mills, and churches. A guidebook in English is available at the gate.

It's easily reached from Platform 8 of Szentendre's bus station, adjacent to the HÉV station (get off at the Szabadság-forrás stop). Buses depart about once an hour. If you're driving, follow Rte. 10 N. Turn left on Sztaravodai út.

Sztaravodai út. © **26/312-304.** www.sznm.hu. Admission 350 Ft ($1.25); family ticket 800 Ft ($3.35). Apr–Oct, Tues–Sun 9am–5pm. Closed Nov–Mar.

WHERE TO DINE

Aranysárkány Vendéglő (Golden Dragon Inn) ✿ HUNGARIAN Located just east of Fő tér on Hunyadi utca, which leads into Alkotmány utca, "The Golden Dragon" is always filled to capacity. The crowd includes a good percentage of Hungarians, definitely a good sign in a tourist town like Szentendre. Indeed, a former chef brought wide fame to this little restaurant with the publication of a cookbook titled *Four Seasons at the Golden Dragon Inn.* He's gone now, but the food remains excellent.

Long wooden tables set with sterling cutlery provide a relaxed but tasteful atmosphere in this air-conditioned restaurant. You can choose from among such enticing offerings as alpine lamb, roast leg of goose, stuffed cabbage, quail, and venison ragoût. Vegetarians can order the vegetable plate, a respectable show of grilled and steamed vegetables in season. The cheese dumplings would round out the meal. Various beers are on draft and the wine list features selections from 22 regions of the country.

Alkotmány u. 1/a. © **26/301-479.** Reservations recommended. Soup 400 Ft–500 Ft ($1.45–$1.80); main courses 1,200 Ft–2,500 Ft ($4.30–$9). AE, DC, MC, V. Daily noon–10pm.

Dobos Museum & Café *Kids* CAFE   Be sure to stop in **Nosztalgia** coffee shop for a slice of authentic *dobos torta,* a sumptuously rich layer cake named after pastry chef József Dobos, who experimented with butter frostings in the 19th century. The success of his recipe was immediate, and he was quickly appointed the official baker for the Habsburg emperor. Photographs of József Dobos and his formerly secret recipe book are on display upstairs in the cafe. The café tends to get crowded in the summer, but it's worth the wait.

Bogdányi u 2. © **26/311-660.** No reservations. Pastries 250 Ft–600 Ft (90¢–$2.15). No credit cards. Sat–Sun 10am–6pm; on weekday by appointment.

Régimódi ✿ HUNGARIAN   If you walk directly south from Fő tér, you'll find another excellent choice for dining. An elegant restaurant in a former private home, Régimódi is furnished with antique Hungarian carpets and chandeliers. Original artworks decorate the walls. Limited terrace dining is available, though you might not want to miss out on eating amid the rich interior decor. The menu offers a wide range of Hungarian specialties, with an emphasis on game dishes.

The wild-deer stew in red wine is particularly sumptuous, while less-adventurous diners might opt for the turkey baked with apples in cheese sauce. The menu also features numerous salad options. There's an extensive wine list.

Futó u. 3. ✆ **26/311-105**. Reservations recommended. Soup 400 Ft–500 Ft ($1.45–$1.80); main courses 1,200–3,000Ft ($4.30–$10.80). DC, MC, V. Daily 9am–11pm.

3 Visegrád ✶

28 miles (45km) NW of Budapest

Halfway between Szentendre and Esztergom, Visegrád (pronounced *Vee*-sheh-grod) is a sparsely populated, sleepy riverside village, which makes its history all the more fascinating and hard to believe. The Romans built a fort here, which was still standing when Slovak settlers gave the town its present name (meaning "High Castle") in the 9th or 10th century. After the Mongol invasion (1241–42), construction began on both the present ruined hilltop citadel and the former riverside palace. Eventually, Visegrád could boast one of the finest royal palaces ever built in Hungary. Only one king, Charles Robert (1307–42), actually used it as his primary residence, but monarchs from Béla IV, in the 13th century, through Matthias Corvinus, in the late 15th century, spent time in Visegrád and contributed to its development, the latter expanding the palace into a great Renaissance center known throughout Europe.

ESSENTIALS

For information on getting to **Visegrád,** see "Exploring the Danube Bend," earlier in this chapter. **Visegrád Tours,** RÉV u. 15 (✆ **26/398-160**) is located across the road from the RÉV ferry boat landing (not to be confused with the MAHART boat landing, about a half mile down the road). It is open daily from April through October, 9am to 6pm; November through March weekdays, 10am to 4pm.

EXPLORING THE PALACE & THE CITADEL

The **Royal Palace** covered much of the area where the MAHART boat landing and Fő utca (Main Street) are now found. Indeed, the entrance to its open-air ruins, called the **King Matthias Museum,** is at Fő u. 29 (✆ **26/398-026**). Admission is 200 Ft (70¢). The museum is open daily 9am to 4:30pm. The buried ruins of the palace, having achieved a near-mythical status, were not discovered until this century. Almost all of what you see is the result of ongoing reconstruction, which has been rigorous in recent years. Aside from the general atmosphere of ruined grandeur, the main attractions are the red-marble base of the Hercules Fountain in the Ornamental Courtyard and the reconstructed Gothic arcaded hallway down below. Exhibit descriptions are in English.

Kids An Annual Festival

Each summer on the second weekend in July, Visegrád hosts the **International Palace Tournament** ✶✶, an authentic medieval festival replete with dueling knights on horseback, early music, and dance. If you cannot make it to this fabulous event, you can enjoy a tournament of a smaller scale combined with a medieval dinner at 6pm. on Thursdays in July and August. For more information, contact Visegrád Tours at ✆ **26/398-160**.

Because of the under-construction aspect of the place, you need to keep a close eye on the kids here.

The **Citadel** ✿✿ (© **26/398-081**), on the hilltop above Visegrád affords one of the finest views you'll find over the Danube. Off to your left you can see the site of the controversial Nagymaros Dam, an abandoned Hungarian-Czechoslovak hydroelectric project (for more information on this dam dispute, see "Esztergom," below). Admission to the Citadel is 400 Ft ($1.45). It is open daily, 9am to 6pm. There are three buses a day to the Citadel, departing from the RÉV ferry boat terminal at 9:26am, 12:26pm, and 3:26pm respectively. Otherwise, "City Bus," a van taxi that awaits passengers outside Visegrád Tours, takes people up the steep journey to the Citadel for the equally steep fare of 2,000 Ft ($7.20) apiece. If you decide to go on foot, keep in mind that it's more than a casual walk to the Citadel, which is suitable for a day-hike.

WHERE TO DINE

Don Vito Pizzeria ✿ PIZZA Don Vito Pizzeria serves very good pizza in a pleasant, relaxed atmosphere. It's a good option if you're traveling with kids. Try the "Don Vito," a delicious ricotta, garlic, and herb pizza. Beer and wine are served.

Fő u. 83. © **26/397-230**. Individual pizzas 550 Ft–880 Ft ($2–$3.15). Daily 11am–11pm.

Renaissance Restaurant ✿✿ *(Kids)* HUNGARIAN In keeping with its name, the restaurant specializes in authentic medieval cuisine. Food is served in clay crockery without silverware (only a wooden spoon) and guests are offered Burger King–like paper crowns to wear. The decor and the lyre music enhance the fun, openly kitsch atmosphere. This is perhaps the only restaurant in the whole country where you won't find something on the menu spiced with paprika. Paprika wasn't around in medieval Hungary. If you're big on the medieval theme, come for dinner on a Thursday (July through August), when a six-course "Royal Feast" is celebrated following a 45-minute duel between knights. No vegetarians, please! Tickets for this special evening are handled by Visegrád Tours. The duel gets underway at 6pm sharp.

Fő u. 11 (across the street from the MAHART boat landing). © **26/398-160**. Main courses range from 1,000 Ft–3,200 Ft ($3.60–$11.50). V. Daily 12am–10pm.

4 Esztergom ✿

29 miles (46km) NW of Budapest

Formerly a Roman settlement, Esztergom (pronounced *Ess*-tair-gome) was the seat of the Hungarian kingdom for 300 years. Prince Géza and his son Vajk, who was crowned by the pope in A.D. 1000 as Hungary's first king, István I (Stephen I), were the first rulers to call Esztergom home. István converted Hungary to Catholicism, and Esztergom became the country's center of the early church. Though its glory days are far behind it, the quiet town remains today the seat of the archbishop-primate—the "Hungarian Rome."

From Esztergom west all the way to the Austrian border, the Danube marks the border between Hungary and Slovakia. There's an international ferry crossing at Esztergom.

ESSENTIALS

For information on getting to Esztergom, see "Exploring the Danube Bend," earlier. **Gran Tours,** centrally located at Széchenyi tér 25 (© **33/413-756** or 33/417-052), is the best source of information in Esztergom. The office is open

ALPS   ASPEN

AT&T Direct® Service

The easy way to call home from anywhere.

Global
connection
with the AT&T
Network

AT&T
direct
service

For the easy way to call home, take the attached wallet guide.

When You Want More Than the Official Line

Over 4 million people rely on the candid star ratings and reviews of the Unofficial Guides for the vacation of a lifetime

Fun Fact Primás-sziget: A Bridge over Troubled Waters

Across the Danube from Esztergom is the Slovak town of Sturovo. The two towns have recently been reconnected by the Mária Valéria Bridge, a wrought-iron construction that was blown up by the Germans in World War II. Until 2001, all that remained was a curious stump, along with four unconnected pylons in the river.

This was the last Danube bridge destroyed by the Germans in World War II to be rebuilt. The grassroots movement in Hungary favoring reconstruction of the bridge, as travel between the two countries in this region was primarily dependent on boats, turned out to be successful. The personal friendship that is said to have developed between the current Hungarian Prime Minister and the Slovakian President seems to have eased the otherwise troubled relations of the two countries.

Reconstruction was not possible during the period in which the Slovak government was controlled by the bellicose former Prime Minister Vladimir Meciar. Meciar took the position that reconstruction of the bridge would be unnecessary if the Hungarians resumed construction of the nearby Nagymaros Dam, a joint Slovak-Hungarian project unilaterally abandoned a decade ago by Hungary, which was to include a roadway across the Danube. As domestic opposition to the project in Hungary coalesced in the 1980s, a modern environmental movement developed in the then-Communist state. In 1997, the International Court of Justice in the Hague (the World Court) ruled that Hungary was at fault for abandoning the dam project, but that Hungary had no obligation to actually build it. The court urged the two countries to come to a formal resolution of the crisis.

The site of the new bridge is halfway between the Hotel Esztergom and Szalma Csárda (see "Where to Dine," below). To get here, walk straight out Táncsics Mihály utca until you hit the river.

in summer, Monday through Friday from 8am to 6pm and on Saturday from 9am to noon; in winter, Monday through Friday from 8am to 4pm.

You can get city maps and concert information, and book private rooms here.

EXPLORING THE TOWN

Castle Museum This museum is next door to the cathedral, in the reconstructed Royal Palace. The palace, vacated by Hungarian royalty in the 13th century, was used thereafter by the archbishop. Though it was one of only two fortresses in Hungary able to withstand the Mongol onslaught in 1241–42, it fell into decay under the Turkish occupation. The museum has an extensive collection of weapons, coins, pottery, stove tiles, and fragments of old stone columns; unfortunately, the descriptions are only in Hungarian. Outside the palace, sections of the fortified walls have been reconstructed.

Szent István tér. ✆ **33/415-986.** Admission 250 Ft (90¢); special exhibits 250 Ft–400 Ft (90¢–$1.45). Tues–Sun 9am–4:30pm.

Esztergom Cathedral ✧ *Kids* This massive, neoclassical cathedral on Castle Hill—Esztergom's most popular attraction and one of Hungary's most impressive

---

Moments   Braving the Tower

Ascending the cramped tower of Esztergom Cathedral can be be a some-what creepy experience; but if you do venture up, you'll be rewarded with unparalleled views of Esztergom and the surrounding Hungarian and Slovak countryside.

---

buildings—was built in the 19th century to replace the cathedral ruined during the Turkish occupation. The intricately carved red-marble, Renaissance-style **Bakócz Chapel** inside the cathedral (to the left) dates from the early 16th century. The chapel survived the Turkish destruction of the former cathedral; when the present structure was being built, the chapel was dismantled (into 1,600 numbered pieces) to be reincorporated into the new cathedral. The cathedral **Treasury** (*Kincstár* contains a stunning array of ecclesiastical jewels and gold works. Since Cardinal Mindszenty's body was moved to the **crypt** in 1991 (he died in exile in 1975), it has become a pilgrimage site for Hungarians; they come to see the final resting place of the uncompromisingly anti-Communist cleric who spent a good portion of the Cold War living inside the American Embassy in Budapest. The **cupola,** has, as far as church towers go, one of the scarier and more cramped ascents, but children seem to love it and the views at the top.

If you happen to be in town during the first week of August, don't miss out on one of the classical guitar concerts performed in the cathedral. The acoustics are sublime. The concerts are part of Esztergom's annual **International Guitar Festival** 🎸🎸.

Szent István tér. © **33/411-895.** Treasury, 250 Ft (90¢); cupola, 150 Ft (55¢). Cathedral, daily 8am–8pm summer; 9am–3pm winter. Treasury, crypt, cupola, daily 9am–5pm summer; 10am–3pm winter.

Keresztény Múzeum (Christian Museum)   This museum, in the neoclassical former primate's palace, houses Hungary's largest collection of religious art and the largest collection of medieval art outside the National Gallery in Budapest. The Lord's Coffin of Garamszentbenedek is probably the museum's most famous piece; the ornately carved, gilded coffin on wheels was originally used in Easter celebrations.

To get to the museum, continue past the Watertown Parish Church on Berényi Zsigmond utca. Even if you don't plan on visiting this museum, it's definitely worth taking a break from the crowds at the cathedral and taking a stroll through the quiet, cobblestone streets of Esztergom's Víziváros (Watertown).

Mindszenty tér 2. © **33/413-880.** Admission 250 Ft (90¢) adults. Tues–Sun 10am–6pm.

WHERE TO STAY

Alabárdos Panzió 🌟   This fine yellow building is located in the heart of Esztergom, just minutes from Castle Hill. Although situated on the town's main thoroughfare, the pension is set back off the road and is much quieter than you'd expect. A restaurant of the same name is in the front of the building. The Alabárdos is far more modern than its rival, the Plátán Panzió, a fact amply reflected in the higher prices. Pension rooms are small but clean and cheery. A cross hangs over every bed, and every room has a toilet and shower. To find the reception, go up the steep cobblestone driveway to the left of the building.

Bajcsy-Zsilinszky út 49, 2500 Esztergom. © **33/312-640.** 21 units. High season 7,500 Ft ($27) single; 9,000 Ft ($32.40) double; low season about 15% lower rates. Rates include breakfast. No credit cards. Free parking. Bus: 1, 5, or 6 from the train station. **Amenities:** Restaurant. *In room:* TV, no phone.

Plátán Panzió √Value   The prices in this nondescript, old-style pension make it the great budget-travel bargain of Esztergom. The pension is located in one wing of a large, institutional, neo-baroque building. The rooms are worn and bare, but clean; all have private baths. The shared facilities are also clean. It's located on a quiet street, just minutes from the city center. If the building's outer door is locked, ring the bell on your right. Once you've been buzzed into the court-yard, turn right and go up the stairs to find the reception.

Kis-Duna sétány 11, 2500 Esztergom. (📞 33/411-355. 16 units. 4,200 Ft ($15.10) double, breakfast included. No credit cards. Free parking. Bus: 1, 5, or 6 from the train station to Rákóczi tér; then walk west on Lörincz utca to Kis-Duna sétány and turn right. *In room:* No phone.

WHERE TO DINE

The food at the recently remodeled and enlarged **Szalma Csárda** ★★★, located at Nagy-Duna sétány 2 (📞 **33/315-336**), is absolutely first-rate, with everything made to order and served piping hot. The excellent house soups—fish soup (*halászlé*), goulash (*gulyásleves*), and bean soup (*babgulyás*)—are all large enough to constitute meals in themselves; they cost from 600 Ft to 900 Ft ($2.15 to $3.25). For main courses, which cost 1,000 Ft to 1,600 Ft ($3.60 to $5.75), the stuffed cabbage (*töltött kaposzta*) and the stuffed pepper (*töltött paprika*) are both outstanding, though not always offered on the menu. Finish off your meal with a dish of sweet chestnut purée (*gesztenyepüré*), a Hungarian specialty prepared here to perfection. There are outdoor tables as well as seating in two dining rooms.

11

The Lake Balaton Region

Lake Balaton may not be the Mediterranean, but don't tell that to Hungarians. Somehow over the years they have managed to create their own Central European version of a Mediterranean culture along the shores of their long, shallow, milky-white lake. Throughout the long summer, swimmers, windsurfers, sailboats, kayaks, and cruisers fill the warm and silky smooth lake, Europe's largest at 50 miles (80 km) long and 10 miles (15km) wide at its broadest stretch. Around the lake's 315 miles (197km) of shoreline, vacationers cast their reels for pike; play tennis, soccer, and volleyball; ride horses; and hike in the hills.

First settled in the Iron Age, the Balaton region has been a recreation spot since at least Roman times. From the 18th century onward, the upper classes erected spas and villas along the shoreline. Not until the post–World War II Communist era did the lake open up to a wider tourist base. Many large hotels along the lake are former trade union resorts built under the previous regime.

Lake Balaton, it seems, has something for everyone. Teenagers, students, and young travelers tend to congregate in the hedonistic towns of the south shore. Here, huge 1970s-style beachside hotels are filled to capacity all summer long, and disco music pulsates into the early morning

hours. The south-shore towns are as flat as Pest; walk 10 minutes from the lake and you're deep in farm country. The air here is still and quiet; in summer, the sun hangs heavily in the sky.

Older travelers and families tend to spend more time on the hillier, more graceful north shore. There, little villages are neatly tucked away in the rolling countryside, where the grapes of the popular Balaton wines ripen in the strong southern sun. However, if you're coming from Budapest, the northern shore of the lake at first appears every bit as built up and crowded as the southern shore. Beyond Balatonfüred, this impression begins to fade. You'll discover the Tihany Peninsula, a protected area whose 12 square kilometers (4¾ square miles) jut out into the lake like a knob. Moving westward along the coast, passing from one lakeside settlement to the next, you can make forays inland into the rolling hills of the Balaton wine country. Stop for a swim—or the night—in a small town like Szigliget. The city of Keszthely, sitting at the lake's western edge, marks the end of its northern shore. All towns on the lake are within 1½ to 4 hours from Budapest by a *gyors* (fast) train, but the trip takes much longer on a *sebes* (local) train (See "Getting Around Hungary by Train," in chapter 2, "Planning Your Trip to Budapest").

1 Exploring the Lake Balaton Region

GETTING THERE & GETTING AROUND
BY TRAIN From Budapest, trains to the various towns along the lake depart from Déli Station. The local (*sebes*) trains are interminably slow, stopping at each

village along the lake. Unless you're going to one of these little villages (sometimes a good idea), try to get on an express (*gyors*). To Keszthely, the trip takes about 4 hours and costs 1,482 Ft ($5.35). To reach Tihany, take a train to Balatonfüred for 1,032 Ft ($3.70) (travel time 2 hrs.), and then a local bus to Tihany.

BY CAR   From Budapest, take the M7 motorway south through Székesfehérvár until you hit the lake. Route 71 circles the lake.

If you're planning a trip to Lake Balaton for more than a day or two, you should consider renting a car, which will give you much greater mobility. The various towns differ enough from one another that you may want to keep driving until you find the place that's right for you. Without a car, this is obviously more difficult. Also, wherever you go in the region, you'll find private rooms to be both cheaper and easier to get if you travel a few miles off the lake. Driving directly to the lake from Budapest will take about an hour and 15 minutes.

BY BOAT & FERRY   Passenger boat travel on Lake Balaton lets you travel across the lake as well as between towns on the same shore. It's both extensive and cheap, but considerably slower than surface transportation. All major towns have a dock with departures and arrivals. Children 3 and under travel free, and those 13 and under get half-price tickets. A single ferry (*komp*) running between Tihany and Szántód lets you transport a car across the width of the lake.

All boat and ferry information is available from the **MAHART** office in Siófok (✆ **84/310-050** or 84/312-907). Local tourist offices all along the lake (several listed below) also have schedules and other information.

BY BUS   Once at the lake, you might find buses to be the best way of getting around locally. Buses will be indispensable, of course, if you take private-room lodging a few miles away from the lake.

WHERE TO STAY IN THE AREA

Because hotel prices are unusually high in the Balaton region, and since just about every local family rents out a room or two in summer, we especially recommend private rooms as the lodging of choice in this area. You can reserve a room through a local tourist office (addresses listed below by town) or you can just look for the ubiquitous SZOBA KIADÓ (or ZIMMER FREI) signs that decorate most front gates in the region. When you take a room without using a tourist agency as the intermediary, prices are generally negotiable. (Owners sometimes prefer hard currency.) In the height of the season, you shouldn't have to pay more than 6,000 Ft ($21.60) for a double room within reasonable proximity of the lake.

In addition to staying in private rooms, many budget travelers pitch their tents in **lakeside campgrounds** all around the lake. Campgrounds are generally quite inexpensive, and their locations are well marked on maps.

All the campgrounds have working facilities, but are probably not as clean as most Americans are accustomed to.

2 En Route to Lake Balaton: Veszprém ✦✦

72 miles (116km) SW of Budapest

Just 10 miles (16km) from Lake Balaton, Veszprém (pronounced Vess-praym) surely ranks as one of Hungary's most charming and vibrant small cities. It often serves as a starting point for trips to the Balaton resort area. In Veszprém, you'll find a harmonious mix of old and new: A delightfully self-contained and well-preserved, 18th-century baroque Castle District spills effortlessly into a

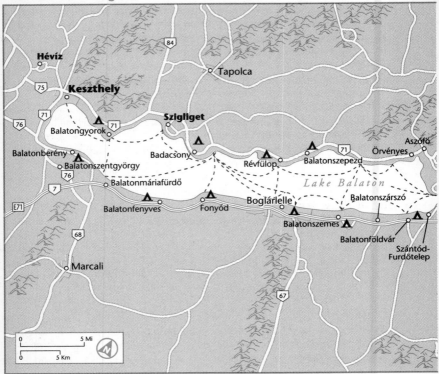

typically modern city center, itself distinguished by lively wide-open pedestrian-only plazas.

The history of Veszprém, like the scenic Bakony countryside that surrounds it, is full of peaks and valleys. The city was first established as an episcopal see in the time of King Stephen I, Hungary's first Christian king, but was completely destroyed during the course of the long Turkish occupation, the Habsburg-Turkish battles, and the subsequent Hungarian-Austrian independence skirmishes. The reconstruction of Veszprém commenced in the early 18th century, though the castle itself, blown up by the Austrians in 1702, was never rebuilt. The baroque character of that era today attracts thousands of visitors who pass through each year.

ESSENTIALS

GETTING THERE   Six daily **trains** depart Budapest's Déli Station for Veszprém, a 2-hour trip. Tickets cost 882 Ft ($3.20).

If you're **driving** from Budapest, take the M7 motorway to Székesfehérvár, and then Route 8 to Veszprém.

VISITOR INFORMATION   **Tourinform,** Rákóczi u. 3 (© **88/404-548**), is open Monday through Friday 9am to 5pm, Saturday and Sunday 9am to 4pm (only weekdays in winter); and **Ibusz,** Kossuth u. 10 (in the odd modern structure marked "KINIZSI ÜZLETHÁZ," © **88/565-540** or 88/427-604), is open

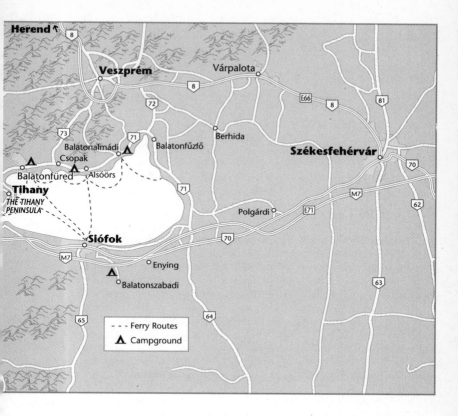

Monday through Friday from 9am to 5pm. Both offices provide information, sell city maps, and help with hotel or private-room bookings.

EXPLORING THE CITY

Most of Veszprém's main sights are clustered along Vár utca, the street that runs the length of the city's small but lovely Castle District. The Bakony Museum, though, is located in the new (low) part of town.

Housed inside the 18th-century canon's house, the **Exhibition of Religious Art,** Vár u. 35, has a fine collection of religious (Roman Catholic) art. Admission is 100 Ft (36¢). It's open daily from 9am to 5pm; closed October to April.

At Vár u. 16, the vaulted **Gizella Chapel,** named for King Stephen's wife, was unearthed during the construction of the adjoining Bishop's Palace in the 18th century. Today, it houses a modest collection of ecclesiastical art, but is best known for the 13th-century frescoes that, in various states of restoration, decorate its walls. Admission is 40 Ft (15¢). It's open daily from 9am to 5pm; closed October to April.

In addition to Roman relics uncovered in the surrounding area, the **Laczkó Dezső Museum,** on Megyeház tér, features local folk exhibits (art, costumes, tools, utensils, and so on). There are also exhibits on the legendary highwaymen of the region, celebrated figures from 19th-century Bakony who share some characteristics with the mythological outlaws of the American West. Admission is 150 Ft (55¢). It's open Tuesday through Sunday from 10am to

6pm; in winter, noon to 4pm. To get to the museum, walk directly south from Szabadsag tér, where the old and new towns converge.

For a wonderful view of the surrounding Bakony region, climb up the steps to the narrow observation deck at the top of the **Fire Tower** ✸, at Óváros tér. Though the foundations of the tower are medieval, the structure itself was built in the early 19th century. Enter via the courtyard of Vár u. 17, behind Óváros tér. Admission is 150 Ft (55¢). Open daily from 10am to 6pm.

The **Veszprém Zoo** (Kittenberger Kálmán Növény és Vadaspark) is located at Kittenberger u. 17 (☎ 88/421-088). It's open daily, in summer 9am to 6pm, in winter 9am to 4:30pm. Admission is 490 Ft ($1.75), children 290 Ft ($1.05). The zoo is set in a small wooded valley at the edge of the city center and boasts 550 animals from 130 species. It's rather sad and depressing by American zoo standards, but the kids will still learn something.

WHERE TO STAY

For a double room in a private home in Veszprém you pay 3,500 Ft to 5,000 Ft ($12.60 to $18). The room price usually does not include breakfast. You can book a private room through either of the tourist offices mentioned above.

Péter-Pál Panzió ✸ (☎ 88/567-790) is a value option conveniently located on Dózsa György u. 3; it's only a 5-minute walk from the center. Don't be put off by the grungy building facade. Inside are 12 tidy but very small rooms, all with twin beds, toilet, shower, and television. Insist on a room in the rear of the building, as the pension sits close to the busy road. Rates are 5,200 Ft ($18.70) double and 6,300 Ft ($22.70) triple. Breakfast is included and is served in the garden in summer. Call ahead for reservations.

Hotel Villa Medici ✸✸ (☎ and fax 88/590-070), at Kittenberger u. 11, is a modern, full-service hotel set in a small gorge on the edge of the city, next to Veszprém's zoo-park. There are 24 double rooms and two suites; each has a bathroom with shower, telephone, minibar, and TV. Rates are 16,000 Ft to 17,000 Ft ($57.60 to $61.20) for a double room; 22,500 Ft ($81) for a suite. Breakfast is included. The hotel also features a sauna, a small indoor swimming pool, and a beauty salon. Credit cards are accepted. Buses 3, 5, and 10 take you as far as the bridge overlooking the gorge. You can walk from there.

WHERE TO DINE

Veszprém does not have many dining options, but at the following places you should be able to find a satisfying meal.

For fast food, try **Mackó Cukrászda,** at Kossuth u. 6 (☎ 88/569-140). Open daily 7am to 7pm (10am to 7pm on Sunday), this quick-stop, no-frills eatery is always bustling. Pizza, hot dogs, French fries, fried chicken, and various sweets are served. There's also a salad counter (heavy on the mayonnaise dressings); salads are sold by the decagram. A meal here will put you back about 600 Ft ($2.15).

Cserhát Étterem ✸ (☎ 88/425-441), also housed in the huge structure that is Kossuth u. 6, is an authentic önkiszólgáló (self-service cafeteria). You'll find this very popular cafeteria behind the Nike store; go up the winding staircase inside the building. Cserhát serves up extremely cheap traditional fare. Hearty meals are available for less than 600 Ft ($2.15). The menu changes daily; it's posted on a bulletin board at the bottom of the stairs. It's open Monday through Friday from 9am to 6pm and Saturday 9am to 3pm.

You can get lunch or dinner at **Óváros Vendéglő** (Old City Guest House), at Szabadság tér 14 (☎ 88/326-790), a traditional Hungarian restaurant with a large outdoor terrace and a number of smaller indoor dining rooms. The food is

Herend: Home of Hungary's Finest Porcelain

About 10 miles (16km) west of Veszprém lies the sleepy village of Herend. What distinguishes this village from other villages in the area is the presence of the Herend Porcelain factory, where Hungary's finest porcelain has been made since 1826.

Herend Porcelain began to establish its international reputation as far back as 1851, when a dinner set was displayed at the Great Exhibition in London. Artists hand paint every piece, from tableware to decorative accessories. Patterns include delicate flowers, butterflies, and birds.

The recently opened **Porcelanium Visitors Center** features the newly expanded **Herend Museum** (© 88/261-801), which displays a dazzling collection of Herend porcelain. A mini-tour of the factory and a porcelain-making demonstration film are also part of the Visitors Center offerings. The Porcelanium is open daily from May to October, 9:30am to 5pm; weekdays only from November to April, 10am to 3pm. Admission is 300 Ft ($1.25). At the **factory store** (© 88/523-223), which accepts credit cards, you might find patterns that are unavailable in Budapest's Herend Shop (see chapter 8, "Budapest Shopping"). Prices will be comparable to those in Budapest, but much less than what Herend costs in the United States. The factory store is open Monday through Saturday, 9:30am to 6pm. In winter, Monday through Friday 9:30am to 4pm, Saturday 9:30am to 2pm. The Porcelanium Visitors Center also has a coffeehouse and upscale restaurant. Food is served on Herend china, naturally. Herend is easily accessible via bus from Veszprém.

fine, and main courses run 800 Ft to 1,300 Ft ($2.90 to $4.70). It's open daily 8am to 10pm.

For something more upscale, **Villa Medici Étterem** ★★ (owned by the same people who own the hotel), at Kittenberger u. 11 (© 88/590-072), is the place. Our American friend who first told us about this place, claiming at the time that it was one of Hungary's best restaurants, liked it enough to have his wedding reception there. It's expensive but worth it. Main courses here are between 2,000 Ft and 3,600 Ft ($7.20 to $12.95). Villa Medici serves Hungarian/continental cuisine daily from 12am to 11pm.

3 The Tihany Peninsula ★★

The Tihany (pronounced Tee-hine) Peninsula, a national park since 1952, has several towns on it, the most notable of which is called, appropriately, **Tihany** (or Tihany Village). Because the peninsula is a protected area, building is heavily restricted; consequently, it maintains a rustic charm that's unusual in the Balaton region.

The Tihany Peninsula also features a lush, protected interior, accessible by a trail from Tihany Village, with several little inland lakes—the aptly named **Inner Lake** and **Outer Lake**—as well as a lookout tower offering views out over the Balaton. Give yourself at least an hour or two to explore the interior.

As you travel west from the Tihany Peninsula, the landscape begins to get hillier.

ESSENTIALS

GETTING THERE   The **rail** line that circles Lake Balaton does not serve the Tihany Peninsula. The nearest railway station is in Aszófő, about 3 miles (5km) from Tihany Village. If you don't have your own car, you can get here by land or by water. A local **bus** comes frequently to Tihany from the nearby town of Balatonfüred. It costs 132 Ft (47¢). You can also go by **ferry** from Szántód or Balatonföldvár, or by boat from Balatonfüred.

VISITOR INFORMATION   Visitor information and private-room bookings for the Tihany Peninsula are available in Tihany Village at **Balatontourist,** Kossuth u. 20 (© and fax **87/448-519**). The office is open May through October only, Monday through Friday from 8:30am to 7pm and on weekends from 8:30am to 12:30pm.

EXPLORING TIHANY VILLAGE

The 18th-century baroque **Abbey Church** ✸ is, undoubtedly, Tihany Village's main attraction. The church stands on the site of an earlier 11th-century Romanesque church (the charter for which contains the first words ever written in Hungarian), around whose remains the crypt of the current church was built. These remains include the marble gravestone of King Andrew, who died in 1060; this is the sole Hungarian royal tomb that remains in its original location. A resident Austrian-born monk carved the exquisite wooden altar and pulpit in the 18th century. The frescoes in the church are by three of Hungary's better-known 19th-century painters, whose work can be viewed throughout the country: Károly Lotz, Bertalan Székely, and Lajos Deák-Ébner.

Next door to the Abbey Church is the **Tihany Museum** (© **87/448-650**), housed in an 18th-century baroque structure, like the church. The museum features exhibitions on the surrounding region's history and culture. You pay a single entry fee of 250 Ft (90¢) for both church and museum. Both are open daily from 9am to 5:30pm.

Tihany Village is also the site of the legendary **Echo Hill,** a scenic spot overlooking the lake (near the Echo Restaurant), which is reached via a winding path that starts from the left side of the Abbey Church. Voices on Echo Hill reverberate back from the side of the church. See for yourself.

Note: Some say the best ice cream on Lake Balaton is to be had at the shop on the road between the Abbey Church and Echo Hill.

4 Szigliget ✸✸

Halfway between Tihany and Keszthely is the lovely village of Szigliget (pronounced Sig-lee-get). If you are as taken as we were by the thatched-roof houses, the lush vineyards, and the sunny Mediterranean feel of Szigliget, you might consider spending the night. **Natur Tourist** (© **87/461-197**), in the village center, is open daily from 9am to 7pm (closing earlier in winter) and can help book private rooms. There are also ubiquitous ZIMMER FREI signs along the roads. **Szőlőskert Panzió,** (© **87/461-264**) on Vadrózsa utca, might be the best option, given its close proximity to the beach. Situated on the hillside amidst lush terraces of grapes, the pension is open only in summer. A double is 9,000 Ft ($32.40).

EXPLORING THE VILLAGE

Szigliget is marked by the fantastic ruins of the 13th-century **Szigliget Castle,** which stand above the town on **Várhegy** (Castle Hill). In the days of the Turkish invasions, the Hungarian Balaton fleet, protected by the high castle, called

Szigliget home. You can hike up to the ruins for a splendid view of the lake and the surrounding countryside; look for the path behind the white 18th-century church, which stands on the highest spot in the village.

A good place to fortify yourself for the hike is the **Vár Vendéglő** ★★, (© 87/ **461-990**) on the road up to the castle. It's a casual restaurant with plenty of outdoor seating, serving traditional Hungarian fare. Main courses run from 800 Ft to 1,500 Ft ($2.90 to $5.40). It's open daily 11am to 11pm.

If you really enjoy hiking, you might take a local bus from Szigliget to the nondescript nearby village of **Hegymagas,** about 3 miles (5km) to the north along the Szigliget-Tapolca bus route. The town's name means "Tall Hill," and from here you can hike up **Szent György-hegy** (St. George Hill). This marvelous vineyard-covered hill has several hiking trails, the most strenuous of which goes up and over the rocky summit.

The lively **beach** at Szigliget provides a striking contrast to the quiet village and is a good place to take the kids. In summer, buses from neighboring towns drop off hordes of beachgoers. The beach area is crowded with fried food and beer stands, ice cream vendors, a swing set, and a volleyball net. Admission to the beach is 300 Ft ($1.10).

Szigliget is also home to the **Eszterházy Wine Cellar,** the largest wine cellar in the region. After a hike in the hills or a day in the sun, a little wine tasting just might be in order. Natur Tourist can provide you with the best directions.

5 Keszthely ⭑

117 miles (187km) SW of Budapest

Keszthely (pronounced *Kest*-hay), which sits at the western edge of Lake Balaton, is one of the largest towns on the lake. Though Keszthely was largely destroyed during the Turkish wars, the town was rebuilt in the 18th century by the Festetics family, an aristocratic family who made Keszthely their home through World War II. The town's main sites all date from the days of the wealthy Festetics clan.

ESSENTIALS

For information on getting to Keszthely, see "Exploring the Lake Balaton Region," earlier. For information about Keszthely, stop in at **Tourinform,** at Kossuth u. 28 (© and fax **83/314-144**). It's open daily, Monday through Friday from 9am to 5pm; and on Saturday and Sundays in high season only from 9am to 1pm. For private-room bookings, try **Zalatours,** at Kossuth u. 1 (© **83/ 312-560**), or **Ibusz,** at Kossuth u. 27 (© **83/314-320**).

EXPLORING THE TOWN

The highlight of a visit to Keszthely is the splendid **Festetics Mansion** ⭑, at Szabadság u. 1 (© **83/312-190** or 83/312-191), the baroque 18th-century home (with 19th-century additions) for generations of the Festetics family. Part of the mansion is now open as a museum. The main attraction is the ornate **Helikon library,** which features floor-to-ceiling oak bookcases—hand-carved by a local master, János Kerbl. The museum also features hunting gear and trophies of a bygone era. The museum is open in summer, daily from 9am to 6pm; in winter, it closes at 5pm and is closed on Monday. Admission for foreigners is 1,400 Ft ($5.05), only 400 Ft ($1.45) for Hungarians. This museum is almost certainly the last in Hungary to maintain this odious Communist-era price discrimination.

The mansion's lovely concert hall is the site of **classical music concerts** almost every night throughout the summer (just two or three times a month

Kids An Excursion to the Thermal Lake in Héviz

If you think the water of Lake Balaton is warm, just wait until you jump into the lake at **Héviz** (pronounced *Hay*-veez) ☆☆, a resort town about 5 miles (8km) northwest of Keszthely. Here, you'll find the largest thermal lake in Europe and the second largest in the world (the largest being in New Zealand), covering 50,000 square meters (60,000 square yards).

The lake's water temperature seldom dips below 85° to 90°F—even in the most bitter spell of winter. Consequently, people swim in the lake year-round. You are bound to notice the huge numbers of German tourists taking advantage of the waters. Héviz has been one of Hungary's leading spa resorts for over 100 years, and it retains a distinct 19th-century atmosphere.

While the lakeside area is suitable for ambling, no visit to Héviz would be complete without a swim (© 83/340-587). An enclosed causeway leads out into the center of the lake where locker rooms and the requisite services, including massage, float rental, and a *palacsinta* (crêpe) bar are housed.

You can easily reach Héviz by bus from Keszthely. Buses depart every half hour or so from the bus station (conveniently stopping to pick up passengers in front of the church on Fő tér). The entrance to the lake is just opposite the bus station. You'll see a whimsical wooden facade and the words TÓ FÜRDŐ (Bathing Lake). Tickets cost 490 Ft ($1.75) for up to 3 hours or 990 Ft ($3.55) for a day pass; however, the latter is not available from November through March. Your ticket entitles you to a locker; insert the ticket into the slot in the locker and the key will come out of the lock. Keep the ticket until exiting, as the attendant needs to see it to determine whether you've stayed a half day or a full day.

Incidentally, there is no shallow water in the lake, so use discretion when bringing children. There is a nice small playground on the grounds that they will enjoy, however.

from September through May). Concerts usually start at 8pm; tickets, ranging all the way from 900 Ft to 5,000 Ft ($3.25 to $18) apiece, are available at the door or earlier in the day at the museum cashier. Another part of the mansion has in the past—and, we are informed, may again—serve as a hotel.

Not far from the Festetics Mansion is the **Georgikon Farm Museum** (© 83/311-563), at Bercsényi u. 67, on the site of Europe's first agricultural college (there is still an active faculty), built by György Festetics in 1797. The museum is devoted to an exhibit of the area's agricultural history. It's open May through October only, Tuesday through Sunday from 10am to 5pm. Admission is 200 Ft (70¢).

Another Keszthely museum worth a visit is the **Balaton Museum** ☆, on the opposite side of the town center from the Festetics Mansion, at Múzeum u. 2 (© 83/312-351). This museum features exhibits on the geological, archaeological, and natural history of the Balaton region. It's open Tuesday through Sunday from 10am to 6pm. Admission is 150 Ft (50¢).

Located down the hill from Fő tér (Main Square), is Keszthely's **open-air market.** Vendors line the street daily. While dawn to mid-afternoon is the busiest time, some vendors stay open into early evening. You'll find fruit and vegetables, spices, preserves, and honey, as well as household appliances, hand-made baskets, and children's clothing. It's a great spot to pick up a good buy.

The center of Keszthely's summer scene, just like that of every other settlement on Lake Balaton, is down by the water on the "strand." Keszthely's **beachfront** is dominated by several large hotels. Regardless of whether or not you're a guest, you can rent windsurfers, boats, and other water-related equipment from these hotels.

WHERE TO STAY

As elsewhere in the Lake Balaton region, private rooms are the recommended budget accommodations in Keszthely. Tourinform, Zalatours, or Ibusz can help in booking you a private room. Rates are from 2,500 Ft to 4,000 Ft ($8.40 to $10.50) per person.

You can also stay at one of several large German-tourist oriented hotels on the beach. Try the **Danubius Hotel Helikon** (℃ **83/311-330**). Rates are $88 for a double room with bath, and breakfast is included. The hotel has a good-size indoor swimming pool, sauna, massage parlor, and outdoor sundeck.

WHERE TO DINE

Oázis Reform Restaurant, at Rákóczi tér 3 (℃ **83/311-023**), is a self-service salad bar featuring adequate (if uninspired) vegetarian fare. There are cold and hot options. Go at lunch time, when the food is freshest. Oázis is open Monday to Saturday, 11am to 4pm.

Csiga Kisvendéglő ✩ (Little Snail Guest House), at Tessedik u. 30 (℃ **83/ 314-799**), a good 15-minute walk from the center, is a small neighborhood restaurant serving a variety of meat and fish dishes. At 500 Ft to 1,000 Ft ($1.70 to $3.80) for main dishes, prices are more than reasonable. Csiga is open Monday through Saturday (through Sunday, in summer), 11am to 9pm.

6 Lake Balaton's Southern Shore

If you're looking for long days at the beach followed by long nights out on the town, the southern shore of Lake Balaton may be the place for you. After all, a million Hungarian students can't be wrong (or could they?)!

Siófok, the largest resort town on Lake Balaton, is at the lake's southeastern end. Its growth dates back to the 1860s, when Budapest was first connected to the southern shore of the lake by rail. Thus, we suppose, nobody alive can remember a time (other than the war years) when Siófok was not overrun by summertime revelers. Today, bustling Siófok caters to a young, active crowd of students and teenagers who fill every inch of the town's beaches all day long and then pack their sunburned bodies into the town's discos until the early morning hours. Large, modern, expensive hotels line the shore in Siófok. You'll find no empty stretches of beach here, but you will find windsurfing, tennis, and boating.

Other popular spots on the southern shore include **Balatonföldvár, Boglár- lelle,** and **Balatonmáriafürdő.**

For information on the southern shore, contact the **Tourinform** office in Sió-fok, at Fő u. 41 (℃ and fax **84/310-117**).

12

Northeastern Hungary: Traveling into the Hills

Northeast of the Danube Bend is Hungary's hilliest region, where its highest peak—Matra Hill at 3,327 feet—can be found. Here you can visit the preserved medieval village of Hollókő; see remnants of the country's Turkish heritage in Eger, also known for its regional wines; or explore the 14-mile (23-km) cave system in Aggtelek.

1 Hollókő: A Preserved Palóc Village ★★

64 miles (102km) NE of Budapest

The village of Hollókő (pronounced Ho-low-koo) is one of the most charming spots in Hungary. This UNESCO World Heritage site is a perfectly preserved but still vibrant Palóc village. The rural Palóc people speak an unusual Hungarian dialect, and they have some of the more colorful folk customs and costumes in Hungary. If you're in Hungary at Easter time, by all means consider spending the holiday in Hollókő. Hollókő's traditional Easter Celebration features townspeople in traditional dress and Masses in the town church.

ESSENTIALS

GETTING THERE   The easiest way to get to Hollókő is by **bus** from Budapest's Népstadion bus station (☎ 1/252-4496). Two direct buses depart daily, at 8:30am and 3:15pm; it takes about 2½ hours on a direct bus. The fare is 900 Ft ($3.25). You can also take a bus from the Árpád Híd bus station (☎ 1/329-1450) to Szécsény, where you switch to a local bus to Hollókő. Six buses ply the Budapest-Szécsény and Szécsény-Hollókő routes every day.

If you're **driving** from Budapest, take the M3 motorway to Hatvan, the M21 from Hatvan to Pásztó, and local roads from Pásztó to Hollókő.

VISITOR INFORMATION   The best information office is the **Foundation of Hollókő,** at Kossuth Lajos út. 68 (☎ 32/579-010). It's open Monday to Saturday 9am to 4pm. You can also get information through **Nograd Tourist** in Salgótarján (☎ 32/310-660) or through **Tourinform** in Szécsény, at Ady Endre u. 12 (☎ 32/370-777).

SEASONAL EVENTS

At **Eastertime** ★, villagers wear national costumes and participate in a folklife festival. Traditional song, dance, and foods are featured. On the first weekend in August, the **Palóc Szőttes Festival** ★★ is held in Hollókő. Folk dance troupes of Nógrád county as well as foreign dance companies perform on an open-air stage. Folk art by local artisans is also on display. In the winter, groups visiting Hollókő can participate in a **wild pig hunt** and subsequent roast. Contact local hunter and guide József Szabó at ☎ 32/379-224 for information.

EXPLORING THE VILLAGE

A one-street town, Hollókő is idyllically set in a quiet, green valley, with **hiking trails** all around. A recently restored 14th-century **castle** is perched on a hilltop over the village.

In the village itself, admire the 14th-century wooden towered church and the sturdy, traditional peasant architecture (normally seen only in stylized skanzens, such as the one near Szentendre), and observe the elderly women at work on their embroidery (samples are for sale). You can also visit the **Village Museum** at Kossuth Lajos u. 82, where exhibits detail everyday Palóc life from the turn of the 20th century. Official hours are Tuesday through Sunday from 10am to 4pm. Like everything else in town, though, the museum's opening times are flexible. Entry is 100 Ft (36¢).

WHERE TO STAY

In Hollókő, traditionally furnished thatch-roofed **peasant houses** are available to rent on a nightly or longer basis. You can rent a **room in a shared house** (with shared facilities), or rent an **entire house.** The prices vary depending on the size of the room or house and the number of people in your party, but 4,500 Ft ($16.20) for a double room is average. Standard **private rooms** are also available in Hollókő. All accommodations can be booked in advance through the tourist office in Hollókő or Salgótarján (see "Essentials," above). If you arrive without reservations (which is not advised), the address and phone number of a room finder is posted on the door of the **Foundation of Hollókő** at Kossuth Lajos u. 68.

WHERE TO DINE

Dining options are limited in tiny Hollókő. The **Vár Étterem,** Kossuth Lajos u. 95 (© **32/379-029**), serves decent Hungarian food at very low prices. Try a dish prepared with the "treasure of the local forests," porcini mushrooms. There is indoor and outdoor seating. The menu is available in English, and the waiters are patient. The restaurant is open daily, noon to 8pm, except Christmas Day.

2 Eger ★★

79 miles (126km) NE of Budapest

Eger (pronounced *Egg*-air), a small baroque city lying in a valley between the Matra and Bükk mountains, is best known for three things: its castle, its wine, and its women—the women of the 16th century, that is. In that dark era of Turkish invasions, the women of Eger claimed their place in the Hungarian national consciousness by bravely fighting alongside István Dobó's army in defense of Eger's castle. Greatly outnumbered by the invaders, the defenders of Eger fought off the Turks for 38 grueling days, achieving a momentous victory that would stall the Turkish advance into Hungary for nearly half a century. Forty-four years later, in 1596, the sultan's forces attacked Eger again, this time taking the castle without great difficulty. Dobó's initial victory, though, and particularly the role of the women defenders, is a much cherished and mythologized historical event, recalled in numerous paintings, poems, and monuments.

As for the wine, the area around Eger is known for producing some fine vintages. Most famous among the regional potions is undoubtedly the heavily marketed *Egri bikavér* (Eger Bull's Blood), a strong dark-red wine, but there are many others worth sampling as well—and no shortage of places in Eger to sample them.

Today Eger's landscape presents a harmonious blend of old and new. The ruined castle, one of Hungary's proudest symbols, dominates the skyline; throughout the summer huge groups of Hungarian children visit the castle. Eger is also home to one of Hungary's most impressive Turkish ruins: a single, tall, slender minaret. The view from the top of the minaret affords a wonderful vista of the town's surroundings. If you wander beyond the confines of the old section, you'll find a small modern city.

ESSENTIALS

GETTING THERE Eger is a 2-hour direct **train** ride from Budapest. Sixteen daily trains depart Budapest's Keleti Station. Tickets cost 1,182 Ft ($4.25).

If you're **driving** from Budapest, take the M3 motorway east to Kerecsend, where you pick up Route 25 north to Eger. There is a 1,400 Ft ($5.05) toll; a toll ticket, valid for a week, is available at all MOL Petrol stations.

VISITOR INFORMATION For information, contact **Tourinform**, at Dobó tér 2 (© **36/517-715;** fax 36/518-815; www.ektf.hu/eger). The office is open in summer, Monday through Friday from 9am to 6pm and on weekends from 10am to 1pm; off-season, the office closes an hour early. For private-room booking, try **Egertourist**, at Bajcsy-Zsilinszky u. 9 (© **36/411-225**). The office is open Monday through Saturday from 10am to 6pm.

EXPLORING OLD EGER

All of Eger's main sites are within easy walking distance of **Dobó István tér** ✶✶, the lovely, dignified square that's the center of old Eger. Dobó István tér is home to the Minorite Church, a fine 18th-century baroque church. You'll also find a statue of Dobó, flanked by a knight and a woman, by Alajos Strobl, one of the country's leading turn-of-the-20th-century sculptors. Strobl's other work includes the statues of King Stephen on Buda's Castle Hill and the poet János Arany in front of the National Museum in Pest. The larger statue in the square, erected in the 1960s, is a more recent—and less subtle—rendition of the fight against the Turks.

The ruined **Eger Castle,** visible from just about anywhere in Eger, can be reached by walking northeast out of the square; enter it via the path out of Dózsa György tér. You can just wander around the grounds, which are always open, or explore two museums on the premises. The **István Dobó Castle Museum** (© **36/312-744**) displays a history of the castle and some Turkish artifacts. The **Eger Picture Gallery** is particularly worth a visit for those who have not yet seen the Hungarian National Gallery in Buda; the same fine 19th-century Hungarian artists are featured in both museums. The museums are open Tuesday through Sunday from 8am to 5pm. Admission to both is 400 Ft ($1.45).

Just to the west of the castle, on Harangöntó utca, is Eger's most visible reminder of the Turkish period, its **Minaret** (© **36/410-233**). Though its mosque was destroyed in 1841, the 14-sided 110-foot-tall minaret survives to this day in remarkably good condition. For 100 Ft (36¢) you can ascend its narrow height. It's a terrifying journey up a steep, cramped spiral staircase; because the space is so narrow, you can't turn back if anyone is behind you. Consequently, the ascent is not recommended for the weak-kneed or weak-hearted. Those who do make the climb, however, are justly rewarded with a spectacular view. Officially, the Minaret is open daily from 10am to 6pm, but the ticket taker in the little booth at the Minaret's base is not always faithful to these hours. If no one is there, you might ask at the nearby Minaret Hotel.

Eger

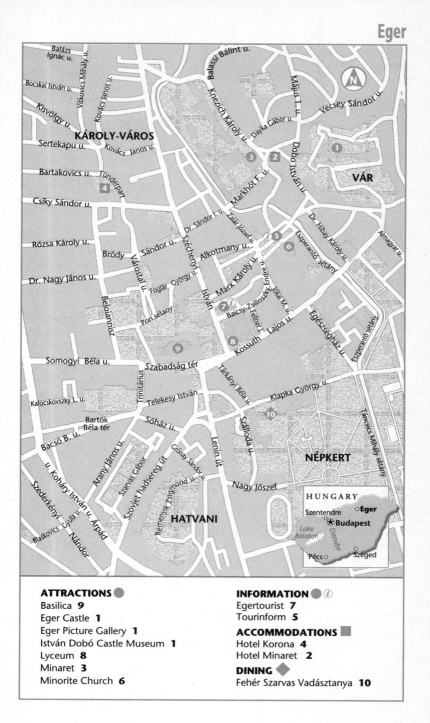

ATTRACTIONS ●
Basilica **9**
Eger Castle **1**
Eger Picture Gallery **1**
István Dobó Castle Museum **1**
Lyceum **8**
Minaret **3**
Minorite Church **6**

INFORMATION ● ⓘ
Egertourist **7**
Tourinform **5**

ACCOMMODATIONS ■
Hotel Korona **4**
Hotel Minaret **2**

DINING ◆
Fehér Szarvas Vadásztanya **10**

Moving from the graceful to the overpowering, you'll find the massive **Basilica**—the second-largest church in Hungary (after Esztergom's Basilica)—a few blocks to the south on Eszterhazy tér. József Hild, who was one of the architects of St. Stephen's Basilica in Pest, built this church in the 1830s in the grandiose neoclassical style of the time. It's open daily from 6am to 7pm. Thirty-minute organ concerts are held in the church in summer, beginning at 11:30am Monday through Saturday and at 12:45pm on Sunday. These times are subject to change; check at Tourinform. Admission is 300 Ft ($1.10).

Opposite the cathedral is the **Lyceum** ✹✹ (✆ **36/325-211**), perhaps Eger's finest example of 18th-century architecture. The library ✹ (*könyvtár*) on the first floor is the highlight of a visit to the Lyceum; the ceiling fresco of the Council of Trent by Johann Lukas Kracker and József Zach ranks among the greatest pieces of Hungarian art. The baroque carved bookshelves are magnificent. The library has a letter written by Mozart, the only one of its kind in the country. It is open to the public: in summer Tuesday through Sunday from 9:30am to 3pm; in winter, Saturday and Sunday only from 9:30am to 13:30pm. Admission is 430 Ft ($1.55). In July and August, concerts are frequently performed in the yard of the Lyceum. Ask at Tourinform for schedule and ticket information.

If you missed visiting a spa or bathhouse in Budapest, try Eger's own Turkish bath at Fürdó u. 1–3 (✆ **36/413-356**). The bath is open to women on Monday, Wednesday, and Friday, and to men on Tuesday, Thursday, and Saturday. Spa services are posted in English. Northeastern Hungary is rich in thermal waters; ask at Tourinform for a list of spas in the region.

WHERE TO STAY

Eger is blessed with several fine little hotels right in the center of town. Two stand out in particular. The **Hotel Korona** ✹, Tündérpart 5, 3300 Eger (✆ **36/ 310-287**; fax 36/310-261), is a clean, cozy establishment on an extremely quiet, residential street just a few blocks west of Dobó István tér. The hotel has a shaded patio, where breakfast is served, and a wine cellar. There are 40 rooms, all with private bath. A double room goes for 60€ to 70€ ($54 to $63), with prices about 20% lower off-season. Rates include breakfast and sauna. Credit cards are accepted. Bus no. 11, 12, or 14 will get you there from the train station; get off at Csiky Sándor utca and you're practically at the doorstep.

On a par with the Hotel Korona is the much less expensive and recently expanded **Hotel Minaret** ✹, directly adjacent to Eger's Minaret, at Harangöntó u. 5, 3300 Eger (✆ and fax **36/410-473**). Just minutes north of Dobó István tér, this hotel offers spare, tidy double rooms for 10,200 Ft ($36.70). Rates include breakfast. All of the 42 rooms are equipped with private bathroom. Credit cards are accepted. Take bus no. 11, 12, or 14 from the train station; after getting off at the Main Post Office (Fóposta), you have to walk 5 minutes or so to the northeast.

For something peacefully removed from the downtown, try the **Garten Vendégház,** Legányi u. 6, 3300 Eger (✆ **36/320-371**). Operated by the Zsemlye family, this guest house is located on a quiet residential street in the hills overlooking the city. The view from their gorgeous garden is splendid. The price of a double room is 8,500 Ft ($30.60). Rates include breakfast.

Travelers on a tighter budget should consider renting a private room through **Egertourist** (see above) or through Express, at Szécseny u. 28 (✆ **36/427-757**). Rates in Eger are as low as 1,800 Ft ($6.50) for a bed with a shared bathroom and as high as 3,500 Ft ($12.60) for an apartment with bath and kitchen.

> ## ⟳ An Excursion to Bükk National Park
>
> Just to the northeast of Eger lies the Bükk mountain range, a lush, rugged terrain of cliffs and forest land. Since 1976 a large part of this region has comprised the **Bükki Nemzeti Park** (Bükk National Park). In addition to numerous hiking trails, area highlights include a visit to the Lippizaner horse-breeding stables in the village of Szilvásvárad and a ride on the narrow-gauge railroad from Szilvásvárad to Szalajka-völgy. This train ride takes you through a serene landscape of mountain streams and waterfalls.
>
> This mountainous national park is best visited in the spring, when countless wildflowers color the landscape. A public bus from Eger stops here. Call ℭ **36/411-581** for information. The area has several pensions and hotels, as well as accommodations in private rooms. Egertourist or Tourinform (in Eger) should be able to help you book a room. Cartografia publishes the best area map; called *Bükk hegység* (Bükk Hills), it shows all the area hiking trails in fairly good detail.

WHERE TO DINE

The **Fehér Szarvas Vadásztanya** (White Stag Hunting Inn) ⭐, located next door to the Park Hotel at Klapka u. 8 (ℭ **36/411-129**), a few blocks south of Dobó István tér, is one of Eger's best-known and best-loved restaurants. The menu offers a full range of Hungarian wild-game specialties. The hearty, paprika-laced stews are especially good. Award-winning regional wines are featured. A piano and bass duet play nightly, amid the kitschy hunting lodge decor. The restaurant is open daily from noon to midnight, and reservations are recommended. Credit cards are accepted.

WHERE TO SAMPLE LOCAL WINE

The best place to sample local wines is in the vineyard country just west of Eger, in the wine cellars of the **Szépasszony-völgy** (Valley of the Beautiful Women). More than 200 wine cellars are here, each offering its own vintage. Some cellars have live music. Although the wine cellars don't serve food, you can grab a meal at a few local restaurants. Generally, the cellars open at 10am and close by 9 or 10pm.

The easiest way to get to the Szépasszony-völgy is by taxi, though you can also walk there from the center in 30 or 40 minutes. You could also take bus no. 13 to the Hatvani Temető (Hatvan Cemetery) and walk from there; it's a 10- to 15-minute walk.

3 Aggtelek: An Entrance to the Caves ⭐

140 miles (224 km) NE of Budapest

Tucked away beneath the Slovak border in northernmost Hungary, about 50 miles (80km) north of Eger, **Aggtelek National Park** (Aggteleki Nemzeti Park) is home to the extensive **Baradla cave network,** one of Europe's most spectacular cave systems. Although the remote and sparsely populated Aggtelek region is also suitable for hiking, people tend to travel to Aggtelek primarily to explore the caves.

Tips **Cool Caves**

Remember, no matter how hot it is outside, the Baradla caves are always damp and chilly (a constant 50° to 52°F), so dress appropriately.

You can enter the Baradla cave system on guided tours from either of two villages: Aggtelek or Jósvafő, which is on the other side of the mountain. The tours are a lot of fun. Call Aggtelek National Park (© 48/350-006) for tour information. If this is your first time in a cave, you'll be astounded by the magical subterranean world of stalactites, stalagmites, and other bizarre formations. Three different guided tours—appropriately called short (*rövid*), medium (*közép*), and long (*hosszú*)—depart at different times throughout the day.

The **Hotel Cseppkő** (© 48/343-075), in the village of Aggtelek, is a popular place to crash after a day in the caves. Double rooms start at 6,500 Ft ($23.40), without breakfast. Though it's nothing to write home about, the Cseppkő is clean and conveniently located. Camping is also popular in the area.

Travelers without cars can get to Aggtelek by bus from Eger. The trip takes 3 hours. From Miskolc, the trip takes 2 hours. Ask about transportation at the local tourist office (such as Eger's Tourinform or Egertourist), where you can also ask for help booking a room in the Hotel Cseppkó (off-season there is no need to book in advance).

Southern Hungary: The Great Plain & the Mecsek Hills

The mainly agricultural region of the Alföld (Great Plain), including the last remnants of the Puszta, Hungary's prairie, lies south and east of the Danube River. The main cities here are Kecskemét and Szeged. The Great Plain comprises approximately 20,000 square miles. On the other side of the river, in southwestern Hungary, are the verdant Mecsek Hills. The city of Pécs is the centerpiece of this hilly region.

1 The 2,000-Year-Old City of Pécs ★★★

123 miles (197 km) SW of Budapest

Pécs (pronounced *Paych*) is a delightful, exuberant place, the largest and loveliest city in the Mecsek Hill region. Situated 20 miles (32km) or so from the Croatian border, the city enjoys a particularly warm and arid climate; the rolling hills around Pécs is the source of some of Hungary's finest fresh fruit. Few places in Hungary possess a more Mediterranean quality than Pécs.

Known as the "2,000-year-old city," Pécs was a major settlement in Roman times, when it was called Sopianae. It was later the site of Hungary's first university, founded in 1367. While that university no longer exists, Pécs remains one of the country's more important centers of learning. The city's present university, Janus Pannonius University (named for a local ecclesiastical poet of the 15th century) was moved here from Bratislava after that city (known as Pozsony to Hungarians) was allocated to Czechoslovakia when Czechoslovakia was created after World War I.

Pécs thrived during the almost 150-year Turkish occupation as well, and reminders of this period fill the city. Although Pécs (like much of Hungary) was almost completely destroyed during the bloody liberation battles between the Ottoman and Christian armies, what did survive—particularly the Mosque of Pasha Gazi Kassim—may well be the best example of Turkish architecture in the country.

The people of Pécs are proud of their city. If you travel just a block or two outside the historic core, you'll see that the place is thriving: People throng the shops and streets; buses thunder past in every direction. Pécs is a city on the move. It exhibits none of the torpor you might notice on a hot summer afternoon in a Great Plains town like Kecskemét or Szeged.

And if you walk up Janus Pannonius utca toward Széchenyi tér, about a block up the street, you'll notice on your left a small metal fence covered with padlocks. Young lovers visiting Pécs have left these locks as a token of their desire to live in this beautiful city.

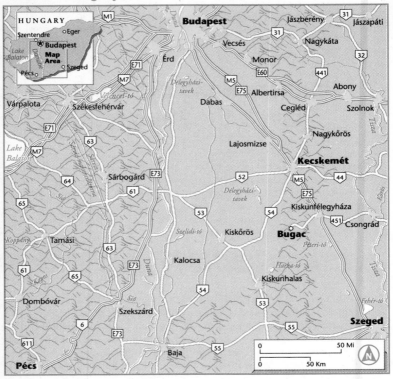

A more recent development in Pécs is the presence of NATO and UN troops, including a sizable American contingent, who are based just outside the city as part of the peacekeeping missions in the former Yugoslavia.

ESSENTIALS

GETTING THERE   Fourteen **trains** depart daily from Budapest's Déli Station; five of these are Intercity trains. The fare is 1,722 Ft ($6.20). On an Intercity train the journey takes about 2½ hours, and you are required to pay an additional 360 Ft ($1.30) for a seat reservation. On a fast train (*gyors*), the trip is more like 3 hours, but you don't need a reservation.

If you are **driving** from Budapest, take the M6 south for approximately 3 hours.

VISITOR INFORMATION   The best source of information in Pécs is **Tourinform,** at Széchenyi tér 9 (© **72/213-315;** fax 72/212-632). Tourinform is open April through October, Monday through Friday from 9am to 7pm and on weekends from 9am to 6pm; in winter, Monday through Friday from 8am to 4pm. Tourinform can provide a list of local private-room accommodations, but you'll have to reserve the room yourself.

If you want to have a room reserved for you or are specifically interested in finding accommodations, visit **Mecsek Tourist,** at Széchenyi tér 1 (© **72/ 513-371;** fax 72/512-373). The office is open Monday through Friday from 9am to 5pm and on Saturday from 9am to 1pm in summer.

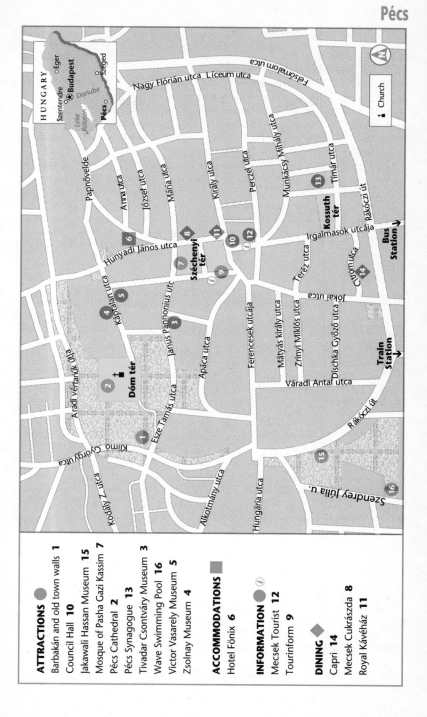

Pécs

HUNGARY

Szentendre ◦Eger
◉ Budapest
◦ Szeged
Danube
Lake Balaton
Pécs ◦

✝ Church

Nagy Flórián utca   Líceum utca

Felsőmalom utca

Papnövelde

Anna utca
József utca
Mária utca
Király utca
Perczel utca
Munkácsy Mihály utca
Timár utca

Kossuth tér
Rákóczi út

6

Hunyadi János utca

8
11
10
ℹ **12**

Széchenyi tér

7
ℹ
9

Irgalmasok utcája

13

Bus Station →

Kápalan utca
4
5

Janus Pannonius utca
3

Teréz utca
Gyöm utca
14

Jókai utca
Aradi vértanúk útja

Kodály Z. utca

Dóm tér
✝
2

Apáca utca

Ferencesek utcája

Mátyás király utca
Zrínyi Miklós utca
Dischka Győző utca

Train Station

Esze Tamás utca

Klimo György utca
1

Váradi Antal utca

Rákóczi út

Alkotmány utca

Hungária utca

15

Szendrey Júlia u.

16

ATTRACTIONS ●
Barbakán and old town walls **1**
Council Hall **10**
Jakawali Hassan Museum **15**
Mosque of Pasha Gazi Kassim **7**
Pécs Cathedral **2**
Pécs Synagogue **13**
Tivadar Csontváry Museum **3**
Wave Swimming Pool **16**
Victor Vasarely Museum **5**
Zsolnay Museum **4**

ACCOMMODATIONS ■
Hotel Fönix **6**

INFORMATION ⓘ
Mecsek Tourist **12**
Tourinform **9**

DINING ◆
Capri **14**
Mecsek Cukrászda **8**
Royal Kávéház **11**

A free weekly magazine called *Pécsi Est* contains lots of useful information; pick it up anywhere. You can also get city information online at **www.pecs.hu**.

EXPLORING OLD PÉCS

Today, the old section of Pécs captivates visitors. One of Hungary's most pleasing central squares is here—**Széchenyi tér** ★★★, set on an incline with the mosque at the top and the powerful equestrian statue of János Hunyadi at the bottom. Hunyadi defeated the Turks in the 1456 Battle of Nandorfehérvár (present-day Belgrade), thus forestalling their northward advance by nearly a century. Grand pastel-colored buildings line the cobblestone streets that border the square.

Old Pécs is known for its many museums and galleries; after Budapest, Pécs is perhaps the biggest center of the arts in Hungary. The large student population contributes greatly to this creative state of affairs. We list several museums below, but there are many more as well, some containing the work of contemporary and student artists. Pécs is also home to the Zsolnay ceramics factory; Zsolnay porcelain, though lesser known internationally than its rival Herend, may be more popular domestically. The Zsolnay Museum, also listed below, is a "must see" in Pécs.

MUSEUMS

Jakawali Hassan Museum This museum is housed inside a 16th-century mosque, the only mosque in Hungary with a minaret still intact (though unfortunately you can't ascend the minaret as you can Eger's mosque-less minaret). Like the much larger mosque up in Széchenyi tér, this mosque was converted to a church after the Turks were driven from Pécs, but in the 1950s it was restored to its original form. The museum's main attraction is the building itself, although various religious artifacts are on display as well.

Rákóczi út 2. ✆ **72/313-853.** Admission 120 Ft (45¢). Thurs–Sun 10am–6pm (closed 1–2pm for lunch). Closed Wed. Closed Oct–Mar.

Tivadar Csontváry Museum ★ Tivadar Csontváry Kosztka (1853–1919), today one of Hungary's most beloved artists, remained unknown during his lifetime, scorned by the art establishment. His mystical postimpressionist landscapes suggest a unique vision of the world, one that is both tormented and idyllic, a talent attributed by some to his schizophrenia. Hungarians like to point out that some time after Csontváry's death Picasso saw an exhibition of his work and referred to him as the "other" artistic genius of the 20th century. This little museum houses an impressive collection of his work.

Across the street from the museum, in the park beneath Pécs Cathedral, is a statue of Csontváry.

Janus Pannonius u. 11. ✆ **72/315-694.** Admission 300 Ft ($1.10). Tues–Sun 10am–6pm; winter Tues–Sun 10am–4pm.

Victor Vasarely Museum ★ The late Victor Vasarely, internationally known founder of "op art," was born in the house where this museum now stands. This is one of two museums in the country devoted solely to his work (the other is in Óbuda; see "More Museums & Sights," in chapter 6, "Exploring Budapest"). While Vasarely's fame was achieved abroad, Pécs proudly considers him a native son.

Kaptalan u. 3. ✆ **72/324-822.** Admission 300 Ft ($1.10). Tues–Sat 10am–6pm; Sun 10am–4pm.

Zsolnay Museum ★★★ This is one of five museums on Káptalan utca, Pécs's "street of museums," and you shouldn't miss it. The Zsolnay Museum displays some of the best examples of Zsolnay porcelain, produced locally since 1852. There are vases, plates, cups, figurines, and even ceramic paintings. Once you've seen the museum, check out the Zsolnay fountain at the lower end of Széchenyi tér.

Kaptalan u. 2. ✆ 72/324-822. Admission 350 Ft ($1.25). Tues–Sat 10am–6pm; Sun 10am–4pm.

HOUSES OF WORSHIP

Mosque of Pasha Gazi Kassim   The largest Turkish structure still standing in Hungary, this former mosque now houses a Catholic church. It was built in the late 16th century, during the Turkish occupation, on the site of an earlier church. The mix of religious traditions is oddly evident everywhere you look, but the effect is rather pleasing. An English-language description of the building's history is posted on a bulletin board on the left-hand wall.

At the top of Széchenyi tér. ✆ 72/321-976. Free admission. Mon–Sat 10am–4pm, Sun 11:30am–4pm; winter Mon–Sat 10am–noon, Sun 11:30am–noon.

Pécs Cathedral   Dating back to the 11th century, this four-towered cathedral has been destroyed and rebuilt on several occasions. During the Turkish occupation it was used as a mosque, sporting a minaret. The neoclassical exterior is the work of the early-19th-century architect Mihály Pollack. The interior remains primarily Gothic, with some baroque additions and furnishings. Various paintings and murals by leading 19th-century artists Károly Lotz and Bertalan Székely are inside. Organ concerts are performed in the cathedral throughout the year. Inquire at the cathedral or at Tourinform for the schedule.

The square in front of the cathedral—as well as the little park beneath it—is a popular gathering place, and occasionally the site of folk concerts or dances.

On Dóm tér. ✆ 72/513-030. Admission cathedral (includes treasury and crypt) 400 Ft ($1.45). For 500 Ft ($1.80), you can have the lights turned on. A guided tour can be arranged in advance for 1,500 Ft ($5.40). Apr–Oct Mon–Sat 9am–5pm, Sun 1–5pm; Nov–Mar Mon–Sat 10am–4pm, Sun 1–4pm.

Pécs Synagogue ⭐   Pécs's grand old synagogue is incongruously situated in what is now one of the city's busiest shopping squares, Kossuth tér (home of the Konsum Department Store). Nevertheless, once inside you'll find it to be a quiet, cool place far removed from the bustle outside. The synagogue was built in 1869, and the original rich oak interior survives to this day. Next door is the former Jewish school of Pécs, now a Croatian school. Prior to World War II, the synagogue had over 4,000 members, of whom only 464 survived the Holocaust. Every year, Pécs's small Jewish community commemorates the 1944 deportations to Auschwitz on the first Sunday after July 4.

Regular services are held in the smaller temple next door at Fürdő 1 (there isn't a sign; go through the building into the courtyard and cross diagonally to the right) on Friday at 6:30pm.

Kossuth tér. ✆ 72/315-881. Admission 150 Ft (55¢). May–Oct Sun–Fri 10am–5pm. Closed Nov–Feb.

SHOPPING

A short stroll through the center of town is enough to see that Pécs is prospering. Several pedestrian-only streets make shopping in Pécs a favorite activity. For a more exotic shopping experience, visit the **Pécsi Vásár** ⭐⭐ (Pécs Flea Market). At this crowded, bustling open-air market you can find everything from antique china and silver to Turkish T-shirts and Chinese baby booties. Tables of homemade preserves and honey stand alongside boxes of used car parts. The main attraction, however, is the animal market. People sell puppies and kittens out of the trunks of their cars. You might also find for sale chickens, rabbits, and even pigs and horses. It's open every day, though Sunday is the biggest and best day (particularly for the animal market).

To get to the flea market, a special bus (marked "Vásár") departs the Konsum shopping center in the center of downtown Pécs regularly. You need two standard city bus tickets for this bus, which are available for 95 Ft (35¢) each at newsstands and kiosks or for 115 Ft (40¢) apiece from the bus driver. You can also take the no. 3 bus from the Konsum (only one ticket required), but you'll have to walk some distance from the stop to the entrance of the flea market.

OUTDOOR ACTIVITIES

If you are visiting Pécs in the summer, you are bound to feel the heat. Cool off in the waves at **Hullám uszoda** (Wave Swimming Pool) on Szendrey Júlia utca (© **72/512-936**). Admission is 400 Ft ($1.45). The pool is open daily from 6am to 10pm. Another swimming pool complex that belongs to the university is at Ifjúság útja 6, (© **72/501-519, ext. 4195**). There is a wading pool for kids, as well as a 25-meter lap pool. Admission is 200 Ft (75¢). After swimming, treat yourself to some of the best ice cream in town, right down the street at Egerszegi Cukrászda.

Pécs is home to perhaps one of the most appealing neighborhood playgrounds in all of Hungary. **Napsugár Játszókert** (Sunshine Playground) is on Vadász utca, a short bus ride from the city center. Built in 1997 by a foundation and with donations from the community, this small grassy playground has a quaint friendly appeal. There are chunky wooden climbing structures, slides, seesaws, swings (including an infant swing), a sandbox, and picnic tables. To get there, take bus no. 27 from the Konsum to the "Ledina" stop.

Nine kilometers west of town, on Route 6, there is a golf course operated by the **Golf Club of Pécs** (© **72/464-136**). You can rent clubs and carts, play 18 holes (17€/$15.30, on weekends 20€/$18), or use the driving range (2€/$1.80 for 30 balls). The club also offers lessons.

WHERE TO STAY

You can book a private room through **Mecsek Tourist** (see "Essentials," above) or Ibusz, across Széchenyi tér at no. 8 (© **72/212-157**).

If you're in the mood for a funky little hotel right in the center, try the popular **Hotel Fönix** ★★, at Hunyadi út 2 (© **72/311-680** or 72/510-226, fax 72/324-113). This unique hotel, just off the top of Széchenyi tér, has 14 rooms, each one with oddly angled walls and sloped ceilings. The rooms are a bit cramped, but all are clean and have refrigerators and TVs. Each room has a shower, but only eight have toilets; the common facilities are well maintained. Three apartments, with full facilities and its own entrance off the street, is also available. A double room costs 6,990 Ft ($25.15), a room with a private toilet is 7,990 Ft ($28.75), and the apartment goes for 15,390 Ft ($55.40). Rates include breakfast. Call several days ahead to reserve a room. Credit cards are accepted.

If the Hotel Fönix is full, the management can book a room for you at a pension they operate, **Kertész Panzió,** at Sáfrány u. 42 (© **72/327-551**). If you'd prefer a smaller, quieter accommodation in the hills anyway, this pension might be just the place for you. A double room is 8,990 Ft ($35.65); a suite with three beds is 10,990 Ft ($39.55), one with four beds is 12,990 Ft ($46.75). Bus no. 32 or 36, which stops in front of the Hotel Fönix, will take you to Kertész Panzió.

WHERE TO DINE

Bagolyvár Étterem ⊕ HUNGARIAN   Bagolyvár, a large, classy restaurant, serves delicious, hearty food in a fabulous setting, high in the hills overlooking the city. The view is excellent, the service is equally good, and there's a well-stocked wine cellar. Bagolyvár was recently extended with a fine pizzeria in the same building (© 72/310-736). *Note:* The same owner operates a second restaurant, **Dóm Vendéglő,** in the city center, at Király u. 3 (© 72/ 210-088 or 72/310-736).

Felsőhavi Dűlő 6/1. © 72/211-333. Reservations recommended in summer. Main courses 950 Ft–2,500 Ft ($3.40–$9). Daily noon–midnight. Bus: 33 from in front of the Konsum shopping center to the last stop.

COFFEEHOUSES & ICE-CREAM PARLORS

Pécs offers numerous places to enjoy coffee and sweets. Try **Mecsek Cukrászda,** on **Széchenyi tér** (no phone), for a quick jolt of espresso and any number of sinfully good and inexpensive pastries. For a more leisurely coffeehouse experience, try the **Royal Kávéház,** at the corner of Király utca and Széchenyi tér (© 72/210-683). There's outdoor seating, but the recently renovated art deco interior makes sitting inside worthwhile. You can also order a more substantial meal here; soups cost 350 Ft to 580 Ft ($1.25 to $2.10), while main courses cost 650 Ft to 980 Ft ($2.35 to $3.50).

For ice cream, **Capri,** a very popular shop at Citrom u. 7 (© 72/319-713), 3 blocks south of Széchenyi tér, serves up various sundaes as well as cones. Some locals, however, claim that the ice cream at Capri is inferior to that of the **Egerszegi Fagylaltozó,** on Rókusalja utca (© 72/325-560), a 15-minute walk from the center. The owners of Egerszegi recently opened a second, easier-to-reach place at Bajcsy-Zsilinszky u. 5 (© 72/327-540). Our current favorite for sweets and ice cream is **Magda Cukrászda** ⊕⊕, at Kandó Kálmán u. 4 (© 72/511-055). This is a bright, bustling neighborhood cukrászda, where the selection and quality of cakes is superb. Notable ice cream flavors include poppy seed, chestnut, blueberry cream, cherry cream, and cinnamon (however they do not sell ice cream in the winter). The slightly out-of-the-way location (near the train station) apparently hasn't deterred customers at all. It's open daily from 10am to 8pm, in winter 7pm.

2 Kecskemét ⊕

53 miles (85 km) SE of Budapest

Kecskemét (pronounced *Ketch*-keh-mate), a city of over 100,000 inhabitants in the western portion of the Great Hungarian Plain, has a decidedly small-town feel to it. A quiet, sun-baked city with wide, open squares and broad avenues, Kecskemét is blessed with some of the most interesting architecture in the Great Plain. The town's dizzyingly colorful art nouveau buildings may be the equal of any in the country outside the capital.

Kecskemét was the birthplace of Zoltán Kodály, the musicologist, teacher, and composer who, along with his friend and colleague Béla Bartók, achieved worldwide renown earlier this century. Today, a music school in town bears his name. Kecskemét is also famous throughout the country for its many varieties of apricot brandy (*barack pálinka*).

ESSENTIALS

GETTING THERE   Twelve daily **trains** depart Budapest's Nyugati Station. The fare is 882 Ft ($3.20). On an Intercity train the journey takes 1¼ hours, and you are required to pay an additional 360 Ft ($1.30) for a seat reservation. On a fast train (*gyors*), the trip is just over 1½ hours, but you don't need a reservation.

If you're driving from Budapest, take the M5 motorway south. You will have to pay a 1,600 Ft ($5.75) highway toll each way.

VISITOR INFORMATION   The best source of information is **Tourinform**, at Kossuth tér 1 (© and fax **76/481-065**). The office is open in summer Monday through Friday from 8am to 5pm and on Saturday from 9am to 1pm, in July and August on Sundays 9am to 1pm as well; n winter weekdays only 8am to 5pm. **Pusztatourist**, at Szabadság tér 2 (© **76/483-493;** fax 76/328-863), will be useful if you're planning a side trip to Bugac. It's open Monday through Friday from 9am to 5pm, and Saturday from 9:30am to 12:30pm.

EXPLORING KECSKEMÉT

The museums mentioned here are in the immediate vicinity of Kossuth tér, Kecskemét's main square.

Photography lovers will not want to miss the excellent **Hungarian Photography Museum**, Katona József tér 12 (© **76/483-221**), featuring the works of contemporary Hungarian photographers, including foreign photographers of Hungarian origin. Admission is 150 Ft (55¢). Open Wednesday through Sunday from 10am to 5pm.

Located inside the Cifra Palace, the city's other art nouveau gem, the **Kecskemét Gallery (Kecskeméti Galéria),** Rákóczi u. 1 (© **76/480-776**), features Hungarian art of the 19th and 20th centuries. Even if you don't go inside, make sure you check out this incredible building. Admission is 200 Ft (75¢). It's open Tuesday through Saturday from 10am to 5pm, on Sundays from 1:30pm to 5pm.

The **Museum of Hungarian Naïve Artists (Naïv Múvészeti Galéria)** ✦, Gáspár András u. 11 (© **76/324-767**), houses the works of local folk artists from the early 20th century to the present. In one gallery, artworks are available for purchase. Admission is 100 Ft (36¢). Open Tuesday through Sunday from 9am to 5pm.

Hungary's largest toy collection can be found at the **Toy Museum (Játék-múhély és Múzeum)** ✦, at the corner of Gáspár András utca and Hosszú utca (© **76/481-469**). This quaint museum has exhibits on toy design and manufacturing. Families with children should try to come on the weekend, when youngsters are allowed to play with some of the toys. Admission is 200 Ft (75¢) for adults, 50 Ft (21¢) for children. Open Wednesday through Sunday from 10am to 5pm, with a lunch break from 12:30pm to 1pm.

Town Hall ✦   Built in 1893 by Ödön Lechner and Gyula Pártos, this delightful art nouveau structure is a "must see" for aficionados of Lechner's later Budapest buildings, the former Post Office Savings Bank (see "Walking Tour 3: Leopold Town & Theresa Town," in chapter 7, "Strolling Around Budapest") and the Applied Arts Museum (see "More Museums & Sights" in chapter 6, "Exploring Budapest"). Like those buildings in the capital, Lechner's Kecskemét masterpiece is generously decorated with colorful Zsolnay majolica tiles. The council chamber (*dísz terem*) contains ceiling frescoes by the artist Bertalan Székely, whose work is also on exhibit in Buda's National Gallery. If the building is closed when you arrive, admire it from the outside while you listen to the bells playing music by Kodály and others throughout the day (usually on the hour).

Just in front of the Town Hall is an odd monument: a stone broken in two to symbolize the heart attack suffered on that spot by József Katona, the beloved early 18th-century playwright and native son, who is recognized as the father of modern Hungarian drama. Katona is best known for *Bánkbán,* a play that was later put to music by Ferenc Erkel, becoming the first Hungarian opera.

Kossuth tér 1. (℗ 76/483-683. Admission 200 Ft (75¢), by appointment only. Mon–Fri 9am–5pm.

WHERE TO STAY

Private rooms can be booked only through Pusztatourist (see "Essentials," earlier). Due to lack of demand there is no other private rooms service in town.

Caissa Panzió ⭐   Centrally located and reasonably priced, the Caissa, named for the goddess of chess, is also the choice for enthusiasts of the game. A family-owned and -operated pension, Caissa hosts official grandmaster tournaments every year. Recent guests have included the Polgar family and Péter Lékó. Bobby Fischer, having chosen Budapest as his place of self-imposed exile, is said to order books regularly from the Caissa chess bookshop. The hotel's reception desk is on the fifth floor, where the kitchen and common room are also located. The small rooms are clean and bright; many overlook the quiet residential park on the front side of the building. Four have TVs, and two have private toilet and shower.

Gyenes tér 18, 6000 Kecskemét. (℗ and fax 76/481-685. 10 units, 2 with private bathroom. 4,900 Ft–5,900 Ft ($17.65–$21.25) double. Breakfast 480 Ft ($1.70) extra (served 7–11am). No credit cards. **Amenities:** Common kitchen. *In room:* TV (4 units).

Hotel Három Gúnár   This is a well-maintained, clean, comfortable hotel, just minutes from central Kossuth tér. Insist on a room above the ground floor to avoid the noise from the bowling alley in the hotel's basement.

Batthyány u. 7, 6000 Kecskemét. (℗ 76/483-611. Fax 76/481-253. 46 units. 11,200 Ft ($40.30) double; from 14,600 Ft ($52.55) suite. Rates include breakfast. V. Free parking. **Amenities:** Restaurant; bowling alley. *In room:* TV, minibar.

WHERE TO DINE

We recommend the **Görög Udvar Étterem** ⭐, a Greek restaurant, housed inside the Greek culture museum, at Hornyik János krt. 1 (℗ **76/492-513**). The authentic Greek fare is delicious. Main courses cost 1,000 Ft to 1,500 Ft ($3.60 to $5.40). Alcohol is served, including Greek specialty liquors and wine. Open daily from 11am to 11pm.

Another good dining option is **Italia,** just down the street at Hornyik János krt. 4 (℗ **76/484-627**). Italia serves great tasting pizza for 380 Ft to 810 Ft ($1.35 to $2.90), as well as pasta, priced at 430 Ft to 600 Ft ($1.55 to $2.15), in a bright, busy atmosphere. There's outdoor seating in summer. Open daily from 10am to 11pm.

HBH ⭐, Csányi u. 4 (℗ **76/481-945**), is the best choice for traditional Hungarian and Bavarian fare at reasonable prices: Soups cost 290 Ft ($1.05), while main courses run 780 Ft to 3,500 Ft ($2.80 to $12.60). HBH also brews its own beer; a half-liter mug, korsó, is 280 Ft ($1). Open daily from 11am to midnight.

3 Bugac & the Puszta

Much of the Great Hungarian Plain was once comprised of open, rugged *puszta* (prairie) country, home to a fondly remembered, much-mythologized culture of nomadic shepherds and fierce horsemen. The vast wilderness of grasslands and marshes has long since given way to the modern era of agricultural reclamation, but pieces of the native terrain—and the puszta way of life—are preserved in national parks in the Great Plain.

Kiskunság National Park (✆ **76/321-777**) and especially the village of **Bugac,** about 25 miles (40km) south of Kecskemét, are well worth a visit. If you're lucky enough to be in Hungary in late spring, you can see one of the region's finest sights: endless fields ablaze with wild red poppies.

You can book a tour to Bugac from Budapest through Ibusz. The scheduled tour includes a traditional horse-riding show featuring Hungarian cowboys (*csikós*), horseback riding on the trails, and a traditional puszta dinner of *bogrács gulyás,* a hearty stew cooked over an open fire.

You can also travel to Bugac on your own by train from Kecskemét; three trains depart and return daily. A local bus also departs Kecskemét for Bugac Monday through Friday at 11am daily. The bus leaves from the main bus station (next to the train station); the trip takes 30 minutes. You can also see the riding show; tickets are 1,100 Ft ($3.95), or 2,200 Ft ($7.90) for a combined ticket, which includes an hour-long horse-drawn carriage ride. Of course, you can always skip the show and hike out into the wilderness, too.

If you want to spend a night on the puszta, you can book a room through **Bugac Tours,** in Kecskemét at Szabadság u. 5/A (✆ **76/481-643**). (Ask them for riding and trail information as well.) Or try the **Gedeon Tanya Panzió** (Gedeon Farm Boarding House) (✆ **76/382-800**), a traditional old farmhouse with three double rooms. An adjoining new building has five double rooms, a large dining room, and a wine cellar. A double room costs 9,400 Ft ($33.85). Gedeon Tanya also has its own stables. Nonguests are welcome to visit just for the horseback riding, it is 1,800 Ft ($6.50) for an hour. **Táltos Lovaspanzió** (Táltos Equestrian Pension) (✆ **76/372-633;** fax 76/372-580) is another accommodation in Bugac for horse lovers. The pension operates a large stable. There are double rooms with private shower costing 8,000 Ft ($28.80), and double rooms with shared facilities for 5,000 Ft ($18). There are also bungalows for 15,000 Ft ($54). Each bungalow sleeps about six people.

No trip to Bugac would be complete without a meal at the **Bugaci Csárda** (✆ **76/372-522**), locally famous for "authentic" Puszta meals: rich, hearty paprika stews. Meals cost between 750 Ft to1,300 Ft ($2.70 to $4.70).

4 Szeged: Hungary's Spice Capital ⭐⭐

105 miles (168 km) SE of Budapest

World famous for its paprika and salami (*Pick Szalami*), Szeged (pronounced Seh-ged) is also home to one of Hungary's major universities, named after Attila József, the brilliant but disturbed interwar poet who rose to artistic heights from a childhood of desperate poverty. As a young man, he was expelled from the university that would later change its name to honor him. Driven by private demons, Hungary's great "proletarian poet" committed suicide at the age of 32 by hurling himself under a train at Balatonszárszó, by the Lake Balaton. József failed to achieve wide recognition during his lifetime; today, though, he is adored in Hungary, particularly by teenagers and students drawn to his rebellious, nonconformist, irreverent spirit. The national book fair each year is traditionally opened on his birthday, April 11th. A wonderfully unassuming statue of the doomed poet stands in front of the university's main building on Dugonics tér. The only other statue of him we know of is next to the Parliament Building

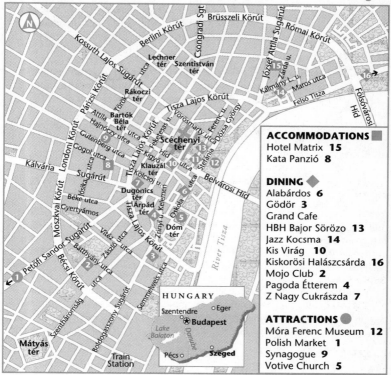

ACCOMMODATIONS ■
Hotel Matrix **15**
Kata Panzió **8**

DINING ◆
Alabárdos **6**
Gödör **3**
Grand Cafe
HBH Bajor Sörözo **13**
Jazz Kocsma **14**
Kis Virág **10**
Kiskorösi Halászcsárda **16**
Mojo Club **2**
Pagoda Étterem **4**
Z Nagy Cukrászda **7**

ATTRACTIONS ●
Móra Ferenc Museum **12**
Polish Market **1**
Synagogue **9**
Votive Church **5**

in Budapest, sitting on the steps of the embankment, evoking the theme of the multicultural Danube, his famous poem written against the specter of nationalism in the 1930s.

In addition to its status as a center of learning and culture, Szeged is the industrial capital of the Great Plain (Alföld), though you wouldn't know it by spending a day or two in the city center. The Tisza River splits the city in two, with the historic center lying, Pest-style, within a series of concentric ring boulevards on the left bank. Indeed, the river looms large in Szeged's history: The city was almost completely destroyed by an 1879 Tisza flood, but with financial assistance from a number of European cities—Brussels, Berlin, Rome, London, and Paris—was rebuilt in the characteristic ring style of the time. The post-flood reconstruction explains why Szeged's finest architecture is of the *fin-de-siècle* art nouveau style. Don't miss the synagogue (see "Exploring the Historic Center," below) and the recently restored Reök Building (now a bank) on the corner of Kölcsey utca and Feketesas utca.

Szeged, the proud capital of the Great Plain, is a hot and dusty but hospitable town. Its people, many of whom are students, love to stroll along the riverside, sit in cafes, and window-shop on the just reconstructed elegant **Karász utca** ★★ , the town's main pedestrian-only street. Dóm tér, a beautiful, wide open square, is home to the **Szeged Summer Festival** ★, a popular summer-long series of cultural events. At the end of July, Szeged also plays host to a theater festival known as **Thealter,** for its focus on alternative performances. An international festival, drawing theater troupes from all over Europe, Thealter was founded by drama students from the university. In 2000, Thealter celebrated its tenth season. Ask about both of these festivals at **Tourinform** or Szeged Tourist.

ESSENTIALS

GETTING THERE   Eleven daily **trains** depart Budapest's Nyugati Station, of which three are intercity. The fare is 1,482 Ft ($5.35). On an Intercity train the journey takes about 2¼ hours, and you are required to pay an additional 360 Ft ($1.30) for a seat reservation. On a fast train (*gyors*), the trip is more like 3 hours, but you don't need a reservation. (Travel times by trains generally seem to have slowed down in the past two years due to the poor conditions of the tracks all over the country.)

If you're **driving** from Budapest, take the M5 motorway south through Kecskemét and Kiskunfélegyháza. You will have to pay 2,500 Ft ($9) in highway tolls each way, in two installments at two different toll plazas.

VISITOR INFORMATION   The best source of information, as usual, is **Tourinform,** at Dugonics tér 2 (© **62/488-690**), in the courtyard, next to Z. Nagy Cukrászda. The office is open Monday through Friday from 9am to 5pm.

If you arrive on a weekend or wish to book a private room, try **Szeged Tourist,** at Klauzal tér 7 (© **62/321-800;** fax 62/420-428), open Monday through Friday from 9am to 5pm.

Pick up *Szegedi Est,* a free weekly magazine with lots of useful information.

MAHART, the Hungarian ferry line company, organizes boat tours up and down the Tisza river from the first of April through mid-October. For information, contact the MAHART boat station in Szeged at © **62/425-834.**

EXPLORING THE HISTORIC CENTER

Móra Ferenc Museum   By the river's edge, this imposing structure houses a varied collection devoted to local history. Of particular note is the display of local folk costumes and the exhibit that reconstructs the nomadic lifestyle of the early Hungarian settlers.

Roosevelt tér 1–3. © **62/549-040.** Admission 200 Ft (75¢). Tues–Sun 10am–5pm.

Synagogue 🔎   A relic of Szeged's once-thriving Jewish community, the great synagogue was completed in 1903. Considered the masterpiece of architect Lipot Baumhorn, a disciple of Ödön Lechner, and the most prolific and renowned synagogue architect in modern Europe, the great synagogue in Szeged exemplifies a confident eclecticism. The building mixes cupolas, turrets, tracery, and other ornamental effects. It occupies a full block in an otherwise sleepy, tree-lined residential neighborhood just west of the city center.

Inside the vestibule is a series of marble plaques, listing by name the local victims of the Holocaust. Behind the synagogue, at Hajnóczy u. 12, stands the Old Synagogue, built in 1843 and badly damaged by the flood of 1879. Its reconstruction was completed in 1998. It serves as a cultural center, a venue for alternative theater groups and chamber music concerts.

If you find the synagogue closed when it should be open, you might go to the address that's posted (from May to September) near the entrance, and the caretaker will open the synagogue for you.

Jósika utca. © **62/423-849.** Admission 200 Ft (75¢). Sun–Fri 9am–noon and 1–6pm. From Dugonics tér, walk right on Tisza Lajos körút, and turn left on Gutenberg utca.

Votive Church   The symbol of Szeged's post-flood revitalization, this church with its two tall, slender clock towers was built in 1912. Its elaborately painted neo-Renaissance interior suggests a much older structure. Inside the church is one of Europe's largest organs, with over 9,000 pipes. Ask at Tourinform or Szeged Tourist about organ recitals.

In front of the church is the Broken Tower, a remnant of the 13th-century Romanesque church that stood on the same spot. Across from the church, there is a wall clock from which wooden figures emerge on the hour to play a Kodály tune.

On Dóm tér. Free admission. Mon–Sat 9am–6pm; Sun 9:30–10am, 11–11:30am, and 12:30–6pm.

OPEN-AIR MARKETS

Szeged, a city situated within 20 miles (32km) of two international borders (Romanian and Serbian), has long attracted shoppers and vendors from a variety of countries. If this kind of open-air market interests you, check out the **Polish Market** ✷✷ (*Lengyel Piac*) at the southwestern edge of town. Once filled with Polish smugglers, this dusty flea market is now home to Vietnamese, Chinese, Romanians, Serbs, Uzbeks, and others. The Poles are gone, but the name has stuck. You never know what kind of junk you might find here—it all depends on what's "in season." Unfortunately, the Cold War souvenirs that once attracted Westerners to markets like this are seldom displayed any longer. The market is open Monday through Saturday from dawn to mid-afternoon. To get to the Polish Market, located in a dusty field at the corner of Petőfi Sándor sugárút and Rákóczi utca, walk straight out Petőfi Sándor sugárút from the center of town or take tram no. 4.

Szeged's **main fruit and vegetable market** ✷✷✷ is located behind the bus station on Mars tér (formerly Marx tér, and still known to many as such). The vendors are local Hungarian farmers. If you haven't tried any Hungarian produce yet, you're definitely missing out on something wonderful. You won't be disappointed with the peaches, apricots, watermelons, cherries, strawberries, plums, or pears. The market is open daily from dawn until mid-afternoon—arrive early for the best selection. Fresh flowers and dried paprika wreathes are also sold here.

You can buy Szeged's signature paprika and salami anywhere food is sold. See "Paprika, Pastry, & Pálinka: Hungarian Cuisine" in "appendix A, "Budapest: The Heart of Hungary," for descriptions of types of paprika.

WHERE TO STAY

Private rooms can be booked through **Szeged Tourist** (see "Essentials," earlier) or **Ibusz** at Oroszlán u. 3 (© **62/471-177**).

Hotel Matrix   This fairly new choice is about 10 minutes from central Dugonics tér by tram no. 1 or trolleybus no. 9. The tasteful, small hotel is clean and pleasant, with a friendly and professional management. Its pleasant rooms all have showers.

Zárda u. 8. © **62/556-000**. Fax 62/420-827. 10 units. 8,000 Ft ($28.80) double. Breakfast 750 Ft ($2.70) extra. AE, V. **Amenities:** Laundry service. *In room:* TV.

Kata Panzió ✷   We highly recommended this lovely little pension, which opened in 1995 in a quiet residential neighborhood a 10-minute walk from central Klauzál tér. It features plenty of common space, sunny balconies on each floor, an enchanting terrace garden, and a friendly German shepherd named Ivan. Four double rooms, one triple, and one quad are available.

Bolyai János u. 15 (between Gogol u. and Kálvária sgt.). © **62/311-258.** 6 units. 8,000 Ft ($28.80) double. Breakfast 500 Ft ($1.80) extra. No credit cards. *In room:* TV.

WHERE TO DINE

Alabárdos HUNGARIAN   Alabárdos is *the* choice for an elegant, upscale dining experience. Hungarian cuisine is served on Herend porcelain; the cutlery is sterling. Locals consider it the town's finest restaurant. Alabárdos has also opened a pub right next door, open 10am to 2am. The pub menu is small but wholesome: salads and cheese-based dishes. Draft beer is available. It's a popular place with Szeged's large foreign student population.

Oskola u. 13. © **62/420-914.** Reservations recommended. Main courses 1,000 Ft–2,500 Ft ($3.60–$9). Mon–Sat noon–midnight.

Gödör ☆ HUNGARIAN   The Gödör is the local university's restaurant; faculty members pack it at lunchtime. The extensive menu of Hungarian specialties (including many vegetarian options) is very reasonably priced.

Tisza Lajos krt. 103 (next to the Hero's Gate). © **62/420-130.** Main courses 540 Ft–1,100 Ft ($1.95–$3.95). No credit cards. Daily 11am–10pm.

HBH Bajor Söröző ☆ HUNGARIAN/BAVARIAN   This is another good option for Hungarian and Bavarian fare. The HBH brews its own beer and is a popular nighttime gathering place. A half liter of beer will set you back 270 Ft (95¢).

Deák Ferenc u. 4. © **62/420-934.** Soups 350 Ft–420 Ft ($1.25–$1.50); main courses 960 Ft–1,500 Ft ($3.45–$5.40). No credit cards. Mon–Thurs noon–11pm; Fri–Sat noon–midnight; Sun noon–4pm.

Kiskőrösi Halászcsárda ☆ HUNGARIAN   In Szeged, you'd do well to sample the local fish fare at this authentic, riverside restaurant. Paprika and onions are the spices of choice for hearty fish stews and bisques alike.

Felső Tisza-part 336. © **62/495-480.** Reservations recommended. Main courses 700 Ft–1,200 Ft ($2.50–$4.30). AE, DC, DISC, MC, V. Daily 11am–midnight.

Pagoda Étterem ☆ CHINESE   This is our favorite Chinese restaurant in all of Hungary. The menu is extensive and the dishes are delicious. The Chinese lanterns and dragon-red tablecloths only add to the appeal.

Zrinyi u. 5. © **62/312-490.** Main courses from 800 Ft ($2.90). AE, V. Daily noon–midnight.

COFFEEHOUSES & ICE-CREAM PARLORS

Szeged is famous for its **Virág Cukrászda,** an Old-World coffeehouse on Klauzál tér. A local petition drive in the early 1990s prevented this Szeged institution from being turned into a car showroom. However, as a result of a dubious economic deal, the place was closed down suddenly one night and its gorgeous antique Herend china espresso machines and all the original furniture were packed up and shipped to an unknown location. Rumor has it that the old Virág will be reopened in 2002. This would be an excellent development. For now, it is only at the **Kis Virág** ☆☆☆ (Little Flower), across the square, that you can pick up a wide variety of delicious pastries and the best ice cream in town for take-out (in winter, there is service on the premises). Their specialty is *rakott rétes* (layered strudle), which is the most divine local variety of the Jewish traditional pastry, *flodni*. In our opinion, it's the best in the whole country.

Rivaling (and some say surpassing in the traditional pastries) the Kis Virág for take-out pastries and cakes is the tiny **Z. Nagy Cukrászda** ★★★, located on József Attila sgt. 24 (just off of Tisza Lajos krt. by the river). It's a good walk from the center but well worth it. Z. Nagy dispenses a scrumptious *Erzsi kocka,* walnut paste sandwiched between two shortbread cookies, dipped in dark chocolate. There is a more spacious Z. Nagy shop right in the center of town as well, on Dugonics tér, just off Karász utca (the pedestrian-only street). Recognizing the gap on the market caused by the temporary shutdown of the nearby Virág, this shop, once a tiny closet-like place, was renovated and enlarged into a proper coffee shop in September 2001. They are planning to open a terrace in the courtyard of the building in summer 2002 as well.

On hot dusty summer days, the line at the most popular ice-cream shop, **Palánk** (on the corner of Tömörkény utca and Oskola utca), snakes out the door and down the street. By all means, join the queue.

SZEGED AFTER DARK

Jazz Kocsma, at Kálmány L. u. 14 (✆ **62/326-680**), is the place for live jazz. Local bands play on Tuesdays. It's a groovy, smoky, student scene. The kitchen serves Mexican food. Open daily, 11am to 2am; no cover. While Jazz Kocsma is one of the hottest venue for the university crowd, **Mojo Club,** Batthyány u. 30, on the corner of Alföldi utca (✆ **62/426-606**), next to the university building of the arts faculty, is the other venue. As the posters in the window proudly advertises, the owners of the place have maintained their close links with their former country of residence, Yugoslavia; you can see the posters of OTPOR, the pioneering Serbian youth organization that successfully organized resistance to the Belgrade university collectives. The sunken rooms have a distinctly bohemian appeal. Local blues bands perform once a week. There's a full bar, and decent pizza and pasta on the menu. It's open Monday through Saturday from 11am to 2pm, Sunday from 6pm to midnight, in summer open daily from 6 pm only. There's no cover, but reservations are highly recommended at both.

Another extremely popular nightspot for the local university crowd is the **Grand Cafe,** at Deák Ferenc u. 18 (✆ **62/420-578**). Part cafe, part movie theater, the Grand Cafe is owned and run by graduates of Szeged's Attila József university. Two features play each day, beginning at 7 and 9pm. You won't find any dubbed movies here. If the films don't interest you, stop in for a coffee and the artsy atmosphere. The Grand Cafe is open Monday through Friday 3pm to midnight; Saturday and Sunday 5pm to midnight. No cover. Reservations are not accepted, and a table can be hard to find. If you happen to be in Hungary on New Year's Eve, this is a great spot to ring in the dawn.

Appendix A:
Budapest, the Heart of Hungary

For much of the 20th century, Budapest languished in relative obscurity, off the itinerary and out of the minds of most European travelers. The dramatic political changes of 1989 irreversibly altered the state of the Hungarian capital. Budapest, awakened after its long slumber behind the Iron Curtain, now ranks as one of Europe's hottest travel destinations. One of the great cities of Central Europe, Budapest embodies all the elements of the region's peculiar and rich cultural legacy. Poised between East and West, both geographically and culturally, Budapest stands proudly at the center of the region's cultural rebirth.

Despite the collapse of the Iron Curtain, Budapest retains an exotic feeling seldom experienced in the "better known" capital cities of Europe.

1 The City Today

With a population of approximately 2.1 million, Budapest is home to one in five Hungarians. Few capitals so dominate the life of their country: Compared to the capital, every other Hungarian city is no more than a provincial town. Present-day Hungary has a population of about 10.5 million, while some 3 million ethnic Hungarians live in neighboring countries.

Hungarians are a predominantly Catholic people; in fact, along with the Poles and Lithuanians, they represent the eastern frontier of European Catholicism. Once the junior seat of a sprawling multi-national empire, Hungary is today more or less ethnically homogeneous. The 1920 Treaty of Trianon, imposed on a defeated Hungary after World War I, delegated most minorities to neighboring countries. Scarcely a generation later, the destruction of Hungarian Jewry in World War II and the departure of thousands of ethnic Germans after the war further homogenized the population. Hungary's 500,000 Gypsies comprise the country's largest minority today, while other minority populations include ethnic Germans, Slovaks, Serbs, Croats, Jews (Budapest is home to the largest Jewish population of any European city outside Russia), and Romanians. The capital city reflects this ethnic mix.

Budapest is in every way Hungary's cultural and economic center—as well as, more or less, its geographical center. All major Hungarian highways and rail lines emanate from Budapest like spokes from the hub of a wheel. The city encompasses 525 square kilometers (203 sq. miles), of which just over two-thirds lies on the right bank in predominantly flat Pest. Buda, on the other hand, is distinguished by its hills—its highest is 529-meter (1,735-ft.) János Hill—and wooded areas.

Oddly enough, this capital of a landlocked country is defined by water. The Danube River cuts a wide swath between its constituent parts, Buda and Pest, while over 100 natural hot springs bubble beneath the city. The river flows through the city at an average width of 400 meters (1,312 ft.), and its 17.4-mile (28-km) stretch at Budapest represents almost 1% of its total length. To the north of Budapest, the Danube alters its west-east course sharply in a series of curves at the celebrated Danube Bend, an area famous for its historic towns and lovely scenery.

Among Hungarian cities, Budapest is the clear leader in the rapid Westernization process. For example, Budapest's fast-food market, as recently as 1991 cornered by McDonald's, is now crowded with outlets of Burger King, Kentucky Fried Chicken, Dunkin Donuts, Pizza Hut, and Wendy's. Most consumer products are now available in the Hungarian capital, but some things do not change so fast. Salaries, for example, have not kept pace with inflation, and as a result many citizens can only look longingly through shop windows at these new goods. A certain amount of bitterness has thus accompanied the rapid development, as Hungarians begin to understand the drawbacks of a consumer society.

Still, Hungary is wasting little time in trying to undo 4 decades of stunted economic development and cultural orthodoxy. The first act was symbolic: Hundreds of streets reverted back to their prewar names, shedding appellations like "Red Army Square," "Road of the People's Republic," and "Lenin Boulevard." Western visitors are also pleased to see new standards of efficiency, service, and cleanliness. Tourists are flocking to Budapest in numbers no one could have imagined even a few years ago.

In 1999, Hungary, along with Poland and the Czech Republic, joined NATO. Membership in the European Union now appears imminent. Troubled by inflation, unemployment, and the fast pace of privatization, however, a significant number of Hungarians fear the darker side of their country's transition to a Western-style free-market economy. The Socialist party, the most successful party in the 1994 elections and the lead party in the governing coalition, remains firmly entrenched in power, even as the prime minister, Gyula Horn, fends off criticism of his ignominious, though minor, role in suppressing the 1956 anti-Communist uprising. In the midst of all these changes, Hungary in 1996 found the time and energy to celebrate the 1,100th anniversary of the Magyar Conquest. Most Hungarians, it seems, can look back more than a thousand years with a clear gaze, but few pretend to know what tomorrow has in store for them.

2 A Look at the Past

THE ROMANS & THEIR SUCCESSORS Although Celtic tribes established themselves in the area around Buda in the 3rd century B.C., the Romans built the first extensive settlements. After conquering present-day western Hungary (Transdanubia), the Romans extended their empire east to the Danube and occupied the Celtic settlement of Ak-Ink (Abundant Waters), renaming it Aquincum. The military camp of Aquincum was near where the Árpád Bridge now stands, while the civilian town was farther north; ruins of both can be seen today. By the early 2nd century, Aquincum had become the capital of

Dateline

- 3rd century B.C. Celtic tribes establish settlements in the area around Budapest.
- 1st to 5th century A.D. Roman Empire extends to the Danube; Aquincum (present-day Óbuda) chosen as capital of Roman province of Pannonia.
- 5th century Huns take over Pannonia, soon to be replaced by migratory tribes.
- 6th to 9th century Avars control Hungary.
- 896 Magyar (Hungarian) conquest of Carpathian Basin.

continues

the Roman province of Lower Pannonia. It was the seat of the imperial governor; the future emperor Hadrian was the first to fill the position in this Roman outpost. The Romans ruled Transdanubia for 4 centuries, building impressive fortifications along the Danube's west bank. They were the first to develop the thermal waters of Buda, building a number of bathhouses. At its height, Aquincum had a population of 50,000 people. As the empire waned, however, the garrisons on the Danube were increasingly subject to attacks from "barbarians" from the east, and Rome evacuated Aquincum in the early 5th century.

THE AGE OF MIGRATIONS

The Huns succeeded the Romans, but their rule here was brief. After the death of their great leader Attila in 453, the Hun empire crumbled and present-day Hungary became the domain of a succession of mostly Teutonic tribes. A conquering tribe from central Asia, the Avars, moved into the area in the 6th century. Under their sponsorship, commerce-oriented Slavic tribes settled in the area of present-day Budapest.

THE MAGYAR CONQUEST

Led by Prince Árpád, whose family line (the House of Árpád) would rule Hungary until 1301, the seven allied Magyar tribes took the entire Carpathian Basin (a natural geological formation incorporating parts of present-day Romania, Serbia, Croatia, Slovenia, Austria, Slovakia, and Ukraine) in 896. Legend has it that the tribes fanned out, each taking control of a different part of the country. Árpád and his tribe are believed to have settled on Csepel Island in present-day Budapest, and another tribe settled in Óbuda, refortifying the Roman town. Once established, the Magyars engaged in a series of successful 10th-century raids on Western Europe, penetrating as far west as the Pyrenees. During these

- **1000** Stephen I becomes Hungary's first Christian king; the House of Árpád is established; the capital is first at Esztergom, and later at Visegrád and Székesfehérvár.
- **12th century** Buda and Pest develop as trading towns.
- **1241–42** Mongol armies under Batu Khan overrun Hungary, leaving it in ashes when they suddenly depart.
- **1242–70** King Béla IV rebuilds the country; a fortress is built in Buda.
- **14th century** Royal court is moved to Buda; late in the century King Sigismund of Luxembourg builds a great Gothic palace at Buda.
- **1458–90** Reign of King Matthias Corvinus, who initiates Golden Age of Buda and introduces ideas and culture of the Renaissance.
- **1541** 150-year Turkish occupation of Buda and Pest begins.
- **1686** United Christian armies drive Turks from Buda, but the city is destroyed in the liberation; Habsburg occupation of Hungary commences.
- **1703–11** Ferenc Rákóczi II's rebellions against Austria defeated.
- **Late 18th century** Buda and Pest begin to undergo rapid growth; in 1777, the University of Nagyszombat moves to Buda and then to Pest in 1784.
- **1825–48** Age of Reform; rise of neo-classical style in Budapest; building of National Theater (1837) and National Museum (1848).
- **1838** Great Danube flood destroys much of Pest.
- **1848–49** Hungarian Revolution defeated by Austrians, with critical aid from tsarist Russia; plans to unite Buda, Pest, and Óbuda into one city are not realized.
- **1849** The first permanent bridge across the Danube, the Chain Bridge, is opened.
- **1867** Austro-Hungarian empire established; Franz Joseph crowned king of Hungary in Matthias Church.
- **1873** Pest, Buda, and Óbuda are united into one city—Budapest.
- **1873–1914** Pest's Golden Age: City Park, Andrássy út, the ring boulevards, Opera House, the continent's first metro, and Parliament are built.

raids they earned their lasting reputation as skilled horsemen; the tricky "feigned withdrawal" was their most famous ploy. The raids ended with a decisive defeat at Augsburg in southwest Germany in 955.

THE DEVELOPMENT OF THE STATE A feudal state was forged under Hungary's first Christian king, István (Stephen) I (later Saint Stephen), who was crowned by the pope in 1000. The forced conversion of the Magyars was not without its darker side: Those who preferred to maintain their traditional ways were treated with the utmost cruelty. Nevertheless, Stephen succeeded in organizing a feudal state apparatus, without which the fledgling Hungarian kingdom certainly would not have survived. After Stephen's death, there was renewed strife between the Christians and the pagans. The iron-fisted Bishop Gellért, who had served Stephen for many years, was killed in 1046 when he was rolled in a barrel into the Danube from the hill in Buda that now bears his name. Despite this, and a number of succession crises in the following centuries, the feudal Christian state remained intact.

In this period, Esztergom, then Székesfehérvár, and briefly Visegrád, had served as Hungary's capital. Not until the 12th century did Buda and Pest begin to develop into major towns, populated in large part by German, French, and Walloon settlers. But in 1241 disaster struck: Rampaging out of Asia, the Mongols overran Hungary. Pest was destroyed, and after crossing the frozen Danube in the winter of 1241–42, the Mongols conquered Buda and all of Transdanubia beyond, burning and looting everything in their path. King Béla IV was forced to flee the country. During his brief exile he vowed his daughter would become a nun if he could return to rebuild Hungary. The Mongols retreated in 1242, and Princess Margit was duly sent to the convent on "Rabbit Island": This island in the Danube, now Budapest's most popular park, bears Margit's name today.

- **1896** Millennial of Magyar Conquest; city is site of great celebrations.
- **1914–18** Austria-Hungary is on losing side of World War I; the Habsburg monarchy disintegrates.
- **1918–19** Country in chaos; Hungarian Republic established; Béla Kun forms a short-lived Communist government, which is succeeded by the reactionary regime of Admiral Miklós Horthy.
- **1920** Treaty of Trianon codifies the enormous territorial losses suffered by Hungary in the aftermath of World War I.
- **1941** Hungary, obsessed with revision of Trianon treaty, enters World War II, joining Germany's unprovoked attack on Yugoslavia.
- **1944–45** Nazis occupy Hungary; Budapest Jews are forced into a walled ghetto; bitter Soviet-German fighting leaves Budapest in ruins; Soviets liberate—and occupy—the country.
- **1945–56** Brief parliamentary democracy is followed by the establishment of a Stalinist state.
- **1956** Hungarian Uprising, led by Imre Nagy and centered in Budapest, is crushed by Soviet troops; János Kádár installed as new Communist leader.
- **1968** Period of internal Communist reform is capped by the New Economic Mechanism, which decentralizes the economy and allows limited private enterprise.
- **1988–89** Kádár ousted by party reformers and Hungary begins transition to multiparty government; Eastern European communism collapses in summer and fall 1989.
- **1990** First free elections since 1945 bring center-right Hungarian Democratic Forum to power.
- **1991** Last Soviet troops leave country; Pope John Paul II visits.
- **1994** Socialist Party prevails in election; forms coalition government.
- **1999** Hungary joins the North Atlantic Treaty Organization (NATO).

Because only hilltop fortresses had withstood the Mongol onslaught, King Béla had a series of new ones built around the country. Buda was one of the spots chosen; in addition to the fortification of Castle Hill, a royal palace was constructed (though it was not Béla's primary residence). German settlers were invited to replace the Hungarians who had been wiped out by invasion. These Germans gave the name *Ofen* (oven) to the town on the Danube's right bank, probably because of the presence there of a lime kiln industry. The Slavic name *Pest*, also meaning oven, is believed to derive from this time. In 1255, Castle Hill was made a city, usurping the name Buda from the former Buda to its immediate north, which was henceforth known as *Óbuda* (Old Buda). Buda became the residence of an increasing number of aristocrats and burghers, while the medieval walled city of Pest continued to develop across the river. In 1301, the male line of the House of Árpád died out; Hungary would be ruled henceforth by a mixed succession of foreign-born and Hungarian kings.

THE GOLDEN AGE OF BUDA   King Charles Robert (1308–42), of the House of Anjou, moved his court from Visegrád to Buda, and his son Louis the Great (1342–82) expanded the palace. The town began to blossom at the turn of the 15th century under the rule of King Sigismund of Luxembourg (who was also the Holy Roman Emperor), who had a glorious Gothic palace built on Castle Hill. But it was King Matthias Corvinus (1458–90), influenced by the Italian Renaissance, who oversaw the Golden Age of Buda. Matthias's palace was expanded in Renaissance style by Italian architects and decorated with the finest European art, while his court became a center of European culture and learning. He amassed an enormous and fabled library, filled with the famous Corvinae manuscripts. The András Hess Press, one of Europe's earliest, was operating in Buda at this time as well. Called "Matthias the Just," the king remains one of the best-loved figures of Hungarian history, and the largest church of the Castle District bears his name.

THE TURKISH PERIOD   After Matthias's death, a divided nobility and the bloody suppression of a peasant revolt severely weakened Hungary. The Ottoman armies swept north up the Danube, and in 1526 routed the Hungarians at the Battle of Mohács. The fortified city of Buda fell in 1541. The 150-year Turkish period that followed is rued by Hungarians as one of stagnation and decay. Little new building, aside from fortification of existing walls and bathhouse construction, was undertaken. Everywhere churches were converted into mosques, and Buda's skyline filled with minarets.

THE HABSBURG PERIOD: LIBERATION BY FIRE   The wry joke "the operation was successful, but the patient died" might describe the liberation of Buda and Pest by the united Christian armies in 1686. The two towns were utterly destroyed, with only a few thousand people remaining alive inside the walls by the time the Turks were vanquished. Having survived the Turkish period intact, the royal palace was destroyed in the siege.

Resettlement and rebuilding were gradual, and formerly Gothic Buda took on a decidedly baroque appearance during the process. Though it would never again be a royal seat, the palace was rebuilt and expanded over the years.

Hungary was to be ruled by the victorious House of Habsburg until the collapse of the Habsburg empire in World War I. Relations with the new Viennese rulers were strained from the outset, flaring into open conflict for the first time when the Transylvanian prince Ferenc Rákóczi II led a series of valiant, but ultimately unsuccessful, rebellions between 1703 and 1711. The beginnings of

Impressions

In the city of Buda, which is extraordinarily high, lies the king's palace, which reaches to the sky.
—Dzhelalshade Mustapha, Turkish chronicler, 16th century

modern Hungarian nationalism, which would explode into revolution in 1848, can be detected in this period.

Budapest's population grew steadily throughout the 18th century, while the university was moved from Nagyszombat (now Trnava, Slovakia) first to Buda, in 1777, and subsequently to Pest, in 1784. Pest expanded beyond its medieval city walls in the late 18th century with the development of Lipótváros (Leopold Town, now considered part of the Inner City).

THE 19TH CENTURY: REFORM, REVOLUTION & COMPROMISE

By the early 19th century, Pest and Buda had become the centers of political, economic, and cultural life in Hungary. Habsburg Archduke Joseph, longtime palatine of Hungary (1796–1847), was a leading force in Pest's development in the early part of the century. The great Danube Flood of 1838 would destroy much of Pest, but it also provided an opportunity for the town to be rebuilt along more contemporary and progressive lines. For the first time, Pest began to surpass Buda as the center of commerce and industry, a role it has never relinquished. Jews played a major part in the early development of Pest and continued to do so until World War II.

The second quarter of the century is known as the Age of Reform in Hungary. Concomitant with the development of modern nationalism, this period saw the construction of many important and grand buildings; first among them were the National Theater (1837) and the National Museum (1848). Emblematic of the era was the construction of the first permanent bridge across the Danube, the Chain Bridge (1839–49). Like the Academy of Sciences, founded in 1825, this project was the brainchild of Count István Széchenyi. One of the period's leading figures, Széchenyi argued for increased Hungarian independence within the Habsburg empire and was the first to call for the union of Buda and Pest. His more radical rival, and the other giant figure of the mid-19th century, was Lajos Kossuth, a lawyer of Slovak ethnic origins, who demanded full independence from Austria in addition to the abolition of Hungary's feudal structure.

Hungary's nationalistic and anti-Habsburg sentiments culminated in the revolutionary events of 1848. Legend has it that the poet Sándor Petőfi rallied the radical forces of Pest by reciting his incendiary "National Song" from the steps of the National Museum. Students seized the university and City Hall. A revolutionary body, the Budapest Committee of Public Safety, was formed. Weakened by revolts spreading throughout their empire, the Austrians initially agreed to Hungarian independence, but as they consolidated power in the summer, it became increasingly clear that Hungary would have to defend its independence militarily. Despite Lajos Kossuth's passionate leadership, the defeat of the revolution was eventually ensured by the defection of most minorities living within Hungary—who saw that their own national aspirations had no future in an independent, ultranationalist Hungary—and the willingness of the Russian tsar to aid the Habsburgs. The tragic heroes of the day—Kossuth, who spent his remaining years in exile; Széchenyi, who went mad; the prime minister Lajos

Batthyány, who was executed by his captors; and the poet Petófi, who was killed in battle—remain among the most revered figures in the land.

A brief but painful period of absolutism followed, during which the Citadel on Gellért Hill was built as an overt symbol of Austrian supremacy. The 1867 Compromise, engineered by Ferenc Deák, established the dual Austro-Hungarian monarchy and brought a lasting peace and a measure of independence to Hungary. Following the coronation of the Habsburg emperor Franz Joseph, the union of the three cities—Buda, Pest, and Óbuda—became a reality in 1873.

PEST'S GOLDEN AGE: 1873–1914   The most intense period of development in the city's history was now under way. The national railway system was developed, with all lines converging in the capital. The distinctive ring boulevards of Pest were designed, as well as the radial road, now called Andrássy út, on which the lovely State Opera House opened in 1884. The City Park was laid out, with Heroes' Square as its entrance, and more bridges were built over the Danube. The first metro on the continent was built underneath Andrássy út; this antique line, renovated in 1996, is still functioning today. Much of this development culminated in the 1896 Hungarian millennial celebration, the greatest expression to date of Hungarian national pride. The predominantly neo-Gothic Parliament building, modeled on London's, was completed in 1902, although only once prior to 1990 did a democratically elected legislature convene in its great hall (in 1945).

A strident Hungarian nationalism fueled this period of frenetic expansion. Under the policy of "Magyarization," ethnic assimilation was encouraged— indeed, coerced—throughout the country. The use of the Hungarian language by ethnic minorities became more widespread; Jews, adopting it for the first time as their mother tongue, continued to play a leading role in the city's rapid expansion.

Population growth in the combined cities reflects the magnitude of Budapest's expansion: In 1867, the city had 270,000 residents; by 1890, there were 500,000 people living in the now unified city; and only 20 years later, in 1910, there were almost 900,000.

If King Matthias Corvinus's day was Buda's Golden Age, the turn of the century was certainly Pest's. The distinctive eclectic and art nouveau buildings that still define the city today date from this brief period when some of the country's greatest architects labored to create a singular Hungarian style. Cafe society was at its peak, rivaling that of Vienna. In the first heady days of the new century, Budapest seemed poised to take its place among Europe's great capitals. But as Matthias introduced the Italian Renaissance to a city in the path of the Turkish armies, so, too, did the burgeoning of Pest occur under the gathering clouds of World War I.

THE WORLD WARS: DESTRUCTION, DESOLATION & LOSS   The advent of war in 1914 and Hungary's alliance with the Central Powers was greeted with great shows of patriotism in the capital. Almost from the outset,

---

Impressions

And when day dawned mournfully on a sea swarming with the remains of a ruined city and hundreds and hundreds of the drowned, the carcasses of cows and horses floated in the pale rays of the rising sun.

—Miklós Wesselényi, hero of the 1838 Danube flood

however, the civilian population suffered great hardships. Under the pressures of wartime production, the nascent workers' movement gained new ground in Hungary.

After Emperor Franz Joseph's death in 1916, the last Habsburg emperor, Charles IV, was crowned in Matthias Church. Juxtaposed against the steadily deteriorating war situation and desperate shortages of food and fuel in the city, the coronation was the last gasp of a dying empire. The winter of 1917–18 was a particularly difficult one for the Hungarians, both on the battlefield and at home. Antiwar protests, usually met by police repression, increased, and opposition forces rallied around Count Mihály Károlyi, a vocal opponent of the war.

The total defeat of the Central Powers in 1918 led to the collapse of the Austro-Hungarian empire, and the new Hungarian Republic was declared on November 16 of that year. Károlyi was elected president, but his position was untenable from the start. Chief among his domestic problems was the increasingly radical position of the labor movement, inspired by the recent Russian Revolution. His unwillingness to enact a land reform program caused unrest in the countryside. The international situation was even grimmer. The victorious powers insisted on treating Hungary as a vanquished nation, much to the delight of the other newly formed successor states (particularly Romania, Czechoslovakia, and Yugoslavia) that were competing with Hungary for disputed territory. Hungary suffered enormous territorial losses (later codified by the Treaty of Trianon) during these postwar days as the country's new leaders stood by helplessly. Károlyi's fall was ultimately caused by the French demand that Hungarian troops withdraw a further 30 miles (50km) from the Romanian border, in order to create a "neutral zone." Unwilling to comply, he resigned.

In 1919, the Hungarian Communist party leader Béla Kun formed a new government and declared a "Republic of Councils." Allied with Bolshevik Russia, the Kun administration initially enjoyed some measure of popular support in Hungary. Industry was nationalized, and the leading figures of Hungarian culture were enlisted to champion the regime. Much of the initial enthusiasm waned with the start of a Red Terror on the Bolshevik model, and the rural population turned against Kun when it became clear that collectivization was his version of land reform.

In reality, the experiment was a generation, or a world war, too early. The Western powers, alarmed at the developments in Russia, were certainly not prepared to permit another Bolshevik government to remain in power in a country over which they exerted some measure of control; and Lenin's infant regime, fighting desperately for its own survival, was in no position to lend fraternal assistance. Kun was banking on the outbreak of a general proletarian revolution in Europe, a dream that, in the ashes of World War I, inspired no small number of radicals. But it was not to be: With tacit French approval, Romania attacked Hungary on April 16, followed by a Czech incursion on the 27th. The Hungarian Red Army scored some initial victories, but Kun also had to contend with counterrevolutionary struggle within the country. The counterrevolution was centered in the town of Szeged, from which Admiral Miklós Horthy launched a "White Terror" of his own, massacring leftists and Jews. In June, a rightist coup was attempted in Budapest, but was defeated. In the end, the Romanian army, entering the city on August 3, overwhelmed the short-lived Republic of Councils; after this brief flirtation with radicalism, Hungary was to be ruled throughout the interwar period by the reactionary Horthy, who was "elected" Regent in 1920 by a rubber-stamp parliament.

Impressions

Bandits are skulking around the city beating, looting, and shooting peo-
ple. Among my staff, I have already had forty cases of people being car-
ried off and abused. . . . We hear the thundering cannons of the
approaching Russians day and night.
      —Raoul Wallenberg, Swedish diplomat, in a letter to his mother

As Hungary drifted inexorably to the right in the interwar period, many of the country's greatest minds would seek their fortunes elsewhere. At the same time, the interwar period was one of enormous, uncontrolled growth for Budapest, its numbers swelled by refugees from the lost territories and the countryside. While the city expanded in all directions, it also suffered the effects of the worldwide recession: Social problems ballooned, hand in hand with increasing poverty.

The 1920 Treaty of Trianon confirmed the massive territorial losses of the past few years: 70% of the former Hungary was ceded to its neighbors, while 60% of the population found itself living beyond Hungary's new borders. Hungarians across all class and political lines were united against the treaty, and every Hungarian government of the interwar period was concerned chiefly with reversing it. This national obsession had the unfortunate consequence of leading Hungary to ally itself in the 1930s with Nazi Germany, which, in its own zeal to redraw the map of Europe, endorsed Hungary's revisionist claims. It was a reckless path, and one about which the Hungarian people remain deeply troubled to this day.

As the war progressed, Horthy began to have second thoughts about the alliance with Germany. The Nazis, unwilling to accept anything other than total commitment to the war effort, occupied Hungary in March 1944. Adolf Eichmann arrived with the Nazi forces and immediately set up a ghetto for Budapest's Jews in the historic Erzsébetváros district. While relatively few Hungarian Jews outside the capital survived the deportations (most perished in Auschwitz in the war's last year), at least half of Budapest's Jews were saved, many through the intervention of the Swedish diplomat Raoul Wallenberg, who at great personal risk issued thousands of false passports and established dozens of "safe houses."

In October, the Horthy regime, caught red-handed by the Germans in a clumsy attempt to negotiate a separate peace with the Allies, was replaced by Hungary's fascist Arrow Cross Party. The next 4 months saw bizarre and wanton acts of cruelty in Budapest, as the city was plunged to a level of barbarism unseen since the Middle Ages. Heavily armed Arrow Cross gangs wandered the scarred city, and hundreds of Jews were taken to the Danube that winter to be shot on its bank or thrown alive into its icy waters.

Meanwhile, the Red Army had penetrated eastern Hungary by late summer, and by Christmas had surrounded the capital. The war all but over, Germany itself breached by Allied forces, the Nazis stubbornly refused an invitation to quit the city honorably. Pest fell to the Russians on January 18, ensuring the survival of those who remained alive in the Jewish ghetto. Retreating to Buda, the Nazis blew up all the Danube bridges and retrenched on Castle Hill. In one of the most bitter sieges of World War II, Soviet artillery pounded the Castle District from the top of Gellért Hill until the Germans were finally driven from the capital on February 13. Budapest was again in ruins; three-quarters of its buildings (including the Royal Palace and most of the Castle District) were damaged or destroyed in the war.

THE STALINIST ERA   After the war, reconstruction was the primary task facing the country. In the absence of clear central authority, a civic spirit characterized the immediate postwar period, as newly formed local organizations assumed control of rebuilding projects, chief among them the reconstruction of the Danube bridges. The postwar days also saw Hungary suffering the most dramatic inflation in world history: Between January and July 1946, the price of a standard postage stamp soared from 100 pengó to 100,000 quadrillion pengó! The introduction of a new currency, the forint, halted the runaway inflation.

Soviet forces remained in the country as an occupation army. The Allied Powers at Yalta relegated Hungary to the Soviet sphere of influence, and by 1949 a Stalinist state was in place. A "cult of personality" surrounded Communist party leader Mátyás Rákosi, now known as Stalin's "wise Hungarian disciple." The next few years would be an oppressive period of secret police activity and party infighting. In 1950, the first Soviet-style Five-Year Plan was introduced, emphasizing heavy industry and massive construction projects. Peasants, forced onto collective farms, became bitter opponents of the regime.

In Hungary, as elsewhere in the East Bloc, Stalin's death in 1953 led to pronounced swings between reform and retrenchment. Rákosi continued to play a major role, although the popularity of reformist Imre Nagy also rose. Following Khrushchev's "Secret Speech" at the 20th Party Congress in February 1956 denouncing Stalin's crimes, the stage was set for political and social upheaval throughout the disenchanted Bloc.

1956–89: REVOLUTION, REACTION & REFORM   Almost all the key events of the 1956 Hungarian Uprising occurred in Budapest. The spark that lit the fire was an October 23 student demonstration in support of reforms unfolding in Poland. Tens of thousands marched from Petófi Square in Pest to Bem Square in Buda. Spontaneously, the students decided to march on Parliament, where they lit torches and called for the reinstatement of the increasingly popular Nagy as prime minister (a post he had held briefly in the aftermath of Stalin's death). Another smaller group collected in front of the Budapest radio station, near the National Museum, and were fired upon by the secret police. Shortly thereafter, outraged crowds toppled the enormous Stalin statue near the City Park and paraded through the darkened streets with the fallen dictator in tow. Army units, called out to protect key buildings, turned their weapons over to the rebels.

The events of the next 13 days would capture headlines around the world, though the simultaneous outbreak of war in the Middle East, at the Suez Canal, significantly detracted attention from Central Europe. In the end, the lack of Western assistance to the Hungarians gave unmistakable notice that the West, in the grip of the Cold War, essentially accepted the division of Europe as defined by Yalta.

Reappointed prime minister on October 24, Nagy found events moving beyond his control. The revolt was no longer aimed at reforming the system, but at overthrowing it. On October 25, the police again fired on unarmed demonstrators, this time at the Parliament. Two days later, a beleaguered Nagy announced the formation of his new government with most of the hard-line Stalinists excluded. Nagy announced the removal of Soviet military units from Budapest, the dissolution of the secret police, and his desire to negotiate with the Soviet Union regarding full military withdrawal from Hungary. In his boldest act, Nagy announced Hungary's unilateral withdrawal from the Warsaw Pact and pleaded for assistance from the West.

There was optimism in the capital as Nagy formed yet another new government. But by November 4, a Soviet invasion was in full swing. Facing little resistance, the Soviets crushed what they were now calling a "counterrevolution." Budapest was heavily damaged by the fighting, and altogether about 2,000 Hungarians died in the uprising while another 200,000 fled the country. Nagy and several of his associates were eventually executed.

János Kádár was placed in control of the government, a position he would maintain for 30 years. A short period of hard-line repression was used to break the spirit of the uprising, but during his long rule, Kádár, who was initially despised for his treacherous role in 1956, was able to achieve a level of public popularity enjoyed by few East Bloc leaders. Because of the many reforms Kádár carried out, Hungary earned the nickname of "the happiest barracks" in Eastern Europe. His easygoing slogan "those who are not against us are with us" was the reverse of the menacing Stalinist catchphrase. By and large, Hungarians accepted the "goulash communism" Kádár practiced, but no longer required to express their support, most people withdrew into political apathy.

Kádár's best-known reform, the 1968 New Economic Mechanism (NEM), encouraged limited private enterprise and partially decentralized the economy. Ironically, while the NEM foreshadowed "perestroika" a generation before Gorbachev, Hungarian troops were sent in the same year to join the Warsaw Pact forces in crushing the Prague Spring. Nevertheless, Hungary soon became known as the most liberal country of the Bloc, and Budapest became a magnet for East Bloc youth. Western tourists, too, found Budapest to be a hospitable place in comparison to other Eastern European cities, and its proximity to Vienna increased its accessibility.

Despite economic difficulties caused by inflation and foreign debt, Hungary continued throughout the 1970s and 1980s to lead a sluggish Eastern Europe in gradual reforms. The advent of Gorbachev in the Soviet Union emboldened the most radical elements within the Communist party; while the world's eyes were turned to Moscow and Warsaw in early 1989, Hungary was quietly playing a key role in the drama. In May 1989, 6 months before the opening of the Berlin Wall, Hungary began dismantling portions of the barbed-wire frontier with Austria, becoming the first country to open a hole in the "Iron Curtain." The reburial of Imre Nagy in June attracted as many as 250,000 to Budapest's Heroes' Square, and helped heal the psychic wounds left by the failed uprising. By September, thousands of East Germans had gathered in Hungary, hoping for permission to flee to the West; when permission was finally granted, more than 50,000 crossed over to Austria. The year, of course, would conclude with the toppling of the East German, Czechoslovak, and Romanian Communist systems. As for the collapse of Communism in Hungary itself, it was far less dramatic, more gradual, and unaccompanied by violence.

POST-COMMUNIST BUDAPEST   Hungary's first free elections since 1945 were held in 1990, marking the end of nearly half a century of Communist rule. The new center-right coalition government was led by the late József Antall's Hungarian Democratic Forum (MDF), a party that used overtly nationalist themes in its campaign. The last Soviet troops left the country in 1991, and Pope John Paul II visited Hungary in the same year. Hungary then joined NATO a few years later and is presently among the first group of countries from the former Eastern Bloc being considered for membership in the European Community.

As the new century dawns, though, the Treaty of Trianon still strikes a deep chord of resentment and discontent in Hungarian society. The twin questions of national borders and Hungarian ethnic minorities abroad still dominate relations with nearly all neighboring states. The false rhetoric of Communism clumsily attempted to bury Eastern and Central Europe's nationality problems, just as Trianon had vainly endeavored to solve them in one fell swoop: Now, civil war has ravaged the former Yugoslavia; the Balkans remain an ethnic tinderbox; and throughout the region, few countries trust their neighbors. Hungary's relations with Romania remain bitter; regarding former Yugoslavia, Hungarian concern is over the very survival of Serbia's Hungarian minority; and relations with Slovakia are strained at best. The neo-fascist right, though small, has deep roots in this land and remains the country's most disturbing manifestation of chauvinistic nationalism.

3 Paprika, Pastry & Pálinka: Hungarian Cuisine

Hungary's cuisine reflects the rich and varied flavors of four major geographic regions. From Transdanubia, west of the River Danube, come rich mushroom sauces, sorrel soups, cottage cheese and onion dumplings, and high-quality goose liver. A host of excellent wild-game dishes come from forested northern Hungary. Bucolic Erdély (Transylvania) introduces spices such as tarragon, summer savory, and fresh dill to the palate. The region is also known for its lamb dishes and sheep's cheese. And, finally, from the Great Hungarian Plain, the home of Hungary's renowned paprika, come hearty fish, bean, and meat stews all spiced with the red powder ground from different varieties of peppers ranging from sweet (*édes*) to hot (*csípós*).

Lunch, the main meal of the day, begins with soup. *Gyümölcs leves,* a cold fruit soup, is excellent when in season. *Sóskakrém leves,* cream of sorrel soup, is another good seasonal choice. *Babgulyás,* a hearty bean soup, and *halaszle,* a fish soup popular at river and lakeside spots, constitute meals in themselves.

The main course is generally a meat dish. Try the *paprikás csirke,* chicken cooked in a savory paprika sauce. It's especially good with *galuska,* a pasta dumpling. *Pulykamell,* turkey breast baked with plums or served in a mushroom gravy, is also delicious. *Pörkölt* is a stewed meat dish, which comes in many varieties. *Töltött káposzta,* whole cabbage leaves stuffed with rice, meat, and spices, is another favorite.

Vegetarianism is gradually gaining acceptance in Hungarian restaurants; many establishments now offer a vegetable plate entree, usually consisting of seasonal steamed and grilled vegetables. Otherwise, vegetarians would do well to order *lecsó tojással* (eggs scrambled in a thick tomato-onion-paprika sauce), *rántott sajt* (batter-fried cheese with tartar sauce), or *túros csusza tepertó nélkul* (a macaroni-and-cheese dish). The kitchen should be able to prepare any of these dishes to order, even if they don't appear on the menu.

Snack foods include *lángos,* a slab of deep-fried bread served with your choice of toppings: sugar and whipped cream, or garlic sauce and cheese. *Palacsinta,* a paper-thin crêpe stuffed with cheese or draped in hot chocolate sauce, is another excellent light bite. *Kalács,* a hollow, tubular honey-cake, made so by wrapping the dough around a bottle, is an old-fashioned treat sometimes available in metro stations or at outdoor markets. *Fagylalt,* ice cream, is the national street food; even early in the morning you'll see people standing in line for cones. Scoops are small, so order more than one. Fruit flavors are produced seasonally:

In the spring, try strawberry (*eper*) and sour cherry (*meggy*); in the fall, plum (*szilva*) and pear (*körte*). A summer regular is delicious cinnamon (*fahéj*).

Hungarian pastries are scrumptious and cost a fraction of what they do in Vienna, so indulge. The light, flaky *rétes* are filled with fruit or cheese. *Csoki torta* is a decadent chocolate layer cake, and a *Dobos torta* is topped with a shiny caramel crust. *Mákos pastry*, made with poppy seeds, is a Hungarian specialty. *Gesztenye* (chestnuts) are another popular ingredient in desserts.

Picnickers should pick up a loaf of Hungarian bread and sample any of Hungary's world-famous salamis. A number of tasty cheeses are produced in Hungary as well: *Karaván füstölt* (a smoked cheese), *Edami, márvány* (similar to bleu cheese), and *jutúró* (a soft, spreadable sheep's cheese similar in flavor to feta). In season, fresh produce is delightfully cheap and high quality. You won't find much fresh fruit or vegetables in the winter or in traditional dishes served in restaurants, but at the wonderful markets you'll be amazed at the abundance and variety. Sour cherries (*meggy*) in July are out of this world.

BEER, WINE & SPIRITS   Unlike its Austrian, Czech, and Slovak neighbors, Hungary does not have a beer culture; as a result its beer is unexceptional. A number of European beers are now produced under license in Hungary. Among them are German beers (Holsten and Hofbrau Munchen), Austrian beers (Gösser, Steffl, Schwechater, Gold Fassl, and Kaiser), a Danish beer (Tuborg), a Dutch beer (Amstel), and a Belgian beer (Stella Artois). Even Rolling Rock is produced in Hungary now! To our taste, however, all these beers tend to be inferior to those under whose license they are sold and only marginally better than the best Hungarian beer—Dreher. Your best bet in Hungary is clearly Czech beer, such as Budvar, Staropramen, or Pilsner Urquell. Czech beers are not produced in Hungary under license; they are the real thing.

Hungarian wines, on the other hand, are excellent. The most renowned red wines come from the region around Villány, a town to the south of Pécs by the Croatian border. As a result of the aggressive marketing strategy of the former Communist regime, many foreigners are familiar with the red wines from Eger, especially *Egri Bikavér* (Eger Bull's Blood). Eger wines, though rich and fruity, are markedly inferior to Villányi reds. The country's best white wines are generally believed to be those from the Lake Balaton region, though some Hungarians insist that white wines from the Sopron region (by the Austrian border) are better. *Tokaj* wines—*száraz* (dry) or *édes* (sweet)—are popular as apéritifs and dessert wines. Travelers seeking advice on Hungarian wines are encouraged to visit La Boutique des Vins, a full-service wine store in Budapest (see p. 166). You can also pick up the free pamphlet "Wine Regions in Hungary" at Vista Visitor Center or Tourinform (see "Orientation," in chapter 3, "Getting to Know Budapest").

Unicum, the richly aromatic bitter that some call "Hungary's national drink," is a taste worth acquiring. The distilled fruit brandy *pálinka* is another variety of Hungarian "fire water," which is often brewed at home from apricots, plums, or pears; in folk wisdom, it's acclaimed for its medicinal value.

COFFEE & TEA   Hungarians drink coffee (*kávé*) throughout the day, either at stand-up coffee bars or in elegant coffeehouses. Until recently, Hungarian coffee drinking borrowed from the Turkish tradition: Alarmingly strong, unfiltered espresso was served straight up, generally without cream or sugar. These days, coffee drinking has expanded to include milder and more refined tastes. In general, though, when ordering coffee in Hungary, you are still ordering espresso. If you ask for coffee with milk (*kávé tejjel*), you are served espresso with cream on the side. Cappuccino (and its variant cappuciner, with chocolate shavings on top) is now available in most coffeehouses, as is decaffeinated coffee (*koffein mentes*). *Tejeskávé,* a Hungarian version of café au lait, is another option.

Tea drinkers will have a difficult time in restaurants; if tea is available at all, it's generally of the strong black variety. For more variety and a peek at Hungary's burgeoning world of herbal medicine, look for teas in any of the numerous shops: *gyógynövény, herbárium,* or *gyógytea.*

WATER   While tap water (*csapvíz*) is safe to drink in Budapest, it isn't generally offered in restaurants, and few Hungarians request it. Instead they drink *Ásványvíz,* a carbonated mineral water, or *szóda víz,* carbonated tap water. Purified bottled water (*szénsav mentes*) is now available at fancier restaurants as well as at delicatessens and grocery stores in tourist areas.

Appendix B:
Help with a Tough Tongue

Part of Budapest's mystery stems from the complex and unusual language of the Hungarians. Magyar originated on the eastern side of the Ural Mountains: Along with Finnish and Estonian, it's one of Europe's few representatives of the Finno-Ugric family of languages. The Hungarian language has long been one of the country's greatest obstacles; nevertheless, the Hungarian people are intensely proud of their language and its charms. Our transcription of Hungarian pronunciations is of necessity approximate. Stress is always on the first syllable, and all letters are pronounced (there are no diphthongs in Hungarian).

a	t*au*t	ó	same as above but held longer
á	b*ahh*	ö	sub*u*rb, minus the r
e	*e*ver	ő	same as above but held longer
é	d*ay*	u	l*oo*k
I	m*i*tt	ú	b*oo*t
í	t*ee*n	ü	like the French fl*eu*ve
o	b*o*ne	ű	same as above but held longer

Most Hungarian consonants are pronounced approximately as they are in English, including the following: *b, d, f, h, k, l, m, n, p, t, v,* and *y*. There are some differences, however, particularly in the consonant combinations, as follows:

c	ge*ts*	r	slightly rolled
cs	*ch*ill	s	*sh*eet
g	*g*ill	sz	*s*ix
gy	he*dg*e	z	*z*ero
j	*y*outh	zs	a*z*ure, plea*s*ure
ny	as in Russian *ny*et		

1 Menu Terms

GENERAL TERMS

Bors black pepper
Főételek main courses
Főzelék vegetable purée
Gyümölcs fruits
Halak fish
Húsételek meat dishes
Italok beverages
Kenyér bread
Levesek soups

Paprika red pepper/paprika
Sajt cheese
Saláták salads
Só salt
Tészták pasta/dessert
Tojás eggs
Vaj butter
Zöldség vegetables

COOKING TERMS

Csípos hot (peppery)
Forró hot (in temperature)
Főzött boiled

Friss fresh
Fuszerezve spiced
Hideg cold

Párolt   steamed
Pirított   toasted
Pörkölt   stew

Sútve   baked/fried
Töltött   stuffed

SOUPS (LEVESEK)

Gombaleves   mushroom soup
Gulyásleves   goulash soup
Húsleves   bouillon
Karfioleves   cauliflower soup
Lencseleves   lentil soup

Paradicsomkrémleves   cream of
   tomato soup
Zöldborsöleves   pea soup
Zöldségleves   vegetable soup

EGGS (TOJÁS)

Kolbásszal   with sausage
Rántotta   scrambled eggs
Sonkával   with ham

Szalonnával   with bacon
Tükörtojás   fried eggs

MEAT & POULTRY (HÚS ÉS BAROMFI)

Agyonsütve   well done
Bárány   lamb
Bécsi szelet   Wiener schnitzel
Borjú   veal
Csirke   chicken
Félig nyersen   rare
Gulyás   goulash
Kacsa   duck

Kotlett   cutlet
Közepesen kisütve   medium
Liba   goose
Marha   beef
Pulyka   turkey
Sertés   pork
Tokány   ragout

FISH (HALAK)

Csuka   pike
Fogas Balaton   pike-perch
Halászlé   fish stew

Pisztráng   trout
Ponty   carp
Tonhal   tuna

VEGETABLES (ZÖLDSÁG)

Bab   beans
Burgonya   potato
Fokhagyma   garlic
Gomba   mushrooms
Hagyma   onion
Káposzta   cabbage

Paradicsom   tomato
Sóska   sorrel
Spenót   spinach
Tök   squash
Zöldbab   green beans

SALADS (SALÁTÁK)

Fejes saláta   green salad
Lecsó   stewed pepper, tomatoes,
   and onion

Paprikasaláta   pickled-pepper salad
Uborkasaláta   cucumber salad
Vegyes saláta   mixed salad

FRUITS (GYÜLMÖLCS)

Alma   apple
Barack   apricot
Cseresznye   cherry
Dinnye   watermelon
Körte   pear
Meggy   sour cherry

Narancs   orange
Öszibarack   peach
Sargadinnye   cantaloupe
Szilva   plum
Szóló   grapes

DESSERTS

Almás rétes   apple strudel
Dobos torta   layer cake with
  caramel candied frosting
Fagylalt   ice cream
Ischler   chocolate-dipped, short-
  bread cookie sandwich

Lekváros palacsinta   crêpe filled
  with preserves
Meggyes rétes   sour-cherry strudel
Túrós rétes   cheese strudel

BEVERAGES

Barna sör   dark beer
Fehér bor   white wine
Kávé   coffee
Koktél   cocktail
Narancslé   orange juice

Sör   beer
Tej   milk
Víz   water
Vörös bor   red wine

2 Basic Phrases & Vocabulary

QUESTION WORDS (IN THE NOMINATIVE)

English	Hungarian	Pronunciation
Where	Hol	hole
When	Mikor	*mee*-kor
What	Mi	mee
Why	Miert	*mee*-ayrt
Who	Ki	kee
How	Hogy	hohdge

USEFUL PHRASES

English	Hungarian	Pronunciation
Good day/Hello	Jó napot	*yoh* napoht
Good morning	Jó reggelt	*yoh* reg-gelt
Good evening	Jó estét	*yoh* esh-tayt
Good-bye	Viszontlátásra	*vee*-sont-lah-tahsh-ra
My name is . . .	vagyok . . .	*vodge*-yohk
Thank you	Köszönöm	*kuh*-suh-nuhm
You're welcome	Kérem	*kay*-rem
Please	Legyen szíves	*ledge*-yen *see*-vesh
Yes	Igen	*ee*-gen
No	Nem	nem
Good/Okay	Jó	yo
Excuse me	Bocsánat	*boh*-chahnat
How much does it cost?	Mennyi bekerül?	men-yee *beh*-keh-roohl?
I don't understand	Nem értem	nem ayr-tem
I don't know	Nem tudom	nem *too*-dum
Where is the . . . ?	Hol van a . . . ?	*hohl* von a . . . ?
bus station	busz állomás	boos *ahh*-loh-mahsh
train station	vonatállomás	vah-not-*ahh*-loh-mahsh
bank	bank	bahnk
museum	múzeum	*moo*-zeh-oom
pharmacy	patiká	*paw*-tee-kah
theater	színház	*seen*-hahz
tourist office	turista iroda	*too*-reesh-ta *eer*-ohda

embassy	**nagykövetség**	*nahdge koo*-vet-shayg
restaurant	**étterem**	*ayt*-teh-rehm
rest room	**wc**	*vayt*-say

RESTAURANT SERVICE

English	Hungarian	Pronunciation
Breakfast	**Reggeli**	*rehg*-geh-lee
Lunch	**Ebéd**	*eh*-bayd
Dinner	**Vacsora**	*vah*-choh-rah
I would like . . .	**Kérnék . . .**	*kayr*-nayk . . .
a table	**egy asztalot**	edge *ah*-stah-lot
a menu	**egy étlapot**	edge *ayt*-lah-poht
a glass(of water)	**egy pohár (vizet)**	edge poh-har (*vee*-zet)
to pay	**fizetni**	*ee*-zeht-nee
I have a reservation	**Foglaltam már**	*fohg*-lawl-tahm mahr

TRAIN TRAVEL

English	Hungarian	Pronunciation
A ticket, please	**Egy jegyet kérek**	*Edge ye*-dget *kay*-rek
Seat reservation	**helyjegy**	*heyh*-yedge
One way only	**csak oda**	*chalk oh*-da
Round-trip	**oda-vissza**	*oh*-dah-*vees*-sah
First class	**elsó osztály**	*ell*-shooh *oh*-stahy
Arrive	**érkezik**	*ayr*-kez-eek
Depart	**indul**	*inn*-doohl
Track	**Vagány**	*vah*-ghine

POST OFFICE

English	Hungarian	Pronunciation
Airmail	**Légiposta**	*lay*-ghee-posh-ta
A stamp, please	**Egy bélyeget kérek**	Edge *bay*-yeh-get *kay*-rek
A postcard . . .	**Egy képeslapot . . .**	Edge *kay*-pesh-law-poht
An envelope . . .	**Egy borítéket . . .**	Edge *bohr*-ree-tay-ket

USEFUL WORDS

English	Hungarian	Pronunciation
map	**térkép**	*tayr*-kayp
police	**rendórség**	*ren*-du(r)r-shayg
hospital	**korhéz**	*kohr*-hahhz
emergency	**szükséghelyzet**	*soohk*-shayg-hey-zet
theft	**lopás**	*loh*-pahsh
passport	**útlevél**	*oot*-leh-vayhl

SIGNS

Bejárat   Entrance
Érkezések   Arrivals
Indulások   Departures
Informácio   Information
Kijárat   Exit
Tilos a dohányzás   No Smoking
Toalettek   Toilets
Veszélyes   Danger
Vigyázat   Beware

NUMBERS

1 **egy** (edge)
2 **kettó** (*ket*-tu(r))
3 **három** *(hahh*-rohm)
4 **négy** (*naydge*)
5 **öt** (*u(r)t*)
6 **hat** (*hawt*)
7 **hét** (*hayt*)
8 **nyolc** (*nyohlts*)
9 **kilenc** (*kee*-lents)
10 **tíz** (*teez*)
11 **tizenegy** (*teez*-en-edge)
12 **tizenkettó** (*teez*-en-ket-tu(r))
13 **tizenhárom** (*teez*-en-hahh-rohm)
14 **tizennégy** (*teez*-en-naydge)
15 **tizenöt** (*teez*-en-u(r)t)

16 **tizenhat** (*teez*-en-hawt)
17 **tizenhét** (*teez*-en-hayt)
18 **tizennyolc** (*teez*-en-nyohlts)
19 **tizenkilenc** (*teez*-en-kee-lents)
20 **húsz** (*hoos*)
30 **harminc** (*hahr*-mints)
40 **negyven** (*nedge*-vehn)
50 **ötven** (*u(r)t*-vehn)
60 **hatvan** (*hawt*-vahn)
70 **hetven** (*het*-vehn)
80 **nyolcvan** (*nyohlts*-vahn)
90 **kilencven** (*kee*-lents-vehn)
100 **száz** (*sahhz*)
500 **ötszáz** (*u(r)t*-sahhz)
1,000 **ezer** (*eh*-zayr)

Index

See also Accommodations, Restaurant, and Coffeehouses & Cafes indexes, below.

COFFEEHOUSES & CAFES

FROMMER'S® COMPLETE TRAVEL GUIDES

Alaska
Alaska Cruises & Ports of Call
Amsterdam
Argentina & Chile
Arizona
Atlanta
Australia
Austria
Bahamas
Barcelona, Madrid & Seville
Beijing
Belgium, Holland & Luxembourg
Bermuda
Boston
British Columbia & the Canadian
    Rockies
Budapest & the Best of Hungary
California
Canada
Cancún, Cozumel & the Yucatán
Cape Cod, Nantucket &
    Martha's Vineyard
Caribbean
Caribbean Cruises & Ports of Call
Caribbean Ports of Call
Carolinas & Georgia
Chicago
China
Colorado
Costa Rica
Denmark
Denver, Boulder & Colorado Springs
England
Europe
European Cruises & Ports of Call
Florida
France

Germany
Great Britain
Greece
Greek Islands
Hawaii
Hong Kong
Honolulu, Waikiki & Oahu
Ireland
Israel
Italy
Jamaica
Japan
Las Vegas
London
Los Angeles
Maryland & Delaware
Maui
Mexico
Montana & Wyoming
Montréal & Québec City
Munich & the Bavarian Alps
Nashville & Memphis
Nepal
New England
New Mexico
New Orleans
New York City
New Zealand
Nova Scotia, New Brunswick &
    Prince Edward Island
Oregon
Paris
Philadelphia & the Amish Country
Portugal
Prague & the Best of the Czech
    Republic
Provence & the Riviera

Puerto Rico
Rome
San Antonio & Austin
San Diego
San Francisco
Santa Fe, Taos & Albuquerque
Scandinavia
Scotland
Seattle & Portland
Shanghai
Singapore & Malaysia
South Africa
South America
Southeast Asia
South Florida
South Pacific
Spain
Sweden
Switzerland
Texas
Thailand
Tokyo
Toronto
Tuscany & Umbria
USA
Utah
Vancouver & Victoria
Vermont, New Hampshire
    & Maine
Vienna & the Danube Valley
Virgin Islands
Virginia
Walt Disney World & Orlando
Washington, D.C.
Washington State

FROMMER'S® DOLLAR-A-DAY GUIDES

Australia from $50 a Day
California from $70 a Day
Caribbean from $70 a Day
England from $75 a Day
Europe from $70 a Day

Florida from $70 a Day
Hawaii from $80 a Day
Ireland from $60 a Day
Italy from $70 a Day
London from $85 a Day

New York from $90 a Day
Paris from $80 a Day
San Francisco from $70 a Day
Washington, D.C., from $80
    a Day

FROMMER'S® PORTABLE GUIDES

Acapulco, Ixtapa & Zihuatanejo
Amsterdam
Aruba
Australia's Great Barrier Reef
Bahamas
Baja & Los Cabos
Berlin
Big Island of Hawaii
Boston
California Wine Country
Cancún
Charleston & Savannah
Chicago
Disneyland

Dublin
Florence
Frankfurt
Hong Kong
Houston
Las Vegas
London
Los Angeles
Maine Coast
Maui
Miami
New Orleans
New York City
Paris

Phoenix & Scottsdale
Portland
Puerto Rico
Puerto Vallarta, Manzanillo &
    Guadalajara
San Diego
San Francisco
Seattle
Sydney
Tampa & St. Petersburg
Vancouver
Venice
Virgin Islands
Washington, D.C.

FROMMER'S® NATIONAL PARK GUIDES

Family Vacations in the National
    Parks
Grand Canyon

National Parks of the American
    West
Rocky Mountain
Yellowstone & Grand Teton

Yosemite & Sequoia/
    Kings Canyon
Zion & Bryce Canyon

FROMMER'S® MEMORABLE WALKS

Chicago	New York	San Francisco
London	Paris	

FROMMER'S® GREAT OUTDOOR GUIDES

Arizona & New Mexico	Northern California	Vermont & New Hampshire
New England	Southern New England	

SUZY GERSHMAN'S BORN TO SHOP GUIDES

Born to Shop: France	Born to Shop: Italy	Born to Shop: New York
Born to Shop: Hong Kong, Shanghai & Beijing	Born to Shop: London	Born to Shop: Paris

FROMMER'S® IRREVERENT GUIDES

Amsterdam	Los Angeles	San Francisco
Boston	Manhattan	Seattle & Portland
Chicago	New Orleans	Vancouver
Las Vegas	Paris	Walt Disney World
London	Rome	Washington, D.C.

FROMMER'S® BEST-LOVED DRIVING TOURS

Britain	Germany	New England
California	Ireland	Scotland
Florida	Italy	Spain
France		

HANGING OUT™ GUIDES

Hanging Out in England	Hanging Out in France	Hanging Out in Italy
Hanging Out in Europe	Hanging Out in Ireland	Hanging Out in Spain

THE UNOFFICIAL GUIDES®

Bed & Breakfasts and Country Inns in:	Florida with Kids	New Orleans
California	Golf Vacations in the Eastern U.S.	New York City
New England	The Great Smoky & Blue Ridge Mountains	Paris
Northwest	Hawaii	San Francisco
Rockies	Inside Disney	Skiing in the West
Southeast	Las Vegas	Southeast with Kids
Beyond Disney	London	Walt Disney World
Branson, Missouri	Mid-Atlantic with Kids	Walt Disney World for Grown-ups
California with Kids	Mini Las Vegas	Walt Disney World for Kids
Chicago	Mini-Mickey	Washington, D.C.
Cruises	New England & New York with Kids	World's Best Diving Vacations
Disneyland		

SPECIAL-INTEREST TITLES

Frommer's Adventure Guide to Australia & New Zealand
Frommer's Adventure Guide to Central America
Frommer's Adventure Guide to India & Pakistan
Frommer's Adventure Guide to South America
Frommer's Adventure Guide to Southeast Asia
Frommer's Adventure Guide to Southern Africa
Frommer's Britain's Best Bed & Breakfasts and Country Inns
Frommer's France's Best Bed & Breakfasts and Country Inns
Frommer's Italy's Best Bed & Breakfasts and Country Inns
Frommer's Caribbean Hideaways

Frommer's Exploring America by RV
Frommer's Gay & Lesbian Europe
Frommer's The Moon
Frommer's New York City with Kids
Frommer's Road Atlas Britain
Frommer's Road Atlas Europe
Frommer's Washington, D.C., with Kids
Frommer's What the Airlines Never Tell You
Israel Past & Present
The New York Times' Guide to Unforgettable Weekends
Places Rated Almanac
Retirement Places Rated